ADVANCE PRAISE FOR

Acting Chekhov in Translation

"Before Chekhov, the fundamental mode of nearly all drama was declamatory. Actors stood up, a distance from the audience and, to one degree or another, attempted to announce how they felt. Their utterances and physical behavior seemed first and foremost public (and therefore guarded). The tone of psychological intimacy introduced to the stage by Chekhov's plays was revolutionary and created a new and far more sophisticated challenge for translators.

For this reason, I think Robin Beth Levenson's choice of Chekhov's four greatest plays for her study is particularly apt. His is a theatre of nuance and silence and yearning (both spoken and unspoken), challenging the translator at every point to capture the meaning under the meaning—and the meaning under that. Chekhov is the perfect ground for her inspired and granular inspection of the choices that translators make, as they move literally from word to word through a script.

People sometimes forget that everything in a play—every movement, every syllable—is the product of a specific, conscious human choice. It is a joy to see a study of this kind that respects the crucial importance of that fundamental reality."

—Lee Blessing, playwright of *A Walk in the Woods*, *Eleemosynary*, *Two Rooms* and *Going to St. Ives*, Pulitzer Prize finalist, Tony Award and Olivier Award nominee, Humanitas Award, and Steinberg/American Theater Critics Association Awards

"This well-documented book on what play translation is all about also delves into the nature of how to interpret a play. Stella Adler, whom I taught acting with for ten years, said 'Actors are script interpreters, if you don't know how to interpret a script, you are not an actor.' *Acting Chekhov in Translation* gives you tools to explore your own acting choices for the plays. Plus, the different points of view from expert actors, scholars, directors and translators makes this book a valuable complement to working on any script, acting study or theatre course."

—Ron Burrus, Master Acting Teacher at Stella Adler Studio of Acting, New York City and Art of Acting Studio, Los Angeles

"Robin Beth Levenson's in-depth analysis of Chekhov in translation will be an invaluable, even necessary, resource for all those involved with Chekhov's plays—directors, actors, drama theorists, teachers, students, literary critics, historians and linguists. She provides a road map to script analysis of the plays in English translation: character development, names, word choice, stage directions and more. Her detailed insights into individual plays and how different translators approached them will encourage the theatergoer to go back to the written work with fresh perspectives on how the scenes develop and to appreciate anew Chekhov's adroit dramaturgy."

—Daniel Caplice Lynch, poet, Professor Emeritus in the English Department at LaGuardia Community College, CUNY, Editor-in-Chief of *New York Stories*, and author of *Ventry*

"I would recommend *Acting Chekhov in Translation* based only on the sparkling and insightful quotes that Robin Beth Levenson has unearthed in literary and theatre history and skillfully includes. But this impeccably documented book, held by Levenson's smart and engaging voice, offers far more—from a brilliant history of translation to a rich analysis of Chekhov's dramaturgical ideas. I appreciate how Levenson brings us close to the mind of Chekhov—an inspiring place for an actor, director, playwright, teacher or theatre lover to be."

—Joanna Rotté, Professor Emeritus of Theatre at Villanova University, member of the Actors' Equity Association, and author of *Acting with Adler* and *Scene Change: A Theatre Diary—Prague, Moscow, Leningrad*

"One can't help but wonder what Anton Chekhov would think of the messy, turbulent world we find ourselves in today. Well over a hundred years since he wrote his plays, we don't seem to know any more about how to live our lives or to be happy, but Chekhov's questions and concerns continue to be timely and important. Robin Beth Levenson has written a welcome and wonderful book for actors and directors who work with Chekhov's seminal texts in translation. The playwright Tom Stoppard said that foreign texts need to be re-translated every few years as the cadences of contemporary speech change rapidly. Levenson's book encourages actors and directors to pay attention to the nuances of Chekhov's words in translation and to forge their own understanding of these astonishing texts."

—Cecilia Rubino, Director and Adaptor of *Uncle Vanya* at Jefferson Market Playhouse (NYPL), Associate Professor of Theater and Director of Arts in Context Program at Lang College/The New School

"Robin Beth Levenson's book *Acting Chekhov in Translation* is perfect for actors who want to know the details about acting the various characters in Chekhov's plays. If you are doing a show—Chekhov or any play in translation—this book is helpful to see how the words in the script affect what you do onstage.

Chapters describe how various translators, actors, directors and teachers approach Chekhov's last four masterpieces—and translating theatre in general. The wide variety of comments from the likes of Ian McKellen, Anne Bogart, Tom Stoppard, David Mamet and many, many others make the book an interesting read, whether you are a theatre professional or just interested in how drama gets from page to stage."

—John Turturro, actor

"I read every page of Robin Beth Levenson's *Acting Chekhov in Translation*. I found it far too compelling to just select a chapter here and there. Her comparisons of variant translations are wonderful! Her knowledge of the fields of acting, drama, speech and voice bring new insights both to Chekhov's four masterpieces and to translation studies. She convincingly points out the pitfalls of translating a play strictly as a verbal text without properly considering all the elements that go into a performance.

Her underlying theory that variations in language result in variations in subtext and action is of critical importance and is far too often overlooked in play translation. Her analysis of Stanislavsky's contribution to acting methods, along with his misunderstanding of some of Chekhov's intentions as well as later practitioners' misunderstanding of Stanislavsky's own concepts, will be illuminating for many, particularly translators who do not have an extensive background in theatre. Her careful analysis of Chekhov's dramaturgy likewise will be helpful to those who do not already have this level of familiarity with the great playwright's works. Her numerous personal interviews and observations drawn from classes she has taken with outstanding teachers are sources of considerable enrichment.

Among her other crucial ideas are:

the interaction of playwright and director;
the question of how to capture source rhythm in the translated text;
her discussion of how playwrights and translators impose themselves on the source text;

the impact for the actor of deleting intentional ellipses and punctuation;
the question of whether characters will speak perfect grammar when they are emotionally distraught;
the impact of deleting elements from the source;
the significance of title and character names and of stage directions.

Levenson's book will attract a range of readers with varying interests: play translation, Chekhov, acting and theatre in general. Its appeal extends throughout the English-speaking world and perhaps to Russians who know English and are curious about how translations work."
—Phyllis Zatlin, literary critic and translator, Professor Emerita at Rutgers University, author of *Theatrical Translation and Film Adaptation: A Practitioner's View*

Acting Chekhov
in Translation

Dear Mike,

I couldn't have wished for a more incisive & articulate interviewer – a friend.

Love,

Robin

This book is part of the Peter Lang Media and Communication list.
Every volume is peer reviewed and meets
the highest quality standards for content and production.

PETER LANG
New York • Bern • Berlin
Brussels • Vienna • Oxford • Warsaw

Robin Beth Levenson

Acting Chekhov in Translation

4 Plays, 100 Ways

PETER LANG
New York • Bern • Berlin
Brussels • Vienna • Oxford • Warsaw

Library of Congress Cataloging-in-Publication Data

Names: Levenson, Robin, author.
Title: Acting Chekhov in translation: 4 plays, 100 ways /
Robin Beth Levenson.
Description: New York: Peter Lang, 2019.
Includes bibliographical references and index.
Identifiers: LCCN 2018024907 | ISBN 978-1-4331-5253-5 (hardback: alk. paper)
ISBN 978-1-4331-5266-5 (paperback: alk. paper) | ISBN 978-1-4331-5267-2 (ebook pdf)
ISBN 978-1-4331-5268-9 (epub) | ISBN 978-1-4331-5269-6 (mobi)
Subjects: LCSH: Chekhov, Anton Pavlovich, 1860–1904—Translations into
English—History and criticism. | Chekhov, Anton Pavlovich, 1860–1904—Criticism
and interpretation. | Russian drama—19th century—History and criticism.
Classification: LCC PG3458.Z9 T375 2019 | DDC 891.72/3—dc23
LC record available at https://lccn.loc.gov/2018024907
DOI 10.3726/b14362

Bibliographic information published by **Die Deutsche Nationalbibliothek**.
Die Deutsche Nationalbibliothek lists this publication in the "Deutsche
Nationalbibliografie"; detailed bibliographic data are available
on the Internet at http://dnb.d-nb.de/.

Cover image: John Turturro as Lopakhin and Dianne Wiest as Mme. Ranevskaya in
The Cherry Orchard, Act III, Classic Stage Company, NYC, 2011. Lopakhin, once a serf
in Ranevskaya's household, buys the estate. Director: Andrei Belgrader.
Translator: John Christopher Jones. Photo Credit: Richard Termine.

© 2019 Peter Lang Publishing, Inc., New York
29 Broadway, 18th floor, New York, NY 10006
www.peterlang.com

Printed in the United States of America

This book is dedicated to the memories of Shirley Eleanor Levenson, Leon and Rose Levenson, Nathan and Rebecca Kline, Richard Kline, Benny and Ida Shapiro, Charlie and Dottie Kline, Shana Dowdeswell, Carol Golnick, Susan Sable and Charlotte Patton.

Rosencrantz: *What are you playing at?*
Guildenstern: *Words, words. They're all we have to go on.*
Tom Stoppard

Words, words, words—they are the skin of our thought.
Bill Moyers

The body says what words cannot.
Martha Graham

Words in the theatre are only a design on the canvas of motion.
Vsevolod Meyerhold

Speech is but broken light upon the depth of the unspoken.
George Eliot

Language determines thought.
Sapir-Whorf Hypothesis

Language disguises thought.
Ludwig Littgenstein

La coeur sent rarement ce que la bouche exprime.
Jean-Galbert de Campistron

The things we say are all unsuccessful attempts to say something else.
Bertrand Russell

The most important thing is to see what's obvious.
George Orwell

Table of Contents

Illustrations

Acknowledgements

I am most grateful for the suggestions and support of New York University professors Dr. Deborah Borisoff and Dr. Nancy Smithner, whose close readings and uncanny abilities to articulate the crux of my work at each stage of its development were stunning. Dr. Joanna Rotté's knowledge of and dedication to acting practice and Chekhov are immeasurable, and she helped me see the path and purpose of this work clearly, and more objectively. I cannot thank all three of them enough.

Neil Postman's generosity, kindness and humor helped me begin writing early on in the work, and to continue through the hardest times. Lowell Swortzell sparked initial ideas for the study, without which it would not ever have come to be. I am thankful they were my mentors and teachers.

My teachers Ron Burrus, Stella Adler, Yevgeny Lanskoy, Allen Schoer, Carol Rocamora, Richard Schechner, Nancy Swortzell, Helen White, Chris Vine, Franz Rijnbout, Slava Dolgatchev, John Harrop, Stanley Glenn, Michael Addison, Richard Rizzo, Richard P. Brown, Jules Aaron, Eric Barr, Rip Parker, Kristin Linklater, Patsy Rodenburg, Ruth Morgenroth, Geneviève DeLattre and Robert Carrelli were among those who shaped my experience of acting, of Chekhov, and views on theatre and literature; their sparks are also present in this study.

I give special thanks to Sharon Carnicke, Phyllis Zatlin, John Turturro, Simon Russell Beale, Jean-Claude Van Itallie, Dakin Matthews, Phoebe Brand, Stephen and Miranda Carnovsky, Paul Lazar, Louis Zorich, Olympia Dukakis, Austin

Pendleton, Liev Schreiber, Andrew Upton, Lee Blessing, Edward Albee, Irene Moore, John Strasberg, Orietta Crispino, Martin Sherman, Tom Donaghy, Anne Bogart, Dina Dodin, Nancy Meckler, Julie W. de Sherbinin, Laurence Senelick, Earle Gister, Chay Yew, John Gould Rubin, John Christopher Jones, Tim Craig, Štepán Šimek, Tom Markus, Royston Coppenger, Ron Sossi, Bella Merlin, Lawrence Sacharow, Stephen Wangh, Katherine Alt Keener, Karen Braga, Tom Oppenheim, Marat Yusim, Tracy Bersley, Nellie McCaslin, Joni Swartz, Tracy Shaffer, Charlotte Patton, Lance Strate, Martin Levinson, the cast of *3 × 3 Sisters* and Allen Schoer with The Actor's Institute (TAI) who graciously furnished the space for our staged reading. The published or unpublished works, interviews, photographs, conversations, classes, rehearsals and stage productions of these artists were all helpful to this study.

Editors Kathryn Harrison and Erika Hendrix at Peter Lang provided insights and support that were elemental in preparing the book for publishing. I am supremely grateful for their tireless patience and encouragement. I am also grateful to Michael Doub for his cheer and reinforcement, and Luke McCord for his detailed comments and suggestions on the final production copy of the book.

The support of family and friends has been extraordinary. I thank Shirley Levenson, an incisive editor, Bob Levenson, Laurie Levenson, Valerie Kane, Gene Zerna and Martha Rodriguez for their counsel and compassion. My husband, Nick Andrews, has sustained and advised me, contributing meaningfully to the work at every turn. I am deeply in his debt.

Introduction

Acting teacher Stella Adler said, "I am a student by nature. I am a scholar as well as an actress" (1999: 195). This is not surprising. Ideally, actors do practical research on their roles; they are "script interpreters" and, Adler declares, "unless you can interpret a script you are not an actor" (4). I am a scholar and an actor as well: acting professionally in Los Angeles and New York and teaching acting, theatre, drama, voice and speech and communication have all contributed to my understanding and study of acting, dramatic literature, and human behavior. This book, however, does not presume to "interpret" Anton Chekhov's work definitively, or to assess which translations of his plays may be the "best." It is, rather, an exploration of how practitioners and scholars may approach script analysis when the play is in translation. Interpretation is up to the individual production, and to the audience. Chekhov's plays provide useful examples for this examination of the playscript.

The study came about in an attempt to explore how language differences in various translations of the text of a playscript might affect "Actions" played by the actor of the text onstage. It has become an investigation into the nature of translation itself, as well as the idea of "Action" as a concept in the theatre, and how notions of play translation and the Action underlying language in a playscript might be applied to the four masterworks of one of the most enigmatic and gifted playwrights in the world since Shakespeare.

While many critical studies on Anton Chekhov's masterworks and translations and/or adaptations of his work continue to appear every year, few address
how language affects performance, or how the Actor—the interpreter of the text
in its final form, which is called the "playscript"—might approach the text, written in English "translation." The title of this exploration of Chekhov's plays is of
course taken from the phrase "*lost* in translation," which is ironically what happens
to many cultural meanings whenever works are transposed from one language to
another. New books on literary translation have been published recently, but few
address translation for the stage, or Chekhov's works. This is bizarre since Chekhov's plays—more than any other Realist writings—changed the way we approach
acting practice on the stage, and in film and television. With the slashing of the
arts and drama in particular from school curricula in the U.S., the learning of
vital communication skills are lost as well. This is devastating for our students
and society at large. This examination of stage work, Chekhov and the nature of
translating foreign cultures is an attempt to open doors to global communication
and understanding.

The study is divided into four parts. The first three chapters examine the
nature of literature translation in general, and then translation for the stage in
particular. The second part, Chapter IV, examines the notion of "Action," which
helps define overall play structure, as well as characters' individual purposes and
movements through a play. Chapter V is the third part of the study, and it explores
Chekhov's distinctive dramaturgy, which has had so much impact on writers and
playwrights since the early twentieth century. Lastly, the fourth part, Chapters
VI through IX, is comprised of explications of Chekhov's canon using elements
described and discovered in parts one, two and three.

More specifically, Chapter I discusses the difficulties of translation from various points of view, describes how it is a transfer of "situations" rather than just
words, and gives views on interpretation. Then, a short history of translation pre-
cipitates discussion of "literal" versus "true to the spirit" styles of translation.

Chapter II delves into the modern age of translation, where dramatic literature is finally seen as a separate area of study. Factors that affect translation for the
stage include the recognition that audiences have individual responses to theatrical signs, with regard to time and cultural perceptions, and that translators have
diverse (and contrary) criteria for translation. Time and culture-bound intricacies
continue to affect translation throughout history. "Intuition" has a place in translation, rather than specific theories or practices. While attempts to formalize translation practice persist with linguists, theatre translators understand that the play is
written to be performed, and must be adapted to particular performance venues.
Some translators still wrestle with notions of "readability" versus "performability,"

though theatre translators see the playscript as only a "blueprint" for performance. Modern critics,' theorists' and directors' outlooks on these issues are presented. Teacher, critic and translator Robert Corrigan and others put forward the idea that plays are structured from Action, and that the actor is the core of the drama. This idea, however, is not yet accepted by many linguists and literary translators.

Chapter III describes how current Chekhov translators have come to the fore as primary artists in remodeling Chekhov's plays, though they do not claim to know the source language. Their uses of interlinear "cribs"—literal translations fashioned by a Russian speaker (often unnamed) and then reshaped for performance by a "playwright-translator"—may greatly affect the translations. While theatre practitioners may create "playable" renditions, literary translators feel it is imperative for a translator or adaptor to know the source language. The value of understanding the rehearsal process and the actor's contribution to the text are addressed, as well as the significance of the audience. Differences among "translations," "adaptations" and "versions" of scripts are described at length. Finally, translators discuss the importance of recreating rhythm in the translated script, and the necessity of "love" or kinship with the source playwright.

If the playscript is only a plan or "blueprint" for the play, what brings the actual performance alive on the stage? The notion of "Action" is explored in Chapter IV (See Appendix A/Glossary),[1] considered the second part of the study. From Aristotle's *Poetics,* and Constantin Stanislavsky's system of acting, the notion of "Action" is proposed as a basic tool of drama, helping to create the "poetry of the theatre." This idea is recognized by critics Bernard Beckerman and Francis Fergusson, and playwright Jean Cocteau, as well as adherents of Stanislavsky. Vasily Toporkov, an actor who was under Stanislavky's direction at the Moscow Art Theatre, along with master teacher Stella Adler and director Jerzy Grotowski, have various views on Action. Toporkov worked with Stanislavsky on the "Method of Physical Action," which began with the actor learning to play simple physical actions truthfully. Adler, an American teacher who has inspired or had an affect on thousands of acting students, has been particularly articulate as a proponent of Stanislavsky's view of Action. She has taught students to play truthfully in the *circumstances* of the play (see Appendix). Adler's and Fergusson's teachers, Boleslavsky and Ouspenskaya, and especially Anton Chekhov's nephew Michael Chekhov, continue to have an impact on actor-training. Michael Chekhov's "Psychological Gesture" helps the actor find appropriate Actions in the circumstances of the play.

---

1   This Glossary defines terms specific to the art form, and of import to the actor working on a role.

Vsevolod Meyerhold, an actor in Stanislavsky's productions, is, perhaps, the best-known Russian practitioner and theorist to develop his own practice in contrast to that of his mentor. Director/theorist Jerzy Grotowski, too, takes ideas from Stanislavsky, and creates his own "poor theatre," as well as his later construct known as "Objective Drama Research." Bertolt Brecht was another admirer of Stanislavsky. Other practitioners, who may not have acknowledged Stanislavsky's notion of "Action" per se, have still used it in their work. Examples include theatre directors Joseph Chaikin and Anne Bogart. Uta Hagen, Morris Carnovsky and Sanford Meisner (the latter two with The Group Theatre) all recognize the importance of Action for actors, while directors Charles Marowitz and Peter Brook use other metaphors to describe stage praxis. Still, Marowitz's "awakening susceptibilities to the play's situations" and Brook's "energy and inspiration" may both be descriptions of Action.

Finally, researchers and practitioners such as Sharon Carnicke, Irina and Igor Levin and Bella Merlin note the work of Stanislavsky's students who worked with him on the Method of Physical Actions in his final years, and taught his methods to other students: directors/teachers Knebel, Kedrov and Tostonogov are names still recognized by Russian and some American teachers and practitioners. Stanislavsky's "Method of Physical Actions" became "Active Analysis" to these later practitioners, but the notion of an actor's Action as "movement with purpose" is common to them all. The point in this chapter is that the notion of Action, replete in Aristotle, has been passed down as "lore" to acting students in the classroom through master teachers, rather than documented in books. Action is a concept put into practice by Stanislavsky, and tested in Anton Chekhov's plays. It was the plays, however, that created the need for a consummate acting theory and practice that could be applied to Chekhov's later works.

Chekhov's last plays have been seen as plays of "mood." The third part of the study, Chapter V, is devoted to Chekhov's dramaturgy—that is, the structures and theatrical poetry—of Chekhov's plays through metaphors of "lace," Impressionism and music. His work is compared to a "feeling of sadness and longing, not akin to pain" (from Longfellow) because his style is neither altogether comedy nor tragedy, but something potent and yet delicate that falls between the two. Many playwrights and writers over the past 100 years have claimed Chekhov as an influence.

Artists as diverse as Russian novelist Leo Tolstoy, poet Andrey Bely and French playwright Jean Cocteau have described Chekhov's works and theatre art in general through the metaphor of "lace." This is because Chekhov's plays are full of "holes"—the pauses, interstices and ellipses seem to thwart attempts to pin down his meanings, or even label his style. Chekhov has, however, been called a "Symbolist," as his "spotty" or lacelike punctuation is seen to imply "deeper meanings" in the playscript. While writers and critics point to Chekhov's "Symbolist" leanings, they leave out that it is the *actor* who must sort out the possible deeper or hidden meanings of Chekhov's dialogue and stage directions, in the playing.

Chekhov's canon (his last four masterpieces) has been labeled "Impressionist" too, by various Russian critics, as well as by English and American writers and theatre practitioners. Maurice Valency (*The Breaking String*) writes that this "impressionism" makes Chekhov difficult for the actor, while actor Ian McKellen (*The Cambridge Companion to Chekhov*) states Chekhov is the actor's "friend." This illustrates how a lack of knowledge of script analysis and of Action as the core of the drama promulgates misunderstandings of Chekhov's work, even by gifted critics.

Meyerhold may have been the first to comment on Chekhov's plays' likeness to music. Musical harmonies are analogous to both the plays' internal dialogue (the characters who don't seem to hear each other) and the scene structure of each individual work. The irony in juxtaposition of scenes and monologues is akin to the strategies of Gustave Flaubert, another pioneering Realist. In the French writer's novels, as in Chekhov's plays, characters say one thing and do another. In the burgeoning "Realist" style, this was seen as "objective" writing, which both Flaubert and Chekhov espouse.

Chekhov puts emphasis on objectivity in a writer. He uses Nature in his plays to point up the need for a healthy objective indifference towards characters. Though his objectivity caused his critics (Tolstoy among them) to accuse him of not taking social or political stands as a writer, Chekhov's dramaturgy does have meaning, and promotes thoughtful reflection on characters presented in all their fullness and fallibility. Though Russian and American critics have considered Chekhov's precursors to be poets and playwrights from Pushkin through Turgenev (coincidentally a friend of Flaubert's), Chekhov's style is unique. Director Stanislavsky admits to having been puzzled by it: while Chekhov considered his plays comedies (with the exception of *Three Sisters*), Stanislavsky imposed heavy "Naturalist" details on productions, and belabored the mood. But key elements of structure and language in Chekhov's plays, discussed in depth, reveal both comedy and pathos in his iconoclastic approach to playwriting. Finally, significant events in Chekhov's life that may have affected his dramaturgy are noted.

Next, in Chapters VI through IX, which comprise the fourth section of this study, elements of Chekhov's dramaturgy are applied to close script analyses of selected scenes in translations of Chekhov's plays, in chronological order: *Seagull*, *Uncle Vanya*, *Three Sisters* and *Cherry Orchard*. The import of play titles and character names, stage directions, actor's Actions, word choice, word meaning, punctuation, pauses, rhythm, syntax, sound, song and allusion are treated variously as they occur in scenes from each play. Translations and scenes have been chosen based on the most variant and divergent examples of language and uses of these elements, observed in available texts of each of the four plays. These last four chapters also incorporate descriptions of the plots, characters and events in each play that provoke Actions.

In Chapter VI on *Seagull*, a discussion of "the well-made play" is included, as Chekhov's works—especially beginning with *Seagull*—were blatant reactions against this formulaic and often overly Romantic style of drama. In these four chapters, notes on particular style choices, the use of leitmotifs, the structures of particular scenes or Acts, character eccentricities or groupings and useful observations from practitioners, critics and translators are also included as they apply to particular plays.

The Conclusion, Chapter X, sums up how the nature of translation for the stage, the notion of Action, and the myriad elements in Chekhov's dramaturgy expressed in diverse translations of his last four plays combine to influence the actor's approach to the text. The significance of this for educators and theatre artists is broached, along with suggestions for further study.

Bibliography

Adler, Stella. *The Art of Acting.* Ed. Howard Kissel. New York: Applause Books, 2000.

———. *On Ibsen, Strindberg and Chekhov.* Ed. Barry Paris. New York: Alfred A. Knopf, 1999.

———. "The Reality of Doing," *Tulane Drama Review*, IX(1): 136–155, Fall 1964.

———. *The Technique of Acting.* New York: Bantam Books, 1988.

Aristotle. *Aristotle's Poetics.* Trans. S. H. Butcher. Intro. Francis Fergusson. New York: Hill and Wang, 1961.

Arrowsmith, William and Roger Shattuck, eds. *The Craft and Context of Translation.* Austin: The University of Texas Press, 1961.

Beckerman, Bernard. *Dynamics of Drama.* New York: Drama Book Specialists, 1979.

Benedetti, Jean, ed. *Dear Writer, Dear Actress.* London: Methuen Drama, 1996.

———. *The Moscow Art Theatre Letters.* New York: Routledge, 1991.

———. *Stanislavski.* New York: Routledge, 1990.

———. *Stanislavski: An Introduction.* London: Methuen, 1982.

Bogart, Anne. *Anne Bogart: Viewpoints.* Eds. Michael Bigelow Dixon and Joel A. Smith. Lyme, NH: Smith and Kraus, 1995.

———. Letter to the author, September, 2006.

Boleslavsky, Richard. *Acting, The First Six Lessons.* New York: Theatre Arts Books, 1963.

Brecht, Bertolt. *Brecht on Theatre.* Trans. and ed. John Willett. New York: Hill and Wang, 1964.

Brook, Peter. *The Empty Space.* New York: Avon Books, 1968.

————. Interview with Genista McIntosh, Royal National Theatre/Olivier Theatre, November 5, 1993a. Also at: website-archive.nt-online.org.

————. *The Open Door*. New York: Random House, 1993b.

————. *The Shifting Point*. New York: Harper & Row, 1987.

Callow, Philip. *Chekhov: the Hidden Ground*. Chicago: Ivan R. Dee, 1998.

Carnicke, Sharon Marie. "The Nasty Habit of Adaptations," Conference: "Chekhov the Immigrant: Translating a Cultural Icon," Colby College, October 8–9, 2004.

————. *Stanislavsky in Focus*. Australia: Harwood Academic Publishers, 1998.

————. "Stanislavsky Uncensored and Unabridged," *Tulane Drama Review*, T137, 13:22–37, Spring, 1993.

————. *The Theatrical Instinct*. New York: Peter Lang, 1989.

Carnovsky, Morris. *The Actor's Eye*. New York: Performing Arts Journal Publications, 1984.

Chaikin, Joseph. *The Presence of the Actor*. New York: Atheneum, 1972.

Chekhov, Anton. *Letters of Anton Pavlovitch Chekhov*. Trans. Constance Garnett. New York: Benjamin Bloom, 1966.

————. *Letters on the Short Story, The Drama, and Other Literary Topics*. Ed. Louis S. Friedland. New York: Dover Publications, 1966.

————. *Notebook of Anton Chekhov*. Trans. S. S. Koteliansky. New York: P. W. Huebsch, 1922.

————. *The Oxford Chekhov*. Trans. Ronald Hingley. London: Oxford University Press, Vol. II, 1967, Vol. III, 1964 and Vol. IX, 1975.

————. *The Personal Papers of Anton Chekhov*. Trans. S. S. Koteliansky. New York: Lear Publishers, 1948.

Chekhov, Michael. "Chekhov on Acting: A Collection of Unpublished Materials (1919–1942)." *Tulane Drama Review*, 27:63 No. 3 (T99), Fall 1983.

————. *Lessons for the Professional Actor*. Arr. by Deirdre Hurst du Prey. New York: Performing Arts Journal Publications, 1985.

————. *On The Technique of Acting*. Ed. Mel Gordon. New York: Harper Collins Publishers, 1991.

————. *To The Actor*. New York: Harper & Row, 1953.

Cocteau, Jean. Preface, *Les Mariés de la Tour Eiffel*. Paris: Editions Flammarion, 1995. See also: https://www.poetryfoundation.org/poets/jean-cocteau.

Coger, Leslie. "Stanislavsky Changes His Mind," *Tulane Drama Review*, 9:63–68, Fall 1984.

Corrigan, Robert W. "Some Aspects of Chekhov's Dramaturgy," *Educational Theatre Journal*, 7:108–114, May 1955.

Fergusson, Francis. *The Human Image in Dramatic Literature*. Gloucester, MA: Peter Smith, 1969.

————. *The Idea of a Theatre*. Garden City, NY: Doubleday Anchor Books, 1953.

————. "The Notion of Action," *Tulane Drama Review*, 9:85–87, Fall 1964.

Flaubert, Gustave and Gerorges Sand. *Flaubert-Sand, the Correspondence*. Trans. and eds. Francis Steegmuller and Barbara Bray. New York: Alfred A. Knopf, 1993.

Flood, Alison. "Tolstoy thought Chekhov 'worse than Shakespeare.' " *The Guardian*, July 11, 2011.

Friedberg, Maurice. *Literary Translation in Russia.* University Park, PA: The Pennsylvania State University Press, 1997.

Gilman, Richard. *Chekhov's Plays.* New Haven: Yale University Press, 1995.

Gottlieb, Vera. *Chekhov and the Vaudeville.* Cambridge: Cambridge University Press, 1982.

Grotowski, Jerzy. *Towards a Poor Theatre.* New York: Simon and Schuster, 1968.

Hagen, Uta. *A Challenge for the Actor.* New York: Charles Scribner's Sons, 1991.

———. *Respect for Acting.* New York: Macmillan Publishing Company, 1973.

Hingley, Ronald. *Chekhov, A Biographical and Critical Study.* New York: Barnes and Noble, 1966.

———. *A New Life of Anton Chekhov.* New York: Alfred A. Knopf, 1976.

Johnston, David, ed. *Stages of Translation.* Bath, England: Absolute Classics, 1996.

Kenner, Hugh. "The Flaubertian Tradition," Class at UC Santa Barbara, English Department, 1973.

Lanskoy, Yevgeny. Interviews with the author, 1999, and Classes, "The Structures of Action," at the Stella Adler Conservatory, 1986–89.

Levenson, Robin. "Afraid to Lie," Unpublished paper, Dr. Richard Schechner's Directing Course, New York University, Tisch School of the Arts, Spring, 1999.

Levin, Irina and Igor. *The Stanislavsky Secret.* Colorado Springs: Meriwether Publishing, 2002.

———. *Working on the Play and the Role.* Chicago: Ivan R. Dee, 1992.

Longfellow, Henry Wadsworth. *The Complete Works of Henry Wadsworth Longfellow,* "The Day is Done," Boston, MA: Ticknor & Fields, 1866.

Magarshack, David. *Chekhov.* New York: Grove Press, 1952.

———. *Chekhov the Dramatist.* New York: Hill and Wang, 1960.

Mamet, David. *True and False.* New York: Vintage Books, 1999.

Marowitz, Charles. *The Act of Being.* New York: Taplinger Publishing Company, 1978.

McCaslin, Nellie. Interview with the author. New York City, June 2, 2003.

Meisner, Sanford. *On Acting.* New York: Vintage Books, 1987.

Merlin, Bella. *Beyond Stanislavsky.* New York: Routledge, 2001.

Meyerhold, Vsevolod. *Meyerhold on Theatre.* Trans./Ed. Edward Braun. London: Methuen & Company, 1969.

Moore, Sonia. *The Stanislavski System.* New York: The Viking Press, 1974.

Nikolarea, Ekaterina. "Performability vs. Readability." *Translation Journal,* 6(4): 1–21, October 2002. www.accurapid.com/journal/22theater.htm.

Rayfield, Donald. *Anton Chekhov.* London: Harper Collins Publishers, 1997.

———. *Understanding Chekhov.* Madison: University of Wisconsin Press, 1999.

Richards, Thomas. *At Work With Grotowski on Physical Actions.* London: Routledge, 1995.

Roberts, J. W. *Richard Boleslavsky.* Ann Arbor: UMI Research Press, 1981.

Rosenfield, Paul. "Stella Adler's Teaching Actors How to Imagine," *The Los Angeles Times,* August 15, 1982.

Rotté, Joanna. "Stella Adler: Teacher Emeritus," *Journal of American Drama and Theatre,* City University of New York, 11:3, Fall 1999.

———. *Acting with Adler.* New York: Limelight Editions, 2000.

Senelick, Laurence, ed. and trans. *Anton Chekhov.* New York: Grove Press, 1985.

————. *The Chekhov Theatre.* Cambridge: Cambridge University Press, 1997.

————. "Chekhov's Plays in English," *The North American Chekhov Society Bulletin,* Vol. IX, Spring, 2000.

————. Correspondence with the author, laurence.senelick@tufts.edu, to robin.levenson@nyu.edu, Boston and New York, March 7 and 11, 2002.

————. *Russian Dramatic Theory from Pushkin to the Symbolists.* Austin: University of Texas Press, 1981.

————. ed. *Wandering Stars, Russian Émigré Theatre, 1905–1940.* Iowa City: University of Iowa Press, 1992.

Simmons, Ernest J. *Chekhov: A Biography.* Chicago: The University of Chicago Press, 1962.

Stanislavsky, Konstantin. *An Actor Prepares.* Trans. Elizabeth Reynolds Hapgood. New York: Theatre Arts Books, 1948.

————. *Building a Character.* Trans. Elizabeth Reynolds Hapgood. New York: Theatre Arts Books, 1949.

————. *Creating a Role.* Trans. Elizabeth Reynolds Hapgood. New York: Theatre Arts Books, 1961.

Steiner, George. *After Babel.* New York: Oxford University Press, 1998.

Toporkov, Vasily Osipovich. *Stanislavsky in Rehearsal.* Trans. Christine Edwards. New York: Theatre Arts Books, 1979.

Turkov, Andrei, compiler. *Anton Chekhov and His Times.* Trans. Cynthia Carlile and Sharon McKee. Fayetteville: University of Arkansas Press, 1995.

Valency, Maurice. *The Breaking String.* New York: Schocken Books, 1983.

Yusim, Marat. *Passing the Torch—Basic Training: Stanislavsky's School of Acting and Directing.* New York: Marat Yusim, 2006.

CHAPTER ONE

Translation

What is translation? On a platter
A poet's pale and glaring head,
A parrot's screech, a monkey's chatter,
And profanation of the dead.[1]

To those who are bothered about adaptations, seeing them as parasitic or even a violation of the original, there is simply only one answer. The history of theatre is a history of adaptation ... theatre has always enjoyed this activity, has seen it as essentially theatrical and it has never felt that the integrity of the original has been damaged in any way.[2]

As one may glean from the comments above, views on the nature and practice of translation vary enormously. Anton Chekhov may have agreed with countryman Nabokov's observation, as Chekhov claimed "indifference" to translation of his

---

1   Vladimir Nabokov, *On Translating Eugene Onegin*, qtd. in George Steiner, *After Babel* (1998), p. 252. Nabokov first published this poem (a 14-line sonnet) in *The New Yorker* in 1955, described as a tribute and apology to Russians and to Pushkin, about the impossibility and insult of translation (Remnick 104).

2   Thomas Kilroy, "*The Seagull:* an adaptation," *The Cambridge Companion to Chekhov*, eds. Vera Gottlieb and Paul Allain (Cambridge, UK, 2000), pp. 89–90.

plays into German, French, British or American English, and regretted that he was unable to prevent their translation abroad (Scolnicov 1). He wrote:

> "I know that we [Russian writers] neither are nor ever will be needed in Germany—however much we may be translated."

> "What's the point of translating my play [*Cherry Orchard*] into French? How grotesque! … they'll only be bored."

> "I present so little in the way of interest to the British public …"

> and

> "Why do you want my work to be published in America? And in a lady's—which means an atrocious—translation?"
>
> (Chekhov 1975: xv)

While translator Ronald Hingley finds Chekhov's comments above ironic (*Ibid.*)[3] translator Michael Henry Heim attributes them to Chekhov's "innate modesty" (Chekhov 2003: xi). Chekhov was patently wrong about a lack of interest in his plays throughout the world; today his popularity in translation is second only to Shakespeare's (Senelick 1997: 1). But Chekhov's concerns ought not to be swept aside. Whatever his reasons may have been, it is clear Chekhov thought that Russian culture would not appeal to foreigners. He also wrote, "*The Cherry Orchard* is being translated for Berlin and Vienna. *But it won't succeed there since they don't have billiards, Lopakhins or students à là Trofimov*" (emphasis added, 1975: xv). Here Chekhov has hit on the core question of translation in general: How might translators "translate," transpose or adapt the essence of Russian (or any country's) character and context for the foreign sensibility?

To consider this question, I begin by attempting to define translation in general, and then to define translation for the stage in particular. The latter has recently been recognized as "not an end in itself, but as a kind of blueprint [that] playwright and translator create."[4] The "blueprint" is for the actor and director. However, there is much controversy over the issue of understanding translation for the stage as "an extension of stage-craft … an integral strand of that multi-layered process of making a play work onstage," which is how theatre practitioners see the play translation (Johnston 7). Linguists, translators and theatre practitioners are not in accord on this issue. Many agree, however, that there is a dearth of scholarship on the subject, and it is worthy of investigation. What is translation, what is the job of the translator, and what, in particular, are the challenges of translating for the stage?

---

3   Hingley allows the "lady's atrocious translation" to go by without comment in his Introduction.
4   John Clifford, "Translating Moments, Not Words," www.teatrodomundo, Feb. 9, 2005.

Definitions

"... Not to *translate* him, but to make him write *English*."

—Gregory Rabassa[5]

"Translation" is defined in Webster's Dictionary as "the rendering of something into another language" (1505). Of course this is true. The process of "rendering"—however we may define it—is key. But George Steiner[6] maintains it may be impossible to "define" the work of the translator, because there is no one set "theory of translation." He asks, "How does the mind move from one language to another? ... A radical indeterminacy characterizes the question ..." (1998a: 293). Beyond indeterminacy, the well-known Italian proverb "Tradutorre traditore" (the translator is a traitor)[7] implies (with Nabokov's observation which opens this chapter) the consensus that the entire enterprise is a betrayal. A Jewish proverb also asserts "He lies who renders a verse as it reads, with strict literal-ness; he blasphemes who makes additions."[8] Implicit in these observations is that the translator is doomed to failure. So, Anna Chilewska, in her thesis on translation, may well state "Torture and translation ... can be worse than death. Strictly speaking, translation is a subtle form of torture."[9] And translator Phyllis Zatlin asks whether readers of her book on theatre translation may "wonder if anyone besides confirmed masochists would want to translate plays at all" (15).

---

5   Famed translator of Gabriel Garcia Marquez' *One Hundred Years of Solitude*, Leonard Lopate Show, WNYC, July 11, 2005. Rabassa also stated, according to translator Edith Grossman in her superb book *Why Translation Matters*, that it is not whether one knows enough about the source language to translate a master like Marquez, but whether one knows enough *English* to do justice to Marquez' extraordinary book. This is also the point that English-speaking playwright translators of Chekhov—who do not know the source language—might make. We want Chekhov to live in *English* as well as Russian.

6   Steiner is scholar, teacher, literary critic and "polyglot"—equally adept at several languages from childhood—who has written a detailed volume on the nature of language and translation: *After Babel*. Interestingly, noted linguist/translator André Lefevere, in 1980 (*Languages of Theatre*), has included *After Babel* in a list of "highly speculative theories of translation formulated on the basis of literary criteria." This would imply that, for Lefevere, "literary criteria" in translation is somehow suspect. We may wonder what Mr. Lefevere might think of theatre craft and acting "criteria."

7   Frank Pohorlak, "Proponents for a Literal Translation of the New Testament," www.concordant.org.

8   *Ibid.*, from the Babylonian Talmud.

9   Anna Chilewska, "The Assessment of Translations," qtd. *The Spectator*, 24 September 1977.

"Profanation," "atrocity," "grotesqueness," "indeterminacy," "blaspheme," "betrayal" and even torture and masochism: these are words attached to the nature of translation. Paul Valéry, poet and translator, insisted that a poet can only be understood "by his own people; he is inseparable from the speech of his nation … A true poet is untranslatable" (Friedberg 70).[10] Maurice Friedberg believes that such views are rare today, because "Theories of the impossibility of translation are 'elitist.' They belong to … the 18th century, when literary culture was limited to a narrow, privileged class, educated in foreign languages and able to read foreign texts in the original" (*Ibid.*). Yet this seems not to be true for modern translators; they proclaim the endeavor "impossible," even as they attempt it.

Zoja Pavlovskis, translator and professor of classics at SUNY Binghamton, describes the impossibility of rendering the "dialectical interplay" of Greek plays and poetry while maintaining that this activity is "indispensable" for future generations (Rose 105–6). Eric Bentley, with Bertolt Brecht, notes the impossibility of translating—it is "ungeheuer delikat" (frightfully delicate)—and nevertheless he agreed to "defy this truth" by translating Brecht (1985: 5–6). Translator, scholar and theatre dramaturg Alex Gross states, "We really need translation. Sometimes it can be a matter of life and death."[11] He also presents "an extremely cogent case" that translation "is ultimately a stage illusion" and "for practical purposes translation simply does not exist."[12] Veteran translator Ranjit Bolt concurs: "Theoretically there is no such thing as translation … it's an impossibility."[13] Translator Eric McMillan explains how translator error can eviscerate an entire work, "yet all translators have to do that to some extent" (2). McMillan notes that translation is considered successful if it manages to get fifty or sixty per cent of what is actually "translatable" in a literary work into a given translation (*Ibid.*). And, while Steiner optimistically claims, "Between verbal languages, however remote in setting and habits and syntax, there is always the possibility of equivalence, even if actual translation can only attain rough and approximate results," fifty-five pages later he announces, "There are no translations. *Pain* is not *bread* … *Home* is not *Heim* … English has no exact equivalent." (1998a: 15, 270).

---

10 Chekhov might also be considered a "poet" of the theatre, especially since his Realist/Symbolist style helped define a new theatrical genre for the 20th century. His dramaturgy is discussed in Chapter V.

11 Alex Gross, "Translation: The Human Utility," language.home.sprynet.com, Jan. 28, 2005c.

12 *Ibid.*, "Translation Theory: Some Images and Analogies."

13 Ranjit Bolt, qtd. by Brian Logan, "Whose Play is it Anyway?" *Guardian*, UK, March 12, 2003.

So, according to many translators, there is no theory of translation, it is a tortuous thing to do, and translation itself does not exist. Yet, it goes on. Those who believe translation does not exist may be referring to the impossibility of a "word by word" translation process; exact equivalences are impossible, because words in different languages have different connotations and etymologies. "Each language frames the world uniquely" (270). Eugene Nida, described as the world's leading scholar on translation (Brislin 1), concurs with linguist J. Catford that "in a strict sense the meaning of any unit of language can only be described in terms of the sets of contrasts within that language. Therefore, there can be no identity of meaning between languages" (64). For example, S. I. Hayakawa, in his well-known work *Language in Thought and Action,* reminds us that "affective" connotations of words are different from "informative" connotations (63–4). "I'm so tired, I'm *dead!*" is understood in English, but, translated literally, it may not have the same effect on the listener or reader in a different language. Clearly, metaphors in one culture may be nonsensical, inappropriate or imprecise in another.

Linguists and translators accept or reject this notion of "equivalence" in translation to varying degrees. Stephen David Ross discusses translation as an "active judgment" on the part of the translator, where "precise equivalences ... are not always available" (Rose 13). He makes clear the "limitations of similarity of meaning" (an aspect of equivalence) as characteristic of translation, versus adaptation or interpretation. He maintains "both paraphrase and adaptation might well preserve the full 'content' of the original" (9). H. Stephen Straight admits linguistic accuracy is "extremely relative" based on the purpose of the translation towards a particular audience (30–2). Joseph Graham maintains that "finding grammatical equivalents across languages" is an "impossible task" (30).

Why should this be so? Steiner tells us that any study of translation is a study of language. And language itself, even intra-lingually (within one language) necessitates "translation." In Communication Studies, we learn that in the most well-known model of communication, the Psychological Model, human beings communicate by encoding (sending) messages that are then decoded by the receiver (Trenholm 26). In other words, the receiver must "translate" what has been said by the sender. "Thus, a human being performs an act of translation, in the full sense of the word, when receiving a speech-message from any other human being" (Steiner 1998a: 48). As humans, we engage in this "translation" activity all the time, by paying attention to communicators' tones of voice, facial expressions and body postures, as well as the connotative meanings of their words. Indeed, as Alex Gross observes, "There is ultimately no earthshaking difference between what translators do with two languages and what everyone else has to do every day even within a single language" and "Almost every act of communication we perform is to some degree also an act of translation."[14] This is because language itself is abstract: it is only a "signifier" for the thing (idea, concept, message) we want to "signify" when we attempt to communicate. So it must be interpreted. And that interpretation is based on, accompanied by, or influenced by the *context* of the semantic environment—that is, the circumstances—of the particular communication. Language theorists refer to this contextual side of communication as "extra-linguistic." In the communication field it is known as "paralanguage," an aspect of nonverbal communication. In theatre it may be described as "subtext" (see Appendix A). In any case, the notion that words are not the only indication of meaning (and may often obscure, contradict or deny meaning) is fundamental to theatre practice.

As mentioned, interpretation, as a form of translation, is necessary to both interlingual and intralingual communication. And the written or spoken words are only a part of the message that must be interpreted in translation. In other words, "This means that translation cannot be viewed *merely as a linguistic undertaking* but as … an aspect of a larger domain, namely, that of communication" (emphasis added, Brislin 65). Mikhail Bakhtin expresses this point of view as well: "From the standpoint of the extralinguistic purposes of utterance, *everything linguistic is only a means to an end* (emphasis added, 109)."[15] When interlingual communication is difficult, or nuanced, we must look to other modalities—beyond the linguistic— to accomplish the goals of the translation. One of these, according to Nida, is "sociolinguistic" (Brislin 65). He explains how understanding the social context— an "extralinguistic context of the utterance"—is a valid approach to translation. Moreover, he admits that with translations that involve wide differences in time, culture and structural complexity, "the translator is almost compelled to think of his task in sociolinguistic terms" (*Ibid.*). This applies demonstrably to playscripts, notably those of Chekhov, who wrote in late 19th century Russia.

Translator/scholar Rainer Schulte also discusses the validity of a sociolinguistic approach to translation in his essay "Translation Studies as Model for Revitalizing the Humanities." He notes that "situational thinking" and "associative thinking" are the basis of translation thinking: "We associate the word with its visual situation" and "the reader must at all times visualize the word in its situational existence before any meaningful interpretation can be initiated." Thus,

---

14   Alex Gross, "Some Major Dates and Events in the History of Translation," www.accurapic. com.

15   M. M. Bakhtin, *Speech Genres and Other Late Essays*. Austin: University of Texas Press, 1986, p. 109. Bakhtin is known as a literary critic, social thinker and philosopher of language. He was particularly interested in the phenomenology of acting.

> Translation is not simply the translation of words, but rather the translation of situations. Meaningful interpretations are the visualizations of words and the situations they project. The translator consistently considers the word as a sign toward something, as a sign beyond itself toward a situation that is in the process of being built. (Mueller-Vollmer 36)

Schulte ends this section of his discussion with the affirmation that "translation is indeed the transferal of situations and *not of words*" (emphasis added, *Ibid.*). And while Schulte is not referring to dramatic literature in particular, his ideas, along with Nida's and Bakhtin's, have significant implications for translation in the theatre. All plays involve particular "situations" seated in a place and time known as the "circumstances" of the play[16] (see Appendix A). The actor's contribution to the play—the use of his/her imagination—is based on the circumstances set up by the playwright. Circumstances also provoke "Action," discussed in Chapter IV. We may explain Schulte's "situation in the process of being built" as the moment to moment unfolding of the circumstances of a play. In this way, a play is compiled of "situations," not words.

Further, and more recently, translator Edith Grossman in *Why Translation Matters* insists:

> Good translations ... are not necessarily faithful to words or syntax ... which can rarely be brought over directly in any misguided and inevitably muddled effort to somehow replicate the original. This is the literalist trap, because words do not *mean* in isolation. Words *mean* as indispensable parts of a contextual whole that includes the emotional tone and impact. ... I believe that the meaning of a passage can almost always be rendered faithfully in a second language, but its words, taken as separate entities, can almost never be. (71)

Grossman goes on to make a case for seeing the translator as an interpreter who goes behind the "mere surface" of the words on the page to "unravel aesthetic mysteries" at the heart of literature (74).

We may pause here to consider the nature of translation as "interpretation." Steiner states that the French "interprète" and English "interpreter" are commonly used to mean "translator." As mentioned, we "interpret" what has been communicated to us even within one language, based on our own memory, experience and understanding. "We remember culturally, as we do individually, by conventions of emphasis, foreshortening, and omission" (1998a: 30). An "interpretation"

---

16 Stella Adler defines two sets of circumstances: the larger set is the time and place that define the world of the play, and the immediate set is the particular place where the actor is at the moment. Both are constructed from reading the playwright's script, and doing the imagination work based on that script.

of Chekhov may be different in 1912 than it is today; our cultures, memories and surely our lexicons are different. This process, when the language is foreign, "is stylized and differently coded by different cultures" as well (*Ibid.*). Russia itself, for example, may mean something different to us today than did the former pre-"glasnost" and "perestroika" U.S.S.R. So we must reinterpret the classics of literature in every generation. Steiner holds that:

> Art dies when we lose or ignore the conventions by which it can be read, by which its semantic statement can be carried over into our own idiom … In short, the existence of art and literature depend on a never-ending, though very often unconscious, act of internal translation … In the absence of interpretation … there could be no culture. … (31)

So Steiner believes that nothing less than our understanding of art and culture is at stake if we do not attempt to "interpret" art for each generation.

On the other hand, Susan Sontag has written a convincing treatise "Against Interpretation." What she is against is what she sees as the artificial or arbitrary—indeed, "philistine"—"refusal to leave the work of art alone" (3). Sontag defines interpretation of art as "plucking a set of elements from the whole work," consciously, to illustrate a certain "code" of translation (*Ibid.*). She eschews the idea of explicating a work of art by assuming there is underlying symbolic meaning therein, beyond what the original artist created. Her solution to avoiding this "overt contempt for appearances" is to pay more attention to "form" in art, rather than "content." Sontag writes:

> If excessive stress on *content* provokes the arrogance of interpretation, more extended and more thorough descriptions of *form* would silence. What is needed is a vocabulary—a descriptive, rather than prescriptive, vocabulary—for forms. The best criticism, and it is uncommon, is of the sort that dissolves considerations of content into those of form. (10)

This study will concentrate largely on the form—a "descriptive vocabulary"—of Chekhov's last four plays, as well as possibilities of "interpretation" for the actor in particular roles. It is not avoiding the issue to pursue descriptions of both form and content; the actor's contribution to the playscript may be interpretive, while the form of the plays contributes to the choices the actor must make. The form of the text on the page influences the actor's work enormously—often "dissolving considerations of content"—but *suggesting* certain content as well. Dramaturgy requires observation of form, as well as explanation of content. Indeed, the actors and director are responsible for creating content, through the playscript of the playwright.[17]

---

17 We notice how "circumstances" are part of the form and content of a play. This process of "creating" content through Action and the actor's contribution to the text are discussed in Chapter IV.

While, as Sontag suggests, "the function of criticism should be to show *how it is what it is,* even *that it is what it is,* rather than to show *what it means*" (12), the actor must make specific artistic choices based on observations of form and perceived content. As Chekhov wrote—and as his last four masterpieces demonstrate—it is important for the artist to pose questions correctly, without giving set answers, while it is up to the audience to make judgments with regard to meaning (Friedland 60). The actor is specific in his/her playing, but ambiguity, in Chekhov's lyrical realism, is written into the plays. This is part of Chekhov's special gift. His "iron grid" of a form, discussed in Chapter V, is too strong to be broken by any one interpretation.

However they may feel about "interpretation," Steiner and Sontag might agree that "only great art both solicits and withstands exhaustive or willful interpretation" (Steiner 1998a: 28). Chekhov's art has managed to do so for over 100 years. In theatre, if an interpretation of a work (in production onstage) is iconoclastic, it can pave the way for "new forms" in the discipline, as Chekhov's plays did for Samuel Beckett and Harold Pinter, among others. In this sense, Steiner's definition of " … 'Interpretation' as that which gives language life beyond the moment and place of immediate utterance" (*Ibid.*) is applicable to the development of theatre art.

Finally, in the search for a definition of translation, it is interesting to look at the numerous connotations of the words "interpreter" and "translator" taken from their ancient etymology. Alex Gross makes a case for the Greek god Hermes as the "god of translators and interpreters."[18] St. Jerome, biblical scholar/translator of the "vulgate" (common language) Bible in 4th century A. D., and known as the patron saint of translation, proposed that translation be "word by word in the case of the mysteries [of the Bible], but meaning by meaning … everywhere else" (Steiner 1998a: 275). Hermes' attributes may give us a broader view of the meaning of translation. This winged messenger god presided over commerce, travel, and was the god of all arts and crafts, magic and matrimonial match-making. He was also the god of thieves and deceit, which spring from these other duties. As a part of the Greek word "Hermeneus" (from which emerges the term "hermeneutics," the science of interpretation), Gross attaches other possibilities of meaning to Hermes: interpreter of foreign terms, dragoman (an ancient Turkish word meaning interpreter, mediator and translator), court interpreter, go-between, broker and an expounder on words. Gross compares "Hermes" with the Latin "Interpres," which means to catch, lay hold of, grasp or take, as well as, literally, "caught in between." Of course, the god Mercury (with his swift, winged feet) is the Roman counterpart to Hermes.

---

18   Alex Gross, "Hermes—God of Translators and Interpreters," language.home.sprynet.com.

Gross notes that all these attributes are assigned to Hermes and Interpres, and, throughout history, translators and interpreters have been expected to perform the tasks mentioned above. Even Plato said, "Hermes has to do with speech … he is the interpreter … or thief, or liar, or bargainer; all that sort of thing has a lot to do with language."[19] So language, through Hermes, is linked to the act of prevarication. This is pertinent to usage of language in the theatre, especially in the genre of Realism. Whether characters are lying or telling the truth, their motives and actions are often revealed (or concealed) through language.

Hermes, apparently, has other names in many cultures: "Thoth in Egypt, Eshu in Africa, Coyote or Raven in Native American folklore, Krishna in India, or China's Monkey King … In other words, Hermes … is worthy of being the god of translators on an international scale."[20] We may say that translators, like Hermes, must perform wily and clever machinations. So, translation is not a simple transference of words. It involves interpretation, both praised and damned by acknowledged scholars on both sides, and it is often a wooly practice as evolved from a trickster god.

If translation is not a "transferal of words," what is it? How do translators "transfer a situation"? As Chekhov's resistance to his plays being translated implies, it is a whole culture that must be translated, rather than just words. Do all translators think of translation in this way? In order to further define this process of translation—specifically for the stage—it is helpful to understand the historical and theoretical influences on translation, and how they shape current translation practice.

A Brief History of Translation

A history of translation goes beyond the scope of this study. But some clarification of the issues involved will help explain current approaches to translation for the stage. While, as Maurice Friedberg states, "literary tastes evolve" (9), the same basic issue recurs in century after century: "In what ways can or ought fidelity to be achieved?" and, specifically, "Whatever treatise on the art of translation we look at, the same dichotomy is stated: as between 'letter' and 'spirit', 'word' and 'sense'" (Steiner 1998a: 275). For literary translation, we may ask even more specifically, "Which should come first, the literary version or the literal; and, is the translator free to express the sense of the original in any style and idiom he chooses?" (251). And, for translation for the stage, where the contemporary "translator" frequently

---

19   *Ibid.*, tr. Benjamin Jowett.
20   *Ibid.*

does not know the source language, we may ask: how is any "translation" to be done at all?

It is significant to a study of theatre translation to note that some of the first translations ever were translations of oral literatures—Homer's *Odyssey* by Livius Andronicus in 250 B.C. from Greek into Latin—and, somewhat later, translations of the Greek plays (Friedberg 19). Aristotle based his *Poetics* on the latter (the original Greek plays), in the fourth century B.C. Of course, *Aristotle's Poetics* has been translated numerous times and variously over the last centuries by literary and theatre scholars alike—as have the plays—and Aristotle's text is "incomplete, repetitious in spots, and badly organized" (Fergusson, *Aristotle's Poetics* 2). It is also the basis for our Western understanding of theatre for the last two thousand years. Such is the irony of "translation."

Gross has suggested that translators have "almost inevitably presided over most exchanges of knowledge from one culture to another ... they were simply the ones in a position to perform this task. Or, in the words of Giordana Bruno, 'From translation all science had its offspring.' "[21] This is evidenced by the works of Aristotle. This makes translators important to human cultural development in general. Though it is also beyond the scope of this study, it must be mentioned that the myriad translations of the Bible are "idiosyncratic," and translated from different points of view and dependent on the issue of "literal" translation versus "paraphrase." (The first English translation was made in the late fourteenth century from the "Latin Vulgate" version, not taken from the original languages of Hebrew and Greek.) Bible scholar/historian Barry Hoberman concludes that both *dynamic equivalence translations* (the paraphrase or idiomatic version) and *formal equivalence translation* (the more "literal" version) are both considered "translations," that is, "acceptable methods of rendering a text" (54–5). However, they have yielded stunningly different versions. Hoberman maintains that "An excellent way to enhance one's understanding of a difficult passage in Scripture is to place a number of English versions side by side and compare their renderings" (55). In these comparisons, it is interesting to see how the fundamental text of so many Judeo-Christian religions (the Old Testament and the New Testament) varies so significantly in various translations.[22] The same is true in translations of Chekhov's

---

21   *Ibid.*, language.home.sprynet.com, and in Steiner's *After Babel,* p. 261.
22   Language choices may irreparably skew a translation. Example: Minister Marianne Williamson, an author and lecturer on esoteric Christianity, observes that the word "sin" in the Bible translates as "mistake." What if a "sin" was replaced with a "mistake"? It bears consideration. Also see translator Philippe Le Moine: "Sin was a very Christian idea ... it carries ... moral baggage which Ancient Greek theology would not have had ..." and Christopher Campbell's reply: "That sort of thing is absolutely at the heart of talking about

canon (Chapters VI–IX). This underscores the importance of the translator—and of comparing diverse translations—in both religion and literature.

The history of translation is a history of language, nations and religion as well. Steiner divides this history into four periods, though there are many overlaps in attempted theory and empirical approaches.[23] The first period includes writings from Cicero, who cautions not to translate "word for word," (1998a: 248) through Alexander Fraser Tytler (Lord Woodhouse Lee), who wrote "the first and only book directly and only on the problems of translation until the end of the nineteenth century" in 1791 (Friedberg 71). This period is more about the practical side of translation.

The second period (spanning 1791 to 1946), which includes A. W. Schlegel (noted German translator of Shakespeare) and Wilhelm von Humbolt (a major thinker who "aims at nothing less than an analytic correlation of language and human experience") is more theory-based, though works of playwrights/poets/philosophers like Goethe, Schiller, Matthew Arnold, Paul Valéry and Ortega y Gasset give practical advice. For example, the earlier years of this period, with Schlegel and Goethe, saw the invention of the "dramaturg" who takes a play from one culture and makes it work plausibly in another, as Gross describes (2005b: 10). Indeed, the history of translation has followed the history of literature itself; they are inseparable. This is especially true for stage translation, where, as noted in this chapter's second opening quote, theatre is a history of adaptation. Steiner thinks this more "philosophical" second era ends with Valéry Larbaud in 1946, who wrote, "Le traducteur est méconnu; il est assis à la dernière place; il ne vit pour ainsi dire que d'aumônes" (the translator is unknown; he's seated at the last place; he lives only on [or because of being given] alms … 1998a: 284). We may remark that, to some degree, this is still true: translators for the stage may not even be recognized.

The third period, after 1946, is considered "modern" by Steiner. It is when translation as a discipline is more recognized, and two influential studies are published: *On Translation*, edited by Reuben Brower, and *The Craft and Context of Translation: A Critical Symposium*, edited by William Arrowsmith and Roger Shattuck in 1961. The latter includes seminal modern essays on "Translating for

---

translation—is there a single word that you can translate from one language to another? I doubt it. Everything we say has so much history and echo and nuance" (Campbell 2003).

23 Scholar/Translator Alex Gross divides his history into 12 major periods, defining them as times when particular cultures "perceived the need to absorb … more knowledge … from [one] another." He includes ancient and eastern cultures (Sumerian, Chinese, Arabian, etc.) and Steiner does not; I've chosen to comment on Steiner's and others' assessments, as they are more pertinent to Chekhov's translators, his dramaturgy, and the development of play translation in English.

Actors" and approaches to play translation as an endeavor distinct from translating other genres of literature. This notion that translation for the stage is greatly different from the translation of novels or poetry is a considerable notion to digest, apparently, for linguists and those not involved in theatre practice. Some translation and language scholars are not convinced of the distinction between play translation versus that of other literatures, even today. The notion that a play is written for actors was common to Shakespeare and Molière, yet some modern translators have ignored or are unfamiliar with the craft that depends so much on the translated text. This issue is addressed in Chapters IV and V.

Steiner situates the latest or fourth period of approaches to translation sometime after the 1960s, as one wherein "the study of the theory and practice of translation has become a point of contact between established and newly evolving disciplines. It provides a synapse for work in psychology, anthropology, sociology and … ethno- and socio-linguistics" (1998a: 284). The field of semiotics is included here; "signs" of theatre—gesture, movement, sounds and images—may be seen as a kind of translation or interpretation of what is in the playscript. However, as actor/director/scholar John Harrop observes, semiotics may be a tool for hermeneutics, but it is "sterile"—thus inaccurate—as a way to understand theatre (1992: 17–18). This issue is addressed in Chapter II, as modern and contemporary semioticians and linguists have attempted to analyze theatre structure, which bears on the nature of translation for the stage.

Along with an overview of each period, it is helpful to understand individual approaches to translation over the centuries in Western Europe and Russia, since they influenced English and American translators, as well as Chekhov. In the Middle Ages, accuracy was not a great concern (with the possible exception of Greek and Latin texts), and, apparently, the "translator" appropriated the original author's work as his own (Friedberg 250). The idea that one translates "with a view to one's own Nation and one's own age" goes back to 1656 with John Denham's translation of Virgil (*Ibid.*).

In every age, we may see that translation encounters the narrow view that one's own language (or style or view) is better than another's, which greatly influences how foreign works may be transposed. In 1663 Katherine F. Philips wrote "The rule that I understand of translation … was to write to Corneille's sense, *as it is supposed Corneille would have done, if he had been an Englishman.*"[24] Pertinently, director/actor Evgeny Vakhtangov (1883–1922) of Stanislavsky's Moscow Art Theatre states that, in directing a play, one should do it in a style for the time one is in, the place in which one has to play it, with the particular actors in the

---

24 In Brower's *On Translation*, cited by Maurice Friedberg, pp. 27–28.

company at hand and the audience for whom one is to perform it.[25] This has great implications for the performance of period and/or foreign plays. How much might we "change" or "improve" a work to make it palatable for our own time and sensibility? Is this idea of manipulating the source text—and labeling it a "translation" or "adaptation"—more acceptable for the time-bound and ephemeral art of the theatre than for text-bound literatures? In any case, the practice of translating for one's own time and nation has historical precedents.

For examples, Homer's *The Iliad* and *The Odyssey* were considered much too vulgar for Madame Dacier (1647–1720), who had Homer's "mouth washed out with soap," and the Neoclassicist translations of the eighteenth century forced authors Homer, Virgil, Chaucer, Tasso, Shakespeare, Milton and Dryden to "all converse in *one* language" (Friedberg 26). Romanticism brought more respectful attitudes towards foreign texts; the idea that nature should be left as it was seeped into literary translation as well. Wilhelm von Humbolt (1767–1835)—among the first to express concern for preservation of the form of the translated literary work—insisted that a translation be faithful to the entire source text, and "moreover, he favored multiple translations, since 'many translations result … in a cumulative approximation of the original'" (27). This is helpful for play production as well: a core tenet of this book is that comparisons of translations help the practitioner score and understand the play. While consulting multiple translations of Chekhov's plays may not result in "a cumulative approximation of the original"—actors must make specific, concrete choices—it opens up possibilities for the practitioner to see a variety of interpretations for particular moments in the play.

Before Humbolt, Steiner tells us, Gottfried Wilhelm Leibniz and J. G. Hamann set forth ideas on language and translation that persist to our time. Leibniz, in 1697, wrote, in his tract on German, that "language is not the vehicle of thought, but its determining medium" (1998a: 78). This is the same idea that contemporary communication theorists Edward Sapir and Benjamin Whorf have posited: language determines thought, and not the other way around (Trenholm 72). Hamann too, in 1750, affirmed that the "lineaments of speech" determine the thoughts and feelings in a community (Steiner 1998a: 79–80). Language, he believed, defines culture. He also identifies "action" with "dynamic linguistic posture or structure,"

---

25 Interview with Marat Yusim, former Moscow Art Theatre director, Spring 2003. His comprehensive book is *Stanislavsky's School of Acting and Directing*, copyrighted 2003. Author Yusim was kind enough to give me a preliminary draft before publication; his published book is *Passing the Torch—Basic Training: Stanislavsky's School of Acting and Directing*, 2006. Yusim quotes Vakhtangov frequently; Vakhtangov was a former member of the MAT, a gifted teacher and director, and was considered the "future leader of the Russian theatre" by Stanislavsky (*The Vakhtangov Sourcebook*, 35).

anticipating Kenneth Burke's *Grammar of Motives* (1945). In other words, language shapes our reality, and influences or informs our actions. This link between language and action is considered throughout this book.

Johann Gottfried von Herder, who wrote a famous essay in 1772, "Sprach-philosophie," used the new nationalism emerging in Europe as the foundation for his view of language. He "called for a general physiognomy of the nations from their languages," especially German, and believed that "National character is 'imprinted on language'" (81–2). This has great implications for translation. If Russian language (or any other nation's language) "imprints" national character, what does it do to that character to take its language away in an English translation? These linguist/philosophers seem to be proving Chekhov's point that translation of his plays would be fruitless for other nationalities. Later, in 1929, Edward Sapir wrote:

> No two languages are ever sufficiently similar to be considered as representing the same social reality. The worlds in which different societies live are distinct worlds, not merely the same worlds with different labels attached. (91)

So, again, we are confronted with the problems of a lack of "equivalency" across language borders, noted throughout translation history. Modern translations presented as equivalent to originals may also "dumb down" or "smooth out" the source work, resulting in the following sorts of translations, as writer/critic Joseph Brodsky said: "The reason English-speaking readers can barely tell the difference between Tolstoy and Dostoevsky is that they aren't reading the prose of either one. They're reading Constance Garnett" (Remnick 98–100).[26] National languages, it would seem, to greater or lesser degrees, are pervasive and often impenetrable for other nationalities.

Steiner maintains that the work of Leibniz, Hamann and Herder lead up to Humbolt's, whose work is in a direct line to that of Benjamin Whorf and Edward Sapir. The gist of it is that "The forms of a person's thoughts are controlled by inexorable laws of pattern of which he is unconscious. ... Every language is a vast pattern-system ... by which the personality not only communicates, but also ... builds the house of his consciousness."[27] So, if our thinking and personalities are communicated by language—which is the basis of our consciousness—the language used by the actor is monumentally important to the characters and action of a play.

---

26 Garnett is the early twentieth century English translator of many Russian writers, including Chekhov. Actor Ian McKellen similarly states: "We don't do Chekhov, we do *translations* of Chekhov" (Gottlieb and Allain 122). For English speakers in the twentieth century, this translator was often Constance Garnett.

27 Benjamin Lee Whorf, *Language, Thought and Reality*, qtd. George Steiner, *After Babel*, p. 93.

This matter of the differences in cultures, based on language, continues to beg the question of a "literal" versus a "true to the spirit" translation of foreign texts. In Russia, Peter the Great (1689–1725), according to Friedberg, was the first to expose Russians to influences of Western Europe. He commanded that Russian translators be clear, rather than lofty, that the language of translation (Russian, in this case) be the translator's native tongue, and that a literal translation be avoided because it destroys comprehensibility and "obfuscates the meaning of the original" (28). Others—notably poets and playwrights—echoed this call for "nonliteral" translations. Vladimir Lukin (1737–94) was notorious for his "free" translations that substituted Russian for Western names, and Russian props for French and German objects. These translators often appropriated the foreign works as "original works," though some (novelist Mikhail Chulkov, 1743–91) called this outright plagiarism (31). Leo Tolstoy, in Chekhov's time, denounced the idea of changing foreign literature to "suit Russian mores," claiming it deprived the works of "their value as documents of non-Russian life and of their realism above all" (35). Yet, in the twentieth century, some writers of Stalin's era went in the opposite direction and claimed that translators should delete from their work anything that was "alien" to the "progressive" notions of Stalin's Russia. We may well ask, when does a "free" translation become censorship? That is, when is a "translation" so "free"—or prescriptive—that it leaves out pertinent information? Though modern translators of Chekhov's canon may not purposefully intend to censor Chekhov's works by "adapting" them for modern audiences, this study will show how "adaptations" or "versions" of his plays may significantly affect style and meaning (Chapters VI–IX).

A reaction to the view promulgated by Stalinist Russia may have been a part of what fueled Vladimir Nabokov to claim "In fact, to my ideal of literalism I have sacrificed everything (elegance, euphony, clarity, good taste, modern usage and even grammar) that the dainty mimic prizes higher than truth" (Steiner 1998a: 331). He also wrote "I have sacrificed to total accuracy and completeness of meaning every element of form save the iambic rhythm, the retention of which assisted rather than impaired fidelity" (Friedberg 123). We may surmise that, for Nabokov, "fidelity" means mostly *semantic* fidelity. In theatre translation, as in poetry, the meaning of the words is important, but rhythm and cadence may be just as significant, since inflection helps define underlying meaning, or subtext. Nabokov is referring to his famous (or infamous) translation of Alexander Pushkin's (1799–1837) *Eugene Onegin*; Pushkin's work is acknowledged as "*the* supreme work of Russian literature of all time" (85).[28]

---

28   Friedberg quotes Pushkin: "Translation is the most difficult and the most thankless of all
     the literary genres I know" (38). Pushkin abandoned his own translation projects, writing:
     "I don't know how to translate; I don't know how to submit to the translator's hard work."
     This is stunning from the creator of the "supreme work of Russian literature," who knows

Friedberg cites the 1964 appearance of Nabokov's literalist rendition of *Onegin* into English as the most publicized event of the century in the sphere of translation.

Nabokov's *Onegin* is noted by many translators to be largely "unreadable."[29] With 256 pages of translated text, Nabokov included 1,175 pages of introduction and commentary. While helpful to the student, some translators believe the copious notes prove the work cannot be "literally" translated. Lefevere states "The footnote, in this case, amounts to the literal translator's admission of defeat" (qtd. Friedberg 153). In literature that is meant to be read, this point of view is debatable; the reader may choose to read notes or not, and notes may well inform meaning and circumstance. In the theatre, the audience will only hear the words and sounds, so notes are unhelpful (though they may be printed in a program), while notes may well help the director and actors conceive and formulate the production.

It is significant to mention Nabokov's own definitions of poetic translation:

1) Paraphrastic: a free version with omissions and additions … [based on] the translator's ignorance … and idiomatic conciseness … but no scholar should succumb to it …
2) Lexical: the basic meaning of the words (and their order) …
3) Literal: rendering, as closely as the associative or syntactical capacities of another language allow, the exact contextual meaning of the original. Only this is a true translation. (85–6)

It must be noted that Nabokov himself was not always a proponent of this type of "literal" translation. Friedberg recalls Nabokov's "cavalier" translation of *Alice in Wonderland*, which Nabokov authorized in a 1976 republication. Nabokov also had views on the requirements of a translator: "First, he must have at least as much talent as the original author [especially difficult with an iconoclast like Chekhov], second, he must know thoroughly the two nations and the two languages involved, the author's manner and methods, as well as the social background of words, their history and period associations, and, thirdly, he must be able to act the real author's part, impersonating his tricks of demeanor and speech … with the utmost verisimilitude" (Nabokov 319).

"hard work." Pushkin defined the translator as "the courier [notice allusion to Hermes] of the human spirit" (Steiner 1998a: 262).

29 Steiner quotes Russian virtuoso Alexander Gershonkron: "Nabokov's translation can and indeed should be studied, but despite all the cleverness and occasional brilliance it cannot be read" (Steiner 332). Translators André Lefevere and Dudley Fitts agree, while Harrison Salisbury, called it "a limpid, literal poetic translation" stating "He has given Pushkin's wondrous lines the glow and sparkle of the original" (qtd. by Douglas R. Hofstadler in "On Pushkin's Eugene Onegin").

Nabokov's views are important to acknowledge, as theatre playscripts—with the elements of rhythm, diction and cadence—are much like poetry in performance. The pitfalls of the translator of poets are similar to those encountered by the translator of plays. And, while some Chekhov translators are talented playwrights themselves and know theatre, they may not "know the two nations and two languages involved" and it may be argued that they do not necessarily "impersonate the tricks of demeanor and speech" of Chekhov. The translator's choices of language significantly affect actors' choices, as speech elements such as cadence, rhythm, etc., are as much at issue in performance as in poetry on the page. We may ask, do Chekhov's translators live up to many (or any) of Nabokov's requirements for poetic translation? (see Chapters VI–IX).

Other key literary historical figures are important to our understanding of the history of translation. John Dryden (1631–1700), who, according to Steiner, refuted blind literalism, defined *paraphrase* as "to produce the text which the foreign poet would have written had he been composing in one's own tongue" (Steiner 1998a: 351). This is reminiscent of Philips' statement about translating Corneille in 1663. Steiner claims Dryden—more than his literalist precursor Ben Johnson—is a "compromiser," choosing paraphrase over literal translation (267). At the other end of the scale, Dryden disparaged the translator who "assumes the liberty not only to vary from words and sense, but to forsake them both as he sees occasion" (267–8). He called this type of translator an "imitator." Of course, the overlap between literal, paraphrase and imitation is indistinct. Still, Steiner states that Dryden's views on translation "laid down ideals and lines of discussion that are with us still" (267).[30]

Johann Wolfgang Goethe (1749–1832) had a three-pronged theory of translation, which culminated in the idea that "the highest and best translation method is one which strives to make the original identical with the translation" (Friedberg 75–6). How this is accomplished is unclear, yet Goethe's process does call for "the transformation of the original into the translator's current idiom and frame of reference" (Steiner 1998a: 271). For example, since Goethe thought "Shakespeare is, above all, a poet to be read; staged, his plays are full of weakness and crudity,"[31] Goethe's famous productions of Shakespeare in Weimar were "drastically amended" to remove all prurient references (401). This is a clear example of the "ethnocentricity" of translations—that is, the translator fits the translation to his/her own

---

30   Poet Kenneth Rexroth too claims "When discussing the poet as translator, from time immemorial it has been the custom to start out by quoting Dryden." This is from "The Poet as Translator," *The Craft and Context of Translation*, ed. Arrowsmith and Shattuck (Austin: 1961), p. 22.

31   Goethe in *Shakespeare und kein Ende*, qtd. Steiner in *After Babel*, p. 401.

ethnic or national standards. Even with these emendations, Schlegel claimed that German Shakespeare translations transformed the native German tongue and the range of German national consciousness (*Ibid.*). In the famed Schlegel-Tieck translations of Shakespeare,[32] the Bard was transformed into a German "classic" poet—and playwright—who was read and played as widely as any German playwright. In other words, Shakespeare, for Germans, became more a German playwright than an English one; Shakespeare's English text was not "translated" into German, it *became* German, fulfilling Goethe's prerequisites for the "best" translations, including eliminating Shakespeare's "crudities." Later, translations of Ibsen and Strindberg helped raise the issues of women's rights at the end of the nineteenth century in Europe. Translation may prompt social development.

The tradition begun by the Schlegel-Tieck Shakespeare translations helped socialize Germany—and other nations—and is testimony to the "potency of translations," in the theatre (Friedberg 202). However, while the nature of translation has not lost its intrinsic potency, discoveries in the field, it seems, have not blossomed much more since Goethe and Schlegel's time. Attitudes and practices with regard to translation of literature still center around questions of "literal" fidelity or capturing the "spirit" of a work, but just how these might be accomplished, especially in translation for the theatre, is dependent on the individual translator.

In modern times, though theatre seems the lesser sibling in the world of translating literature, disagreements about the nature of the translation continue to spark interest and acrimony. Popular publications—Remnick's "The Translation Wars" in *The New Yorker* (2005), Logan's "Whose Play is it Anyway?" in *The Guardian* (2003), Bellos' *Is that a Fish in Your Ear?* (2011), Jiayang Fan's "Han Kang and the question of translation" in *The New Yorker* (2018)[33] and many more—are testimony to the fact that translation in general, and translation for the theatre in particular, continue to be issues of interest for the public as well as in academic circles. In the

---

32   A. W. Schlegel, contemporary of Goethe, translated seventeen of Shakespeare's plays (published 1797–1810); the rest were translated by Count von Bandissin and Dorothea Tieck with father Ludwig Tieck.

33   Korean author Han Fang and her translator Deborah Smith were both awarded the Man Booker International Prize for Fang's 2016 novel, *The Vegetarian*, but the paper Huffington Post Korea claimed the translation was completely "off the mark." Interestingly, author Fang had read and approved the translation. Smith defended herself, saying "I would only permit myself an infidelity for the sake of a greater fidelity." Also, as author Jiayang Fan notes, "what Smith describes is the effect that any writer might hope to coax from her reader: a feeling so visceral that it's as if she had absorbed the text into her own experience." This might be what Chekhov's translators and adaptors hope their audiences might feel as well.

next two chapters, contemporary scholars and theatre practitioners continue to face the quandary of translation, and particularly that for the stage.

References

Aristotle. *Aristotle's Poetics.* Trans. S. H. Butcher. Intro. Francis Fergusson. New York: Hill and Wang, 1961.

Arrowsmith, William and Roger Shattuck, eds. *The Craft and Context of Translation.* Austin: The University of Texas Press, 1961.

Bakhtin, M. M. *Speech Genres and Other Late Essays.* Austin: University of Texas Press, 1986.

Bellos, David. *Is that a Fish in Your Ear? Translation and the Meaning of Everything.* New York: Faber & Faber, 2011.

Bentley, Eric. *The Brecht Memoir.* Evanston, IL: Northwestern University Press, 1985.

Brislin, Richard. *Translation: Applications and Research.* New York: Gardner Press, 1976.

Burke, Kenneth. *A Grammar of Motives.* New York: Prentice-Hall, 1954.

Campbell, Christopher. *Platform Papers on Translation*, Royal National Theatre, November 11, 2003.

Chekhov, Anton. *Chekhov: The Essential Plays.* Trans. Michael Henry Heim. New York: Modern Library, 2003.

———. *Letters on the Short Story, The Drama and Other Literary Topics*, Ed. Louis S. Friedland. New York: Dover Publications, 1966.

———. *The Oxford Chekhov.* Trans. Ronald Hingley. London: Oxford University Press, Vol. II, 1967, Vol. III, 1964, and Vol. IX, 1975.

Chilewska, Anna. "The Assessment of Translations: Examples from Chekhov, Zoshchenko and Sienkiewicz." M.F.A. Thesis. University of Alberta, Canada, 2000.

———. "The Assessment of Translations …" *The Spectator*, 24 September 1977.

Clifford, John. "Translating Moments, Not Words," www.teatrodomundo.com, February 9, 2005.

Fan, Jiayang. "Buried Words: Han Kang and the Complexity of Translation." *The New Yorker,* January 15, 2018.

Friedberg, Maurice. *Literary Translation in Russia.* University Park, PA: The Pennsylvania State University Press, 1997.

Gottlieb, Vera and Paul Allain. eds. *The Cambridge Companion to Chekhov.* Cambridge University Press, 2000.

Gross, Alex. "Hermes—God of Translators and Interpreters," language.home.sprynet.com, April 26, 2005a.

———. "Some Major Dates and Events in the History of Translation," www.accurapic.com, January 28, 2005b.

———. "Translation: The Human Utility," language.home.sprynet.com, January 28, 2005c.

———. "Translation Theory: Some Images and Analogies," language.home.sprynet.com, January 28, 2005d.

Harrop, John. *Acting.* London: Routledge, 1992.

Hayakawa, S. I. *Language in Thought and Action.* New York: Harcourt Brace Jonanovich, 1939.

Johnston, David, ed. *Stages of Translation.* Bath, England: Absolute Classics, 1996.

Kilroy, Thomas. "*The Seagull:* An Adaptation," *The Cambridge Companion to Chekhov,* eds. Vera Gottlieb and Paul Allain. Cambridge University Press, 2000.

Logan, Brian. "Whose Play is it Anyway?" *Guardian,* UK, March 12, 2003.

Mueller-Vollmer, Kurt and Michael Irmscher. *Translating Literatures, Translating Cultures.* Berlin: Erich Schmidt, 1998.

Nabokov, Vladimir. "On Translating Eugene Onegin," *The New Yorker,* 1955.

Pohorlak, Frank. "Proponents for a Literal Translation of the New Testament," www.concordant.org.

Rabassa, Gregory. Trans. *100 Years of Solitude* by Gabriel Garcia Marquez, Interview on the Leonard Lopate Show, WNYC, July 11, 2005.

Remnick, David. "The Translation Wars," *The New Yorker,* November 7, 2005, pp. 98–109.

Rose, Marilyn Gaddis, ed. *Translation in the Humanities.* Binghamton: State University of New York, n.d.

Scolnicov, Hannah and Peter Holland. *The Play Out of Context.* Cambridge: Cambridge University Press, 1989.

Senelick, Laurence. *The Chekhov Theatre.* Cambridge: Cambridge University Press, 1997.

Sontag, Susan. *Against Interpretation and Other Essays.* New York: Picador USA, 2001.

Steiner, George. *After Babel.* New York: Oxford University Press, 1998a.

Trenholm, Sarah. *Thinking Through Communication,* 4th ed. Boston: Pearson Education, 1995.

Vakhtangov, Yevgeny. *The Vakhtangov Sourcebook.* London and New York: Routledge, 2011.

Zatlin, Phyllis. *Theatrical Translation and Film Adaptation, a Practitioner's View.* UK, USA, Canada: Multilingual Matters Ltd., 2005.

CHAPTER TWO

Modern Approaches to Translation

I live in fear of not being misunderstood.

—OSCAR WILDE

With time, a translator gets used to promising the impossible
the way a loan shark gets used to promising carnage.

—TRANSLATOR INDRA NOVEY[1]

In spite of innumerable comments on translation and language by scholars and translators throughout history, as we approach the modern age there are relatively few new observations on the art and craft of translation.[2] William Arrowsmith

---

1   Novey translated Han Kang's book *Ways to Disappear* in a lauded and criticized version. Critics accused Novey of "over-reaching" in the article by Jiayang Fan, "Han Kang and the Complexity of Translation" in *The New Yorker*, Jan. 15, 2018.

2   For more examples, Steiner states "[D]espite this rich history, and ... the caliber of those who have written about the art and theory of translation, the number of original, significant ideas in the subject remains very meager" (1998: 251) and "the range of theoretic ideas, as distinct from the pragmatic notation, remains very small ... it has figured marginally ..." (283–4); Friedberg claims "very few theoretical studies of translation exist in any language" (71); Mueller-Vollmer and Irmscher observe "translation ... has been accorded only scant and sporadic attention within the established academic institutions" (IX).

and Roger Shattuck claim: "Intelligent comments on translation ... tend to be unavailable or scattered, tucked away in odd corners, and their arguments diffused. The crucial, comprehensive volume of pioneering scholarship **has yet to be written** (emphasis added)."[3] Steiner's *After Babel*, first published in 1975, may be this "comprehensive volume," but it does not address the translation of the playscript, written to be acted.

Arrowsmith and Shattuck's *The Craft and Context of Translation* brings us into the modern age of translation, where dramatic literature as a separate area of study is finally recognized. Three of the twenty-two essays in this volume deal with the nature of theatre translation. If translation itself has been given "meager, scant and sporadic" attention, as Steiner suggests, translation for the stage has had even less. The introduction of Realism—and Stanislavsky's acting theory issuing from this new genre—has helped to put more focus on the subject, since Ibsen and Chekhov were translated throughout Europe. Chapters IV and V discuss Action, its relation to Realism, and Chekhov's dramaturgy.

Scholars, linguists and theatre practitioners have only recently begun to discern and comment on the differences between theatre texts—that is, the playscript—and other genres of literary writing such as poetry, novels or short stories. Practitioner John Harrop tells us that, interestingly, while actors have always known that it is through action, not just language, that theatre communicates with its audience, the critical community has just recently been catching up to acting practice (1992: 10). Though the science of semiotics now includes a Semiotics of Theatre and Theatre Translation,[4] semioticians miss the "subjective interpretation or decoding" that happens "when looking at the actor alone onstage ... placed within the sociocultural conventions of a scenic space" (17). Like use of sound, inflection and gesture in speech, use of space, movement and voice onstage may evoke different reactions and communicate different ideas to each member of the audience. Steiner also makes this point about language in general:

> Private connotations, private habits of stress, of elision or periphrase make up a fundamental component of speech. Their weight and semantic field are essentially individual. Meaning is at all times the potential sum total of individual adaptations. ... Different human beings ... will always relate different associations to a given word. ... The words we speak as individuals take on a specific gravity, specific to the speaker

3 Steiner, 1998; 286, qtd. from Arrowsmith and Shattuck at the University of Texas Symposium, 1961.
4 See Ekatarina Nikolarea's "Performability vs. Readability: A Historical Overview of a Theoretical Polarization in Theater Translation," *Translation Journal*, Vol. 6, No. 4, Oct. 2002, and accurapid.com.

alone, to the unique aggregate of association and preceding use generated by his total mental and physical history. ... This is precisely the way in which all of us put mean- ing into meaning. ... More often than not, the active sources of connotation remain subconscious or outside the reach of memory (1998: 206–7).

In normal social interaction, our associations of words are our own, whether we consciously acknowledge this or not. This is just as true for us when we partici- pate in theatre performance, as an audience member or as an actor. In the theatre, gesture, sound and setting also communicate meaning. The idea that we assign meanings to words and signs individually makes the notion of Theatre Semiotics— that we may assign meanings to particular "signs" in the theatre—especially prob- lematic, because our interpretation of "signs" is subjective, and based so much on culture. Uses of language and gesture and how they are evoked from the playscript by the actor are individual, and affect audience members diversely.

Something else that greatly influences how a translation might be received onstage—in our time or previous ones—is the fact that translation is almost always a transport over time: "Inevitably, the spectrum of connotations is that of [the trans- lator's] own age and locale. Even when he finds the precise chronological equivalent, the objects or facts of feeling are imbedded in his own modern perception of them" (1998: 352). Arrowsmith reminds us too that "we translate into the literary con- ventions of our own age" (122), and we translate the specific theatre conventions of our age as well. Chekhov will be translated according to different conventions than Molière, for example. And he will be translated anew for each generation according to our accumulated understanding of the past. Steiner insists "We are so much the product of set feeling-patterns, Western culture has so thoroughly stylized our per- ceptions, that we experience our 'traditionality' as natural" (1998: 486). This has to do with our own time and culture-bound perceptions. Poet Kenneth Rexroth, too, dis- cussing the poet as translator, reminds us of the ethnocentricity of our English trans- lations. We must, he claims, communicate directly to our own audience (Arrowsmith 22). He echoes Vakhtangov's advice for stage performance described earlier, where the director is advised to direct a play for his/her own time and circumstances.

Interestingly, this idea of perpetrating our traditional perceptions may be aligned with Stella Adler's idea that, as actors, we have a "collective conscious- ness:" we all have pre-life experience, we know more than we think, we are a continuum of previous knowledge, and we draw on millions of years of human experience from our past human history. Adler writes, "... the collective mem- ory of man is such that he forgets nothing he has ever seen, heard, read about or touched." Adler insists "Your life is fractional compared to your experience" (1988: 16–17). We have, in us, historical memory. While memory and traditions may skew our perceptions to what is familiar to us culturally, it may also expand our understanding of the wealth of human experience. These two possibilities are not necessarily mutually exclusive, especially for the actor working onstage. Stanislavsky also believed in a cumulative understanding beyond that of our own time and place (1961: 83).[5] This understanding is vital to the actor: it involves his/her creative imagination, which is sparked by the text.

Modern translators, seeing that notions of the value of "literal" and "free" translations have tottered back and forth according to the tenor of the times in a particular culture, have attempted to come up with some ground rules for the discipline. It is not unusual that I. A. Richards has claimed that translation is "probably the most complex type of event yet produced in the evolution of the cosmos" (Brislin 1,79), because it demands so many concurrent skills of the translator.[6] Often, these skills demand contradictory implementations. Maurice Friedberg describes how modern translators rarely follow any one translation theory strictly because dictates of translation may be mutually exclusive.[7] Here is his list:

1. A translation must give the [literal sense of the] words of the original.
2. A translation must give the ideas of the original [departing from the text if necessary].
3. A translation should read like an original work.
4. A translation should read like a translation.
5. A translation should reflect the style of the original.
6. A translation should possess the style of the translator.
7. A translation [of a non-contemporary work] should read as a contemporary of the original.
8. A translation [of a non-contemporary work] should read as a contemporary of the translator [avoiding stylized or archaic language].
9. A translation may add to or omit from the original [if this would improve it].
10. A translation may never add to or omit from the original.
11. A translation of verse should be in prose.
12. A translation of verse should be in verse.[8]

---

5   Stanislavsky believed the actor reached the "creative state" through conscious work that established "some sort of communion with the superconscious" and that true inspiration was thus born of conscious preparation on the role (1961: 83).

6   Susan Bassnett, a translation theoritician, denies the necessity of some skills, with regard to play translation, later in this chapter.

7   I include these amusing and contradictory lists to show the breadth of the endeavor, and how scholars are fond of making lists.

8   Maurice Friedberg, *Literary Translation in Russia*, (University Park, PA, 1997), p. 110, originally assembled by Theodore Savory, *The Art of Translation* (London, 1957).

We may compare it to Alex Gross' list, entitled:

I. **Recurrent Ideas About Translation Over the Last 2,500 Years**
1. The never-ending battle between "translating words" vs. "translating ideas," AKA "Literalism" vs. "Liberalism."
   1A. Translating ideas is better than translating words.
   2B. Translating words is better than translating ideas.
2. Translation is virtually or ultimately impossible because no two languages are alike.
   2A. Only fools, scoundrels or traitors translate.
   2B. Translation violates natural or divine law.
   2C. Translation can never work because Language A (*your language*) is inferior to Language B (*my language*).
   2D. No humans can possibly do it, so let's invent a machine that can do it.
3. Perhaps translation is possible, but most translations are bad, and most translators are just as bad (or at best poorly trained).
   3A. To improve matters, all translators must be carefully trained and strict rules must be followed. The training method and rules are usually provided by the person or persons making this statement.
4. Academics—including even translation scholars—have no real knowledge of practical translation problems. This position is held even by a number of academics and translation scholars.
5. Whatever problems may exist, translation is nonetheless of great value to society.
6. There must be some great and majestic theory of universal knowledge or universal grammar to account for all of the aforementioned problems and contradictions.
   6A. There can be no such theory.
7. The art and craft of translation are greatly misunderstood and translators are largely ignored.
8. It is nonetheless possible to provide general advice and specific tips to help translators improve their translations.
   8A. Most such advice and/or tips is (are) contradictory or mutually exclusive.[9]

---

9   Alex Gross, language.home.sprynet.com.

Also of interest are the "main premises of literary translation" from what Soviet translator/scholar Vladimir Rossel called the Gorky-Chukovsky-Kashkin[10] doctrine of literary translation:

1. *Any* literary text is translatable.
2. A translator, like an original author, should study not only the text, but life itself.
3. In literary translation, literary aspects are more important than linguistic ones.
4. A literary translation should be neither "precise" (that is literal) nor "free," but should strive to achieve an artistic impact on readers of the translation that equals the impact of the original on the author's countrymen. (Friedberg 95).

As Friedberg points out, the latter is more easily said than done. The impact, for example, of Chekhov's plays on his countrymen was varied to begin with, and changed over time. Chekhov had many detractors during his lifetime, in his own country (Mirsky 380–3). To this day, critics discuss the fallout of Chekhov's works on his countrymen, and debate his plays' meanings for our country and our times. Dictum two above is true for the actor as well: we are observers of life, and so may copy or create behavior appropriate for the play at hand. The translator must do the same, and understand deeply the original playwright's style and background in order to do so.

With regard to language, whether or not Chekhov's canon should be translated as a "contemporary of the original"—that is, as period pieces—or with contemporary colloquialisms, is perennially at issue. As noted in Chapters VI–IX, contemporary usages of language in Chekhov's plays are sometimes mixed with more "old-fashioned" language usages and syntax. For the actor, this may make for confusing performance choices that unintentionally take the audience out of the

---

10 Maxim Gorky, famous "naturalistic" playwright and contemporary of Chekhov, was a spokesman of the short-lived "World Literature" project in 1918 in the Soviet government, establishing a studio for the training of translators. Chukovsky was a novelist and translator who bemoaned the unacknowledged state of Soviet translators. Kashkin was a leading translator and theoretician of the Stalinist era, and a proponent of sticking to the "norm" and thus the censorship of his era. This list was first published in Jiri Levy's *Iskusstvo perevoda* in 1963 in Czech and in 1969 in German (Friedberg 95).

context of the play.[11] The translator's language choices can support or corrupt the fluidity of the style of performance.

In any case, the three lists of dictums noted above show markedly how, as Steiner says, "Every general statement worth making about language invites a counter-statement or antithesis. In its formal structure, as well as its dual focus, internal and external, the discussion of language is unstable and dialectical. What we say about it is momentarily the case" (1998a: 129). Thus, we see that "translation may be far harder than anyone had imagined. It may be the one field of learning where two thousand years have brought no real advances."[12] The issues regarding translation noted by the ancients are still hotly debated today. Chekhov's plays are a pointed example of the time-bound intricacies involved in current translation practice.

Indeed and nonetheless, much of the actual work of translation can be about the translator's own intuition, rather than any specific theory or practice. This is noted by many translator/critics, even those who have attempted to write about translation in terms of linguistic theory. H. Stephen Straight puts forth a "dimension" of translation "somewhat *reluctantly* (emphasis added)" which he labels "*intuition:* is the translation satisfying?" and concedes that translation is an art as much as a skill. He states that some elements of translation are "ineffable" and "beyond scientific investigation" and that those who believe in the irreconcilability of science and art are possibly "wrong ... in principle ... although ... right in practice" because "our present ignorance of the bases of language use is too great for anyone to feel terribly sure of himself in accounting for it scientifically" (Rose 1981: 48). For linguists, the notion that translation should be a "scientific" endeavor is important, and not easily renounced.[13]

---

11 Example: in Tom Donaghy's adaptation of *Cherry Orchard*, characters spoke in contemporary, colloquial speech—epithets like "Shit!" were expressed—while actors were in Edwardian costume. Some characters wore the clothes easily, while others seemed as if they'd been dropped into another time, against their will. How might the aristocratic Ranevskaya respond to Lopakhin, once a serf on her land, when he screams an epithet in her presence? The actress, inexplicably, just seemed to ignore Lopakhin. This was odd and uncomfortable for the audience, who expected a response from Ranevskaya.

John Gielgud (who translated a "version" of *Cherry Orchard*) defined style as "knowing what kind of play you are in." How can the actor know this in a translated text? If the translator has given few or contradictory clues, prudent directors and actors will make choices on this in rehearsal. Their creative contributions to the text and action of the play are crucial to the performance.

12 Alex Gross, language.home.sprynet.com.

13 Sirkku Aaltonen's *Time-Sharing on Stage* states that "scientific models promoted by linguistics-oriented approaches are insufficient for the study of [contextual codes for theatre

Thus, translator/semiotician Patrice Pavis—after a heady "scientific" attempt to define stage translation—concludes "theatre translation is never what one expects it to be: not in words, but in gesture, not in the letter, but in the spirit of a culture, ineffable, but omnipresent" (Scolnicov 42). I suggest that what Straight and Pavis label as "ineffable" may be the understanding of "Action" (which is psycho-physical) in play translation, defined and discussed in Chapter IV (and Appendix A). Action may be "ineffable" *on the page* to the scholar unfamiliar with acting practice, but clear to the theatre practitioner who works with the actor and playscript in rehearsal and production.

Straight concludes "we [linguists, apparently] shall simply have to accept the fact that there is an essentially 'intuitive' component in our evaluation of translations, a component that lies outside and beyond the more familiar and discernible dimensions of knowledge and purpose [of translation]" (Rose 1981: 50). André Lefevere concurs, claiming "Many scholars in the field are becoming increasingly disenchanted with the proliferation of attempts to formalize and schematize what cannot be formalized, not in any way that goes much beyond the intuitive knowledge of the process ..." (54). Moreover, Steiner states categorically that whether or not there is a genuine "science of language" is a moot point. He suggests there is no real "analogy" with science underlying the notion of scientific linguistics, because human speech "is not of this order" (1998a: 115). Translation is a "motion of the spirit" (75) and there are no scientific criteria for the humanities, which is an entire "discipline of intuition" (xv).[14]

Attempts to "formalize" translation practice persist in the field of linguistics. Translators of plays who are also theatre practitioners, however, understand that plays are bound by the given circumstances—cultural, social and temporal—of the works, and so see the entire enterprise as a much different endeavor. It is replete with what linguists call the "extralinguistic" factors mentioned previously. These factors include the audience ("receptors" in linguistic-speak) as well as the notion of Action: the play translator's "intuition" is based on the fact that the play is written to be performed.

Christopher Hampton, a playwright and more recent play translator, uses his "imagination" in translating; this may be another aspect of "intuition." He states he tries to "rather rigidly ... reproduce whatever it is that I imagine the playwright

---

translation]" (3). The fact that Aaltonen's study was published in 2000 documents how the controversy among linguists persists into the 21st century.

14   In the humanities and the arts, PhD dissertations are still written in the scientific format (Problem, Methodology, etc.) though the literary subject matter may not be "of this [scientific] order."

wants to say" (Logan 2003) while Kevin Halliwell (translator of the Gate Theatre's *Witness*, a Swedish play about the art of translation) aims for "an equivalent effect. You want to produce the same effect on the English-speaking audience as the play would have had on its native audience" (*Ibid.*). Again, what this effect might be is debatable, but it is often considered and addressed by translators, as well as directors and dramaturges.

Playwright/translator John Clifford's website article "Translating Moments, Not Words" is subtitled "Imagine." He calls his "perception" of a play "the largely invisible web of connections that make up the structure of the play" (2005). He claims that harnessing the "spirit of the play"—"unspoken shared values that make communication possible within a language at a given time"—relies on an ability to "learn how to translate the unspoken" (*Ibid.*). This may be intuitive, but also relates to understanding the nature of Action, which, I maintain, *is* the web of connections underlying the dialogue of the playscript. In Chekhov's four plays, what is unspoken—or transmitted with gesture, setting, costume, lighting and mood, rather than words—is the core of the plays. The "unspoken" is understood by the actors, director and dramaturge, and is rendered by the translator. A translator who does not understand this "poetry of the theatre" is likely to make awkward mistakes in translation.

Literary translator Lila Ray disparages both the "brick by brick" style of translation, literally translating each word with little attention paid to the overall meaning, and the so-called "intuitive" method that "comes mysteriously right if the translator runs through the text a number of times and regurgitates it in an unobstructed flow of fluent verbiage" (Brislin 262).[15] While Ray claims her process of translation is her own, she, perhaps unwittingly, borrows basic precepts from the idea of structures of Action inherent in the playscript. She states that any translation needs a blueprint, which is based on "the examination of the event that has resulted in an experience and perception the author feels the urge to communicate" (264; and see "event" in Appendix A). Structures of action are based on events. She also mentions the importance of sound and syntax, and the meanings associated with certain vowels and consonants. Her work is tightly based on an understanding of context. In explicating both form and content—based on form—Ray's personal process is similar to that of the actor, director and dramaturge. While she lays "intuition" at the feet of the poet, she claims the translator's task of restructuring a

---

15 Translator/playwright Jean-Claude Van Itallie, in an interview in Spring 2003, actually described to me how he works in a similar way in translating Chekhov's plays, as a way of "channeling" Chekhov into English.

poem in another language requires detailed and accurate knowledge of form and style (278). This is also true for the translator of plays.

More recently, literary translator Edith Grossman too writes:

> By now it is a commonplace, at least in translating circles, to assert that the translator is the most penetrating reader and critic a work can have. The very nature of what we do requires that kind of deep involvement in the text. Our efforts to translate both denotation and connotation, to transfer significance as well as context, means that we must be engaged in extensive textual excavation, and bring to bear everything we know, feel and intuit about the two languages and their literatures ... And this kind of close critical reading is sheer pleasure for the shameless literature addicts like me, who believe that the sum of a fine piece of writing is more than its parts and larger than the individual words that constitute it. ... [W]e have to ... weigh and consider each element within its literary milieu and stylistic environment. ... [S]omething more lurks behind mere surface ... I think this kind of longing to unravel esthetic mysteries lies at the heart of the study of literature. It is surely the essence of interpretation, of exegesis, of criticism, and of translation. (73–4).

Like Pavis, Straight, Aaltonen, Lefevere, Steiner, Hampton, Clifford and Ray, Grossman admits to a more "intuitive" approach to translation, rather than a "word-by-word" process.

Translator/scholar Rainer Schulte does not write of the use of "intution" per se in creating a translation, but mentions "acts of visualization" and "moments of ambiguity." As mentioned previously, Schulte is an advocate of a "situational" or a "sociolinguistic" approach when it comes to translation of literature. A translator is encouraged to visualize the entire situation in translating, rather than searching for words that are "equivalent" to those in the source text. Schulte cites "moments of ambiguity" as moments when a different choice of words is used in various translations. He claims the author, at these moments, has "created an environment of directed ambiguity" which necessitates multiple translations in order to encourage the reader to see the "subtle nuances" and "reconnect with the internal progression of the poem" (Mueller-Vollmer 38). In other words, multiple translations are helpful in getting the reader to "think through the poem" as a work beyond the "strictures of one definitive interpretation" (Ibid.). Multiple translations are helpful to the actor too, in script analysis of translated texts. "Intuition" and creative acting choices may be sparked by noting the different uses of language in various playscripts. This is exemplified in Chapters VI through IX.

Language—and so translation—may be time and culture-bound and personal, and the navigation of its process considered "intuitive." These and other considerations, such as whether to translate to the "letter" or to the "spirit" of a text—or somewhere in between—continue to make the translation process a difficult one.

In translation for the stage, some current theorists do not recognize that plays are written to be performed. Well-known playwrights, who do understand performance, translate Chekhov's last four plays without knowing the Russian language. The polarizations between theorists who see the written text of a play as complete in itself, and those who see it as simply a blueprint for performance, *and* those between translators who know the source language and those who don't, continue today. These issues are pertinent to a definition of Action as the structure of drama, and understanding translation of the playscript as a particular and distinct form of creative writing.

Some translator/scholar/linguists may finally come to the idea that plays are different than other written genres of literature, but warily. Noted translator/scholar André Lefevere, in 1980, writes the summation of *Languages of Theatre, problems in the translation and transposition of drama.* He observes that, after the nineteen-sixties, texts were "inextricably bound up with contexts" rather than linguistics alone, but that this greatly "complicated the task" of translation for the stage (Zuber 160). He suggests, after naming several linguistic approaches to literary translation, that both linguistic and what he calls "metaliterary"[16] approaches to the text of a play may be more or less viable, but that, finally, "the study of translated dramatic literature has been treated extremely superficially by translation studies" since "literary analyses of translated dramatic texts very often were confined *to its textual dimension, to what was on the page*" (160, emphasis added). Without discussing the structure, "non-literary" or performance elements of drama, Lefevere ends the volume with no nod to or definition of any "language of the theatre" at all. He suggests more studies be done.

In the same volume, Ortrun Zuber acknowledges that translations "must be actable" (*Ibid.*). She is concerned with many practical problems of translation—or transposition—from one culture to another. She asks "Why has the translated text to be tried out onstage?" and "Why has the intention of the author of the original to be respected and maintained?" (*Ibid.*) These questions reveal the point of view of previous translators, in Zuber's opinion: many do *not* see the import of "trying out" the translation onstage, nor of maintaining the "intention of the original author," whatever that may be. So gaffes might be made, unforeseen by the translator at his/her table, and the original author may complain and shut down a production that transposes characters and changes events. Still, Zuber does not

---

16 This approach is based on the "scientific study of literature," not on critical theories of literature, and is particularly time-bound, according to Lefevere. As we have seen, however, a *"scientific* study" of dramatic literature—because of the pragmatic requirements of the theatre—may be oxymoronic.

address the underlying question of what makes drama different from other genres, nor why the audience is important to the production. Though Zuber recognizes that "this piece of literature requires action and movement," she sees in drama a "coalescence of literature and theatre," not a different genre in itself (*Ibid.*). There is no understanding of "poetry *in* the theatre" versus "poetry *of* the theatre." This concept, as a component of dramatic structure, will be addressed in Chapter IV on Action (see also Appendix A).

Semioticians and translation theorists have wrestled with the idea of whether the notions of "performability" or "readability" may be applied to theatre scripts, and so distinguish the play from other written literatures. Translation theorist Susan Bassnett first claimed (in the early 1980s), with semioticians of the Prague School,[17] that a theatre text should be read differently than a prose text, because a play is "fully rounded only when it is performed" (Nikolarea 7). So, the play translator must consider the "*function* of the text as an element for and of performance" (8).

Then, in 1985, Bassnett decided that translators were only using this theory to justify variations in language choices that considered "performance" more important than linguistic structures. She reversed her former position, calling "performability"—"decoded by the actor and encoded into gestural form"—a "vexing … loose and wooly concept" because "there are infinite decodings possible in any playtext" (8–9). Tellingly, she argues that if the idea of performability were taken seriously, it would mean that "during the translation process it is the translator's responsibility to decode the gestic text while he sits at a desk and imagines the performance dimension" and, "in Bassnett's opinion, this situation does not make any sense at all!" She states too that this makes the translator's task "superhuman!" (14).[18]

Translators and theorists throughout the history of translation might well agree with Bassnett about the enormity of the task. At the same time, in play translation, imagining actors performing onstage, with actions, sets, costumes, lights and all aspects of performance, is exactly what is required of the translator.

---

17 In 1931, Otamar Zich published *Aesthetics of the Art of Drama* and Jan Mukarovsky published "An Attempted Structural Analysis for the Phenomena of the Actor." These works laid the foundations for theatrical theories of the Prague School of the 1930s. These publications changed semiotic analysis of theatrical theory by claiming that the written text had no special prominence over other aspects of performance. They claimed the text was one aspect of the theatrical system, and that elements such as "acoustical perception," i.e., sound and movement, lights, etc. were integral to the theatrical experience of a play ("Performability vs. Readability: A Historical Overview …" Ekaterini Nikolarea, accurapid. com). These elements are part of the "poetry of the theatre" described in Chapter IV.

18 In Bassnett's articles "Translating for the Theatre" (1990) and "Translating for the Theatre: The Case Against Performability" (1991).

Moreover, reading a play requires the imagination of the reader, as well as that of the performer, so that one may "see" the play unfolding on a stage. There are two volumes devoted in large part to this idea: *How to Read a Play* by Ronald Hayman, 1977, and *How to Read a Play* by Tom Markus, 1996. It is fundamental that theatre students—like critics and translators—learn an approach to the art that recognizes the form and function of performance.

Current theorists and translators disagree with Bassnett's latest point of view. It is largely accepted that plays are written to be performed. In Pavis' "Problems of Translation for the Stage: interculturalism and post-modern theatre" from *The Play Out of Context*, he makes the case that it is the *mise en scène* of a play, its "performability" that must be addressed in translation (Scolnicov 25–42).[19] The text alone is "unrealized" until it is performed. Bassnett now argues the entire notion of "performability" is only an excuse for "English translators, directors and impresarios" to justify substantial variations, to "hand over a supposedly literal translation to a monolingual playwright" to rewrite the play, and to make the text "speakable" for actors. Pavis, a theatre semiotician, has, alternately, focused on "the *process* of translating, staging and receiving a theatre text" (Nikolarea 16), which includes the *mise en scène*. Since a script is dialogue based on Action, it must be translated with a view to performance. As scholar Nikolarea points out, historical texts, on the page and in performance, have not suffered from any polarization between "readability" versus "performability." What all three theorists (Bassnett, Pavis and Nikolarea) have left out of their approaches to play translation is an understanding of the function and contribution of the actor.

Translation for Actors

Robert Corrigan may have been the first modern American translator, scholar, practitioner and critic to comment articulately and in detail on the importance of the actor to translation for the stage. His essay, "Translating for Actors," is in *The Craft and Context of Translation*, which Steiner claims begins the modern phase of the history of translation in 1961 (1998: 250). Corrigan states that, though theatre has been thought of as a branch of literature, it is actually a *performed text* based on a theatre language which is not of "words," but goes deeper than spoken language.

---

19 Pavis names the "union of word and gesture" the *language-body*. He writes it is "the orchestration, peculiar to a language and culture, of gesture, vocal rhythm and text." (36). He is, it seems, actually describing the notion of *Action* or *subtext* used by actors, described in Appendix A and Chapter IV. Word and gesture come together when we have a *purpose* to speak.

It is a "language that speaks directly to our senses" (Arrowsmith 96). He claims we have still not managed to understand the difference (not recognized by Bassnett) between "literature for reading and literature for the theatre" (*Ibid.*). This is still true for some scholars today.

Corrigan cites Antonin Artaud and Vsevolod Meyerhold[20] as theatre practitioners who understood that, in theatre, "In the beginning was the Gesture!" and not the "word." Corrigan suggests that it is the *avant-garde* theatre that is a theatre of gesture (*Ibid.*).[21] Actually, *all* theatre is "gestural." That is, all theatre—as opposed to novels, short stories, poems or journalism—is written to be performed, and thus involves the underlying motive of the character, as enacted by the actor. Corrigan quotes writer/critic R. P. Blackmur: "Words are made of motion, made of action or response … gesture is made of language—made of the language beneath or beyond or alongside the language of words … When the language of words most succeeds it *becomes* gesture in its words" (97–8). This has great implications for the nature of translation for the stage, as it is the actor who "achieves the fullness of the dramatist's intention. … *The actor is the playwright's most valuable means of expression*" (emphasis added, 99).[22] In the theatre, the importance of the actor and language as gesture would seem to be intrinsic to the art.

Even established contemporary directors may not have considered the idea of language as gesture, as it relates to words of plays in translations. British director Nancy Meckler, of the well-known Shared Experience company, has used British playwright Pam Gems' translations of two of Chekhov's plays in two separate productions over the past twenty-five years.[23] Meckler believes that it is important for

---

20 Artaud, heralded as a theatre theorist more than a practitioner, wrote the seminal *The Theatre and Its Double*, which lauded gesture and sound as more endemic to expression in the theatre than language alone. Meyerhold was a student of Stanislavsky, and a prominent actor in the Moscow Art Theatre, who challenged Realist style with his physical practice "Biomechanics," based on movement and gesture.

21 Chekhov, Corrigan notes, has an affinity to the *avant-garde*; many critics (Gilman, Kataev, Valency, et al.) see Chekhov's last four plays as precursors to the works of Beckett and Pinter, among others.

22 Director Peter Brook begins his much-quoted *The Empty Space* with the idea that only a space, an actor and someone watching him or her is needed for an act of theatre to take place. The actor is primary.

23 Shared Experience was founded by Mike Alfreds in 1975 "to restore the actor's identity and freedom to create" (Miles 170). He directed Ian McKellen in *Cherry Orchard* at the National Theatre to acclaim in 1985. The company is known for identifying the actor as the "central creative energy and generating force" of theatre, their productions are particularly physical and stripped of scenery, and Alfreds, in particular, is devoted to Chekhov and "the Russian quality of the writing and the characters" (*Ibid.*).

the play translator to be a dramatist, as "you have to write dialogue" (Mekler 2004). Meckler explained that Gems used a "literal" translation by a Russian woman, Tonia Alexander, whose name does not appear in the published versions.[24] Both Gems and Alexander were present for Meckler's rehearsals, and helped answer actors' questions on word usage. Meckler stated, "People just work from 'literals,' don't they. Which is, you know, not out of the question, really." When I asked Meckler if Gems translated these plays—*Vanya* and *Cherry Orchard*—with a view to play construction, Meckler responded: "You don't have to understand construction. Why would you? It's all constructed. You would know it [the form of the play] if you had a 'literal' [translation]" (*Ibid.*). Meckler would seem to think that the *words* of a literal translation give one the construction of the play. But "translation" is not only about translating the words; as we have seen, it's about translating circumstances, culture and the style of the play. Translators Lindsay Bell and Hale and Upton agree that "the translator's authorship of a new dramatic text implies a capacity to manipulate *not just words but also structure*. A translation, in rhythm, tone, character, action and setting, implicitly or explicitly contains the framework for a particular *mise en scène*" (Upton 9). Words—the result of Actions—can change structure.

Meckler certainly understands that actors provide action—she describes this as the actor's "want"—but, apparently, she does not see how the overall actions that make up the structure of the playscript, as *perceived by the translator*, can influence the choice of words, and so affect the performance of the actor. This is interesting to note, as Meckler's company is especially known for its dynamism and use of movement—physical and psychological—onstage.

In Chekhov's last four plays, his work in Russian and in translation has often been criticized for a "lack of action"; this is usually in reference to plot. This is a misunderstanding of Chekhov, and his uses of "indirect action" have spawned a new dramaturgy in the 20th century. Early English and American translations of Chekhov's plays (and modern ones too) have been criticized for stilted language as well, and Chekhov cannot be blamed for this. His language in Russian is considered graceful, fluid and deceptively simple.[25] How important is it for the translator to understand that words come out of *Action*, and that this affects translation?

---

24 Alexander's claim to fame, Meckler told me, was that Alexander's mother was Gorky's mistress.

25 Theatre practitioners have noted this fact. Nemirovich-Danshenko cites Chekhov's "grace and lightness," "sunny and simple … quality" and "lyricism" (Senelick 1997: 68). Actor Meyerhold, an original cast member of his plays, seemed to understand Chekhov's style and language best of all: "The secret of Chekhovian mood was written in the *rhythm* of its language …" (1969: 75). Capturing Chekhov's uses of language in English for individual

Corrigan concludes "Language in the theatre must always be gestural; it must grow out of the gesture, must always act and never be descriptive. The theatre is dead the moment there is a substitution of statement for dramatic process" (Arrowsmith 96). This puts the actor at the center of the art of theatre, and this dramatic process. And if translators cannot envision the actor on the stage, they have, according to Corrigan, "lost the sense of their theatre's physics." This is because "the playwright—and also the translator—cannot really be concerned with 'good prose' or with 'good verse' in the usual sense of those terms. *The structure is action*; not what is said or how it is said, but *when*" (first emphasis added). Corrigan insists that if the playwright does not create what is done and when, it will necessarily be imposed by the actors and/or director. The way the words appear on the page—with particular grammar, syntax, spacing and punctuation— are significant for the actor. Spoken prose has rhythm, just as poetry does. It will be noted, for example, how the translations of Chekhov that dismiss his ellipses, pauses, repetitions and even stage directions may change the drama and Action written into the text of the plays.

Corrigan also reminds us that the Greeks, Shakespeare and Molière had no stage directions beyond entrances and exits. This is because "the motive, meaning and gestures were in the words themselves." But with the advent of Realism, we become more aware that words on a page do not always give us meaning; Action does. While modern actors have been instructed never to pay attention to the playwright's stage directions,[26] the "directions" implicit in the text will be interpreted

---

characters is a challenge—Senelick criticized Jean-Claude Van Itallie, among others, for making all Chekhov's characters sound the same (personal email, March 2002), though it is easy to speak Van Itallie's translations in English. Van Itallie consulted Russian Chekhov scholar/translator Vitaly Vouloff—not named in published translations, nor in my interview with Van Itallie (spring, 2003)—but claims not to have consulted others' translations (Carnicke 2004: 6). Yet, translator Ann Dunnigan threatened to sue Van Itallie in 1978 for allegedly using *her* translations in his *Cherry Orchard* (Senelick 2000: 12, 13).

26 The fact is that many stage directions in modern and contemporary plays are added by the Stage Manager, after the first production of the work. With playwrights such as Chekhov and Samuel Beckett, the directions are written in the script by the *playwright*, so actors ignore them at their peril. How directions are interpreted is determined by the contribution of the actors and director. Tom Stoppard has written, in an Introduction to his *The Seagull*, that he omitted "nearly all of Chekhov's stage directions ... on the ground that instructions to actors (*stamps his foot*, etc.) and to designer (e.g. *bushes to right and left*) nowadays seem over-instructive" (1997: viii). We may wonder, then, how many more of Chekhov's words Stoppard may have cut, feeling they were "over-instructive," and why Stoppard did not feel that the actors, designers and directors may not judge for themselves what may or may not be of import in the play, based on Chekhov's original directions in the Russian

and incorporated into performance based on the actor's choices of Action. The import of Chekhov's stage directions will also be discussed in Chapters VI–IX.

Corrigan believes that it is a mistake to think that these ideas above are "far removed from the problems of translation" because "the theatre is always a matter of scenic materialization in space," and it is the actor who moves and lives in that space. This is why Corrigan emphasizes that "The first law in translating for the theatre is that everything must be speakable (Arrowsmith 101)." Speakability, playability and performability are all required "techniques" for the translator:

> It is necessary at all times for the translator to hear the actor speaking in his mind's ear. He must be conscious of the voice that speaks—the rhythm, the cadence, the interval. He must also be conscious of the look, the feel and the movement of the actor while he is speaking. He must, in short, render what might be called the whole gesture of the scene. To do this it is important to know what words do and mean, but it is more important to know what they cannot do at those crucial moments when the actor needs to use a vocal or physical gesture. Only in this way can the translator hear the words in such a way that they play upon each other in harmony, in conflict and in pattern—and hence as dramatic. I suppose what I am saying is that it is necessary almost to direct the play, act the play, and see the play while translating it. (*Ibid.*)

These words of Corrigan's are among the most quoted by translators, critics and scholars who understand the nature of the theatre. According to Corrigan, the translator's job is more than just being a dramatist who can "write dialogue," as Meckler said. Without mentioning "Action" per se, Corrigan has noted the elements of stage performance that are the results of Action: cadence, ellipses as possible "intervals" of *subtext*, the movement of the body, resulting in the overall "action" of a scene, based on the superobjective of the play. The way in which the translator "hears the words" in "harmony, conflict and pattern" also denotes the elements of *scansion*—noting the rhythm, sounds, syntax, intonation and inflection of words, as in the explication of a poem—which the actor uses to find appropriate speech and gesture for the character.

We may note how Corrigan's requirements of "speakability" and "performability" include elements absent in Bassnett's view of "readability" in the playscript. Yet Corrigan's essay on "Translating for Actors" was written thirty years before

---

playscript. Also, directions to the actor in speeches are distinguished, in the theatre, from set descriptions. It is helpful, however, that Stoppard *does*, at least, document many of his changes in his Introduction. Other translators do not.

Bassnett wrote her essays on the problems of "performability."[27] Other theorists and practitioners have noted the special issues involved with play translation, and have echoed Corrigan's concerns. It is as important for the reader too to understand the differences between plays and other written literatures as it is for the actor.

"Readability" of a play necessitates the ability of the reader to "respond to symbols by hearing in his inner ear the sounds of the words and the rhythms ... so he may create the play" and "to supply the tempo, the gestures" of the characters, as they read (Rosenblatt 13). Louise M. Rosenblatt's well-known *The Reader, The Text, The Poem* (1978) acknowledges "Plays are to be acted, not read" but also supplies the incontrovertible argument that "*before they are acted they must be read*—first by the author evoking his intended work and, second, by the director and actors, who, before they interpret must go through the process," both imaginative and practical, of taking the text off the page in their mind's eye (*Ibid.*).

Rosenblatt spends much of her book describing this process in reading poetry and drama. She emphasizes the fact that the "finding of meanings involves both the author's text and *what the reader brings to it*" (emphasis added, 14). The actor, first a "reader" of the play, must bring "voice, tone, the rhythms and inflections" to the playscript, which, I propose, comes from an understanding of the "Actions" inherent in the play. The point is that "reading" a play is indeed imagining the performance off the page, which Bassnett describes as not making "any sense" and a "superhuman" task for the translator. It is a common and most human task, as Rosenblatt describes:

> The reader of a text who evokes a literary work of art is, above all, a performer, in the same sense that a pianist performs a sonata, reading it from the text. ... The performer's attention is absorbed in what he is producing *as he plays*. ... Is this not the "condition of music" to which the reader of the literary work of art should aspire: a complete absorption in the process of evoking a work from the text, and in sensing, clarifying, structuring, savoring, that experience as it unfolds? ... In the literary work of art ... what the words point to cannot be disassociated from the total lived-through experience in all its immediacy (28–9).

The comparison of the playtext to music—as musical notes on a page—is echoed often by translators and critics, especially with Chekhov's plays, which

---

27 Linguists and semioticians may not be familiar with theory or practice for the theatre, as they may feel the realm of "language" is their territory alone. Interdisciplinary studies on theatre and translation have been called for by scholars and language "generalists" alike, notably George Steiner and André Lefevere.

are considered particularly lyrical. The "lived-through experience" Rosenblatt mentions is the moment-to-moment action of the play that includes the actor's contribution to the text. Both these ideas—a play as music and "lived-through experience" (Action)—are applied to Chekhov's playscripts and described in subsequent chapters. The translator, like the reader, must be a "performer," as he must put himself in the place of the author. The translator, quite naturally, as Rosenblatt describes, must play all the parts. It follows that it would be helpful for the translator to know something about acting, and the actor's contribution to the text.

For some linguists, translators and theatre critics, the idea that the actor contributes to the expression of the playwright—through the translator in a translated text—may be ignored or misunderstood. As scholar/translators Carole-Anne Upton and Terry Hale note in *Moving Target*, "translation theorists are generally unaware of the extent, richness and diversity of theatrical tradition" (12). They believe the words on the page are all, and that the written play on the page is a complete work in itself. This is because they may not understand the nature of drama. It is not a literary genre made up solely of language on a page; it is dynamic, and realized in performance. It is quite practical, therefore, for the play translator to study the nature of performance, the art and craft of the actor, the structure of drama, as well as the words therein.

In 1980–81—twenty years after Corrigan's essay—one volume of essays and one article on translating for the stage were published and are pertinent to this study. The volume *Languages of Theatre, problems in the translation and transposition of drama* discusses various literary aspects of translation for the stage, with some few references to actors and acting. Ortrun Zuber's Introduction claims "This is the first book focusing on translation problems unique to drama. Experts in this *new discipline* [drama in translation studies] have collaborated from all over the world ... [It] considers non-verbal, verbal and cultural aspects as well as staging problems, for a play is written for a performance and must be actable and speakable" (emphasis added, xiii). Oddly, in spite of its nod to these aspects of play translation, *Languages of Theatre* does not mention the seminal *Craft and Context of Translation* or Corrigan. This does not diminish the import of Corrigan's observations for theatre translation.

The fact that Zuber considers the translation of drama as a "new discipline" in 1980 is telling. Translation has been recognized as an art and/or a craft at least since Alexander Fraser Tytler (Lord Woodhouse Lee), in 1791, wrote the first book dealing directly with problems of translation. Plays have been translated—and acting theory and practice have contributed to translations—for thousands of years. *Languages* is testimony to some misunderstandings of the nature of stagecraft by those outside theatre practice. The following examples are cases in point.

Reba Gostand's essay, "Verbal and Non-Verbal Communication: Drama as Translation" observes that the physical aspects of the theatre production—lighting, setting, costume—may be symbolic and "involve processes of translation," but does not discuss how; she notes that actors provide another "filtering" for the translation process, but does not discuss the actor's contribution to the play (Zuber 2). Zuber's article "Problems of Propriety and Authenticity ..." recalls Corrigan's requirements for "speakability" and "performability," but the body of the article is devoted to her discovery of a "definitive text" for a German production of Williams' *Streetcar Named Desire* (92–3). It is evident that Zuber's underlying purpose is a literary explication of this German translation, which "authenticates" the written translation of the play. Her over-riding concern is with the words in a script, rather than the work of actors or other practitioners in a production. The structure of action in a play is not addressed.

A lengthy article by an English Professor, Franz H. Link, is also geared to explaining the literary aspects of language usages in the theatre. Though Link recognizes that "communication is possible as gesture, as language, as music," he "limits his focus to communication by language" (26). His focus is not actual production for the stage. In the only short note on "Acting," Link states "acting involves the way of speaking the text, facial expression and gesture accompanying it, and the movement of the characters on the stage" (*Ibid.*). It may be argued that this is *not* acting, any more than the words on the page are the play. Link's article, though titled "Translation, Adaptation and Interpretation of Dramatic Texts," is more a literary discussion, and does not confront the issues of theatre practice.

Lefevere acknowledges in his essay, "The State of the Art," his final chapter, that the notion of linguistic "equivalence" has been all but abolished, and that the end of the 1960s brought linguistics to consider "beyond the sentence" to "contexts" of a text (155). This is significant for an analysis of the playscript, which must be performed in set "circumstances." Lefevere's key observation is "the study of translated dramatic literature has been treated extremely superficially by translation studies" and he notes:

> None [of those in translation studies], to my knowledge, go beyond treating drama as simply the text on the page. There is, therefore, practically no theoretical literature on the translation of drama as acted and produced. It is hoped that the present volume may help direct the attention of scholars to this *virtually virgin field of research.* (emphasis added, 177)

Based on the mostly literary observations in this volume, Lefevere's point is well made. Lefevere makes no mention of the *Craft and Context of Translation* or Corrigan's "Translating for Actors," and claims Steiner's *After Babel* to be one of many "highly speculative theories of translations formulated on the basis of literary criteria" (176). In any case, it seems that *"Languages of Theatre"* does not address the fundamental "language" of the theatre: that of Action.

Other critics' views are noteworthy, in that they are examples of how linguists who may not recognize the significance of theatre craft to translation for the stage have helped create this "virtually virgin field." George E. Wellwarth's "Special Considerations in Drama Translation," 1981, does not discuss the Action of a play, but points up the importance of "speakability" ("for want of a better term") and style. His definition of style, however, is "that which causes a play to sound as if it had originally been written in the target language" and the chief problem he identifies is the "transposition of the original language's syntax" (141). Also important to Wellwarth in a translation is a "sense of rhythm" and "the ability to recreate poetic imagery ... without loss of semantic nuance" (140). Language is considered the most important part of the play. In Chekhov's plays, however, which have changed the face of modern theatre, the "semantic nuance" and rhythm are created in part by the *action* underneath the words, and not the meaning of the words themselves. This underscores the import of the actor's contribution, which Wellwarth neglects.

Wellwarth advises the translator to "read his translation aloud to someone totally unacquainted with the play, preferably an actor," as they distinguish what "lies easily on the tongue" (*Ibid.*). But then Wellwarth states actors "tend to come to such readings without preconceptions about the play, even if it is a well-known one, since *they rarely read or permit their minds to become contaminated by any indulgence in critical thought about the little they may have read*" (141). Wellwarth is a theatre and literature professor at SUNY Binghamton, so one may hope he is joking. Critical thought is requisite for the actor, in script analysis and in performance. The stereotype of the un-schooled actor is trounced by the likes of Ian McKellen, Annette Bening (both quoted herein), Meryl Streep, Wallace Shawn, and Simon Russell Beale (Chekhov players all), and, of course, hosts of other trained actors all over the world.

Another of Wellwarth's surprising assertions is that, he states, in the majority of modern plays, a "toning down" is required in the English translation. Laurence Senelick is one of many translator/critics who warns that a "toning down" or "smoothing out" of the original author's work is exactly the wrong path to take (2005: xi–xv). It is unclear what "toning down" may mean for the playscript, though it could reveal an ethnocentric bias on Wellwarth's part. He states this is true "51% of the time," and "the important thing to remember is ... one must always write in such a way as not to grate on the ears of the audience." He also holds that plays that must be adapted to other cultures or venues outside the setting of the original play "are better left untranslated" (145). Chekhov's plays have been replanted to soils foreign to Russia many times, and successfully so. (Note Kilroy's *Seagull* removed to Ireland in 1981, Tom Markus' *Sisters* to the American West in the 1990s and Chay Yew's *Orchard* to China in 2004.) Once again, Wellwarth's focus is primarily semantic, and not theatrical.

A contemporary article from Brigitte Schultze (1998) in *Translating Literatures, Translating Cultures* notes the lack of "theoretical premises of drama translation," but asserts the "*dual* nature of the theatrical text" and "coexistence of 'both a literary and performance text'" (Mueller 177). Significantly, she recognizes stage translators "have to do the job of theatrologists before they can move on to the specific questions of translation studies" (178). She does not explore what this job entails. She is intent, rather, on reconciling the "dual context of dramatic language" (189): oral communication and literature.

Schultze does not go to theatre practitioners for answers, but philologists and semioticians.[28] Her essay takes us back to the "performability vs. readability" dichotomy. Throughout her article, Schultze reaches for definitions of terms such as "Theatrical Potential" (from translator Sophia Totzeva), "effectiveness on the stage," "playability," "speakability" and even "playable speakability" and "verbo-corps," from Patrice Pavis (noted as *language-body*), a "sort of union between language and gesture" (179–83). Author David Birch describes the issue:

> Meaning should not be restricted to simply what words mean, but to the many levels of meaning involved in *language as action*; in the social and institutional transactions and interactions of people involved in communication. Most of these meanings never find their way into a dictionary—they are meanings involving body movement, facial expressions, voice quality, speed of delivery. (emphasis added, 178)

The physical skills mentioned here involve *action*, as Birch suggests above. But instead of pursuing a definition of the "language of action," Schultze describes "deviations from norms within the lexical field," "grammatical and semantic gaps" and "dialogue and non-dialogue [scene directions? movement?] text." She admits many of these terms "have not led to any breakthroughs in research" (182), but claims "Theatrical Potential" provides a novel approach, which includes "grammatical gaps that open up opportunities for gesture and other forms of non-verbal communication" (192). Of course, these are part of any play, regardless of the text, translated or not. "Grammatical gaps" are not faults in the text, but the natural uses of the body and mind in communication. In fact, non-verbal communication is not

---

28 Schultze consulted both Pavis and Bassnett; the latter told Schultze she has "given up hope of ever gaining access to this 'labyrinth'" of finding a theory for translating drama (178). The notion of "Action" might untangle the path here.

there to fill in "gaps," but is *continuous*[29] throughout the life depicted onstage, just as in "real life." It is the actor who provides this "Theatrical Potential," based on Action underlying the words. But Schultze does not mention the actor's contribution to the playscript.

The idea of the playscript as only a blueprint for performance is not entertained by Schultze. Finally, she admits that "creating a translation replete with theatrical meaning" is now common to "translators of dramatic texts" (193). But Action—which includes but is not limited to physical action—as the key to the translator's understanding of meaning and performance in a play, is not yet recognized by Schultze or other critics in the fields of literature and/or linguistics.

References

Aaltonen, Sirkku. *Time-Sharing Onstage: Drama Translation in Theatre and Society*. Clevedon: Multilingual Matters, 2000.

Adler, Stella. *The Technique of Acting*. New York: Bantam Books, 1988.

Arrowsmith, William and Roger Shattuck, eds. *The Craft and Context of Translation*. Austin: The University of Texas Press, 1961.

Artaud, Antonin. *The Theatre and Its Double*. Trans. Mary Caroline Richards. New York: Grove Press, 1958.

Bassnett, Susan. "Translating for the Theatre: The Case Against Performability," *TTR: Traduction, Terminologie, Redaction*, 4(1), 1st Semester, 1991.

Brislin, Richard. *Translation: Applications and Research*. New York: Gardner Press, 1976.

Brook, Peter. *The Empty Space*. New York: Avon Books, 1968.

Carnicke, Sharon Marie. "The Nasty Habit of Adaptations," Conference: "Chekhov the Immigrant: Translating a Cultural Icon," Colby College, October 8–9, 2004.

Chekhov, Anton. *Anton Chekhov's Selected Plays*. Trans. and ed. Laurence Senelick. New York: W. W. Norton & Co., 2005.

———. *The Cherry Orchard*. Adapt. Tom Donaghy. Unpublished draft, December, 2004.

———. *The Cherry Orchard*. Version. Pam Gems. UK: Oberon Classics, 2007.

———. *The Cherry Orchard*. Version. Sir John Gielgud. New York: Theatre Arts Books, 1963.

———. *The Seagull*. Version. Tom Stoppard. London: Faber and Faber Limited, 1997.

———. *Uncle Vanya*. Version. Pam Gems. London: Nick Hern Books, 1992.

Clifford, John. "Translating Moments, Not Words," www.teatrodomundo.com, February 9, 2005.

Corrigan, Robert. "Translating for Actors," in William Arrowsmith and Roger Shattuck, eds. *The Craft and Context of Translation*. Austin: The University of Texas Press, 1961, pp. 95–106.

---

29 In communication studies, all non-verbal communication is continuous; it *accompanies* verbal communication, and is the "physical extension of our bodies" (Trenholm 106).

Fan, Jiayang. "Han Kang and the Complexity of Translation." *The New Yorker*, January 15, 2018.

Fergusson, Francis. *The Idea of a Theatre*. Garden City, NY: Doubleday Anchor Books, 1953.

Friedberg, Maurice. *Literary Translation in Russia*. University Park, PA: The Pennsylvania State University Press, 1997.

Gilman, Richard. *Chekhov's Plays*. New Haven: Yale University Press, 1995.

Gross, Alex. "Some Major Dates and Events in the History of Translation," www.accurapic. com. January 28, 2005.

Grossman, Edith. *Why Translation Matters*. New Haven and London: Yale University Press, 2010.

Harrop, John. *Acting*. London: Routledge, 1992.

Hayman, Ronald. *How to Read a Play*. New York: Grove Press, 1977.

Kataev, Vladimir. *If Only We Could Know!* Trans./Ed. Harvey Pitcher. Chicago: Ivan R. Dee, 2002.

Logan, Brian. "Whose Play is it Anyway?" *Guardian*, March 12, 2003.

Markus, Tom. *How to Read a Play*. Dubuque, Iowa: Kendall/Hunt Publishing Company, 1996.

Mekler, Nancy. Interview with the author. Brooklyn Marriott Hotel, November, 2004.

Meyerhold, Vsevelod. *Meyerhold on Theatre*. Trans./Ed. Edward Braun. London: Menthuen & Company Ltd., 1969.

Miles, Patrick., ed. and trans. *Chekhov on the British Stage*. Cambridge: Cambridge University Press, 1993.

Mirsky, D. S. *A History of Russian Literature*. Ed. Francis J. Whitfield. Evanston, IL: Northwestern University Press, 1999.

Mueller-Vollmer, Kurt and Michael Irmscher. *Translating Literatures, Translating Cultures*. Berlin: Erich Schmidt, 1998.

Nikolarea, Ekaterina. "Performability vs. Readability." *Translation Journal*, 6(4), October, 2002, pp. 1–21. www.accurapid.com/journal/22theater.htm.

Rexroth, Kenneth. "The Poet as Translator," in William Arrowsmith and Roger Shattuck, eds. *The Craft and Context of Translation*. Austin: The University of Texas Press, 1961, pp. 22–37.

Rose, Marilyn Gaddis, ed. *Translation Spectrum*. Albany: State University of New York Press, 1981.

Rosenblatt, Louise M. *The Reader, The Text, The Poem*. Carbondale: Southern Illinois University Press, 1978.

Scolnicov, Hannah and Peter Holland. *The Play Out of Context*. Cambridge: Cambridge University Press, 1989.

Senelick, Laurence. *The Chekhov Theatre*. Cambridge: Cambridge University Press, 1997.

———. "Chekhov's Plays in English," *The North American Chekhov Society Bulletin*, Vol. IX, Spring, 2000.

Stanislavsky, Konstantin. *An Actor Prepares*. Trans. Elizabeth Reynolds Hapgood. New York: Theatre Arts Books, 1948.

———. *Building a Character*. Trans. Elizabeth Reynolds Hapgood. New York: Theatre Arts Books, 1949.

———. *Creating a Role*. Trans. Elizabeth Reynolds Hapgood. New York: Theatre Arts Books, 1961.

Steiner, George. *After Babel.* New York: Oxford University Press, 1998a.

Upton, Carole-Anne, ed. *Moving Target: Theatre Translation and Cultural Relocation.* Manchester: St. Jerome Publishing, 2000.

Vakhtangov, Yevgeny. *The Vakhtangov Sourcebook.* London and New York: Routledge, 2011.

Yusim, Marat. *Passing the Torch—Basic Training: Stanislavsky's School of Acting and Directing.* New York: Marat Yusim, 2006.

Zuber, Ortrun, ed., *The Languages of Theatre.* Oxford: Pergamon Press, 1980.

CHAPTER THREE

The Translator as Artist

When, in 1902, a friend casually commented in public to Proust that his translation of Ruskin "must be full of mistakes, because you don't really know English," Proust was stung.

"I don't claim to know English," Proust fired back in a letter. "I claim to know Ruskin." … A vibrant affinity bound him, heart and mind, to his chosen author. When Proust went on to say "I learned English with my eyes," he meant that he had learned how to see the world afresh. And isn't that in the end what a great translator does—give us new eyes with which to see the world?

—ERIC ORMSBY[1]

Michael Scammell, translator of Nabokov's novels, writes "Translators are the ghosts of the literary profession, invisible men who don a mask and pretend to be someone else" (1). Scammell has, inadvertently, made reference to the translator as an actor who is a ghost. Indeed, in the theatre, both translator and actor are "masked," to some degree, by definition. But in contemporary theatre translation, especially with Chekhov's plays, the American and English translator has become less "invisible." Chekhov translator Sharon Carnicke states:

Whether translating or adapting him [Chekhov], playwrights put their own stamps upon his plays. While one could argue that all translators reflect themselves through

---

1   "Still a Great Translation," *New York Sun*, November 3, 2004, p. 17.

the inevitable linguistic and cultural compromises that the very act of translating entails, I would argue that playwrights do so in spades. Unlike professional translators who expect to become the invisible medium of the author, playwrights struggle over the course of their careers to develop recognizable voices of their own. Their reputations depend on it. Playwrights can ill afford to lose themselves in Chekhov. (2004: 8)

Famous playwrights are hired by producers or theatre companies to translate Chekhov's plays for particular productions; these translations are copyrighted, so they receive royalties. With Chekhov, this is possible because his works are in the public domain; he is not alive to oversee new "versions" or "adaptations" that may be performed or printed. The "translator" or "adaptor" is not challenged by the original author.

It may be for these reasons, in part, that playwrights who translate Chekhov recently have returned to the idea of the "translator" as primary artist, as has been the case throughout periods of translation history. When Tom Stoppard, David Mamet, Brian Friel or Lanford Wilson—well-known playwrights all—were hired to write translations of Chekhov, it is playwriting skills and name recognition that prompted their hiring, rather than knowledge of the Russian source language.[2] This goes to the heart of the definition of translators of Chekhov's theatre: is it more important for them to understand dramatic structure, the music of words in English (the "target text"), the particularities of stagecraft, and to be famous, rather than to know Russian?

Playwrights who "translate" Chekhov but do not speak the Russian language are proliferating.[3] Carnicke notes "A list of those who have 'translated' and adapted Chekhov reads like a who's-who of modern and contemporary drama" (4). These playwrights often use English translations of Chekhov's plays, rendered by Russian speakers who are *not* playwrights themselves. While these non-Russian-speaking "translators" give credit for writing the original play to Chekhov, many playwrights

---

2   In the case of Lanford Wilson, he wrote that he made a great effort for "two months ... three hours a day, six days a week" to learn Russian, while he was translating *The Three Sisters* (x).

3   Actor John Gielgud, poet Randall Jarrell, directors Tyrone Guthrie and Emily Mann and playwrights Clifford Odets, Brian Friel, Michael Frayn, Lanford Wilson, David Mamet, Tom Stoppard and Martin Sherman (*Cherry Orchard* at L. A.'s Music Center, 2006) have "translated" Chekhov. Playwright Lee Blessing told this researcher he too would like to translate Chekhov in the future (May, 2004). He has more recently written a play in tribute to *Uncle Vanya* called *Uncle*—a delightful and ingenious comedy and love story, including main characters from Chekhov's play.

often do not credit the original *literal* translator at all.[4] These initial translations are known as "interlinear trots," "cribs," "ponies" or "intermediate"—some say "literal"—translations of the words of a foreign work, done by one who knows the foreign language intimately. These are then given to an "artist"—usually a playwright—who then fashions the crib into "speakable" or "playable" English for the actual playscript. These secondary scripts, crafted from literal translations, can make lexical, scene and even structural changes that change the plays enormously. Also—as Carnicke notes—the voice of the "translator" often comes through the translation. David Mamet's adaptations of Chekhov sound like Mamet's own plays (with short, concise, almost brutal emendations) and Brian Friel's versions are said to be "Irish" in voice (Mendes 2003; Beale 2003). In Friel's *Vanya*, I've observed he often substitutes "subtext" (see Appendix A) for the text written in the playscript. This affects Chekhov's indirect style immensely.

The emendation of Chekhov's originals are notorious in Mamet's adaptations. Mamet takes advantage of the actor's attention to the text as written on the page. Carnicke states Mamet's uses of punctuation, repetition, "broken sentences, capital letters, italics" may "reveal his dramaturgical interest in controlling his actors through rhythms and graphics" (9).[5] Carnicke accuses Mamet of trying to "insure specific line readings and intonations. He famously asks his actors to trust his texts. He transfers this technique to Chekhov as well, and, in effect, directs the plays that he adapts" (9).[6] These written elements of the playscript—punctuation, ellipses, spaces, pauses, etc.—are at issue in any translation of Chekhov; they are crucial as signposts for the translator and the actor. We shall see textual differences in various translations in detail in Chapters VI–IX. Departures from Chekhov's originals are

---

4   David Mamet is among the few exceptions. He credits Vlada Chernomirdik for *Vanya* and Peter Nelles for *Cherry Orchard*. Their names are in smaller letters, under Mamet's name, on the title pages of these plays. Whether they receive royalties, along with Mamet, is another question. Typically, they do not. Scholar/translator Jacek Laskowski quotes a friend who believes "theatre is a ... collaborative venture and it's simply not right that any one name should be printed in letters bigger than the others ... we should return to pre-Renaissance days when artists never put their names to anything, thereby tacitly admitting that their work was produced as much by society ... as by their own individual effort" (Johnston 190).

5   Senelick accuses Paul Schmidt too of "emphatic punctuation which impose[s] interpretations on actors."

6   WNYC radio host Leonard Lopate notes Mamet said actors should just "read the lines" rather than trying to add "meaning" in acting his plays (Spring 2006). But Mamet explains in his book *True and False:* "It doesn't matter how you say the lines. What matters is what you mean. What comes from the heart goes to the heart" (63). Mamet *is* concerned with "meaning;" he's discussing underlying Action.

possible in any translation, but are perhaps aggravated by the use of "literal" or "intermediate" translations. How often do punctuation, rhythm, sound and syntax get lost, when the "translator"—using a crib—can't see them?

Though Friedberg claims that "interlinear trots are used rather rarely in the English-speaking world" (177)[7] he goes on to document their use throughout Russia and Europe, and does not seem to be aware of this common practice in the English-speaking theatre world. He calls the practice "team translation" when "native informants" who know the source texts assist American poets in "translating" Russian verse. For example, heralded poet Richard Wilbur—who knew no Russian—was helped by well-known Russian translator Max Hayward. Friedberg calls Hayward "the best and most prolific translator of Russian prose into English since Constance Garnett"—though he is not a translator of Chekhov, unlike Garnett.[8] Wilbur insists that, with Hayward's help, he spent as much time "thinking" on three Russian poems as he would have in producing his own (Friedberg 178–9). The time spent, of course, does not guarantee an effective translation. Hayward was not pleased with the result (179).

Objections to this "intermediary" method of translating come from many corners of the world of translation. Literary translators and play translators alike argue that translation is impossible without a command of the original source language, though many contemporary Chekhov play translators do not know Russian (173).[9] Even while some translators, like Lanford Wilson, claim to know a smattering of

---

7   Friedberg tells us even Ibsen has never been translated directly into Polish from Norwegian, but only from "inferior" (according to Friedberg?) German cribs. Now, the same is done for (or to) Chekhov. The quality of the "crib" is not known to the actor, and perhaps not to the playwright who uses it.

8   Garnett's translations are considered "Edwardian" by Senelick, and "less colourful than the original" (1997: 103, 140). Magarshack writes "Garnett's ... admirable zeal and indefatigable perseverance was only equaled by her inadequate knowledge of Russian which never rose above the dictionary level" (1972: 13). Today, her translations seem old-fashioned, but are performed, possibly because they are in the public domain. Her *Three Sisters* appeared in 2004 in New York City in an engaging production (2econd Stage Theatre); competent actors may overcome a stilted translation.

Remnick ("Translation Wars," *The New Yorker*) notes that, without Garnett, the 19th century Russian writers would not have exerted such influence on American 20th century literature, while Garnett's critics—Nabokov and Brodsky—pronounce her translations "a complete disaster" (98).

9   Phyllis Zatlin, in her Chapter entitled "Out of the Shadows: the Translators Speak for Themselves," writes: "In 2002–03 I distributed a questionnaire to a selection of theatrical translators in several countries ... including both playwrights and other theatre professionals as well as academics ... They speak in one voice on the need to know the source language

Russian, Senelick—Russian scholar, translator and theatre practitioner—imagines this is like "a Muscovite taking a score of English lessons to turn Tennessee Williams into playable Russian" (1997: 302). Carnicke, also a scholar, translator and theatre practitioner, concurs (2004: 7). The challenges to "interlinear" translation are daunting.

These and other critics have complained that the "name" translators who use a literal translation to work from may not be able to judge the extent to which their final version may or may not have captured the letter and spirit of the original (Friedberg 175). Friedberg maintains that a "translation based on interlinear trots is naturally quite different from one made directly from the source language." He cites translation scholar K. G. Kelly's emphasis: *The essential act here is not one of translation, but one of literary creation from an unpolished original.* It is doubtful whether this is translation in the full sense" (176). The definition of translation is continually debated.

There are play translators, like Ranjit Bolt, who maintain that "People have translated from literals and what they've produced has been said to have been closer to the original than the literal translation. It can be done by feeling how the play works and how the characters work" (Johnston 250). Bolt is an accomplished British translator of verse drama, described as a "translator as star" and "the most ubiquitous and flamboyant" translator of European texts.[10] He also states:

> What matters [in how theatre works] is a sense of theatre and character and the functioning of stage language, more than an academic knowledge of language, words pinned to meaning in its most literal sense. ... One of my tags is that if poetry is 'what is lost in translation' it's also what's added. You can't really translate poetry and be totally literal, totally faithful. (250)

Chekhov's plays are described as "poetical;" translators have justified what may be called more whimsical translations, adaptations or versions by claiming they must go far afield of lexical meanings to be more faithful to the spirit of the text. The "poetry" added to or deleted from Chekhov's plays may change his style, and/or his meanings.

Bolt, however, maintains that the style and personality of the translator must come through in a translation to make it work onstage (Croft 1991: 28); when one can identify the translator of a work, the original is the better for it:

---

themselves. Many of them also express their strong preference for translation, and not 'adaptation'" (3).

10 *Platform Papers*, Interviewed by Giles Croft, Royal National Theatre, November, 1991.

> If you were to try and pin me down, as to why it's better for translators to have their own presence, I'd find it hard to give specific reasons, but I don't think you're going to be making the thing work unless you have some sort of literary identity of your own. (28)

Bolt then argues that Dryden put his own stamp on Virgil, as Pope did with Homer, so, Bolt reasons, "if it's good enough for the greats it's good enough for us." Perhaps tellingly, Bolt insists emphatically that he sees translation very much as a business (28).

Though it is beyond the realm of this study to address the "business" of play translation, it is pertinent to note that translators and theatre practitioners observe the underrating of translators in general and of the "literal" translator of plays in particular. Philippe Le Moine, head of Britain's National Theatre Studio, admits "there is a problem: a schism between academic and theatre worlds. Translators feel spurned, and ask: 'Why do we work with playwrights who don't speak the language, when there are trained professional translators who could do the work themselves?'" (Logan 1). Le Moine cites "commercial pressure … theatres need to have something saleable" (*Ibid.*). Translator/scholar Zatlin calls Le Moine's answer "startling" (1). She responds:

> Apparently spectators, who for centuries did not object to invisible translators, now demand famous adaptors … Yet, is it not possible to produce a stageworthy script without being a playwright per se? Does one have to be a playwright to have dramatic insight? Isn't knowing the original language essential to producing a good translation? Isn't it possible to be both a playwright and a real translator: one who knows the source language and is sensitive to the original text? And where do we place professors of theatre if we accept a split between academics and theatre practitioners? (*Ibid.*)

While one may not be able to answer for all spectators, stageworthy translations not written by playwrights have been cited—though this concept may be hard to define, certainly "non-playwright" versions of Chekhov have been played successfully.[11]

Perhaps one does not have to be a playwright to have "dramatic insight," but there are theatrical skills involved in the creating of any work for the stage. The

---

11 For examples: Schmidt, a Russian speaker whose Chekhov translations are performed often, was an actor (with the famed Wooster Group of NYC) and a professor (University of Texas), but not a playwright. My husband Nick Andrews enjoyed Schmidt's "Poetry in Translation" course at UT in 1969–70. Rocamora's more literary renditions have been staged successfully (as in CSC's *Uncle Vanya*, 2009); Garnett's translations—for all their Edwardian-isms—continue to be performed (*Three Sisters* in the successful turn at Second Stage in Manhattan, 2004), no doubt because they are in the public domain.

jury is still out on whether knowing the original language is *essential*, as there are so many "translations" of Chekhov (and others) that work well in performance. There are playwrights—Michael Frayn, for example—who know Russian and the theatre, but this may or may not guarantee a "good" translation. With regard to professors of theatre, it is germane to point out that many *are* practitioners as well as scholars, teachers and translators. (Sharon Carnicke, Paul Schmidt and Laurence Senelick are cases in point.) In fact, it would be odd to come across a theatre professor who had not some experience in acting, directing or playwriting, though it is possible that professors of theatre limit themselves to research. The nature of teaching theatre art demands its practice.

The key to answering Zatlin's valid questions are in finding the definitions to the concepts of "stageworthyness" and "dramatic insight." Indeed, we must return to a definition of theatre itself as a performance-based art. What is theatre made of? Many writers and theatre practitioners have noted that it is necessary for the translator to understand the art of the actor in order to write dialogue for actors. Le Moine insists that translators who are not of the theatre need to "translate for particular types of performance and staging. These are specific skills. There's a big divide and the two sides don't understand each other very well …" (Logan 2).

Yet, Zatlin finds that the translators surveyed worldwide in her study "take dramatic skills very seriously, even if they are not playwrights; and they consider knowledge of the source language imperative, even if they are playwrights" (Zatlin 3). Zatlin outlines numerous applications to working on language—including the importance of rhythm that correlates with gesture, the tone of the play, differentiation of character voices—as well as the uses of setting, allusions, song, names of characters, and all the outside trappings of any production, modern or historical. Zatlin recognizes that language is only one aspect of play translation, as she insists "a play must be translated as a whole. The elements cited above are like pieces of a jigsaw puzzle … The quality of the theatrical language can be compared to the edge pieces that outline the puzzle and thus facilitate its completion" (7). This analogy is similar to the idea of the text as a blueprint for the play: we begin with the outline of the words, and work to fill in the center of the puzzle.

What is missing from Zatlin's articulate description of the process is the concept of underlying Action—intention, desire, engine, the "feeling how the play works and how the characters work" and the "sense of theatre and character and the functioning of stage language" described by Bolt—that fuels the language for the characters. Action may be understood by the practitioner who translates a play—whether or not he/she uses this term—and not, in some cases, by the translation scholar. Understanding and experience of stagecraft are mandatory for the translator; a name playwright may work from a "literal" translation—steps away from the original's words—and still come up with a playable work because Action creates the play, whatever the original words are. Fidelity to the original playwright is another issue.

Translator Joseph Farrell, part of Johnston's "Roundtable on Translation" in 1994, maintains that there may not be such a thing as a "literal" translation, "because at each point you must be making an interpretation ..." (Johnston 284). Then, the "translator" working from "literals" makes choices based on the "literal *interpretation*" before him or her. Translators consulted in Zatlin's survey note that "the current fad of adapting from a literal translation appears to abandon the concept of a faithful rendering of the source text" (6). Zatlin describes the "related strategy" of comparing previous translations, to which Stoppard admits (Chekhov 1997: v), and Senelick has described the result as a "cobbling together" which makes "the adaptations twice removed from the original."[12] Moreover, Zatlin laments the problems of publisher demands to "novelize" a "stageworthy" translation for publication, and the issue of plagiarism (6).[13] As she observes, the controversy goes on.

However, for the actor, director and dramaturg, more helpful than the search for the perfect translation for a production might be what Senelick suggests, with a nod to Nabokov: "an authoritative text that contains variants, accurate cultural annotation, references to original stage practice, and connections of key words and phrases to Chekhov's work" (2000: 13). Why not give actors and directors more choices, by comparing translations and so telling them as much as possible about the original?

Friedberg quotes Russian translator Herold Bel'ger who thinks there are advantages to an interlinear trot if it's heavily notated:

> An interlinear translation is very much in need of all kinds of annotation, explanations, and footnotes. For instance, "familiar usage," "archaic," "dialect." Or else—literally it means such-and-such, and figuratively this and that. Or else—"this is an idiom," or "a reference to such-and-such event," or else that it's an echo of this or of that. Or that this particular word has two meanings. Geographical terms should be deciphered, as should historical terms. Synonyms should be suggested whenever these are especially apposite—on condition that the extra bunch of synonyms should not be translated bodily into the text of the rendition, as sometimes happens. These are the charms of the interlinear trot, its true attributes which richly compensate for "gracefulness" and "poetic quality." (177)

---

12 Email Interview, March 7, 2002.

13 Scholar/translator/practitioner Senelick wrote to this researcher: "My own translations are revised every time someone wants to stage them so that the latest versions are not in print. And I do not distribute them to anyone other than production companies, because I do not want my best solutions to linguistic problems filched, a common practice (cf. Van Itallie)."

We recall that Nabokov also insisted on copious notes for translations, which he thought should be as "literal" as possible. For the scholar, notes on foreign texts can be welcome and revealing, though not a "compensation" for the grace of the original playwright. Of course, such a "crib" as Bel'ger describes above would be helpful to the non-speaking "translator," as he/she works on a final, "playable" translation, version or adaptation, and to the actor—and director—who wants to know more about the original play.[14] Chekhov's last four plays are replete with allusions, song and local and timely references, and their derivations could be of help to both scholar and practitioner.

In a playscript, however, these notes may or may not be appreciated by the reader. For some actors and directors, used to "clean" scripts with few notes, annotations may be confusing: Zatlin claims "a [commercial] director will quickly discard a script that requires footnotes" (4). But this is not true for all practitioners: this study itself was prompted in part by a comment from actor Ian McKellen, who, according to dramaturg/translator Vera Gottlieb, has played more Chekhov roles than any other actor of his generation. As an actor, he *wants* to know more. McKellen claims:

> The big problem with Chekhov is that we don't do *Chekhov*—we do *translations* of Chekhov. Very few translators—at least those I've worked with—work with the original. Instead they come from literal translations. It varies: Pam Gems doesn't know Russian while Michael Frayn and Richard Cottrell both do … That explains the skepticism about English or American or German actors talking about playing Chekhov. It's constantly frustrating not to know how close you are to his [Chekhov's] intentions … Also you cannot be certain about the rhythm. So Pam Gems and a lot of other translators *adapt* Chekhov, cut him without you knowing. When you are doing a production you are very much in the hands of the translator as well as the director. So you cannot connect the plays in the way that you might connect Shakespeare's where the acting problems are common to all the works. I couldn't say that about Chekhov's plays because I've never read them! It is a major problem. (Gottlieb and Allain 2000: 122)

This goes to the core of the issues described in this study: with foreign texts we are always "acting in translation." In working on *Seagull*, McKellen had specific questions on word usage—whether Konstantin is actually "dead" after he has "shot" himself—that had never been answered satisfactorily for him by any translator.

---

14 Bel'ger points out that "heavily annotated trots restrict the translator's artistic latitude" and some translators "prefer poor trots" as they allow "translators" to mold translations to their own style. Bel'ger, in 1976, states the provider of an annotated crib should be acknowledged as a *co-translator* of the text (Friedberg 180–1). "Co-translators" are not noted in translations of Chekhov's plays by playwrights.

In the interview, Gottlieb told him that the Russian is deliberately ambivalent (*Ibid.* 133). Surprisingly, later in this interview with Gottlieb, in a footnote, she apologizes to McKellen for giving him "a misleading response to his translation question"—she decides that Kostya *is* understood to be dead—"which, however, does prove his [McKellen's] point" about the problems with translation (133). The language or syntax chosen by particular translators may indeed be misleading to the actor. When conscientious actors are doing their research, copious notes in the text of a playscript—with footnotes pointing to further research—may be extremely helpful. The actor is indeed a scholar of the playscript.

Gottlieb says to McKellen, "It's vital that you find it frustrating not being able to work from the originals" (123). It seems McKellen mirrors Gottlieb's own frustration with the difficulties of translating Chekhov for the stage. There are so few comments from actors on the pitfalls of acting in translation. This interview with McKellen and Gottlieb is one of the few times—the only instance I discovered outside of my own interviews—that an *actor's view* is documented in a conversation with a translator regarding problems with acting in English in Chekhov's plays.

Actors and translators have a lot in common: they are both, ideally, involved in detailed script analysis of the work at hand. Translator Timberlake Wertenbacker says, "Only actors know writers that well, I mean understand a play as well as you do as you translate" (Croft 4). Actors, in rehearsal, may give translators helpful suggestions and clues to the actions of a play from the actors' discoveries in the playing, onstage. An intimate understanding of the play and characters is forged in the acting, in the physical *doing* of the play itself. And this "doing" is not only about speaking words in the script.

Many translators do realize the helpfulness of working with actors in rehearsal. Actors, ideally, know how to read a script "to ferret out the action—to read it not as the audience does, or as an English professor does, but as one whose job is to bring it to the audience" (Mamet 1999: 99). Mamet is writing to actors in his *True and False* on the art of acting, but his point is just as pertinent to play translators. This is another thing play translators and actors have in common: their goal is to bring the play to the audience. Laurence Senelick, a translator, academician and practitioner, states:

> [W]hen it comes to Chekhov's drama, I have usually found the plays in production and the remarks of directors, designers and actors more illuminating than most academic critical studies … The pressures of the rehearsal room, the actual configuration of bodies in space, the adventitious discoveries of a performer's imagination can force insights unavailable in the closest reading. *The only comparable experience is to translate a play*, paying close attention to such things as lexical repetition, sentence structure

and levels of discourse. Watching even the most hopeless staging of Chekhov, I have come upon connections and insights that eluded me in years of poring over texts. (emphasis added, Clayton 6)

Why should this be true? Because, as noted, it is the actor's body in space and his/her imagination—his/her *actions*—that give us the meaning of the words, and the play. Chekhov knew this, and crafted his plays accordingly. We may only truly discover the play on its feet.

The Rehearsal and The Audience

"Being faithful to the work has nothing to do with being faithful to the text."

This quote is presented as "Provocative words from German director Michael Thalheimer, a radical reductionist who pares classic works to their essence, stripping them of all excess language, gesture, and historical content." [15] He is not directing Chekhov, but the sentiment of the quote, which I've explored, is significant. It may not be the "text" of a play that determines its fidelity to the original playwright. The "spirit," rather than the "letter" of a translation is important to capture.

The most contemporary approaches to translation take this fact into consideration. Zatlin notes that "absolute fidelity" to a source may result in unplayable—and unspeakable—translations (3). Contemporary translators observe that especially for "texts that belong to another period or culture," it is impossible to take a literal approach.[16] The translator must take into consideration the anticipated response from an audience, and that the rehearsal work of practitioners will shape the play.

Zuber, with Corrigan (Arrowsmith 95–106), not only states "In the process of translating a play, it is necessary to mentally direct, act and see the play at the same time" but "Ideally, the translator would be present at rehearsals and participate in

---

15 Thalheimer's version of *Emilia Galotti* premiered at the Brooklyn Academy of Music (BAM) in October, 2005. Quotes are from the BAM flyer, June, 2005. The play was certainly stripped of all but its primary character relationships: the daughter, her lover, her husband, her father and mother, in a presentational and stark but graceful mise-en-scene. The play became a dance, and each speech an aria. See also Pamela Renner's review, "Lessing is More" in the Village Voice, Oct. 4, 2005.

16 Spanish playwright/director Ernesto Caballero, qtd. in, Zatlin, *Theatrical Translation*, Chapter 1, p. 3.

the discussions and the work of transferring the written translation on to the stage"
(93). Translators, with practitioners, "adapt" plays off the page of the script.

> Drama, as an art form, is a constant process of translation: from the original concept
> to script (when there is one), to producer/director's interpretation, to contribution by
> designer and actor/actress, to visual and/or aural images to audience response ... there
> may be a number of subsidiary processes of translation at work.[17]

Actors, director and designers all have contributions to a production. The process
of rehearsal—with all contributors taking part—is a part of the process of translation, culminating in the performance onstage.

In David Johnston's *Stages of Translation* he notes that all contributors to his
volume believe in the "inseparability of play and performance," and the "impact
of immediate reception" (8). Translators write for the space where plays will be
performed, "with specifically envisaged audiences as well as actors" (11). The playwright writes for *now*; the translator can do no less. So play translations have a
shorter shelf-life than other genres of literature. Masters like Chekhov must be
"translated" for every generation.

Thus we may say there is no such thing as translating a play in a "period" style;
whatever "style" the translator may adopt, the audience who will see it is living in
the present. The idea of pursuing a "style" of writing when a play to be translated is
from another era, as with Chekhov, is described by translator Steve Gooch as "the
unspoken connections from line to line in the dialogue, originating in the author's
mind, which as spectators we're drawn into and then follow" (19). The audience
gets "plugged in" to these connections—"that original engine"—and is allowed
to share the "subjective world of the author ... In the end, a translator's love for a
play, like that of a director, actor or member of the public, can only be requited by
a wider public enjoyment of the dynamic of those synaptic connections" (*Ibid.*).
This "engine" with "synaptic connections" may be a reference to Action in a play,
in which the audience takes part.

Gooch also refers to language as carrying an "energy" which may aid or
"undermine rehearsal." He says actors need to "feel a style for themselves." Words
may seem "tedious" on the page, but "sometimes it takes work on the rehearsal
floor to reveal what is really going on in a scene ... the text frequently represents
the tip of a rehearsal iceberg" (17). The "Action" is discovered in the playing:

> It's not so much a question of the literal meaning of the words as being able to *plug
> into the condition of which the words are a symptom*. There is an act of translation in

---

17 *Ibid.*, Cobos Castro, Esperanza, *Teatro y traduccion en el siglo XIX.*

THE TRANSLATOR AS ARTIST | 59

this for the actor, too. Each word onstage operates like a signpost guiding the actor (and, indeed, the audience) from moment to moment along a cognitive journey. And, ultimately, the journey is more important than the signposts. (emphasis added, *Ibid.*)

The *words* are a *symptom* of the Action the actor is playing; the Action comes before the words. The words themselves do not give meaning. This force or "engine," revealed by the text, but not caused by it, is presented in Appendix A and discussed in Chapter IV on Action. Gooch is describing here—with reference to a "journey"—both the Action of the play as a whole and the individual character Action that "*does* you" rather than you (the actor) *doing* the action.[18]

Finally, Gooch states "The real point is that actors must be able to wear the language of the play like clothes. They must be able to put the text on and feel they can breathe in it, move around freely and find its physical expression from within themselves" (17–18). This is a reference to playing Action. One sees how closely the translator's work is like the actor's, in their attempt to discover the motor or "Action" of the play. Translator John Clifford calls actors one of the "main alarm systems the playwright possesses" and notes "how closely the two processes—of translating theatre and creating it—are intertwined" (5).

Gooch's: metaphors of "energy" and "clothes" fitting the actor are echoed by translator Laurence Boswell, who feels that "one of the most creative ways of doing anything in the theatre—whether it's composing, writing or acting—is through a kind of mutuality … I think that things often work best in rehearsals … the shoe of the language can be fitted much more tightly to the situation." So Boswell also believes the director and translator should both contribute to the play in rehearsal. Further, he states:

It is impossible to say that you know a play until you have gone through the dynamics of testing it in rehearsal … you inevitably come back to the *central energy* of the play— perhaps that's a better word than 'meaning' for the translator (146).

Both Gooch's and Boswell's uses of the term "energy" may also be linked to the idea of Action.[19] Coming to that "central energy" or "original engine" are comparable to Stanislavsky's terms "throughline," "superobjective" or "spine," which are part of his approach to play analysis (see Appendix A). Understanding how play structure is composed of Action is as important for the translator and director as it is for the actor and playwright. The concept of Action may be inherently understood by

---

18 Russian acting teacher/director Yevgeny Lanskoy, Adler Conservatory, 1987–90.
19 Professor/scholar/director Earle Gister, head of Yale Drama School for twenty years, also described Action as a "release of specific energy," in a June 8, 2004 interview at The Actor's Center in NYC.

the play translator, even though the terms used are different: Action is the "energy" or "engine" (desire or purpose) that runs the play.

Implicit in these ideas about performance is the notion that "the theatrical experience consists of a series of moments of complicity between performer and spectator" (153). Kenneth McLeish states:

> The spectator's participation is as crucial as the performer's; they work together to make the show, and without their complicity, there is no show. Even when we read dramatic material alone to ourselves at home, we 'perform' it in our minds, we give it emotional (and sometimes physical) blocking in ways quite different from when we read poetry, say, or novels (153).

The same idea has been put forth by Rosenblatt (see Chapter II) regarding reading a play. The play itself—which is, after all, the *performance* of the play—cannot exist without the spectator, even while one reads the script. In rehearsal, the reactions of the spectator are kept in mind by the director and the actors, and the physical presence and input of the translator can be helpful in creating the performance. McLeish tells us "The texts have to be worked, mined for comic potential,[20] and the translator is there both to assist in this and to pull the process back when it moves too far from (what seem to be) the original author's intentions" (155). Thus the rehearsal of a play and the anticipated audience reaction are inextricable. The translator, by contributing to rehearsal, can be, ideally, part of the realization of his or her translated text.

It has been noted that translators over the centuries do not always share the same methodologies or approaches to translation. This is also true for contemporary translators for the stage (Johnston 7). However, most current translators of plays—including Chekhov's plays—do agree on two main points that have been discussed as jumping-off points for modern translation: plays are translated with a view to the *mise-en-scène* or performance of the playscript, and plays are written for actors (9). These two pronouncements are inextricable, of course: the actor is the core of the scenic depiction of a play. The playscript—the words on the page—is considered a blueprint for performance. These concepts bear repeating, as they are the basis for an understanding of the importance of the rehearsal process and the audience in producing a translation, adaptation or version of a play. It is important to the art form that both the reading and viewing public—as well as theatre practitioners—understand possible differences between translations that result from

---

20 Chekhov considered his last four plays—with the possible exception of *The Three Sisters*—comedies. There is great humor throughout his canon, sometimes lost in production. (See Stanislavsky 1948b: 345–50.)

"translation," "adaptation" or "versions" of a play, whether they are read or seen in performance.

Translation, Adaptation or Version?

Johnston considers structural changes made to the original work to be "adaptations" (273). But these three terms are sometimes used interchangeably, and other times separately, to define the process and result of translating a play. Just as various views of fidelity to the original author—whether to the "letter" or "spirit" of the work—are held by contemporary translators, what a translator calls his or her rendition varies from writer to writer.

Playwright Nick Dear translates from literal renditions, but states he does not consult these translators, as he doesn't think "the process of creating a new version of a classic play for the stage is about fine points of style at all" (272). Dear considers himself an adaptor. He believes the term "translator" may be reserved for poets who practice a "pure" and "much more serious and very respectable tradition of translation" (272). He also explains that elsewhere in Europe (outside Britain) it is the dramaturge who does the adapting that Dear has done with foreign plays, and this dramaturge "receives no credit, no royalties" (273). He concludes that English-speaking "adaptors" are "clearly not classic translators or academic translators" (*Ibid.*). And, apparently, Dear doesn't mind being called an "adaptor" rather than a "translator."

So, for Dear, anyone who uses someone else's "literal" translation would have to be labeled an "adaptor." He goes so far as to say that "it's slightly cozy that adaptation has become almost as applauded as original playwriting" because it is easier to adapt a play than to write one, and more profitable! (*Ibid.*) When confronted by adaptor Jean-Claude Carrière,[21] who stated there is no difference in quality between adaptations and original plays, and that *all* plays are an adaptation of something, Dear disagreed. Dear states that, though Shakespeare adapted from other plays and historical sources, *The Cherry Orchard* and *Waiting for Godot* were, for example, "pure and original dramatic poetry and imagination," and "not adaptation[s] of anything" (275).[22]

Translator Joseph Farrell maintains "the genuine adaptor is a co-creator who forges his own work in the light of the sun. For some theatre-goers, the prime

21 Carrière adapted Peter Brook's French production of *La tempête* from Shakespeare's *The Tempest*.
22 Johnston writes (275) *Godot* may be an "adaptation" of musical hall sketches (Vaudeville, we would say). It is my contention that *Godot* is redolent of Act II of *Cherry Orchard*, with regard to dialogue and set, as well as overall tone. See Chapter IX.

concern in an evening's theatre is the quality of the work staged before them, not with whether it corresponds to some unknown original written in a far-off land for which they care little" (55). But he also asks, how can a true "translator" attain that title if he/she is "not familiar with the tricks of speech of the original characters?" He believes the adaptor too is responsible for "allowing foreign writers to remain foreign and slightly strange" (55) so the audience may not lose all that is the original playwright.

On that note, translator Jacek Laskowski lauds the Chekhov translations of playwright Michael Frayn, calling them "perfection." However, a director told him:

> They are very good, of course they are. But they are *too* English. Reading his translations, I get no sense of otherness, no sense of foreignness … So I get no sense of *Russia*. And if I get no sense of *Russia*, then the plays make no sense to me. The plays are about Russians living in Russia. If the English is so flawlessly, idiomatically English then my audience will not perceive its fundamental nature; its Russianness. The audience will be baffled by the play. (189)

Laskowski begs to differ with his director friend. Other translators agree with the friend. Whether a translation/adaptation should resemble the source or target culture is at issue. Frayn's "translations" (his word) are English, but they are impeccably British. For that reason, they may seem quaint to American audiences. Frayn's plays are included with other English translations and versions in Chapters VI–IX.

Translator Peter Meyer tells us "Colloquial language in a period play is always a problem. Aggressively modern words must be avoided and so must the archaic. One has to tread a delicate path between these two extremes, while at the same time avoiding neutral flatness" (133). Translator/playwright Van Itallie, we recall, is accused by Senelick of making all Chekhov's characters sound the same. In a summer 2005 adaptation by Tom Dohagny of *Cherry Orchard* for the Atlantic Theatre in New York City, Lopakhin yells "Shit!" in a preview of the play. Dohagny later told this researcher he took that particular exclamation out of the final script. It is indeed a delicate path.

Translator Eivor Martinus holds that the "first prerequisite for a translator must then, surely, be a thorough knowledge of both the source language and the target language" and would call anyone who uses a "literal translation" the "adaptor," (as does Dear above) even though the latter gets the biggest billing (110). Martinus, like previous translators mentioned, questions translators/adaptors who "recreate … whole scenes and change the name and nature of characters," and calls for their plays to be labeled "version" or "adaptation." Martinus asks of these, "Does it actually present the original author in a true light? In other words, how far should we as translators go? When does a translation cease to be a translation, when does it become an adaptation?" (113). When indeed.

Scholar/translation theorists Hale and Upton, editors of the aptly named *Moving Target*, call into question the "reverse hierarchy" of conferring higher status (and remuneration, it must be added) on the "adaptor" than the "translator" in play translation. They ponder "Perhaps the implication has been that an adaptation requires a level of dramaturgical skill and creative vision, which, in a 'mere' translation, are solely attributed to the original playwright?" (10). One's understanding of dramaturgy is certainly a consideration, according to theatre practitioners. Hale and Upton are startled at what they call the "dismissiveness" of playwright/translator Christopher Hampton's observation that "It's a terminology problem ... I don't much like 'new version' ... the problem is there isn't a terminology which says I haven't done anything to this play except put it in English" (10).[23] But an "adaptation" can change a play summarily. Because plays are performed, the terms "translation, adaptation and version" have different meanings in the world of play translation than they do in literary translation, and even among play translators themselves.

Perhaps the most significant concept to understand, treated throughout this chapter, is that, as translator John Clifford describes in "Translating the Spirit of the Play," "We are not just translating words. Words in a dramatic text are not an end in themselves; they are a kind of scaffolding on which the actor constructs his or her performance" (Johnston 263–4). The text on the page is a scaffold, a blueprint, the clothes and shoes that fit easily on the body of the actor. Clifford continues: "And what counts are not just the words themselves, but the gaps between the words. The feeling behind the words. What is left unsaid matters as much as what is said: and as translators we have to be sensitive to both" (264). The actor too must be sensitive to both, and Clifford recognizes their contribution to the text. This contribution is key especially in Chekhov's plays, which, with Ibsen's, instigate the concept of Realism on the stage. Realism results from Action, which underlies the text, and which the actor draws on, rather than the words alone.

What is "between the words" is Action, and the experienced translator knows that the job of the actor is to fill in what is left unsaid, as well as to give meaning to what is spoken out loud. Clifford finally maintains that "the best plays ... don't come from the writer: they come from the characters," and "the task of translating remains the basic creative task; to feel with the characters. And listen to what they have to say. That is the foundation of a good translation" (266). These sentiments are also articulated by Chekhov's translators, explored in the chapters on the individual plays.

---

23 Yet Hampton later agrees, apparently, that his *Seagull* on Broadway in October, 2008 is indeed a "new version" of the play—in his interview with Robert Segal of NPR.

Much like Gooch's "unspoken connections," Clifford states that the spirit of the play is made up of "the web of unspoken understandings, unquestioned shared values" of which language is composed (6). He concludes "while it matters to translate the words with accuracy, passion and a sense of theatre, what matters perhaps more is to learn how to translate the unspoken" whether this means "translating" the script in the setting delineated by the original playwright, or "adapting" it to a new venue, more familiar to the target audience (7). As translator Neil Bartlett has stated, it depends on what kind of "night out in the theatre" one is looking for (Johnston 74).

Johnston tells us that this is one distinction between "translation" and "adaptation": often the adaptor changes the venue or time period of the original play, to make it more relevant to the contemporary theatre-goer. A "translation" would preserve the venue of the original playwright. However, as Johnston articulately illustrates, a translator who knows the dramaturgical structure of the play could preserve the "spirit" of the play, even while transporting it to a place known better by the target audience.

Johnston maintains that theatre—pragmatically—is "language in *action*, or language in stage-function" (emphasis added, 57). The alleged "duality" of theatre—as a written text and a text for performance—"imposes a deformation on the play by ignoring the patterns for performance which are encoded in its scripting" (57–8). This is a concept often not recognized by the linguist or philologist, but it is the key to translating a stageworthy play. Johnston, along with most contemporary translators of Chekhov, sees the playscript as "a special form of scripting, which, even from the pen of the most prescriptive of dramatists,[24] cannot be taken as anything other than providing a springboard towards performance" (58). Johnston insists that only with a full dramaturgical interrogation can drama be recreated with something approaching its original impact. So, this means that the translator, adaptor or version-creator must see the play as a producible whole "which functions as theatre and not solely as a piece of linear narrative" (59). We see that Director Meckler's comment that the translator need only "translate" *words* in the dialogue of a play to reproduce the *structure* of a play is mistaken. This dramaturgical analysis is even more important for a playwright like Chekhov, whose last four plays are so deeply embedded in the time, place and language of his country, and the poetry of the stage.

The inseparability of definitions of translation, adaptation and version is demonstrated by the disagreements of respected practitioners in the field. Not

---

24 Such as Samuel Beckett, who demanded, and whose estate demands, that his plays be produced precisely as written, with no deletions or emendations.

all translators address a dramaturgical analysis of the play in question. Playwright Timberlake Wertenbaker notes that "adaptation" means "to fit something for an audience—to fit it into something else. Translation means to transport … you try to transport an audience into the play, as opposed to trying to fit the play to an audience. Why not go for the whole world of the playwright?" (Croft 17). Noel Clark too wants to hear the playwright's voice, not the translator's, and so feels any translation done from a "literal" is "adapting" someone else's translation (Johnston 26). On the other hand, Ranjit Bolt feels "there is a spurious idea that translation is a faithful rendering … I prefer to think that all good translation is really transformation … the adaptation/ translation distinction creates unwanted red herrings" (Croft 33). Yet, Joseph Farrell reasons "there ought to be little dissent over the need to maintain the distinction between translation and adaptation, and to publicize it as clearly as health warnings on cigarette packets. The distinction is under threat …" (Johnston 50).

Johnston agrees, maintaining that many translators call for a "common definition of all these words—translation, adaptation, version—or at least to agree that one should always be open about the process …" (66). He recognizes the difficulty of making distinctions, "unless it is to refer to translation as the first stage of linguistic and broadly literary interrogation of the source text, and adaptation as the process of dramaturgical analysis, the preparation for re-enactment" (66). Interestingly, many of the translations of Chekhov's last four plays are labeled "versions,"[25] while the playwrights may refer to them as "adaptations" as well. Sometimes a "version" is seen as being a version of the original playwright's play—and so closer to a "translation" in style—while other translators feel a "version" is beyond the adaptation. For example, Joshua Logan's *Wisteria Trees* (labeled "based on" Chekhov's *Cherry Orchard*) or Chay Yew's *A Winter People* (based on *Cherry Orchard*), both of which change characters, scenes, settings and endings of the original plays, may be versions *or* adaptations. These differences will be discussed in Chapters VI–IX.

Johnston believes a common definition of these words would be "of interest to all of those who work in the theatre" (66). I agree. More specifically, a "translation" of a play could be viewed as the more literarily (and more literal) word-based interpretation of Chekhov's text. An "adaptation" will be viewed as a work that may consciously change the structure, characters or setting of the play. Examples of an adaptation of a Chekhov play is, as mentioned above, Joshua Logan's *Wysteria Trees* that places Chekhov's orchard on an American southern plantation, and

---

25   Pam Gems, Trevor Griffiths, Brian Friel, Tom Stoppard and Jean-Claude Van Itallie, for example.

changes whole speeches and characters freely in the text. More recently, Tennessee Williams' *The Notebook of Trigorin* also changes speeches and characters, as well as events, while maintaining the setting of a Russian estate; it may be considered an adaptation. "Versions" of Chekhov's plays could be viewed as something in between a "translation" and an "adaptation," or something more radical than an adaptation. Examples are in a range from David Mamet's *Uncle Vanya*, which uses the sparse and idiomatic language that may be associated with this contemporary playwright, and Brian Friel's *Uncle Vanya*, which changes/eliminates whole patches of dialogue while retaining and concretizing the actions of the characters. In any case, we see that these definitions are often overlapping, interchangeable, and used differently by each translator. Such is the territory we explore.

Finally, a crucial element in play translation must be addressed. Theatre scholars and practitioners have made much of the importance of rhythm in the spoken text of a translation. Senelick names "harmony and rhythm" as the greatest loss in English translations of Chekhov's major plays (2005: xii). These include the "echoes" of language and allusions in and amongst his plays, the cadences of characters, the emphasis or stress on important words, lost irony in word meanings, and the pregnant sounds of particular words that are difficult to match in English translation (2000: 13). For translator Boswell, rhythm is also significant; he considers "language is the very surface of the play ... a kind of wrapping" and "the physical rhythm of theatre for me is like a dance, a three dimensional structure which happens in time ... I come at it, like someone making a wheel, trying to look at the hub of the play" (Johnston 283). It is the actor who carries all these elements of harmony and rhythm through the play.

Other translators also wax metaphorical in reaching for ways to describe translating the rhythm of a foreign language. Neil Bartlett states "I don't translate plays to get them onto the page. I translate plays to get them into the mouth. So cadence, stress and the theatrical use of punctuation is something I'm obsessive about" (68). Translator Anthony Vivis[26] insisted:

> The rhythm of dramatic dialogue ... is a complex and living organism. Rhythm is the energy, the heartbeat, the metabolism of language. Variations in rhythm alter emphasis, pace and through them, at times, meaning. The relatively simple element of word order can change a rhythm, and with it the whole accent of a sentence. (39)

Vivis goes on to describe how he sees the play as one long sentence, "paced and pitched" by the actor. "If the rhythm ever sags, the line, the speech, the scene will

---

26 Anthony Vivis died suddenly in 2013. He was known for his translations of Brecht, Schiller and many others.

lose its springyness, and as a result the audience's attention will wander" (40). We see how closely the actor's job is dependent on the translated text, and the translator on the actor. This is why, in his article "Theatre Pragmatics," Johnston repeats three times "It's about writing for actors" (57–66). This is the crux of the issue of translating for the stage.

Playwright/actor David Hare is also concerned with rhythm, and his method has a bearing on the actor: "All dramatic dialogue is plainly about rhythm … think about what the actor is trying to find. Usually the actor thinks he's looking at psychology, but if he doesn't have the rhythm of the writer then he is wasting his time … To me this is as true of prose drama as it is of poetic drama. I spend more time thinking about rhythm than I do about meaning" (142). As an actor, the rhythm of a phrase can *give* one the meaning, along with purposeful punctuation. In translations of Chekhov, the differences in word choice, word order (syntax) and punctuation can change the actor's approach to a role.

One last intention of the play translator must be mentioned. The notion of "fidelity," whether to the letter and/or spirit of the original playwright, must come from love. As Gooch reasons, "If you love a person … you hate to see your view of them misrepresented or misunderstood—even if you yourself are blind to their worst qualities … translating plays can only be an act of love" (14, 19). And Johnston notes "the creature created from that love … has to function under public scrutiny." To do so, Eivor Matinus advises, "one should confine oneself to authors with a kindred spirit" (121). Many authors—Russian speakers and others—feel this special kinship with Chekhov, and profess fidelity to his canon in translating the plays.[27]

Steiner claims that "There are no translations." But he does acknowledge:

> Great translators—and they are disastrously rare—act as a kind of mirror. They offer to the original not an equivalence, for there can be none, but a vital counterpoise, an echo, faithful yet autonomous, as we find in the dialogue of human love. An act of translation is an act of love. Where it fails, through immodesty or blurred perception, it traduces. Where it succeeds, it incarnates. (1998a 270–1)

---

27 In *The Kindness of Strangers*, author Daniel Spoto writes Tennessee Williams claimed kinship with Strindberg and Chekhov (50); in *Stopped Rocking* Williams himself writes "I have not been subjected to any influence but that of Chekhov in my profession" (3). Friel is known as the "Irish Chekhov" (Kerwin 236, 247). Wilson claims *Three Sisters* is his favorite play and *Vanya* his second favorite (Chekhov 1984: ix–xiii). Van Itallie claims to have "channeled" Chekhov (Interview, Spring, 2002). Almost all the Chekhov translators in this study claim some special feeling for the playwright.

The actor too "incarnates." The next chapter will define the underlying energy, motor, engine, the "condition of which the words are just a symptom" (Gooch in Johnston 17) that allows him or her to do so.

Throughout the history and theories of translation, and pragmatic approaches to it discussed in this chapter, the discussion has returned to issues of fidelity, lack of equivalence between languages, and the fact that faithfulness to words does not necessarily mean faithfulness to the work itself, especially in writing for the stage. Translators disagree on definitions of "translation," "adaptation" or "version," and on assessments of translations from non-speakers of the source language. Poet Paul Valéry said of writing poems that they are never actually "finished;" they can only be abandoned (Arrowsmith 168). One may say the same for this discussion on the subject of translation. Now, in an attempt to clarify the actor's contributions to acting in translation, the nature of the actor's work on the stage will be addressed.

References

Arrowsmith, William and Roger Shattuck, eds. *The Craft and Context of Translation.* Austin: The University of Texas Press, 1961.

Beale, Simon Russell. Interview with the author. Brooklyn Academy of Music, March 9, 2003.

Blessing, Lee. Interview with the author. Rutgers University, May, 2004; phone Interview, July, 2017.

———. *Uncle,* Reading at the Arkansas New Play Festival, Theatre Squared, Fayetteville, 2015.

———. *Uncle,* World Premiere by New Ground Theatre, Davenport, IA, 2016.

Carnicke, Sharon Marie. "The Nasty Habit of Adaptations," Conference: "Chekhov the Immigrant: Translating a Cultural Icon," Colby College, October 8–9, 2004.

Chekhov, Anton. *Anton Chekhov's Selected Plays.* Trans. and Ed. Laurence Senelick. New York: W. W. Norton & Co., 2005.

———. *Chekhov, Four Plays.* Trans. Carol Rocamora. Lyme, NH: Smith and Kraus, 1996.

———. *Chekhov, The Major Plays.* Trans. Jean-Claude Van Itallie. New York: Applause Books, 1995.

———. *Chekhov Plays.* Trans. Michael Frayn. London: Methuen, 1988.

———. *The Cherry Orchard.* Adapt. Tom Donaghy. Unpublished draft, December, 2004.

———. *The Cherry Orchard.* Version. Pam Gems. UK: Oberon Classics, 2007.

———. *The Cherry Orchard.* Version. Sir John Gielgud. New York: Theatre Arts Books, 1963.

———. *The Cherry Orchard.* Version. Trevor Griffiths/Trans. Helen Rappaport. London: Pluto Press Ltd., 1978.

———. *The Cherry Orchard.* Trans. Tyrone Guthrie and Leonid Kipnis. Minneapolis: University of Minnesota.

———. *The Cherry Orchard*. Adapt. David Mamet from a literal trans. Peter Nelles. New York: Grove Press, 1985.

———. *The Cherry Orchard*. Adapt. Emily Mann. New York: Dramatists Play Service, 2000. Press/Minnesota Theatre Company, 1965.

———. *The Cherry Orchard*. Trans. Martin Sherman. Unpublished manuscript for the Music Center production in Los Angeles, California, 2006.

———. *The Cherry Orchard*. Trans. Jean-Claude Van Itallie. New York: Dramatists Play Service, 1979.

———. *The Plays of Anton Chekhov*. Trans. Constance Garnett. New York: The Modern Library, 1929.

———. *The Seagull*. Trans. Michael Frayn. London: Methuen Publishing Ltd., 1986.

———. *The Seagull*. Version. Pam Gems. London: Nick Hern Books, 1994.

———. *The Seagull*. Version. Tom Stoppard. London: Faber and Faber Limited, 1997.

———. *Three Sisters*. Version. Brian Friel. New York: Dramatists Play Service, 1981.

———. *The Three Sisters*. Adapt. Christopher Hampton. UK: Samuel French, 2004/2015.

———. *The Three Sisters*. Trans. Randall Jarrell. London: Collier-Macmillan Limited, 1969.

———. *The Three Sisters*. Adapt. David Mamet. Trans. Vlada Chernomirdik. New York: Samuel French, 1990.

———. *Three Sisters*. Acting Version. Clifford Odets. Unpublished manuscript from Phoebe Brand Carnovsky, The Group Theatre, New York City, c. 1939.

———. *Three Sisters*. Trans. Lanford Wilson. Lyme, NH: Smith and Kraus, 1984.

———. *Uncle Vanya*. Version. Pam Gems. London: Nick Hern Books, 1992.

Clayton, J. Douglas, ed. *Chekhov Then and Now*. New York: Peter Lang, 1997.

Clifford, John. "Translating Moments, Not Words," www.teatrodomundo.com, February 9, 2005.

Cocteau, Jean. Preface, *Les Mariés de la Tour Eiffel*. Paris: Editions Flammarion, 1995. See also https://www.poetryfoundation.org/poets/jean-cocteau.

Corrigan, Robert. "Translating for Actors," in William Arrowsmith and Roger Shattuck, eds. *The Craft and Context of Translation*. Austin: The University of Texas Press, 1961, pp. 95–106.

Croft, Giles. *Platform Papers*. London: Royal National Theatre, 1989 and 1991.

Friedberg, Maurice. *Literary Translation in Russia*. University Park, PA: The Pennsylvania State University Press, 1997.

Giona, Dana. "A Translator's Tale," (Interview with Richard Wilbur) *American Theatre Magazine*. New York: TCG, April, 2009.

Gister, Earle. Interview with the author. The Actor's Center, New York City, June 8, 2005.

Gottlieb, Vera and Paul Allain, eds. *The Cambridge Companion to Chekhov*. Cambridge University Press, 2000.

Johnston, David, ed. *Stages of Translation*. Bath, England: Absolute Classics, 1996.

Kerwin, William, ed. *Brian Friel, A Casebook*. New York: Garland Publishing, 1997.

Lanskoy, Yevgeny. Interviews with the author, 1999, and Classes, "The Structures of Action," at the Stella Adler Conservatory, 1986–89.

Lessing, Gotthold Ephraim. *Emilia Galotti.* Adapter/Director Michael Thalheimer. Brooklyn Academy of Music, NYC, October 2005.

Logan, Brian. "Whose Play is it Anyway?" *Guardian*, March 12, 2003.

Logan, Joshua. *The Wisteria Trees, based on Anton Chekhov's The Cherry Orchard.* New York: Random House, 1950.

Lopate, Leonard. "The Leonard Lopate Show," Interview with David Mamet, WNYC Radio, Spring, 2006, retrieved December 23, 2008.

Magarshack, David. *The Real Chekhov.* London: George Allen & Unwin, Ltd., 1972.Mamet, David. *True and False.* New York: Vintage Books, 1999.

Mekler, Nancy. Interview with the author. Brooklyn Marriott Hotel, November, 2004.

Mendes, Sam. Interview with the author. Brooklyn Academy of Music, March, 2003.

Ormsby, Eric. "Still a Great Translation," *New York Sun,* November 3, 2004.

Remnick, David. "The Translation Wars," *The New Yorker*, November 7, 2005, pp. 98–109.

Renner, Pamela. "Lessing is More," Village Voice, October 4, 2005.

Rosenblatt, Louise M. *The Reader, The Text, The Poem.* Carbondale: Southern Illinois University Press, 1978.

Scammell, Michael. "The Servile Path –Translating Vladimir Nabokov," *Harper's Magazine,* www.findarticles.com.

Segal, Robert. "Writer Hampton Transforms 'The Seagull' On Stage," All Things Considered, NPR News, October 3, 2008.

Senelick, Laurence. *The Chekhov Theatre.* Cambridge: Cambridge University Press, 1997.

———. "Chekhov's Plays in English," *The North American Chekhov Society Bulletin,* Vol. IX, Spring, 2000.

———. Correspondence with the author, laurence.senelick@tufts.edu, to robin.levenson@nyu. edu, Boston and New York. March 7 and 11, 2002.

Spoto, Daniel. *The Kindness of Strangers, The Life of Tennessee Williams.* New York: Da Capo Press, 1997.

Stanislavsky, Konstantin. *An Actor Prepares.* Trans. Elizabeth Reynolds Hapgood. New York: Theatre Arts Books, 1948a.

———. Stanislavsky, Konstantin. *My Life in Art.* Trans. J. J. Robbins. New York: Theatre Arts Books, 1948b.

———. *Building a Character.* Trans. Elizabeth Reynolds Hapgood. New York: Theatre Arts Books, 1949.

———. *Creating a Role.* Trans. Elizabeth Reynolds Hapgood. New York: Theatre Arts Books, 1961.

Steiner, George. *After Babel.* New York: Oxford University Press, 1998a.

Upton, Carole-Anne, ed. *Moving Target: theatre translation and cultural relocation.* Manchester: St. Jerome Publishing, 2000.

Van Itallie, Jean-Claude. Interview with the author. New York City, November 19, 2003.

Williams, Tennessee. Trans. Hale, Allean. *The Notebook of Trigorin: A Free Adaptation of Anton Chekhov's Seagull.* New York: New Directions Publishing, 1997.

———. *Stopped Rocking and Other Screenplays.* New York: A New Directions Book, 1984.

Yew, Chay. *A Winter People*. New Adaptation of Anton Chekhov's *The Cherry Orchard*, Unpublished Draft, September 28, 2004.

Zatlin, Phyllis. *Theatrical Translation and Film Adaptation, a Practitioner's View*. UK, USA, Canada: Multilingual Matters Ltd., 2005.

Zuber, Ortrun, ed. *The Languages of Theatre*. Oxford: Pergamon Press, 1980.

CHAPTER FOUR

Action

Below the surface-stream, shallow and light,
Of what we *say* we feel—below the stream
As light, of what we *think* we feel—there flows
With noiseless current strong, obscure and deep,
The central stream of what we feel indeed ...
>   —MATTHEW ARNOLD, FROM "ST. PAUL AND PROTESTANTISM"[1]

"In an art that is temporal as well as spatial, we have hardly any terms
for designating the sequential features of a play, let alone the subtle
interactions of the presentation itself. Our vocabulary is inadequate,
our descriptions of the theatrical process imprecise, and our definitions
of what constitutes the art of drama virtually nonexistent ... despite
heritage and volume, drama lacks a system of practical aesthetics."
>   —(BECKERMAN 1979, VII)[2]

Though critical studies on Anton Chekhov's plays abound, as do studies on the
nature of translation, few theorists or theatre critics have concerned themselves
with how Chekhov's plays, or other plays in translation, may actually be **acted**.

---

1   *St. Paul and Protestantism: with other essays* by Matthew Arnold, London: Smith, Elder, 1889.
2   Bernard Beckerman is a longstanding theatre teacher, critic and stage director. He is a
     featured essayist in editor Hobgood's *Master Teachers of Theatre*, 1988.

Translation scholar Lefevere writes: "Literary analyses of translated dramatic texts very often were confined to its textual dimension; to what was on the page. Neither discipline (linguistics or literary analysis) developed the necessary tools to deal with other dimensions in a satisfactory way" (Zuber 160). As discussed in Chapters II and III, the "other dimensions" often so difficult for literary critics and linguists to describe are the theatrical ones.

This chapter will discuss the most important of these: the notion of "Action." Action is not an intellectual concept, but a functional tool for actors and other theatre practitioners that helps define the nature of the play itself, and the psycho-physical work of the performer. An understanding of Action is necessary in describing how language in various translations may influence the actor's work on Chekhov's plays in translation, addressed in Chapters VI through IX.

According to teacher/director Bernard Beckerman quoted above, drama lacks the necessary tools that would allow us to define the aesthetics of theatre. This is not wholly true. We do have some terms and techniques—such as Action—to help describe the "sequential features of a play," and the theatrical elements that make up the drama. The notion of Action comes to us largely from Aristotle, Stanislavsky and his successors, and other contemporary artists, critics and teachers who understand the difference between drama and other written literatures. For example, modern artists (and teachers and critics) as diverse in their backgrounds as Francis Fergusson, Polish director/theorist Grotowski (self-proclaimed proponent of Stanislavsky[3]), members of the Group Theatre of the '30s (Adler, Clurman, Lewis, Strasberg, Carnovsky, Meisner, Brand), and contemporary Russian acting teachers (Yevgeny Lanskoy, Marat Yusim and Slava Dolgatchev[4]) all teach and propound a view of Action as the basis of drama.

Beckerman begins his treatise on the nature of drama (*Dynamics of Drama*) with Aristotle and Stanislavsky; he gives his definitions of theatre and Action based on these masters (3–5, 11, 17–23). This effectively belies, in part, his statements about a lack of practical aesthetics for the theatre. It is not that we have *no* terms to describe drama; rather, it is that the literary world skews the discussion differently than performance-based scholars and practitioners. Beckerman notes that "even Susanne Langer sees drama as an art of poesis," albeit "an *enacted* poem," while critic/writer Francis Fergusson states "drama, as distinguished from a lyric, is not primarily a composition in the verbal medium" and Elder Olson warns flatly

---

3   Grotowski claims he continued Stanislavsky's work: "some Russians say that 'Grotowski *is* Stanislavski.'" (Richards, 105).

4   These are my teachers/directors from the Moscow Art Theatre who now teach and/or reside in the United States.

that "a play is *not* a literary composition" (17–18).[5] Semiotician Roland Barthes also returns to Aristotle when he defines a "character" in drama and narrative literatures "not as a 'being' but as a 'participant' ... in a sphere of actions" (Barthes 104–7). Barthes notes "characters" may be classified "not according to what they *are* but according to what they *do*" (106). Russian teacher and director Yevgeny Lanskoy also insisted to his students "Now you will never again describe the character you play by saying how they *feel*, but only by what they *do*" (Class, 1987). This description of character follows Aristotle's dictum that "character comes in as subsidiary to the actions" in a play (Aristotle 22), and so character is defined in terms of *Action* rather than qualities or personality.

Stanislavsky paid particular attention to Aristotle's axiom, and with his practical research on acting, according to Fergusson, based his "system" on Aristotle's idea (1964: 86). Among interesting suggestions expressed by Fergusson about Action—as used by the theatre practitioner—is that the notion has indeed come to us from the words of Aristotle's *Poetics* (*Ibid.*). Fergusson's observations on the link between Aristotle's definition of Action and Stanislavsky's work on Action in actor-training are particularly telling:

> The purpose of any good technique of acting is to help the actor to perceive the action of the character he is portraying, and then to recreate it in his own thought and feeling, as Aristotle says the playwright must do. The best-known acting technique of this kind is that of the Moscow Art Theatre ... The late Jacques Copeau taught such a technique, and so did the best theatre schools in Germany before Hitler. Each school tends, unfortunately, to develop its own technical vocabulary, but I think their basic assumptions may all be expressed in Aristotelian terms. They all assume that the actor's art consists in "taking the mold" of the character to be portrayed, and then responding to the situations of the play as they appear to that character. Only in that way can the actor achieve "lifelike reality." Superficial mimicry cannot produce psychological truth, fidelity to the playwright's imagined people and situations, or emotional effect on the audience. The masters of acting technique have a subtle and practical lore of action. There is no better way to understand "action," as the concept

---

5   In Danchik's 1991 Dissertation "The Distinction Between the Written and Performed Dramatic Text ..." he dismisses Langer's and Fergusson's idea that the dramatic script is *not* complete in itself, but only a map to the actions of a play (217–20). Danchik does not recognize that plays are written to be performed; he sees the written script as "complete" in itself (222).

Beckerman notes what Danchik has missed: while "dramatic literature concentrated on the play as a written text, that is, as a completely finished work of art," we now see "the script is a scheme for performance," and is based on "relationships and actions rather than fixed messages" ("The Play's the Thing, But What's a Play?" Bernard Beckerman in Hobgood, 32–3).

is used in Aristotle's *Poetics,* than by studying its practical utility in the art of acting. (Fergusson's Introduction in Aristotle 31–2)

And, conversely, it is helpful to the art of acting to understand how Aristotle used the concept of Action in his *Poetics.* Fergusson states that Aristotle knew that the poet, in the act of creating his or her play, has to be an actor: the *doing* of an Action forces him or her to "imitate each character in his own inner being and 'believe' the situations, just as a good actor does" (Aristotle 22–3). While Aristotle uses the term "action" (*praxis[6]*) to designate sequential movements of the drama (Richard Schechner describes this as "an interior action of the plot"[7]), this movement inherent in the play informs the actor's individual character Actions as well: the character has a purpose behind his behavior, just as the play has a purpose which drives its plot.

In spite of Aristotle, critics may not share a terminology to describe *what,* exactly, drama *is,* though actors with training are familiar with the term "Action" as an actual means of "playing" the script. As both Beckerman and Fergusson point out, the vocabulary of the stage actor and director, based in the praxis of theatre art, and that of the literary critic—each from different schools of thought—may not be concordant. [8]

In Chapters I–III it is put forth that drama is a different animal than other written literatures. This is so because the dialogue in a play is based on the underlying desires or wants of the characters. The actor's job, as Gooch has described it in *Stages of Translation,* is to define and act on the situation or "*condition* [of the character] *of which the words are a symptom*" (Johnston 17). In other words, the

---

6   *Praxis* comes from the Greek word for "deed, act or action;" it means practice, as distinguished from theory, and the application or use of knowledge or skills (Webster's 1129). It is particularly apt for this study, as it has broader connotations than the word "practice" alone. It means what is "doable," both physically and psychologically. It is Aristotle's Greek word for "action," meaning, as Fergusson points out, "the whole working out of a motive to its end in success or failure" (Aristotle 9). Thus it is also related to the ideas of *purpose* and *intention.* It is not mere motion or "kinesis," which describes the purely physical, but what is volitional and intentional (Rayner 131, 138). It may be described as a tool for doing empirical and pragmatic work on the play.

7   From Schechner's notes to me on my paper "Afraid to Lie" for his Directing class, 1998.

8   For example, Fergusson's view of drama is quite unlike that of T. S. Eliot, who has written extensively on drama. Fergusson attempts "to extend Aristotle's definitions to subsequent forms, and to cling to Hamlet's view of drama as an *art of playing,* while Mr. Eliot … starts rather with the Idealist conception of art. …" In other words, Fergusson is interested in the structure of drama from the point of view of the performer (1953: 21). Beckerman too acknowledges that his view of drama "owes a good deal to the working methods of the theatrical director [and thus to the actor]," rather than the literary critic (36–7).

dialogue is what we come upon *first* when we see or read a play, but the actor who says words onstage must understand that they are the logical *result* of the past and present circumstances that promote Action. Further, as Arnold's poem at the opening of this chapter suggests, what we *say* and even what we *think* may not be what we actually feel. As in real life, words in drama—especially in Realism—are often used to conceal, twist, or obfuscate characters' "true" desires and to influence and manipulate other characters, so words alone may not be taken at face value. It is the underlying Actions of the character—and of the plot—that propels the play, and not the words themselves. Actors may know this consciously in the playing of a role, or may not label their technique as playing "Actions." Onstage, the actor is only aware of what he or she is *pursuing* in the moment. In any case, Action impels characters' behaviors, and creates the words he or she speaks.

Fergusson holds that it is "the notion of 'action' [that] is the most basic, and potentially the most valuable, part of the Moscow Art Theatre technique" developed by Constantin Stanislavsky (1964: 85).[9] Though Fergusson claims that it is hard to be sure exactly what Stanislavsky meant by his terms—his disciples interpreted them in various ways, and Stanislavsky himself changed his rehearsal techniques at the end of his career[10]—Fergusson clearly describes the meaning of the word "action" as Richard Boleslavsky and Maria Ouspenskaya (members of Stanislavsky's First Studio[11]) defined it in classes Fergusson took with them from

---

9   The Moscow Art Theatre was founded by Constantin Stanislavsky and Vladimir Nemirovich-Danchenko from their famous 18-hour conversation in 1897 in Moscow's Slavic Bazaar. Its signature play, Chekhov's *The Seagull,* opened in 1898. The MAT's realistic style in Chekhov's plays and Stanislavsky's subsequent work on actor-training changed the face of American acting: Stella Adler, Lee Strasberg, Sanford Meisner, Morris Carnovsky, Phoebe Brand, and other members of the Group Theatre of the 1930s taught aspects of the "system," with their own emendations. Adler alone worked with Stanislavsky himself in 1934.

10 It is now understood that Lee Strasberg's "Method" is taken from Stanislavksy's early experiments with affective memory, largely ignoring Stanislavsky's later work on the Method of Physical Actions (Carnicke 1998: 62–6). Unfortunately, Strasberg's "Method" is often mistaken for Stanislavsky's "system," though Strasberg never worked with nor met Stanislavsky himself (*Ibid.*; see also Levenson, "Afraid to Lie"). Stella Adler's actor training is based on Stanislavsky's later praxis.

11 The First Studio of the MAT (1918) was headed by Stanislavsky's colleague Leopold Sulerjitsky, "humanist and Tolstoyan," who influenced Stanislavsky and brought Yoga and an eastern spiritual practice to the system (Gauss 79–94). The Studio was developed apart from the Art Theatre, as a place where Stanislavsky could work with students on his emerging system. Younger students Richard Boleslavsky, Maria Ouspenskaya, Evgeni Vakhtangov and Michael Chekhov (Anton's nephew) were members of this Studio, with

1926–1930 in New York (*Ibid.* 86). Stella Adler, with Harold Clurman and Lee Strasberg, also took these classes at the American Lab Theatre. These members (among others) of the Group Theatre of the 1930s brought Stanislavsky's techniques and theatre ethics to their work, and later to that of countless American actors through classes and writings.[12] Most actor-training in the United States is based on, or acknowledges, Stanislavsky's approach (Monos 1989).

Professor Richard Schechner at New York University wrote to me "the word/concept 'action' is a very complicated notion."[13] However, playing Actions onstage is understood by the actor in the *doing* of it. To move with purpose is not complicated; we do it every moment in life. The actor understands too the distinction between the individual character "Actions" and the "dramatic action" of the whole play to which character Actions are linked. An understanding of the nature of Action in a play, as applied in this study, requires an understanding of dramaturgy and play structure, as well as an understanding of the actor's function onstage. In defining these two uses of the word—dramatic action and the actor's Action—we continue the discussion of Aristotle's use of the term, as interpreted by Stanislavsky and later practitioners.

Definitions

"The complex structure of signifiers that makes up a performance is always greater than the sum of its parts, and those parts, being interdependent, can never validly be viewed discretely." (Harrop 1992:12)[14]

---

productions taught/produced by "Suler." Vakhtangov became a master of Stanislavsky's system and a director. Actor Michael Chekhov went on to teach in the U.S. (Benedetti 1990: 206–8). His "Psychological Gesture" portrays the inner action of the character.

12 These include Adler's *The Technique of Acting* and *The Art of Acting*, among others, Strasberg's *A Dream of Passion* and *Strasberg at the Actor's Studio*, Meisner's *The Reality of Doing*, Lewis' *Method or Madness?*, Carnovsky's *The Actor's Eye* and Boleslavsky's own *Six Lessons*. Stanislavsky's books, *An Actor Prepares*, *Building a Character* and *Creating a Role* are also used by many acting programs in the U.S. (See Aldridge, 1993 and Pang, 1991).

13 From my paper "Afraid to Lie," Theories of Directing, May, 1998. Dr. Schechner is a gifted writer/director, but not an actor.

14 John Harrop, author of the noted *Creative Play Direction* (with Cohen), *Acting with Style* (with Epstein), and *Acting*, was a PhD from the well-known Theatre Dept. of Tulane University (in the 1960s), and an actor. He was this researcher's acting and directing teacher at University of CA at Santa Barbara, 1971–76. His books are commonly required for acting and directing classes throughout the country (see Pang 1991).

Drama is dynamic. The word is taken from the Greek root "dran," meaning "to do" (Carnicke 1998: 147). A drama *does* something; it accomplishes an Action. Aristotle would say the drama "imitates action" (Aristotle 7–30). According to Aristotle, the core of drama is not language, but Action (62–3). Language, as one of the key elements of drama, provides a *map* to the Actions of the play, but language, provoked by thought, is a *result* (or "symptom") of having an Action. Fergusson notes, "*Character* is defined as 'habitual action'" in Aristotle's "*Poetics*" (22). That is to say, we *are* what we *do*. Whether or not we agree with this description of character in "real life," it is a helpful way for the actor to consider the characters in a play: it means that if we can *do* something on the stage, we can create the human condition. Actors need not *feel* onstage; they *act* and the audience attributes feeling or motivation to those acts.[15]

Fergusson explains:

> One must be clear, first of all, that *action (praxis)* does not mean deeds, events, or physical activity: it means, rather, *the motivation from which deeds spring*.[16] This description is the most clear, telling and significant of definitions with which to begin a discussion of Action for the theatre artist. Butcher[17] puts it this way: 'The *praxis* that art seeks to reproduce is mainly a psychic energy working outwards.' It may be described metaphorically as the focus or movement of the psyche toward what seems good to it at the moment—a 'movement of the spirit,' Dante calls it. When we try to define the actions of people we know, or of characters in plays, we usually do so in terms of motive. (emphasis added, Aristotle 1961: 8–9)

This "movement of the spirit" is also applied, by Aristotle, to the overall dramatic action of the play. The movement of a play, as Fergusson describes it, has a "rational purpose" and is part of what Aristotle means by the word "praxis" (9). In other words, there can be no "praxis," or action, without a reason or *purpose*. Humans act with purpose, and a play progresses because of its larger purpose as

---

15 Director/teacher Yevgeny Lanskoy stated: "Unless he is lying or crazy, an actor feels only one of two things onstage: He feels good if it's going well, and lousy if it's going badly." This makes sense, as the actor can only "feel" *his/her* feelings, and not those of an imaginary character. Anecdotally, actors may dispute this idea, and insist they feel what the character written in the play purports to feel.

16 Critic Martin Esslin also states in *The Field of Drama*, "Thus the 'meaning' of the words spoken in drama … derives … from a consideration of *who* does *what* with those words *to whom* under *which circumstances*. Or, more concisely, in drama the meaning of words derives ultimately from the *situation* from which they spring" (1987: 86–7).

17 Fergusson notes Butcher's translation of the *Poetics* is "probably the best of the standard texts available in English" (3). It was originally published as *Aristotle's Theory of Poetry and Fine Art*, 4th ed. Butcher, London, 1932.

well. This larger purpose is the dramatic action, or, as Stanislavsky called it, the *Superobjective* of the play. Fergusson explains, "The notion of action and the imitation of action [from Aristotle] is the connecting link between the art of the dramatist and the interpretive art of the actor" (1953: 253).[18] The actor plays his/her Actions, which are part of the cohesive whole—the dramatic action—of the play.

The distinction between the Action of the actor's character and that of the play as a whole is essential to our understanding of play structure, and also necessary for the stage translator, as mentioned in previous chapters. The overall dramatic action of a play, its "praxis," purpose or Superobjective, is composed of elements of the *plot*. These elements of plot are the happenings or *events* which support and lead up to an overall dramatic action that the poet or playwright has decided is the point of the play. For instance, the plot of Sophocles' *Oedipus Rex* includes these happenings: Oedipus hears that the gods are visiting plagues on Thebes because they are angered that the murderer of King Laius was never found and punished. Oedipus resolves to find this culprit; he discovers that he is the culprit himself; Oedipus puts out his eyes. The overall action of *Oedipus Rex* might be "to save Thebes from its plague by finding the unknown culprit" (Aristotle 24). This dramatic action of the whole play—a *unity* of action, we may say—is described as the Superobjective, Spine, Through-line or Ruling Idea of the play.[19] (These terms are often used interchangeably.) Notice that this Superobjective moves through an action that is "whole"—it is relevant to everything that happens in the play—and is understood through the use of an *infinitive verb* ("*to save* Thebes"). Oedipus has the Action "to find the culprit" in order to *save Thebes*. There is a rationale or *justification* for every Action. Oedipus' Action is actually part of the whole Superobjective. This idea of a Superobjective—the larger Action of the whole play—is important to the actor because all his or her individual character Actions are related to it, along the "spine" of the play. Thus the structure of plot—part of the dramaturgy of a play—helps guide the actor to Actions, which are also described with an active verb.

---

18 Fergusson has written a comprehensive Introduction to Butcher's translation of *Aristotle's Poetics* (1961) wherein he links Aristotle's notion of Action to that developed by Stanislavsky of the Moscow Art Theatre at the turn of the 20th century. This is a discussion Fergusson began in his 1949 critical work, *The Idea of a Theatre*. This work, which includes Fergusson's well-known essay on *Cherry Orchard* as a "Poem of the Suffering of Change," is a touchstone for any critical discussion on the nature of modern Realism, and its practical application on the stage.

19 Adler uses this term, "Ruling Idea," which she defines as "why the playwright wrote the play" in her *The Technique of Acting*, p. 38. She observes therein, "All the actions within a play are interconnected, and they all lead the actor to the ruling idea or overall action." This is the main idea and thrust of the play.

Plot structure is also described by Aristotle as "the arrangement of the incidents" (Aristotle 14). This is important to understand, as modern or contemporary
drama may not always move forward with a cause-and-effect-type plot in the way
that *Oedipus* does. Whatever the performance, we see that incidents are always
"arranged"—most performances onstage are planned and rehearsed—but they
may not be in chronological order, nor in a logical order that is immediately or
easily discerned by the reader or audience. Ibsen, for example, follows the Aristotelian method in the use of his plot points: one incident breeds another. Chekhov's
dramaturgy is different: it is the juxtaposition of scenes which helps illuminate
character relationships and defines motivation—often with irony—as the plays
move forward. His plays are more like music that proceeds through the harmonies
and/or dissonance created by the order of individual scenes rather than definitive,
chronological plot points.[20] In other words, "plot" alone may not be the only element that helps define or inform the movement of a play.

Jean Cocteau called the theatrical elements of a playscript "the poetry of the
theatre" (Fergusson 1953: 179). This poetry includes the sounds, gestures, language, lights, costumes, set and all aspects of the theatrical event, including, we
may say, the imagination of the audience. It also is made up of "the music of
the action, the underlying poetry of the composition as a whole," i.e., the "*scenes*
[which] are integrated like the *words* of a poem" (*Ibid.*).[21] Cocteau distinguished
this "poetry *of* the theatre" from "poetry *in* the theatre," which is simply the words
written—however poetically—in the text of a play. He knew theatrical "poetry"
includes the non-verbal aspects of performance. Action creates visual and aural
aspects, which include gesture, tone, volume, pitch, rate and duration of speech,
and all the physical attributes of the actor's body and voice. We may recall that
Corrigan too understood this "poetry" in the prose of a play, where "language [is]
gestural" (Arrowsmith, 96). Critic/practitioner Martin Esslin[22] sums up the idea
of poetry of the theatre as follows:

> The total structure of a dramatic work thus depends on a very delicate balance of a
> multitude of elements, all of which must contribute to the total pattern and all of
> which are wholly interdependent. A scene which is very quiet may appear boring after

---

20 Perhaps for this reason, playwright Edward Albee stated to me: "Ibsen is still of the 19th
    century; it is Chekhov, I believe, who is the first playwright of the 20th century." Interview,
    Lincoln Center, New York City, Dec. 7, 2005.
21 The quote is from Cocteau's preface to the ballet based on his play *Les Mariés de la Tour
    Eiffel*, 1922. See also: https://www.poetryfoundation.org/poets/jean-cocteau.
22 Best known for his critical study *Theatre of the Absurd*, 1961. Chekhov may indeed be
    considered a precursor to "absurdist" playwright Samuel Beckett and, arguably, Harold Pinter.

another quiet scene: it will come as a welcome relief after a very noisy one. Context is all: in the right context an almost imperceptible gesture may move mountains, the simplest phrase may turn into the most sublime poetic utterance. That is the true miracle of drama, its true poetry. (1976: 53)

In exploring Chekhov's dramaturgy in Chapter V, and the particular scenes in each play in Chapters VI–IX, we will see that his "poetry" is couched in "contexts"—or circumstances—which create the underlying Actions of the characters, and the dramatic actions of the plays—or Superobjectives—as a whole.

Stanislavsky also understood how "The notion of action and the imitation of action [from Aristotle] is the connecting link between the art of the dramatist and the interpretive art of the actor" (Fergusson 1953: 253). While Fergusson writes in 1949 that "I cannot discover whether Stanislavsky and Nemirovitch-Dantchenko got their concept of action from Aristotle or not" (*Ibid.*), Sharon Carnicke states, in 1998, that Action is at the heart of Stanislavsky's system (88). Stanislavsky claims to "hearken back to Aristotle" when he enforces his notion of Action as drama's distinguishing feature, and traces the Russian root of "to do" (*deistivie*) back to Aristotle's Greek "*dran*" (*Ibid.*). This passage is left out of the American version of Stanislavsky's first book, *An Actor Prepares*.[23] This lost passage gives Fergusson the evidence he sought, proving Stanislavsky indeed linked his ideas on Action to those of Aristotle (201).[24]

Stanislavsky developed and practiced his Method of Physical Actions at the end of his life. While "action" was always at the forefront of his system,[25] he changed

---

23 This seminal volume, published in 1936, along with *Building a Character* (1949) and *Creating a Role* (1961) describes Stanislavsky's system, and remains a staple of American actor-training (see Monos 1981; Pang 1991).

24 Carnicke's *Stanislavsky in Focus* explains how Stanislavky's writings were misinterpreted and amended by translator Hapgood and her publisher for American readers. Instead of the common Russian word "to play" (*igrat'*), Stanislavsky preferred "to act" (*delat'* meaning "to do") and "to take action" (deistvovat') (88). Schechner maintained "Stanislavsky's notion of Action is different than the Aristotelian notion" (Levenson 1999) while Fergusson and Carnicke are aware of the link between Stansialvsky and Aristotle. Schechner asks "Is the word Stanislavsky uses [for 'action'] early in his career the same as the one he uses late? If so, this would be a powerful argument for consistency over his long life; if a different word, this would suggest that 'physical action' is different than Aristotelian action" (*Ibid.*). Stanislavsky *was* consistent in the use of the word, throughout his life. According to Fergusson, "Action," from Aristotle and Stanislavsky, is not only physical: it includes "*the motivation from which deeds spring*" (Aristotle 1961: 8).

25 Sonia Moore, prominent acting teacher and student of the MAT's Third Studio (1920), claims "Though it was at the end of his career that Stanislavski gave the name [Method of

his rehearsal techniques. This goes to the core of the schism between Stella Adler and Lee Strasberg (both members of the Group Theatre), who saw Stanislavsky's system differently: Strasberg saw Stanislavsky's early work on "affective" or "emotion" memory as a basic tenet of the Stanislavsky method, while Adler, working with Stanislavsky near the end of his life, was introduced to the idea that truthful Action in circumstances—requiring that the actor use his or her imagination— was the key to Stanislavsky's system.

Actor Vasily Osipovich Toporkov worked with Stanislavsky closely in these final years at the Moscow Art Theatre, from 1927–38. The Method of Physical Actions, as described by Toporkov, was employed in Stanislavsky's last productions, notably Gogol's *Dead Souls* and Molière's *Tartuffe* (hardly "Realist" works). Instead of endless "table work," where actors and director sat and discussed meanings and interpretations of the play, Stanislavsky put the actors on their feet in the circumstances of the script and had them play their physical actions truthfully early in the rehearsal period (Toporkov 42–3). The result was *"the transference of the actor's attention from the search for feelings inside himself to the fulfillment of the stage task which actively influences his partners ..."* (58).[26] In a play, there is always a conflict, a struggle, which has a certain logic to it: playing an Action is a psycho-physical effort to *influence* others. To grasp the "logic of the character's behavior," Toporkov tells us:

> An actor is required to examine the material of the role analytically and to deepen his powers of communication and imagination. His account of a play's events must not seem that of an observer, but of a person closely involved in what is taking place. In other words, it should be a 'living through' of the events; there should be the desire to interest the listener in their development ... We were asked to prepare ... written accounts [where] the more literary form forced us to a deeper penetration and analysis of the actions. (164)

From Toporkov's description, we see that the Stanislavsky actor is expected to work with both practical and analytical approaches to the role. Stanislavsky's work thus

---

Physical Actions] to this key of the sub-conscious, it was not a late addition to his System. His teachings on action impregnate the whole technique, from beginning to end" (1974: 13).

26   Carnicke claims the "task" (*zadacha*), has been incorrectly translated as "objective" in Hapgood's version of *An Actor Prepares* (1998: 88). Marat Yusim (of MAT) explained that "zadacha" is *"Action,"* while "Superobjective" is, an "overall intention." He states: *"Intention* is outside the scene; it gives perspective. *Actions* are always the [smaller] intentions within the scene. For instance: to go to meet you is an action. To meet you for the purpose of getting a job from you is an *intention.*" (Interview, '05). But Lanskoy (1987–9) used "Action" to include the underlying "intention" of the character. Actors may use "action," "objective" and "intention" interchangeably; the point is to move with purpose to influence others.

upholds the intelligence as well as the instinctual attributes of the actor: defining Actions for the character requires "living through" the role on its feet, and clear understanding—through textual analysis—of the concept of Action.[27]

Perhaps Adler is the most ardent and articulate American proponent of Stanislavsky—more than Grotowski,[28] Meisner or Lee Strasberg—because she is lucid and expressive on the subject of script analysis, and believes this exploration of text is the actor's job. She said, "It's his job to understand the play. *The most important thing you teach actors is to understand plays.* You can't have a stupid actor. You have to be of absolute intelligence and you must understand plays" (emphasis added).[29] She was the only American to actually study acting with Stanislavsky himself, in private meetings for five weeks in Paris, within the same period (1934) that Toporkov was directed by Stanislavsky at the Moscow Art Theatre. During that time, Stanislavsky "turned her attention to the through-line of action that should inform her entire performance" and gave Adler a chart showing how "the truth within the given circumstances of the play" creates this through-line (Smith 179–80).[30] Returning to the Group Theatre, Adler taught Meisner, Carnovsky, Brand, Kazan, Lewis, Odets and other actors, who brought their understanding of Stanislavsky and Action to so many students over the last seventy years.

Strasberg declared Stanislavsky's ideas were "all wrong," stating: "We don't use the Stanislavsky system; we use the Strasberg method. ... If you are unable to bring in emotion, then what is the point of action?" (181–2).[31] But Adler and other

---

27 Wellwarth's note that actors *"rarely read or permit their minds to become contaminated by indulgence in critical thought about the little they may have read"* (Zuber 54) is untrue for the trained actor.

28 Grotowski worked with American acting students at University of CA at Irvine, 1986–92 (Schechner & Wolford 1997: 35).

29 Russell Vanderbrouke, in an Interview with Stella Adler, *Yale Theatre* 8, nos. 2 and 3 (Spring, 1977): 34, op.cit. Malague, Rosemary, "Getting at the Truth ..." Diss., City University of New York, 2001, p. 215.

30 The Group Theatre is described in detail in Smith's *Real Life Drama*, 1990. It is an objective companion to Clurman's *The Fervent Years*, which is, necessarily, Clurman's view of the times. Adler also describes meeting Stanislavsky in her books, *The Technique of Acting* and *Adler on Ibsen, Strindberg and Chekhov*.

31 Coger's 1984 article "Stanislavsky Changes His Mind" in the Tulane Drama Review, which describes how Stanislavsky dropped his use of "affective memory," is not so much about a "change of mind"—or being "wrong"—as a growth in practice. As Ron Burrus, Adler's assistant for over 10 years, states: "They say it took Stanislavsky 21 years to develop his technique ... By the time Stella worked with him, Stanislavsky said they had done affective memory in the work, and he found that the actors were not emotionally healthy because of it ... So Stanislavsky directed [Adler] to select a place, do 3 things in that place, decide

members of the Group were troubled by Strasberg's stress on "affective memory" exercises, which compelled the actor to recall emotional moments in his or her *own* life and apply them to the characters they played onstage. Brand, Carnovsky and other Group actors were bothered by this approach, and felt it psychologically unhealthful for the actor (179). Bobby Lewis quipped "Stanislavsky practiced psychology; Strasberg practiced psychiatry" (1984: 281).[32] Moreover, Strasberg did not emphasize script analysis. He focused on the actor's personal characterization, to the exclusion of study on the dramaturgy of the playwright.[33]

Adler's understanding of the modern playwright—Ibsen, Strindberg, Chekhov—is penetrating and comprehensive.[34] She delineates not only the actor's approach to roles in the plays, but describes the intrinsic purpose and worldview of each playwright, which defines the style of work. Moreover, she insists that the actor discover the life-force of the playwright as well. She lectured eloquently on Williams, Shaw, Odets, O'Neill, and others. She said of Chekhov, "I think [he] is most wanted in terms of performance ... he's misunderstood. He's the most interesting and most wanting to be understood" (1999: viii). Understanding the playwright is the actor's job, as well as that of the translator and director. Adler, with Stanislavsky, was a proponent of the intelligent, thinking actor.

While Adler's emphasis is on Actions, imagination and playing truthfully in the circumstances of the play, and she taught the logic of Actions, the definition of Action may not always be clear to the uninitiated. "Action" is a *practice* and, for the actor, is learned and experienced empirically, often in stages. Adler's definitions of

---

whether they were to be on a light level or a dark level, then build a plot and justify it. There was not talk of affective memory" (Monos 1981: 65). Stella's work with Stanislavsky was simply playing *actions* in *circumstances*, i.e., the core of acting praxis.

32   Adler states: "the use of emotion as a teaching aid is unhealthy," ("The Reality of Doing," *TDR,* 141). Strasberg's "method" is also denigrated by Brustein in "The Heritage of MXAT," *The New Republic,* 29, Hornby in *The End of Acting,* 5–9, Harrop in *Acting,* 38–44, and Marowitz in *The Act of Being,* 14.

33   Richard Hornby's *The End of Acting* accuses Strasberg of an "outright anti-literary bias" (175): "Strasberg [stated]: 'One can have brilliant theoretic, literary, critical, or philosophical concepts of a play and not be able to create reality on stage' (Strasberg 1987: 160). That the opposite might be true, that one can ... botch a performance because of not understanding the play, never occurred to him. The subliminal message to his students was clear: Don't study literature. It only distracts you from your job of creating emotional intensity on stage." Hornby maintains Strasberg practiced "perverse avoidance of plays" and often commented on student's work "without ever mentioning the play at all" (176). See also director Anne Bogart's letter to this researcher, in footnote 56 herein.

34   See *Stella Adler on Ibsen, Stringberg and Chekhov,* edited by Barry Paris (New York: Knopf, 1999).

simple physical actions—such as "raking the leaves"—do not contain the underlying "intention" of *why* the leaves are being raked (Rotté 2000: 80). This is because Adler, like Stanislavsky, has practical definitions of "simple physical actions," "inner action," and "verbal actions" as part of an overall approach to Action in general. While this study is not meant to be a comprehensive approach to actor-training, it is helpful to understand the various terms used in discussing Action, so we may apply them clearly in an encounter with Chekhov's last four plays in various translations.

"Action" is one of the first lessons presented in Stanislavsky's *An Actor Prepares*. He distinguishes "inner psychological actions" from "outer physical actions":

> Every physical action has an inner psychological action which gives rise to it. And in every psychological inner action there is always a physical action which expresses its psychical nature; the unity between these two is organic on the stage (Gorkachov 119).

The physical action alone may be described as an "activity"—such as "raking the leaves," or "setting the table," or "correcting papers," as Olga is doing at the opening of *The Three Sisters*. Physical actions are often described by the author (or inserted later by a Stage Manager) in stage directions in the text of the play. A very small physical action, such as smoking, would be considered "business." Stanislavsky is adamant that physical actions not be performed without an inner purpose: Olga may be reminiscing about the past as she is also "correcting the papers," so that the *way* in which she corrects the papers is influenced by her reminiscence. It is just as important not to leave the physical action out of playing an inner purpose: the activity with the papers helps the character Olga to express to the audience exactly *how* she feels about the past. Does she cross out large portions of a student's paper? Does she throw another paper to the ground? Might she be frustrated with these essays, or do they make her laugh? What she *does* with the activity gives us clues as to how she feels. This is why Stanislavsky later considered the score of Physical Actions so important to his system. We can work from the outside *in* (physicalizing the activity truthfully), as well as from the inside *out*: physicalizing an inner psychological Action is imperative. We know that "raking the leaves" is only an activity (without inner purpose in itself) because we can do it *as* we "reminisce," "plan to escape," or pursue some other intention.

With Stanislavsky, Adler believed that the actor began by performing small, physical actions truthfully—this is often a beginning of both actor-training and/or rehearsal. If one is "raking the leaves," for example, the actor then learns to add *complications* to the physical action (your hold on the rake handle gives you a splinter), the discovery of both the larger ("Where is the play set?") and the immediate *circumstances* ("Where am I?"), a possible *attitude* towards the action (my mother always makes me do the raking), *justification* of the action (I will please my mother, and so she will lend me money I need to buy a car), the theme of the play (the independence of children from their parents), and the nature (anatomy) of the action with regard to all other actions in the play (the child's innate desire to escape parental control and go out into the world). Adler also designated an understanding of various Actions as integral to the actor's toolbox: Inner Action (to Dream, to Reminisce, to Unmask, to Expose, to Reveal, to Confess), Verbal Actions (to Explain, to Advise, to Chat, to Attack or Attack with words, to Denounce, to Arouse) and Physical Actions (to Help, to Take Care, to Escape). She defined the "deepest and most complex" of the foregoing Actions as *to Confess, to Arouse* and *to Escape* (Rotté 2000: 125–6). She stated, with great emphasis, "The most important Action you can have is to tell someone the Truth" (Class, 1981).

Adler's observations on Actions—however insightful and helpful—are not necessarily definitive. Adler herself warned that it is the individual actor him or herself who must choose how they define and *play* Actions. She reiterated: "Your talent is in your choice." Her definitions of the Actions above are linked inextricably to the purpose of the playwright. For example, the ultimate Action "to Escape" may be that of Medea, Ophelia, Hamlet and MacBeth (Rotté 2000: 126), but they will be different for each character. We may also see a more modern attempt "to Escape" in Chekhov's *Three Sisters*, in the sisters' attempt to "go to Moscow" and escape their lives and suffering. Indeed, the Superobjective of Chekhov's play may be "to escape," as it is in *Oedipus Rex* "to save." The *way* the actor "translates" the Action of escaping at each instance in the play is their *contribution* to the text. If the actor has a different Superobjective for the character (perhaps it could be to "find love," or "recapture the past" in *Sisters*), the logic and meaning of the role and the play could change. The point is: choice of a Superobjective—or Ruling Idea—will define the tenor of the performance.

The foregoing theorists, critics and practitioners—Aristotle, Stanislavky, Torpokov, Fergusson, Cocteau, Beckerman, Strasberg, Adler and others mentioned—have comparable views of the nature of Action, though they describe them in their own terms. In the United States, in the early and mid-20th century, other teachers and theorists have also greatly affected the way the idea of "Action" is presented to students of the theatre. The following practitioners were teachers of Adler and other Group Theatre members, and had a permanent impact on how acting was taught in the U.S.

Teachers and Theorists

[Boleslasky's writing] was not the product of a dramatist's mind, turned narrator, but of an actor's mind. One is almost the converse of the other. The actor is usually word-shy and inarticulate. Often he does not know what it is he does or how he does it, that makes him an actor. Even when he knows, it is difficult for him to say it or write it. He can only express it in action. His language is a language of movement, of gesture, of voice, of the creation and projection of character by things done or left undone. The dramatist, on the other hand, works easily with words, writes fluently, interprets character, situation, and events, manner and method in his own terms. So far as the art and craft of acting have been written of at all, it is usually the dramatist or the critic who has written of them. That is why there is so little in print really to explain the actor to himself and to his fellows. Edith J. R. Isaacs[35]

It is difficult to write about what is more easily demonstrated in practice. Adler, Clurman, Strasberg and Fergusson first got their ideas on "Action" from Richard Boleslavsky and Maria Ouspenskaya, through practicing acting technique, or viewing it, in class. Adler recounts: "Strasberg and Clurman attended Boleslavsky's lectures, but I was the only one who actually was a student of his" (Hirsch 217). Fergusson, though not a professional actor, was required, with the other students, to take technique classes with Maria Ouspenskaya, and gained a deep understanding of "the notion of action" from her as evidenced by his later writings.[36] Boleslavsky's and Ouspenskaya's understanding of "Action" is confirmed by Adler in Adler's later work with Stanislavsky himself in 1934. Adler stated, "Stanislavsky said not to start with the language, start with the movement. Acting is action, action is doing: find ways to *do* it, not to say it" (Hirsch 217). Ouspenskaya's familiar question to her students was always "How 'tis about Auhction?" at the start of her classes (recalled by Fergusson in Roberts 148). Teacher and author Nellie McCaslin, who studied with Ouspenskaya in the 1940s, remembered Ouspenskaya's query as well (Interview, 2004).[37] This testifies to the import of "Action" in the very beginning classes taught by Russian expatriates, whose work was the foundation of the American understanding of Stanislavsky's system.[38]

---

35 From the "Introduction" to *Acting, the First Six Lessons* by Richard Boleslavsky, 1963, p. 6.

36 These include "The Notion of Action," *The Idea of a Theatre,* the comprehensive Introduction to *Aristotle's Poetics* and *The Human Image in Dramatic Literature,* all noted in the Bibliography.

37 Though McCaslin is known as a teacher and theorist of "Creative Dramatics," she told me that she is concerned with the art of acting, and with teaching theatre as an art, not only applying it to other disciplines, or using it for "conflict resolution" or "process drama." (Interview, June 2, 2003). McCaslin was a strong advocate for the artist and the art form in the field of drama in education.

38 See Laurence Senelick's *Wandering Stars, Russian Émigré Theatre,* 1992. In his Introduction, Senelick notes: "As students note to their cost, the Russian language makes nice distinctions between completed action and continuous action ..." (xi). Senelick here means to describe a metaphor for the genius Russian émigré (Boleslavsky and M. Chekhov included) who has lost his or her country, rather than to describe Stanislavsky's meaning of "Action," but

Though Boleslavsky's name may not be as familiar to today's acting student as it was to those who received actor-training in the 1960s–1970s (when his students Adler, Clurman, Fergusson and Strasberg were in their prime), his approach, with that of his colleague Ouspenskaya, is still taught, as is that of Michael Chekhov, under the aegis of Stanislavky technique. Boleslavsky described *an ideal "structure of action"* as a tree with the main trunk or *idea*, coming from the director. The branches are elements of the idea (character Actions), coming from the actor, and, thirdly, the foliage, as the result of the previous two, becomes the *presentation* and "bright conclusion" of the foregoing ideas (Boleslavsky 57). Like his teacher Stanislavsky, Boleslavsky saw the idea of Action as pieces of a *spine* (to compare metaphors) growing off from a central idea emanating from the *playwright*, whose main thrust would be the *sap* of the tree, or the marrow of the bone of the spine (*Ibid.*). This idea of a "structure" of action is also used more currently by Russian practitioners who use different metaphors and/or descriptions of "structure" to describe the process of finding and portraying Action.[39] Other practitioners may not understand the idea of "structures of action" in the actor's work, and see the approach to acting differently.[40] Stanislavsky's notion of "action," however, permeates these other approaches as well.

Michael Chekhov, Anton's nephew, son of Anton's oldest brother Alexander, is probably more well-known today than Boleslasky, as Michael Chekhov's books and persona have had a resurgence in the last few years. He was one of Stanislavsky's most creative students, and a genius in his own right (Senelick 1992: 15). His proponents have domestic and international "Chekhov Associations" and studios in New York and Los Angeles.[41] Michael Chekhov is best known for his "psychological gesture" exercise, a full body/facial pose or gesture that expresses the inner feelings and outward image of the character to be played. It is a psycho-physical

---

the Russian concern for the movement of the will, mind and memory which is part of "Action"—in its *grammar* as well as theatre practice—is noteworthy.

39 Lanskoy's two-and-on-half-year course was entitled "Structures of Action" at the Adler Conservatory in NY in the 1980s; Merlin, Carnicke and the Levins discuss "Active Analysis" in their books on Stanislavsky.

40 Stephen Wangh, head of the Experimental Theatre Wing of Tisch School of the Arts, told me he deals more in "images" (Interview, Fall, 2003), and John Strasberg, son of Lee Strasberg, speaks of purposeful "dreaming" (Interview, Spring, 2002) in his biography, *Accidentally on Purpose*. These are two other analogies that result in "Action" for the actor onstage.

41 Beatrice Straight and Deirdre Hurst, benefactors and students of Michael Chekhov, helped establish a school where Chekhov could teach his "method," first with an international gathering of students at Darington Hall in Devonshire, England, and then, due to WWII, in Ridgefield, Connecticutt in 1938–9. Chekhov moved to Los Angeles and set up another studio in 1942.

shortcut to a visceral understanding of the role, and a key to finding the Actions and Superobjective of the character. Just as Stanislavsky, in his Method of Physical Actions, proposed the actor get on his feet and *do* the physical action of a character in order to grasp the *inner* Action, M. Chekhov suggests that the actor's body is always active in pursuing every *objective*[42] in the role, and it is in "gestures, gestures and more gestures" that the character's inner psychology is revealed.

Michael Chekhov claims if actors can construct an "all-embracing gesture which leads and inspires them," incorporating the *atmosphere*[43] and desires (Actions) of the character as a whole, or for a scene in the play, the actor will have a *language of gestures* which frees them from the "killing stiffness" born of dealing with the lines alone. He states, "In using the gesture, we have the greatest opportunity to receive everything which comes to us from our partners, and from the director and the author" (1985: 111). This gesture may come from our idea of an archetype of the character, or a physical image; the most important thing to understand is that it is the imagination of the actor that is fed by inspiration rather than intellect. Chekhov maintains it is the process of *synthesizing* rather than *analyzing* the role that is of import in creating a psychological gesture:

> When the actor gets the part, if he is conscientious, he starts to analyze it. It is a great illusion. Our art is quite the opposite—it is a synthesis. It is the *process of synthesizing* and *not of analyzing*. What do we have to analyze? What do we have in our soul, in our creative imagination? There is nothing to be analyzed or dissected. It is a great illusion which actors have, hoping to get through their work more easily. It is the wrong way. The right way, as I understand it, is to synthesize everything which our soul, our super-conscious, our creative individuality—call it what you like—can prompt us, being influenced by something, absolutely intuitively created, as the simplest and the first bell which we ring, and this is the gesture. (110)

As theatre critic Mel Gordon stated, Michael Chekhov's technique deals primarily with *images* that are presented to the actor, encouraging the psycho-physical nature of the actor's pursuit, or "a profound technical understanding of the actor's intellect and consciousness" (18). Though M. Chekhov insists the key to character is not "analyzing," the actor's ability to express the nature of a role with his or her body uses the intellect as well as the intuition. The point is to do it on one's feet, and not only in one's head.

---

42 Michael Chekhov describes an objective as something we want to get or accomplish (1985: 108). It is also another term for "Action," as it is described in this study.

43 This may be described as the feeling of the place and the attitudes of the characters therein; i.e., the feeling created by the *circumstances* of the scene. An atmosphere can be heavy or light, for example, and can also be communicated or experienced as part of a psychological gesture.

The language used by Michael Chekhov is important to the actor's understanding of the image or gesture. For example, in encouraging the actor to expand his or her physicality, instead of commanding the actor to "sit up straight," M. Chekhov would say "think *up*" (17–18). This is similar to the Alexander technique, so popular in acting programs today, which is also a psycho-physical practice meant to grant ease and grace to an actor's deportment and vocalization. As Gordon notes, "the dissimilarities between Chekhov's linguistic approach and others may seem petty to the non-actor," but, in teaching acting or directing the actor, the way a directive is expressed can be crucial to the actor's understanding and portrayal of a character (18).[44] This is why the language of the playscript is so important: words influence our physical and psychic responses.

Aristotle, Stanislavsky, Boleslavsky, Ouspenskaya, Fergusson, Michael Chekhov, Adler and other members of the Group Theatre, along with current Russian practitioners, have all recognized a fluid and similar definition of Action, as it is understood by the actor and theatre practitioner. Though their emphases and approaches vary, they all understand the concept as psycho-physical, and that it is "the motivation from which deeds spring" rather than just physical movement alone. This is a crucial distinction. The difficulty with some modern and contemporary definitions is that they may not take this fundamental observation into account.

For example, while Beckerman takes his understanding of Action from Aristotle and Stanislavsky, his definitions of "action" and "activity" are different from those in this study. While he recognizes that the theatre practitioner uses "action" to mean "pursuing an intent" (50), he eschews this definition in favor of seeing "action" as "a result, not a tool" (*Ibid.*). But a "tool" is exactly what Action is: a tool for the actor, director and, one may say, the translator, to "designate the sequential features of a play" and to help them describe and perform in a medium that is "temporal as well as spatial" (vii). "Action"—the underlying purpose of a drama— is the basic medium of theatre.

---

44   Mel Gordon stated "it was among the Group Theatre actors in 1935 that Michael Chekhov made his largest impact. Stella Adler, Morris Carnovsky, Bobby Lewis, Sandy Meisner and others borrowed basic scenic ideas and exercises from Chekhov's demonstrations and workshops ... [and they] provided the strongest intellectual counterweight to Strasberg's much criticized Method ... To a larger degree, the variations between the three methods [of Stanislavsky, Michael Chekhov and Lee Strasberg] are not necessarily in scenic outcome, but in language and process" (Gordon in M. Chekhov's *Lessons for the Professional Actor*, 17). Of course, the acting process is of utmost importance to the actor, and it is precisely the "language and process" of understanding Action that are significant to this study.

Beckerman maintains "activity" is the basic medium of theatre (13), which he defines as the physical movement of the performer, distinguished from the underlying "purpose of motion" which he understands is called "action" by practitioners (13). Beckerman uses the term "activity" to express "what the actor does"—confusing this term with Action—and "inner life" or the "imagined act" to describe what the practitioner would call "Action" (19, 36). But, for the actor, as mentioned above, an "activity" is a composite of movements—such as "raking the leaves," "correcting the papers," "preparing for Nina's performance" (as Kostya does at the start of Seagull)—that define a specific *physical* task. Action, as defined in this study is, rather, the "inner life" of the character, with movement that accompanies it. Actions are performed *with* and *through* activities. In other words, "activities" are the physical manifestation that we see on the stage, while "Action" is the motivating energy beneath these activities.[45]

While Beckerman argues for clear definitions, he muddies the issue by providing his own personal definitions of words used differently by practitioners. His language is frequently more that of the academic or critic than that of the practitioner; Beckerman stands outside the play to define its movement, rather than seeing it from the point of view of the actor or character. This is not to disparage Beckerman's clear observations on dramatic tension and its "rhythmic character," which he describes fluently: he illustrates the necessary ebb and flow of climax (labeled "crux") and dénouement as an "intensification-relaxation pattern" (51). This is a description of how the overall Action in a play may appear to the audience. However, it is essential for the *actor*—and those who would study the theatre from its praxis—to understand the science of human behavior that distinguishes drama *from the inside*. This distinction is experienced as Action on the stage: humans move and react with purpose, to influence others. It is applicable to every style of stage practice that involves human beings.

Critic Martin Esslin, writing three years before Beckerman (in 1976), sees theories and systems of aesthetics "as far as ... humanly possible" from the point of view of "practical experience as a director of drama" (1976: 7). He states, "there is no drama without *actors*" (11), so, it makes sense to define drama from the actor's point of view. Esslin also claims "that the art, *activity, human craving or instinct* which embodies itself in drama is ... deeply enmeshed in human nature itself" (10, emphasis added). As human beings, we *crave*, we desire, and so are moved to influence others: this is Action.

---

45 In her linguistic study, *To Act, To Do, To Perform,* 1994, Alice Rayner states "The attribution of motive or intention is the basis for the distinction of *act* as opposed to *activity* in philosophy since Aristotle" (42).

Esslin acknowledges that "words (the literary component of the dramatic fragment) are secondary. The real information ... lies in the *relationship*, the *interaction* of two characters, the way they react to each other" (16). He goes on to describe how tone of voice and gesture—not the dialogue—create meaning in a play, and how "a really good playwright needs immense skill to convey the mood of the gestures, the tone of voice he wants from his actors through the dialogue he writes. But this leads into very much more technical and complex areas ..." (16). And these "areas" are those of Action, and how it is practiced onstage. When an actor *has* "Action," appropriate and believable gestures and tone are incorporated into the performance; playing Actions gives the physical/vocal shape to a character. With Aristotle and Stanislavsky, Esslin believes:

> The characterization always comes from what the characters do ... Analyze any skillfully written play and you will find invariably the characterization is in the action. In drama, of course, language very often *is* action. One could go further and claim that all language in drama of necessity *becomes* action. In drama we are concerned not only with *what* a character says—the purely semantic meaning of their words—but with what the character *does* with his words. (Esslin 40)

Esslin also insists that "What makes drama drama is precisely the element which lies outside and beyond the words and which has to be seen as action—or *acted*—to give the author's concept its full value" (14). This is particularly true of the plays of Anton Chekhov, and it bears repetition from varying points of view.

Directors and Stanislavsky

> Definitions—and thinking about definitions—are valuable and essential, but they must never be made into absolutes; if they are, they become obstacles to the organic development of new forms, experiment and invention. (11)

Many practitioner/theorists have incorporated their understanding of Stanislavsky with their own practice of acting or directing, either consciously, or by default. Those who have been seen as "anti"-Stanislavsky actually included the notion of "Action" in their practice, and in their writings. Vsevolod Meyerhold,[46] for example,

---

46 Meyerhold played Treplev in Chekhov's original *Seagull*, Tusenbach in *Three Sisters,* and began a new experimental Studio for Stanislavsky. He later established his own theatre, and created Bio-Mechanics. He is recognized as an influence on Brecht, Grotwoski and a precursor to avant-guard theatre. He was murdered by Stalinists in 1940, two years after Stanislavsky's death. Meyerhold was an admirer of Anton Chekhov, whom he considered a

whose methods have been seen as the antithesis of Stanislavsky with regard to acting technique, was actually an admirer of his teacher throughout his career, and insisted that his own Bio-Mechanics students learn Stanislavsky's technique first (1969: 250–1 and Hodge 5). Meyerhold held that, had Stanislavsky lived longer, he would have come around to Meyerhold's way of thinking about acting and the physical body (299–300).[47] With Stanislavsky's Method of Physical Actions, it may be argued that Stanislavsky already had done so; Stanislavsky found working "from the outside in" valuable for the actor. Equally, contemporary Russian director/playwright Valéry Fokin relates:

> Later in his life, Meyerhold began to move away from his original ideas. In the 1930's, he said that our biomechanics of the 1920s was actually *too* mechanical—it did not take into account our thought processes. So, very gradually, Meyerhold began to agree with Stanislavsky; he started to accept the fact that there must be a reason you do a certain action. (Sacharow 2004: 99)

Meyerhold also finally saw the value of the actor working "from the inside out."[48]

Grotowski felt similarly to Meyerhold. He said "some Russians say 'Grotowski *is* Stanislavsky' ... because I *continued* his research and did *not just repeat* what he had already discovered" (Richards 105). Grotowski claims he pursued the idea of Action as Stanislavsky might have done, if Stanislavsky had lived.[49] Grotowski is concerned with the *impulse* that precedes the playing of a full physical action,

---

lyric Symbolist. Senelick claims Meyerhold advanced the idea of the "director as 'author of the spectacle'" (1981: xxvii). This idea persists today (Sacharow 2000).

47   In editor Braun's seminal volume on the work of Meyerhold, he states of Meyerhold and Stanislavsky: "[D]espite the popular conception of their complete incompatibility, the relationship ... had never been marred by the acrimony which separated Meyerhold and Tairov. Neither ever questioned the other's integrity, and Meyerhold never lost an opportunity to express the love and gratitude he felt for his first and only teacher ... from 1936 onwards a distinct rapprochement was observed" (Meyerhold 1969: 250–1).

48   Anatoly Smeliansky, dean of the School and Artistic Director of the MAT, states: "Meyerhold and Stanislavsky started Russian theatre together. Their lives formed a kind of circle: At the start of the 20th century, their teaching kept them apart. The two men believed they were opponents ... But ... at the end of Stanislavsky's life ... through decades, through continents, through all of their differences—because they were absolutely different personalities, though both geniuses—their teachings were moving to the direction of the other" (Sacharow 2004: 101).

49   Fokin, artistic director of the Meyerhold Center in Moscow, declares "Stanislavsky endowed Grotowski with everything that has to do with the human spirit and inner life ... Stanislavsky was someone who was very much alive, and very flexible, always experimenting—he was an artist" (Sacharow 2004: 101).

claiming that the impulse *is* the Action, and that it is "rooted in the body" (95). Grotowski states:

> Before a small physical action there is an impulse. Therein lies the secret of something very difficult to grasp, because the impulse is a reaction that begins inside the body and which is visible only when it has already become a small action. The impulse is so complex that one cannot say that it is only of the corporeal domain. (94)

So, Action begins with the mental impulse—or thought—that one wants to do something; it may even be subconscious. Michael Chekhov states it similarly, asking students to:

> Take a certain gesture such as "to grasp." Do it physically. Now, do it inwardly, remaining physically unmoved ... Now, on the basis of this gesture, which you will do inwardly, say the sentence, "Please, darling, tell me the truth." While speaking, produce the gesture inwardly. The more you do these gestures, the more you will see that they suggest a certain kind of acting. They call up feelings, emotions and will impulses. Now do them both together—the gesture and the sentence. Then drop the physical gesture and speak, having the gesture inside only. (1983: 63)

If one does this exercise, one sees that it takes concentration and imagination. Can we "think" the physical sense of "grasping" while we say a line that does *not* have the words "to grasp" in them, but could be about *psychologically grasping* the partner? Yes, we can. And we can do it five times, and the line may come out differently each time, still having the intention of "grasping." This could be the *subtext* of such a line in a play. It is the underlying *demand* that one character makes of another, perhaps never revealing (in words) the true purpose of one's thought. Thus we see the overlapping understandings of Grotowski and Michael Chekhov, who both claim Stanislavsky's system as their foundation. The import of inner Action is understood.

Like Stanislavsky, Grotowski has various periods of work: *Towards a Poor Theatre* documents his earlier theories and practice; his "Objective Drama Research" was conducted at the University of California at Irvine from 1983–86, and involved "people working with material connected to their own cultural traditions" with efforts to create and perform "inner action" (Richards in Schechner and Wolford 1997: 452–3). Later in his career, *Action* was a project that combined a ritual, spiritual approach to vocal expression that Grotowski's actors performed for chosen audiences.[50] Grotowski is considered one of few—with Stanislavsky—theorists of

---

50 *Action* was performed for select audiences in The Workcenter of Jerzy Grotowski, Pontedera, Italy, beginning in 1986 (Schechner & Wolford 1997: 498).

acting in modern times.[51] His contribution to our understanding of "Action"—in the theatre and "paratheatrical" venues—is significant.[52]

Bertolt Brecht wrote much about theatre, but as director and playwright he constantly changed his concepts, and recognized that he did not develop a consistent theory of acting as Stanislavsky did (Zarrilli 228). He admits he had less concern for the actor than he had for the text (229). Brecht used "an assimilation of Stanislavsky's acting methods to Brechtian interpretational ends" (232). Brecht's practice, like Meyerhold's and Grotowski's, is not antithetical to that of Stanislavsky. Rather, as Duane Krause explains it, Brecht, in his epic theatre with an emphasis on "gestus," embraces the same need for passion and physical-actions-played-truthfully by the actor as Stanislavksy does.[53] Brecht acknowledges "we shall get superficial, formalistic, mechanical acting if in our technical training we forget for a moment to portray living people" (Brecht 1964a: 234). He wrote "Stanislasky's 'method of physical action' is most likely his greatest contribution to a new theatre" (Brecht 1964b: 160). Brecht was particularly impressed with Stanislavsky's stress on an understanding of the "Superobjective"; he states unequivocally that his actors could benefit from using Stanislavsky's methods (166). This is another acknowledgment by a formidable force in modern theatre that supports the significance of the idea of "Action"—as Stanislavsky understood it—as a basis for drama and the actor's art.

It is interesting to note how various other practitioners over the last fifty years have defined and used the notion of Action in their work and/or writings. Some of those who do not acknowledge Stanislavsky outright tend to use the terms like "images/ing," "dreaming" or "energy"—all aspects of motivating Action—in an

---

51 Artaud had theories and descriptions of possible approaches to theatre and performance, but was not a practitioner, and never saw his visions achieved (Schechner & Wolford 1997: 11). Fokin states, "The tragedy of this man [Artaud] was that he actually didn't create a system. He had an inspiration for the theatre—a dream—and it was very moving, but it was no system" (Sacharow 2004: 101).

52 Grotowski's biographer/critic Lisa Wolford affirms: "the final phase of Grotowski's practice was characterized by a renewed emphasis on the actor's craft; the results of this research are by no means insignificant for practitioners involved in more conventional forms of theatre practice" (Hodge 207).

53 Krause defines "gestus" as "the means by which ... social attitudes ... become visible to the spectator," and compares it to Michael Chekhov's Psychological Gesture, which is also "non-realistic" and "expansive" (Zarrilli 269). Brecht has asserted "that everything to do with the emotions has to be externalized; that is to say, it must be developed into a gesture" (Brecht 1964: 139). Michael Chekhov would agree with this idea, so "[M. Chekhov's] 'method' is not necessarily at odds with an epic style" (Krause in Zarrilli 269). Michael Chekhov based his concept of "Psychological Gesture" on Stanislavsky's notion of Action.

attempt to "simplify" or suggest a "new" approach to the creation of character for their students (Wangh and J. Strasberg, 2003, Interviews). Others maintain that acting practice has gone "beyond Stanislavsky," admitting that his fundamental research is the basis for their own (see Merlin in *Beyond Stanislavsky*, the Levins in *The Stanislavsky Secret*, Carnicke in *Stanislavsky in Focus*, Lanskoy in Classes, 1986–9). Still others consider the physical body to be the center of all acting work (this is undeniable), and teach skills in juggling, acrobatics, and deepening vocal range and resonance in an effort to prepare the actor for every challenge of contemporary acting styles, including performance art (Bogart xv-12). This may result in actors who can juggle and turn flips, but who may be lost when called upon to approach the style of Realism, or any style of drama, where an inner reasoning or motivation is required.[54]

Some training programs or acting companies steer clear of what they believe to be Stanislavsky technique. Teachers or directors of these groups may have had experience with Stanislavsky's system, but are unaware of its emphasis on physical action, confusing it with Strasberg technique.[55] Others believe it only applies

---

54 Columbia University MFA students struggled to create relationships in Brecht's *Caucasian Chalk Circle* at La Mama (1998), directed by Andrei Serban. Actors could move, dance and sing, but seemed at a loss in scenes with dialogue. As Brecht wrote, technical training is no help without attention to portraying "living people." A way to do this is through playing the *Actions* of a scene. Serban's students had little help in this area of their training (Interview with students at Kristin Linklater's presentation [Chair, Columbia U. Theatre Dept. and famed voice teacher] at American Communication Association conference, NY, 1998).

On the other hand, Will Bond, in Bogart's play *Bob*, appeared to be intensely concentrating on an underlying *objective* or Action in a scene of the play. When I asked him whether he was "pursuing an Action" in his performance, he replied that he was simply *counting*, in his head, how many steps he had to walk in a certain direction onstage. His approach is not necessarily "anti"-Stanislavskian; he had a "subtext." The fact that Bond's "purpose" was not related to the seeming "circumstances" of the scene did not lessen the audience's fascination with his execution (Interview, 1998).

Thirdly, we note Stanislavsky's own reaction to an open-air entertainment of jugglers and acrobats: "This is real art! This is beauty! Oh, if the actors would only understand the true meaning of this kind of precision of movement. An acrobat does nothing haphazardly. He leaves nothing to chance. He knows very well that he has only to make one slip and he will break his neck. That is why he is always working to perfect his body. Actors don't seem to realize this is no less important to them!"

(Magarshack, *Stanislavsky*, 331–2, op. cit. Vosgerchian, "Physical Training of the Actor …" 294).

55 I've noted this in the classes/workshops of Ron Sossi (Odyssey Theatre Ensemble, Los Angeles), Stephen Wangh (NYU), Richard Schechner (NYU), and John Strasberg (New York City), for examples.

to *Realism*, and so propose forms of physical training alone, without giving the younger student or performer a foundation—to which the teacher him or herself has been exposed—in what has come before. In this way, knowledge of or practice in inner technique is denied the student and a traditional handing down of an acting praxis to a new generation is forsaken. Abandoning a technique that addresses "inner work"—which Stanislavsky and others considered organic and helpful to previous generations—may be limiting for the student.[56]

Stanislavsky held his system was not meant only for Realist drama. He directed opera, Maeterlinck, and works by other Symbolist playwrights (Magarshack 1975: 250, 266). The "lore" of Action, as Stanislavsky practiced it, crosses stylistic boundaries and teaches the nature of human behavior (Carnicke 1998: 28). As human beings, we have desires that propel us to act, and the need to influence others. The same is true with characters onstage in Realism, Absurdism, Asian theatre, performance art, dance, puppetry or forms of "experimental" theatre. Whatever one may call it—energy, presence, inner work, motivation, desire, subtext, etc. (see Appendix A), what moves us is always Action. Again, as master teacher Lanskoy held, "It's not *you* who does the Action. When it is done truthfully, *Action* 'does' *you*" (Class, 1986–88).

All actors may not act Chekhov using Stanislavsky's system, but the director vowed his work came from nature, and would apply to any actor drawn to the art of the stage (Magarshack 1975: 375). He said:

> Simple physical actions form the firm basis of everything people do in life. Their value to our art lies in the fact that they are organic in any given circumstances. But the actor must never forget that physical actions are merely an excuse for evoking inner action.

---

56   Porter Anderson writes in Bogart's *Viewpoints* that "Bogart's specific goal is to free her theatre of the curse of the American Method developed from the Stanislavsky system" (115–6). Bogart mistakenly attributes Lee Strasberg's "Method" to Stanislavsky. Anderson continues, "In order to achieve any emotional life onstage, she [Bogart] believes the structure of a work must be concretized. Once that happens, the artist will have her physical bearings so confidently moored that they can be open to the tides of human vulnerability that make for rich dramatic life" (115). This physical approach is exactly what Stanislavsky proposed with his Method of Physical Actions: "concretizing," or setting the truthful physical actions of a role, frees the actor. Thus Bogart, Meyerhold and Stanislavsky share an approach to acting.

    Bogart wrote to me: "I am a huge admirer of and studier of and follower of Stanislavsky, especially late Stanislavsky. I particularly love the Michael Chekhov work. Also I admire Stella Adler's understanding of Stanislavsky. My problems surround Strasberg's interpretation, particularly the emphasis on affective memory. While great for film and television, I believe that it has robbed the stage of extroversion, precision and generosity" (August, 2006).

When you have learnt to create this line of action and when your whole attention is
directed towards it, we shall be able to guarantee that on coming out on the stage you
will always do that which is necessary and for the sake of which your art exists. (*Ibid.*)

The idea that Action is psycho-physical is not exclusive to Stanislavsky's view
of stagecraft; "purpose" is inherent in human nature. This is fundamental for the
theatre practitioner, whether he or she uses Stanislavsky's terminology or not.

The ethic in theatre practice is, traditionally, to do whatever works: praxis
is all. Language can shape an actor's "praxis," or behavior. Just as "think *up*" will
yield different results in the actor than "sit up straight!" the way in which Action
is explained can free or shackle the young actor. Language influences thought,
which influences our ability to act. The way in which we talk about "Action"—or
whatever we may call the basis for *presence* on the stage—may define the scope and
perspicacity of the work.

Action in Practice

We must be able to go somewhere else—where, we don't know. The danger is that we
will get lost. Plan on it: count on it.
　　　　　　　　—JOSEPH CHAIKIN, *THE PRESENCE OF THE ACTOR* (67)

They don't want to see you *relaxed*. They want to see you *in danger*.
　　　　　—UTA HAGEN, QUOTED FROM A NOTICE POSTED AT THE LUCILLE LORTEL THEATRE,
　　　　　　　　　　　　NY, THE DAY AFTER HER DEATH (JAN. 15, 2004)

You don't want to scare the audience. You want to *terrify* them.
　　　　　　　　—ARTHUR MILLER, WNYC, LOPATE SHOW INTERVIEW (2000)

Playing Actions onstage creates life that is exciting and engaging for the audience.
Director Joseph Chaikin, with actor Uta Hagen and playwright Arthur Miller—
from different styles of performance—acknowledge that it is a sense of danger
and unknowing that connects the spectator to the performance. When the actor
is thoroughly "in the moment," and concentrating his full attention on a task,
he draws the audience into his world, which is one of pursuit and anticipation.
Chaikin is remembered by some as an actor/director/theorist who "countered the
years of the Stanislavsky 'method' acting style" (Shapiro 16). Yet, his concentration
on process, like Grotowski and Meyerhold, brought him to an understanding he
shares with Stanislavsky: that much is contained in the physical body. He wrote:

When I make a motion with my arm, from where do I draw the energy in order to
perform the motion? If I go across the room to open the window, it's my interest in the

outside that releases the energy for the walk across the room. The "impulse," in this case, is that which starts a *motion-toward* … [The actor] is given energy by his inner promptings, associations, that part of his life which is already lived. (8–9)

This is much like the work of Stanislavky, as described by Toporkov.[57] While Chaikin may describe this "energy," prompted by an inner desire, as a part of the actor's "presence," it also may be seen as another way to describe "Action." As Beckerman wrote: "As a mode of theatrical art, the medium of drama is *not* language, but human presence" (18). Drama itself is, then, the *doing* of human beings; in life, our very survival depends on it. It's what gives us allure, and makes the audience want to watch. "Presence" on the stage may be seen as an actor's pursuit through Action.

Hagen describes Action as "Animation," not "separate from the body but emanat[ing] from it," a "physical destination *consciously* motivated by events, by basic wishes, by what is done to us and by demands of others" (1991: 100–2). Much like Adler, she defines types of action, describing how thoughts must "keep … traveling toward our targets as they interact with our physical, psychological and verbal actions" (108). She refers to "inner objects" as visualizations which help to "contact the sources that trigger actively traveling thoughts" which are meant to "keep [the actor's] attention on the events of the play" (110). Much of each of her two books on acting contain specific exercises and descriptions of how particular actions are arrived at and performed, with the concept of "endowment" of objects and events figuring highly on the list of ways to achieve viable Action in a play. The term "objectives" is described as "conscious, instinctive, and subconscious needs, wishes, desires, aims, goals [originating] in the body or the soul" (278). An objective, she writes, "will stimulate not only your feelings but the will to do something about it, imaginatively suggesting many possible actions" (280). In her parlance, having an "objective" gives the actor an "action;" they are, in practice, the same thing: pursuit of one's desire.

Morris Carnovsky had much the same interests and practice, though he defines Stanislavsky's approach, "in a nutshell: Self, Object, combined by given circumstances and propelled by *Action*" (39). He quotes Stanislavsky on these three ideas:

What we need are simple, expressive actions with an inner content. … Energy, heated by emotion, charged by will, directed by the intellect, moves with confidence

---

57 Bella Merlin relates Toporkov's view in *Beyond Stanislavsky*: "Through this *forward-moving* impulse, all the actor's apparatus was aligned almost effortlessly, making it a truly psychophysical technique, where body and psychology (brains, emotions and imagination) were mutually dependent" (2001: 16).

and pride, like an ambassador on an important mission. It manifests itself in conscious action, full of feeling, content, and purpose, which cannot be carried out in any slipshod, mechanical way, but must be fulfilled in accordance with its spiritual impulses. (35)

We may note how Carnovsky—with other practitioners—recognizes a "spiritual" element in the pursuit of Actions. There is something in human desire that reaches below or beyond the corporal.

Carnovsky writes that he credits his understanding of acting "—namely action, atmosphere, and all the technical elements I had inherited [to] the Group Theatre" (15). Like other Group members, he worked with Michael Chekhov, and remembered Chekhov's suggestion: "Examine the relationships of the characters" (136). Contemporary teacher/director Lanskoy also cautioned: "You don't rehearse the *lines*; you rehearse the *relationships*" (Class, 1988). Actions onstage come out of desires of each character to influence others, and when the actor understands how each character relates to another, the conflict between them—and the conflict of the entire spine of the play—becomes clear. Of course, these discoveries are made on one's feet, in the *doing* itself.

Sanford Meisner (also of the Group Theatre) took this idea of relationships and developed it into his proviso for actor-training, the "Repetition Exercise." It is described as an improvisation where two acting partners repeat lines back and forth, wherein the short scene would eventually give rise, organically, to something new (183). The point is to observe the partner closely, to make sure responses are based precisely on what one partner gives to the other.

Currently, "Meisner Technique" is one of the most popular approaches to actor-training in schools in the United States. This may be because it is workable and accessible: it is based in the practice of sense memory (remembering how things look, feel, taste, sound, etc.) and true communication with a partner onstage. Meisner disassociates himself from the practices of Lee Strasberg, his colleague in the Group:

The result of [Adler's work in Paris with Stanislavsky] ... was to de-emphasize the importance Strasberg had placed on "affective memory"—which might be defined as the conscious attempt on the part of the actor to remember the circumstances surrounding an emotion-filled event from his real past in order to stimulate an emotion which he could use onstage. Rather, Miss Adler said, Stanislavsky now thought that the key to true emotion was to be found in a full understanding of the "given circumstances"—the human problems—contained in the play itself. This shift of emphasis was critical, and it led directly to a diminution of Strasberg's hold on the acting company and to his eventual resignation from the Group in 1935. On this issue, Meisner sided with Stella Adler, who was later to become a noted acting teacher and close friend, and affective or emotional memory plays no role in the system Meisner has evolved. (9–10)

In his book *On Acting*, Meisner notes the importance of using Stanislavsky's idea "as if" (136–44). An actor behaves *as if* he or she were responding to the circumstances of the character in the play. Meisner underlines the fact that the text is the actor's "greatest enemy" (136). This is because we are to understand that the actor *does* so much more than is seen in the text of the play alone. Meisner describes the script as only a libretto, to which the composer adds music. The actor is the composer: "What you read in the book is only the merest indication of what you have to do when you really act the part" (179). This is central to the idea of "Action": acting is the "reality of *doing*" in *circumstance*—dialogue is only secondary.

Playwright/director David Mamet is another proponent of the idea of Action. He describes it—speaking to the actor—as pursuing the punchline of a joke (1999: 82–3). He calls this "punchline" an "*objective*, which means '*What do I want?*'" And when the actor thinks only of the objective, all concerns of *belief, feeling, emotion, characterization and substitution* become irrelevant, in pursuit of the Action (82). Action, as Mamet describes it, is then "the commitment to achieving a single goal" (84). Also important for the actor—according to Mamet—is that he/she choose an Action that is *fun*, and something the actor *wants to do*. He likens it to what we did as children, i.e. playing a game that had to be fun; there is no "mystery" to playing actions, as long as they're "something like what the author intended" (84). He insists: "not only is it the simple solution to a seemingly complex problem [interpreting the text], it is the right solution. Not only is it the right solution, it is the only solution" (85). Using Action is thus the only viable way to play a role. Other practitioners are less didactic, but just as much involved.

Charles Marowitz and Peter Brook, who have worked together,[58] are also advocates of pursuing Action on the stage. Marowitz disdains the literary scholar's view that the actor's or director's approach of "sub-textualizing"—another way to describe pursuing Action, "underneath" the text—is inappropriate. In his book on the work of the director, *Prospero's Staff*, he quotes Shakespearian scholar Maynard Mack:

The sound notion that there is a life to which the words give life can with very little stretching be made to mean that the words the author set down are themselves simply a search for the true play, which the director must intuit in, through, and under them. Once he has done so, the words become to a degree expendable. (4)

---

58   Marowitz was Assistant Director on Brook's *King Lear*, and his "Theatre of Cruelty" season with productions of Genet's *The Screens* and Peter Weiss's *Marat/Sade*.

Marowitz counters that "If the director is able to 'intuit in, through and under' the words, that makes them *not* expendable, but capable of *infinite variety* … It is the passage of time and the accuracy of a director's perception that determine the 'trueness' or 'falseness' of a play" (4). In other words, "creative process is what confirms or transforms a writer's meaning …" and the actor, as well as the director, is a master of this process, through the technique of Action. The subtext of characters' words is the cause or intention that results in the words being spoken; the process of discovering these underlying intentions is another way to describe finding Action. Marowitz also believes "The business of the director is to restore to the work of the poet whatever was lost on the way from the dream to the manuscript" (6). In comparing translations of Chekhov's plays, this researcher will explore the same possibilities: with the variant "results" of language on the pages of myriad translations, the subtext or Actions in scenes may vary as well.[59]

Marowitz, like Adler, Meisner and other contemporary practitioners, is particularly wary of Strasberg's use of emotion in approaching character. Marowitz claims it is a misunderstanding and mistaken "literal" approach to an early experiment of Stanislavsky's; he writes, "it probably crippled ten actors for every one it aided," when used by inexperienced performers (1978: 11–12). He quotes Vakhtangov, considered Stanislavsky's brilliant student: "The actor, Stanislavsky taught, must think first of … what he wants to obtain at a particular moment, and what he is to do, but not about what he's going to feel" (13). Marowitz sums up the process in *The Other Way*:

> An actor "doesn't so much 'become a character' or 'live a role' as absorb actions, feelings and experiences relative to his character and, in so doing, triggers like-actions, like-feelings and like characters in his own being; that the actor is a conductor-of-energies *already mobilized* and ready to leap into parallel situations; that he doesn't 'perform' so much as allow the psychic functioning of his character to release universal information bred in his bone and echoed in his memory; that phylogeny precedes psychology and that the physical is only the most conspicuous aspect of the metaphysical." (222–3)

The "phylogeny" Marowitz mentions may be likened to Adler's idea about "collective consciousness," linked to the imagination: we know much more than we think we know (Adler 2000: 17). Stanislavsky was interested in how the "conscious"

---

59 Marowitz gives an example of how modern associations may change the meaning of images in Chekhov's *The Cherry Orchard*: Chekhov could not have known, for example, that "the crunch of axes [on the orchard trees] … has as much environmental repercussion for modern audiences as it does nostalgic …" (5).

technique of pursuing Actions was the key to the "subconscious" (Magarshack 1975: 81). Lanskoy stated the "Action does *you*" and Marowitz concurs: "Being an actor is not so much a question of 'training' and 'development' but of *awakening susceptibilities to the play's situations* (emphasis added), stated and implied; the play-wright's intentions, latent and overt; the director's interpretation, articulated and inchoate ... Acting was not something you 'do' but something done *to you* if you were free enough ..." (223–4). Marowitz is not alone in seeing a metaphysical side to acting process.

Peter Brook, in a presentation at Britain's National Theatre,[60] describes how actors only use a small part of themselves, when in actuality "there's a very deep part of him, which isn't only the Freudian sub-conscious but something infinitely more ... There is a vast area which is himself that he doesn't know." Brook illustrates this idea with a brief exercise with an audience. He asks them to stand up, wait a moment, then sit down together. The audience does so. Their movements are not in sync. But when he asks them to use their peripheral vision and their "natural timing instinctively," their efforts result in a more cohesive move, where they all move together. And Brook states,

> If we did this for even twenty minutes, it would be astonishing to see how it's possible for a large number of people to become more sensitive, more alert, more perceptive to one another than when they started, just by each person making a very special effort himself. If we did this everyday for three weeks, there would come a quite uncanny moment when an enormous group of people could in fact do quite difficult things together. (1993a: 1–3)

With this exercise, Brook has given a brief "actor" experience to this audience, and allowed them to see what it is to work collectively, which is, he says, what matters in the theatre; the point is to make each person in the group more sensitive. Sensitive actors on the stage also make the *audience* more sensitive when they go back out into the street. Brook says theatre is "about giving everyone who is together at the moment when there's a performance, a taste of being finer in their feelings, clearer in their way of seeing things, deeper in their understanding, than in their everyday isolation and solitude ... This is something that can only exist because a group of people are living something together" (2–3). In acting in Chekhov's last four plays, this is overwhelmingly true: the plays are each about a *group* of people, and understood as *ensemble* works. In each play, there is an *ensemble protagonist*, rather than *one* person who is affected by the events. Lanskoy insists

---

60   With Genista McIntosh, Olivier Theatre, November 5, 1993; also at website-archive. nt-online.org.

that this is the definition of the word "event" in a play: that it is a happening that affects every character (Class, 1987). Understanding the events in Chekhov's plays is essential to understanding his characters' Actions (See Appendix A).

Brook's exercise demonstrates the need for perception, group communication and purpose in executing a simple physical action. It could begin the work of Chaikin, Grotowski, Michael Chekhov and many other teacher/directors. It is a simple way to do Action with others—and "feel" awareness—which may give us "presence" onstage. It is about experiencing, which is another way to define "Action."

Brook describes the nature of Action in many ways.[61] In *The Open Door* he writes of how the simplest expression can be "full" or "empty" (90): "One can say 'Good day' to somebody without feeling either 'good' or 'day', and without even feeling the person one is speaking to. One may shake hands in an automatic manner—or else the same greeting can be illuminated with sincerity" (90). The difference, we may say, is whether or not the person has a "purpose," having to do with the other person; that is, an "Action." Brook rightly notes, "We can inform a gesture with quality and meaning ... [and] Quality is found in detail. The presence of an actor, what it is that gives quality to his listening and his looking, is something rather mysterious, but not entirely so" (91). It is not completely mysterious; we may say it is having an Action, which points the actor's concentration and attention to a desire he/she intends to accomplish, and people he or she wants to *influence*. Lanskoy points out "If acting is a mystery, it's not a profession" (Class, 1988). That is, if there is no way to quantify or qualify what an actor does, there is no way to study the art of acting as an occupation. This study attempts to describe how an approach to acting may indeed be quantified to a large degree. This in no way diminishes the "awe" Brook and others retain for the art of theatre; but Brook recognizes "the craft of theatre cannot remain mysterious ..."; the "rungs of the ladder to be climbed" with regard to the levels of "quality" in theatre work are the "details, moment by moment. Details are the craft that leads to the heart of

---

61 In *Systems of Rehearsal*, Shomit Mitter pits Brook against Stanislavsky, labeling Stanislavsky's work as "cerebral" and Brook's "somatic." Mitter claims this is a misunderstanding of the Russian's work by Brook. Yet Brook, like Stanislavsky, believes that Action underlies the words of a text; he writes in *The Empty Space*: "A word does not start as a word—it is an end product which begins as an impulse, stimulated by attitude and behavior which dictates the need for expression. This process occurs inside the dramatist; it is repeated inside the actor ..." (15). This is in keeping with Stanislavsky's Method of Physical Actions, and shows how it is Action that creates the dialogue in the playscript, and not the other way around. As with Meyerhold, Brecht and Chaikin, Brook and Stanislavsky are in tandem in their practice.

the mystery" (92). The *details* of Actions in Circumstances are part of what will be examined in translations of Chekhov's plays in later chapters.

Brook states repeatedly that theatre is about "making the invisible world visible" (1993b: 69 and 1987: 234), and that it takes "special skills" to do this: he writes of "energy," "inspiration" and how "only the actor is capable of reflecting the subtle currents of human life" (234). These "currents" may also describe the playing of Actions onstage. Brook finally elucidates stagecraft when he writes "Art only becomes useful to man and society if it contains within it an *urge to action*" (emphasis added, 234). His discussion stresses both the universal phenomenon of Action, and the particular use of it by the actor. Without attributing this discovery to Stanislavsky, Brook suggests his way of working on acting:

> If I had a drama school, the work would begin very far from character, situation, thought or behavior. We would not try to conjure up past anecdotes of our lives so as to arrive at incidents, however true. We would search not for the incident, but for its quality: the essence of this emotion, beyond words, below incident. Then we would begin to study how to sit, how to stand, how to raise an arm. This would have nothing to do with choreography or aesthetics, nor would we be studying psychology—we would just be studying acting. (231)

This puts me in mind of one of the ending class pronouncements of Russian acting teacher Lanskoy in his two-year course entitled "Structures of Action." He declared, "Do you see, now, that Action is *not* what you say, and it is *not* what you do?" (Class, 1989). Action was, rather, understood to be the inner impulse, energy, desire, or interest that moved the actor inside, even when he or she was, perceptibly, unmoving or still on the stage. Brook, too, writes:

> To me what matters is that one actor can stand motionless on the stage and rivet our attention while another does not interest us at all. What is the difference? Where chemically, physically, psychically does it lie? Star quality, personality? No. That's too easy and it's not an answer. I don't know what the answer is. But I do know that it is here; in this question we can find the starting point of our whole art. (232)

It is my suggestion that the answer is to be discovered in practical research on the notion of Action.[62]

---

62 Action may be seen in all works of art: the underlying allure and dynamic can be seen and/ or heard and felt in the still-life paintings of Cezanne, the music of Mozart, the singing of Placido Domingo and the dance of Mikhail Barishnikov. The notion is not exclusive to the theatre.

Back in the U.S.S.R.

Other noted researcher/practitoners like Michel Saint-Denis, Robert Lewis, Jean Benedetti, Sonia Moore, Jack Poggi, William Ball, Robert Benedetti, Viola Spolin, Robert Cohen, Richard Brown, Richard Hornby, Sharon Carnicke, Irina and Igor Levin, Bella Merlin, with my Russian teachers—Yevgeny Lanskoy, Slava Dol-gatchev, Marat Yusim, and no doubt many others—have much more to say about the notion of Action in the theatre.[63] The definitions of Russian practitioners is of particular interest, as these practitioners worked closely with Stanislavsky's actual students, with a knowledge of the cultural milieu.

Carnicke, the Levins and Merlin all recognize and note the significance of the observations of those artists who worked with Stanislavsky in his final years. All three have written about the work of Maria Osipovna Knebel (1898–1985) and Mikhail Nicholoaevich Kedrov (1893–1972), two actors, along with Vasily Toporkov (1889–1970), who worked closely with Stanislavsky in his final rehears-als of *Tartuffe*. Carnicke remarks that it is rather upon the "authority of Russia's classrooms and the lore that developed among his last students" that we may understand Stanislavsky's Method of Physical Actions, and the subsequent "Active Analysis" (1998: 153). While Kedrov (Stanislavsky's Assistant Director and player in the title role in his final *Tartuffe*), according to his student Albert Filozov (born 1937), dogmatically emphasized the logic of physical actions, Knebel was far more interested in "analysis through action: ... the actors analyzed their roles actively by using their bodies, imaginations, intuition and emotions on the rehearsal–room floor" (Merlin 2003: 33–4).

Merlin states there is considerable overlap between the two modes of working: while the Method of Physical Actions—so painstakingly described by Torpokov in his *Stanislavsky in Rehearsal*—was concerned with finding the logical score of physical actions of the character, the "analysis through action," or Active Analysis, is, rather, "Anything" that provides "the actors with valuable clues—the structure of a scene, the 'anatomy' of the play, the very *medium* of drama itself. So the logic of the sequence was less important than the experimental discoveries made through active research" (34). The point is that the actor discovers the role *on his/her feet*, in the playing.

---

63 The volumes *Acting (Re)Considered*, ed. Phillip Zarrilli and *The Method Reconsidered*, ed. David Krause, for example, contain absorbing essays on acting with regard to semiotics and post-modern views, but these articles do not often address Stanislavsky's practical work; they deal largely with theory rather than practice. They often mistakenly throw Strasberg's approach at the feet of Stanislavsky.

I have learned much about Action through the "lore" of contemporary Russian teachers. Lanskoy, Dolgatchev and Yusim, all directors, formerly of the Moscow Art Theatre, impressed on students the significance of the events, inciting incidents and objectives in "assessing the facts" of the play (*Ibid.*). Dolgatchev used stories of Anton Chekhov to help students define these terms in detailed investigations, which may also be applied to the playtext.[64] Lanskoy concentrated on the intricate nature of Action itself, while Yusim writes about the importance of the director's work with actors and on the script, in detailed "analysis through action" whereby the actor is able to "do it"—as a "chain of uninterrupted facts, events and actions" on the stage (250).

The Levins depend largely on the methods espoused by Georgii A. Tostonogov. He was a student of the MAT Department of Directing, who witnessed the work of Kedrov and Stanislavsky in 1938 and later became director of the St. Petersburg Bolshoi Drama Theatre, well-known in the Soviet Union. The Levins write that Tostonogov used a "variant of the method of analysis by action" which he understood from Kedrov (2002: 20). The Levins are "among the inheritors of that tradition" (3). We see how the "tradition of lore," as Carnicke calls it, comes down, "generation to generation, from master to student" (1). Stanislavsky's legacy has thus been established through praxis, rather than a strict following of his writings. The practitioners discussed in this chapter are in a direct line to current acting teachers. It is important to understand how Stanislavsky's later practice and view of Action were handed down from generation to generation. They continue to develop in the hands of the students of his students, of which I am one.

In this study, the elements and structures of Action described above, and others, will be applied to Chekhov's plays in translation. As discussed in this chapter, an understanding of Action is necessary to help describe how language in various translations may influence the actor's work on Chekhov's plays. But a practical knowledge of Action is necessary for playing in *any* style of theatre. Fergusson notes that the purpose of the Moscow Art Theatre, where Chekhov's plays were produced, was "to teach the actor to perceive and imitate *action* so that he can play accurately the roles which dramatists of all kinds have written" (1953: 252). Chekhov's plays provided the nest in which the modern notion of Action was born and nurtured. Fergusson concludes:

> It is necessary to emphasize the fact that a technique of acting, even so fundamental a one as this, merely leads to the literature of drama, just as the performer's technique

---

64   Three-week Workshop with Dogatchev, Spring, 2004 in the Department of Music and Performing Arts, School of Education, New York University.

of the violinist leads to the literature of the violin, where the possibilities of the instrument are explored. (253)

In fact, as Meyerhold too notes, it is not "the stage [that] inspires literature," but *literature* that has always "broken down dramatic forms" and led the way to innovation on the stage (Meyerhold 1969: 34). So it is Chekhov who helped or led Stanislavsky to develop his system, while Stanislavsky's theatre allowed Chekhov's works to achieve the public prominence that ultimately gave his dramaturgy to the world.

So, this discussion of Action leads to an exploration of Chekhov's "instrument"—that is, an exploration of his plays. Therein, one sees his hidden poetry, or "poetry of the theatre," is "not a poetry of words … It is based upon the histrionic sensibility and the act of acting: it can only be seen in performance or by imagining a performance" (160). A discussion of Chekhov's dramaturgy in his masterpieces will help us to do just that—to "imagine the performance," as the actor does, from the first reading of the text.

References

Adler, Stella. *The Art of Acting*. Ed. Howard Kissel. New York: Applause Books, 2000.

———. Interview with Russell Vanderbrouke, *Yale Theatre* 8 (2 and 3), Spring 1977.

———. *On Ibsen, Strindberg and Chekhov*. Ed. Barry Paris. New York: Alfred A. Knopf, 1999.

———. "The Reality of Doing," *Tulane Drama Review*, IX(1): 136–155, Fall, 1964.

———. Scene Study/Technique/Rehearsal Classes, Pan-Andreas Theatre, Santa Monica, CA, 1981–84.

———. *The Technique of Acting*. New York: Bantam Books, 1988.

Albee, Edward. Interview with the author. Lincoln Center, New York City, December 7, 2005.

Aldridge, Joyce Spivey. "The Tradition of American Actor Training and Its Current Practice in Undergraduate Education." Dissertation, University of Colorado, 1993.

Aristotle. *Aristotle's Poetics*. Trans. S. H. Butcher. Intro. Francis Fergusson. New York: Hill and Wang, 1961.

———. *Aristotle's Theory of Poetry and Fine Art*, Trans. S. H. Butcher, 4th ed., London: Macmillan & Co. Ltd., 1932.

Arrowsmith, William and Roger Shattuck, eds. *The Craft and Context of Translation*. Austin: University of Texas Press, 1961.

Artaud, Antonin. *The Theatre and Its Double*. Trans. Mary Caroline Richards. New York: Grove Press, 1958.

Ball, William. *A Sense of Direction*. New York: Drama Book Publishers, 1984.

Barthes, Roland. *Image Music Text*. London: Fontana Paperbacks, 1984.

Beckerman, Bernard. *Dynamics of Drama*. New York: Drama Book Specialists, 1979.

———. "The Play's the Thing But What's a Play?" in Burnet M. Hobgood, ed. *Master Teachers of Theatre: Observations on Teaching Theatre by Nine American Masters.* Board of Trustees, Southern Illinois University, 1988, pp. 32–33.

Benedetti, Jean, ed. *Dear Writer, Dear Actress.* London: Menthuen Drama, 1996.

———. *The Moscow Art Theatre Letters.* New York: Routledge, 1991.

———. *Stanislavski.* New York: Routledge, 1990.

———. *Stanislavski: An Introduction.* London: Menthuen, 1982.

Benedetti, Robert. *The Actor at Work.* Englewood Cliffs, NJ: Prentice-Hall, 1970.

———. *The Actor in You.* Boston: Allyn and Bacon, 1999.

———. *Seeming, Being and Becoming.* New York: Drama Book Specialists, 1976.

Bogart, Anne. *Anne Bogart: Viewpoints.* Eds. Michael Bigelow Dixon and Joel A. Smith. Lyme, NH: Smith and Kraus, 1995.

———. Letter to the author, September, 2006.

Boleslavsky, Richard. *Acting, The First Six Lessons.* New York: Theatre Arts Books, 1963.

Bond, Will. Interview with the author. Anne Bogart's SITI Company at the New York Theatre Workshop, New York City, February, 1998.

Brand, Phoebe. Interview with the author. Manhattan Plaza, New York, NY, May, 2005.

Brecht, Bertolt. *Brecht on Theatre.* Trans. and ed. John Willett. New York: Hill and Wang, 1964a.

———. "Notes on Stanislavsky," *Tulane Drama Review,* 9:157–166, Fall, 1964b.

Brook, Peter. *The Empty Space.* New York: Avon Books, 1968.

———. Interview with Genista McIntosh, Royal National Theatre/Olivier Theatre, November 5, 1993a. Also at website-archive.nt-online.org.

———. *The Open Door.* New York: Random House, 1993b.

———. *The Shifting Point.* New York: Harper & Row, 1987.

Brown, Richard P. *Actor Training 1.* New York: Drama Book Specialists, 1972.

Brustein, Robert. "The Heritage of the MXAT," *The New Republic,* 217.6–7, 29–31, August 11, 1997.

———. *The Theatre of Revolt.* Boston: Little, Brown and Company, 1964.

Carnicke, Sharon Marie. "Stanislavsky Uncensored and Unabridged," *Tulane Drama Review,* T137 13:22–37, Spring, 1993.

———. *Stanislavsky in Focus.* Australia: Harwood Academic Publishers, 1998.

Carnovsky, Morris. *The Actor's Eye.* New York: Performing Arts Journal Publications, 1984.

———. "Statement to House on UnAmerican Activities Committee," n. d., 1950s.

Chaikin, Joseph. *The Presence of the Actor.* New York: Atheneum, 1972.

Chekhov, Michael. "Chekhov on Acting: A Collection of Unpublished Materials (1919–1942)." *Tulane Drama Review,* 27:63 No. 3 (T99), Fall, 1983.

———. *Lessons for the Professional Actor.* Arr. by Deirdre Hurst du Prey. New York: Performing Arts Journal Publications, 1985.

———. *On The Technique of Acting.* Ed. Mel Gordon. New York: Harper Collins Publishers, 1991.

———. *To The Actor.* New York: Harper & Row, 1953.

Clurman, Harold. *The Collected Works of Harold Clurman.* Eds. Marjorie Loggia and Glenn Young. New York: Applause Books, 1994.

———. *The Fervent Years*. New York: Harcourt, Brace, Jovanovich, 1975.

———. *Lies Like Truth*. New York: The Macmillan Company, 1958.

Cocteau, Jean. Preface, *Les Mariés de la Tour Eiffel*. Paris: Editions Flammarion, 1995. See also https://www.poetryfoundation.org/poets/jean-cocteau.

Coger, Leslie. "Stanislavsky Changes His Mind," *Tulane Drama Review*, 9:63–68, Fall, 1984.

Cohen, Robert. *More Power to You*. New York: Applause Theatre and Cinema Books, 2002.

Cohen, Robert and John Harrop. *Advanced Acting*. Boston: McGraw Hill, 2002.

Corrigan, Robert. "Translating for Actors," in William Arrowsmith and Roger Shattuck, eds. *The Craft and Context of Translation*. Austin: The University of Texas Press, 1961, pp. 95–106.

Danchik, Roger L. "The Distinction Between the Written and Performed Dramatic Text from Suzanne Langer's Perspective," Dissertation, NYU, 1991.

Dolgatchev, Slava. "Workshop in Acting." NYU, Department of Music and Performing Arts, 2004.

Esslin, Martin. *An Anatomy of Drama*. New York: Hill and Wang, 1976.

———. *The Field of Drama*. London and New York: Methuen, 1987.

———. *The Theatre of the Absurd*. Garden City, NY: Anchor Books, 1961.

Fergusson, Francis. *The Idea of a Theatre*. Garden City, NY: Doubleday Anchor Books, 1953.

———. "The Notion of Action," *Tulane Drama Review*, 9:85–87, Fall, 1964.

Gorchakov, Nikolai M. *Stanislavsky Directs*. Trans. Miriam Goldina. New York: Funk & Wagnalls, 1954.

Gordon, Marc. "Stanislavsky in America: Russian Émigré Teachers of Acting." Dissertation. Cambridge: Tufts University, 2002.

Gordon, Mel. "Nine Misconceptions About Stanislavsky and His System," *Soviet and European Performance*, 9 (2 and 3), Fall, 1989.

———. *The Stanislavksy Technique: Russia*. New York: Applause Theatre Book Publishers, 1987.

Gottlieb, Vera and Paul Allain, eds. *The Cambridge Companion to Chekhov*. Cambridge University Press, 2000.

Grotowski, Jerzy. *Towards a Poor Theatre*. New York: Simon and Schuster, 1968.

Hagen, Uta. *A Challenge for the Actor*. New York: Charles Scribner's Sons, 1991.

———. Posters on Lucille Lortel Theatre, January 15, 2004. Quotes and Stories of Uta Hagen.

———. *Respect for Acting*. New York: Macmillan Publishing Company, 1973.

Harrop, John. *Acting*. London: Routledge, 1992.

Hirsch, Foster. *A Method to Their Madness*. New York: W. W. Norton and Company, 1984.

Hobgood, Burnet M., ed. *Master Teachers of Theatre*. Board of Trustees, Southern Illinois University, 1988.

Hornby, Richard. *The End of Acting*. New York: Applause Theatre Books, 1992.

Johnston, David, ed. *Stages of Translation*. Bath, England: Absolute Classics, 1996.

Kazan, Elia. "Outline from Elementary Course in Acting, 1935," *Tulane Drama Review*, T104, 28:34–37, Winter, 1984.

Langer, Susanne K. *Feeling and Form*. New York: Charles Scribner's Sons, 1953.

Lanskoy, Yevgeny. Interviews with the author, 1999, and Classes, "The Structures of Action," at the Stella Adler Conservatory, 1986–89.

Levenson, Robin Beth. "Afraid to Lie," Unpublished paper, Dr. Richard Schechner's Directing Course, New York University, Tisch School of the Arts, Spring, 1999.

Levin, Irina and Igor. *The Stanislavsky Secret*. Colorado Springs: Meriwether Publishing, Ltd., 2002.

———. *Working on the Play and the Role*. Chicago: Ivan R. Dee, 1992.

Lewis, Robert. *Advice to The Players*. New York: Harper & Row, Publishers, 1980.

———. "Emotional Memory," *Tulane Drama Review*, T16:54–61, Summer, 1962.

———. *Method or Madness?* New York: Samuel French, 1958.

———. *Slings and Arrows*. New York: Stein and Day, 1984.

———. "Would You Please Talk to Those People?" *Tulane Drama Review* 9:104–113, Fall, 1964.

Linklater, Kristin. *Freeing the Natural Voice*. UK/USA: Drama Publishers, 1976.

———. Workshop at American Communication Association Conference, NYC, 1998.

Magarshack, David. *Chekhov*. New York: Grove Press, 1952.

———. *Stanislavsky*. Westport, CT: Greenwood Press, 1975.

Malague, Rosemary. "Getting at 'the Truth:' A Feminist Consideration of American Actor Training." Diss. City University of New York, 2001.

Mamet, David. Interview, David Mamet, "The Leonard Lopate Show," WNYC Radio, February 12, 2007.

———. *True and False*. New York: Vintage Books, 1999.

———. *Writing in Restaurants*. New York: Penguin Books, 1986.

Marowitz, Charles. *The Act of Being*. New York: Taplinger Publishing Company, 1978.

———. *The Other Way*. New York: Applause Books, 1999.

———. *Prospero's Staff*. Bloomington: Indiana University Press, 1986.

McCaslin, Nellie. Interview with the author. New York City, June 2, 2003.

Meisner, Sanford. *On Acting*. New York: Vintage Books, 1987.

Merlin, Bella. *Beyond Stanislavsky*. New York: Routledge, 2001.

———. *Konstantin Stanislavsky*. New York: Routledge, 2003.

Meyerhold, Vsevolod. "The 225th Studio," *Tulane Drama Review*, 9:22–23, Fall, 1964.

———. *Meyerhold on Theatre*. Trans./Ed. Edward Braun. London: Menthuen & Company Ltd., 1969.

Miller, Arthur. Interview. "The Leonard Lopate Show," WNYC Radio, 2000.

Mitter, Shomit. *Systems of Rehearsal*. London: Routledge, 1992.

Monos, Jim. "The Use of Stanislavsky Techniques in Professional Actor Training in New York City." Dissertation, City University of New York, 1981.

Moore, Irene. Interview with the author. New York City, February 28, 2002.

Moore, Sonia. *Stanislavski Revealed*. New York: Applause Theatre Books, 1991.

———. *The Stanislavski System*. New York: The Viking Press, 1974.

Olson, Elder, ed. *Aristotle's Poetics and English Literature*. Chicago: University of Chicago Press, 1965.

Pang, Cecilia Jessica. "The Angst of American Acting: An Assessment of Acting Texts." Dissertation. Berkeley: University of California, 1991.

Poggi, Jack. "The Stanislavsky System in Russia," *Tulane Drama Review* 28:124–133, T104 Winter 1984.

Rayner, Alice. *To Act, To Do, To Perform.* Ann Arbor: The University of Michigan Press, 1994.

Richards, Thomas. *At Work With Grotowski on Physical Actions.* London: Routledge, 1995.

Roberts, J. W. *Richard Boleslasky.* Ann Arbor: UMI Research Press, 1981.

Rotté, Joanna. *Acting With Adler.* New York: Limelight Editions, 2000.

———. "Stella Adler: Teacher Emeritus," *Journal of American Drama and Theatre,* City University of New York, 11:3, Fall, 1999.

Sacharow, Lawrence. "Enemies: A Russian Love Story," *American Theatre,* January, 2004.

———. "For Russians, A Process of Constant Rediscovery," *The New York Times,* December 2, 2001.

———. Interview with the author. Fordham University, New York, NY, May 12, 2003.

———. "Students Get Taste of Acting's Raw Power," *The New York Times,* August 20, 2000.

———. "Uncertainty is the Most Lethal Weapon," *The New York Times,* December 3, 2001.

Saint-Denis, Michel. "Stanislavsky and Shakespeare," *Tulane Drama Review* 9:77–84, Fall, 1964.

Schechner, Richard. "Already Reworking Classics of Modern Realism," *New York Times,* Feb. 13, 2000.

———. and Lisa Wolford, eds. *The Grotowski Sourcebook.* New York: Routledge, 1997.

———. *Performance Theory.* New York: Routledge, 1988.

Senelick, Laurence, ed. and trans. *Russian Dramatic Theory from Pushkin to the Symbolists.* Austin: University of Texan Press, 1981.

———. *Wandering Stars, Russian Émigré Theatre, 1905–1940.* Iowa City: University of Iowa Press, 1992.

Shapiro, G. "Memories of Joseph Chaikin and Hume Cronyn," *New York Sun,* September 18, 2003, p. 16.

Smith, Wendy. *Real Life Drama: The Group Theatre and America, 1931–1940.* New York: Alfred A. Knopf, 1990.

Stanislavsky, Constantin. *An Actor Prepares.* Trans. Elizabeth Reynolds Hapgood. New York: Theatre Arts Books, 1948.

———. *An Actor's Work. A Student's Diary.* Trans. and ed. Jean Benedetti. New York: Routledge, 2008.

———. *Building a Character.* Trans. Elizabeth Reynolds Hapgood. New York: Theatre Arts Books, 1949.

———. *Creating a Role.* Trans. Elizabeth Reynolds Hapgood. New York: Theatre Arts Books, 1961.

Strasberg, John. *Accidently On Purpose.* New York: Applause Books, 1996.

———. Interview with the author. New York City, April 1, 2003.

Strasberg, Lee. *A Dream of Passion.* New York: Plume/Penguin Books, 1987.

———. *Strasberg at The Actor's Studio.* Ed. Robert H. Hethmon. New York: The Viking Press, 1968.

———. "Working With Live Material," *Tulane Drama Review,* 9:117–135, Fall, 1964.

Tairov, Alexander. *Notes of a Director.* Trans. William Kuhlke. Coral Gables, FL: University of Miami Press, 1969.

Toporkov, Vasily Osipovich. *Stanislavsky in Rehearsal.* Trans. Christine Edwards. New York: Theatre Arts Books, 1979.

Vakhtangov, Yevgeny. *The Vakhtangov Sourcebook.* London and New York: Routledge, 2011.

Wangh, Stephen. *An Acrobat of the Heart.* New York: Vintage Books, 2000.

———. Interview with the author. New York University, March, 2003.

Yusim, Marat. *Passing the Torch—Basic Training: Stanislavsky's School of Acting and Directing.* New York: Marat Yusim, 2006.

Zarrilli, Phillip B. *Acting (Re)Considered.* London: Routledge, 1995.

Zatlin, Phyllis. *Theatrical Translation and Film Adaptation, a Practitioner's View.* UK, USA, Canada: Multilingual Matters Ltd., 2005.

Zuber, Ortrun, ed., *The Languages of Theatre.* Oxford: Pergamon Press, 1980.

CHAPTER FIVE

Chekhov's Dramaturgy

> A feeling of sadness and longing,
> That is not akin to pain,
> And resembling sorrow only
> As the mist resembles the rain.
> —FROM "THE DAY IS DONE" BY HENRY WADSWORTH LONGFELLOW

Longfellow's feeling goes a long way in describing Chekhov's dramaturgy in the last four plays, in both content and form. (The stanza is a definition of "wistful.") While Chekhov's plays have been seen as plays of "mood" (*nastroenie* in Russian), the definition of what this mood may be and how it is achieved have been points of debate since the plays were first produced. Like Longfellow, who paradoxically describes "sadness and longing" that are not painful, and a "sorrow" that is only misty, Chekhov renounced pat "Naturalism" and wrote complex characters layered with the minutiae of behavior that, as Senelick writes, is a *symbolist* technique (2005: xxxii). This has resulted in the unique "tragicomedy" genre that Chekhov created. It is an understatement to proclaim, as Senelick does, "there is no school of Chekhovian playwriting" (xxvii). While playwrights and short story writers claim kinship with Chekhov, none have managed to capture the same style and subtle under-text actually anchored in a "grid-iron structure."[1]

---

1   Critic Eric Bentley comments on Chekhov's "grid iron" in *The Theatre of Commitment*, 1967, pp. 43–4. The term "under-text" is from Hodgson/Richards' *Improvisation*,

Playwrights as diverse as G. B. Shaw (who modeled his *Heartbreak House* on *Cherry Orchard*[2]), Lillian Hellman (whose *Autumn Garden* was inspired by *Cherry Orchard*) Sherwood Anderson, Tennessee Williams, William Saroyan, Eugene O'Neill, Clifford Odets,[3] William Inge, Lanford Wilson, Brian Friel, John Guare, Romulus Linney and others have claimed kinship with or influence from Chekhov, as have writers Franz Kafka, James Joyce, Katherine Mansfield, Eudora Welty, John Cheever, Bernard Malamud, Katherine Anne Porter and Raymond Carver.[4] Comic writer Woody Allen said, "I'm crazy about Chekhov. I never knew anyone who wasn't" (*Ibid.*). One notable dissenter is Ernest Hemingway, who claimed: "Chekov wrote about 6 good stories. But he was an amateur writer" (*Ibid.*).

Hemingway was mistaken; Chekhov even anticipated Bertolt Brecht's "Vefreundungseffekt" ("estrangement," instead of the more common "alienation") technique and what has been called Samuel Beckett's "dramatic stasis and derealization" (*Ibid.*). Chekhov, in his use of seemingly cryptic language, is also recognized as a distinct precursor of Harold Pinter.[5] Both Beckett and Chekhov (Chekhov first) stole comic characters and style from Vaudeville and *commedia dell'arte*. Chekhov's plays, combining previous styles of performance and a new lyric, or "poetic" symbolic Realism (Senelick 1981: xli), were thought of as windows into twentieth century dramaturgy (Interview, Albee 2005), and, no less so now, inform theatre of the twenty-first century. Chekhov's plays continue to plumb the nature of human behavior.

1966, p. 174—it is another word for "subtext" and thus for Action: see Appendix A: Glossary.

2   Shaw admired Chekhov's canon; he wrote "these intensely Russian plays fitted all country houses in Europe … the same nice people, the same utter futility … when they could, they lived without scruple on incomes which they did nothing to earn" (Shaw 615). *Heartbreak* is revived in NYC in Fall, 2006.

3   Odets' *Awake and Sing*, revived at the Roundabout Theatre NYC in 2006, follows Chekhov's "ensemble protagonist" structure, among other similarities. The importance of the house (estate), family and a play where people eat, drink and joke while their lives are falling apart, might also be considered "Chekhovian." Odets penned a little known translation of *Three Sisters* in 1939. I used it as the basis for my re-imagined *3x3 Sisters*, which I adapted for a staged reading in NYC in 2007.

4   From the website: Taganrog Local Government, taganrogcity.com/Chekhov's Legacy Chekhov was born in Taganrog, Russia.

5   Pinter received the Nobel Prize in 2006, as did Eugene O'Neill in 1937; Chekhov influenced both (Byrd 1995: 13–5). Chekhov received the Pushkin Award from Russia's Academy of Sciences in 1900, but resigned it in protest when Gorky's award was "annulled" from this Academy. (P. Callow 331, 372).

Chekhov's Dramaturgy as Metaphor

Critics and practitioners have attempted to describe Chekhov's dramaturgy through metaphors of "lace," Impressionism and music. His dialogue and structure are graceful in their economy, woven gently like delicate lace. His method is soft, pointillist, fuzzy up close, but clear at an objective distance, using "glancing enigmatic strokes" rather than sharp outlines (Senelick 2005: 493). Rhythms, sounds and silences create the music of Chekhov's dialogue, which are the result of the underlying Actions of the characters; whole scenes juxtaposed to others create a musical point and counterpoint to these Actions. These metaphors help us understand Chekhov's approach to theatre art.

Playwright Maxim Gorky relates how Leo Tolstoy thought Chekhov's writing was "like a piece of lace worked by a chaste girl" with patterns of love "knitted into the lace ..." (Koteliansky 40–1). Russian Symbolist poet Andrey Bely (1880–1934) writes that Chekhov reproduced "the texture of an instant ... of life," and that "The lace of life, composed of discrete loops, becomes a series of doors in parallel corridors, leading to something else ..." (Senelick 1981: 89–90).[6] Bely describes this as Chekhov's "mystical symbolism," using the metaphor of lace to describe how Chekhov's "minutiae" helps us "see through" the banality of his characters, making symbolism "inevitable" (91). With "Symbolism" we are in the realm of the poetic. Jean Cocteau concurs:

> The action of my play is in the images (*imagées*) while the text is not: I attempt to substitute a 'poetry of the theatre' for 'poetry in the theatre.' Poetry in the theatre is a piece of lace which it is impossible to see at a distance. Poetry of the theatre would be coarse lace; a lace of ropes, a ship at sea. *Les Mariés* should have the frightening look of a drop of poetry under a microscope. *Scenes* are integrated like *words* of a poem.[7]

As Fergusson notes too, it is the *scenes*, setting or developing story in Chekhov's plays that are composed in such a way as to make a poetry "of the theatre"—while the text, read literally, is not (1953: 179); the text contains the simple quotidian language of the characters, stuck in their circumstances of everyday life.[8] Their underlying Actions provide the "skein" for each movement of the plays.

---

6   From Bely's collection *Arabeski*, Moscow, 1911, which included an essay on *The Cherry Orchard*.

7   From Cocteau's Preface to his play *Les Mariés de la Tour Eiffel*, noted in Fergusson (1953: 179).

8   Translator Stark Young notes "The vocabulary could hardly be simpler than it is in Chekhov ... Of all the dramatists Chekhov least deserves the muddle of the various styles

Not to overplay the "lace" metaphor, Senelick suggests Bely means that real details from life are so closely scrutinized they become transparent, and deep meanings are revealed (2005: xxxii). Senelick writes:

> Bely's earlier brief piece on *The Cherry Orchard* contains the provocative image of life as a skein of lace whose elaborate fabric must be penetrated before one can see through a single loop into the genuine reality beyond. The meaningless warp and woof of everyday life in a Chekhovian drama is riddled with interstices—pauses in dialogue, eruptions of flurried action—which expose the terrifying absolute that lies behind them. If Bely and Samuel Beckett had been contemporaries, the Russian might have quoted the Irishman's essay on Proust, to speak of "the perilous zones in the life of the individual, dangerous, precarious, painful, mysterious and fertile, when for a moment the boredom of living is replaced by the suffering of being." (xlii)

This "suffering of being" in Chekhov's plays—reminiscent of Longfellow's wistfulness—is noted by other critics and theatre practitioners: Yevgeny Lanskoy's acting classes began with the assertion that all life is suffering; this is what would help us, as acting students, to understand the nature of Action.[9] "Suffering" as a part of life, and particularly as a part of Chekhov's dramaturgy, is noted too in Fergusson's insightful essay on *The Cherry Orchard, A Theatre-Poem of the Suffering of Change* (1953: 170–90). It is, of course, the actor who reveals this suffering, using Chekhov's interstices to "make that direct and total response which is the root of poetry in the widest sense: [the Moscow Art Theatre] cultivated the histrionic sensibility in order to free the actor to realize, in his art, the situations and actions which the playwright had imagined" (189). So, Chekhov's dramaturgy demands the *actor's contribution* (see Glossary).

Senelick describes how Russian critic S. Sergeev, in 1900, proposed that the "center of gravity [in Chekhov's plays] is transferred to the mood [nastroenie]" of the play, and "if the play grips us and yet is devoid of regular stage action, it must *conceal an **inner action** more significant than that which is palpable*" [emphasis added] (1981: xli). In other words, the plays have "inner" Action not readily recognized as "action" by Chekhov's audiences at that time. But Chekhov's plays *do* have Action; as discussed in Chapter IV, it is the *inner* Action of the characters that propels the plays, along with the overall dramatic Action (Superobjective), embedded in them

---

that have been foisted on him in English—the involved, for instance, or the elevated, or the psychological-gloomy, or the turgid-soulful, or the flat, or the lacking in lyricism or wit" (Chekhov 1956: viii). The well-known lyrics of Gershwin's song "But Not for Me" illustrate this misunderstanding: "... With love to lead the way, I found more clouds of gray than any Russian play could guarantee ...".

9   Lanskoy's Class, Stella Adler Conservatory, New York City, 1987.

by the playwright.[10] The "pauses" and "interstices" in Chekhov's plays were also seen as a symbolist technique, described as "characters' souls calling to one another as unheard words sped homeward on airy wings" (*Ibid., op. cit.* critic Yuly Aikhenvald, *Russian Thought*, no. 2, 1904). Though it sounds ephemeral, this "calling" of souls with "unheard words" is simply—and quite concretely, in performance—the playing of Actions onstage. When we are silent, Action doesn't stop; we pursue purpose non-verbally. What Senelick and other critics leave out is that it's the *actor* who studies and reveals "deeper meanings" in the play, through the method of Action described in the previous chapter. The actor's art is exciting and temporal, but the *doing* of it is not a mystery. This is why Chekhov's plays may seem dry, flat or inscrutable on the page: they *require* the contribution and physical presence of the actor.

The parallel between impressionist landscape paintings and Chekhov's dramaturgy is addressed often in modern criticism.[11] In Chekhov's lifetime, Tolstoy compared Chekhov to Gogol[12] (1809–52) and French short story writer Guy de Maupassant[13] (1850–93): "His pieces produce the impression of a stereoscope ... like an impressionist artist he achieves wonderful results with the strokes of his brush" (P. Callow 334). Senelick cites Boris Zingerman (1928–2000), "expert on Stanislavsky and Meyerhold," as drawing these parallels (2005: 490–1),[14] and references to Chekhov's last four plays as "impressionist" are also noted by critics

---

10 Magarshack explains in his *Chekhov, The Dramatist* (1960) how Chekhov's plays of "indirect action" (the last four) contain a "tension"—i.e., the inner Actions of the characters—that was (and still is) often unrecognized by actors or directors of his plays (163). Chekhov's dialogue—or, the *subtext* of the dialogue (see Glossary)—creates this tension, which prepares the audience for the development of the action (162). Other elements such as "invisible characters," arrivals and departures, the use of the "messenger," the chorus, the "peripetia" or "reversal of situation" before the denouement, and "literary undertones" or echoes, all contribute to the strong action in Chekhov's canon (164). These elements— from Aristotle—may be "infinitely subtle" (173). Some are discussed herein, and in chapters devoted to the individual plays.

11 Matt Merkel's "Reinventing Chekhov: The journey from realism to impressionism ..." 1998, defines Chekhov's style, "within the framework of postmodernism." Chekhov crosses every "ism" in literary style.

12 Gogol, novelist/playwright, wrote the searing, comic *Inspector General* (or *The Revizor*) in 1836, which installed him as "the father of Russian realism" according to Valency (28). He is a precursor of Chekhov.

13 Henri Renée Guy de Maupassant (1849–92), is known as a master short story writer, and considered a "Naturalist." Like Chekhov, he died at a young age 43. Unlike Chekhov, he died from syphilis.

14 Senelick labels Zingerman a socialist art/theatre writer, who compared Chekhov's plays, in a "sophisticated analysis," to the impressionist landscape paintings of Chekhov's time.

and practitioners George Calderon, first English translator of Chekhov's plays (Chekhov 1912: 7), Fergusson, poet Randall Jarrell, Maurice Valency and many others, including theatre designers. For example, Parisian designer Yannis Kokkos, in 1984, states Impressionism was the "aesthetic starting point" for his production of *The Seagull,* based on works of the landscape painter Levitan, a friend of Chekhov's. Kokkos explains, "I did not want to work in the outdated, stereotypical cameo style which is associated with Chekhov, which would have drowned the design in nostalgia ... [T]he design comes [from] French Impressionism: ... colored light compositions made of grains of primary colors as in the first color photographs" (Gottlieb & Allain 2000: xiii). Though language written in the playscript is called the "dramaturgy" of a play, it is also the scenic design—set, props, sounds, etc., created from Chekhov's *stage directions*—along with the actor's presence—that help create the "poetry of the theatre" the playscript represents.

In his *The Breaking String*, Valency cites Chekhov's impressionism and musicality repeatedly, describing *The Three Sisters* as "Chekhov's masterpiece, the flower of impressionism in the drama" (219). Valency is referring to the dialogue written in the playscript. As we have come to understand, dialogue alone is not the "play." Valency equates "impressionism" with a surface "imprecision" that he believes shows "Chekhov's reluctance to assign precise motives for the actions of his characters," insisting that the "surface" behavior of his characters makes no "obvious reference as to what, if anything, lay beneath it" (230). However, if one knows, as many actors do, how to analyze a play with regard to Action, the subtext of the playscript becomes evident *in the playing.* Script analysis—knowing how to read a play—is mandatory for the actor, and anyone who wants to plumb the depths of Chekhov's works. While Valency believes that Chekhov's "impresssionism" makes Chekhov difficult for the actor (231), actually, as Ian McKellen relates so articulately, "Chekhov is 'a friend to the actor' " if one knows how to read a playscript (Gottlieb & Allain 2000: 121). Chapters VI–IX discuss signposts in the script that reveal possibilities for characterization and performance.

Lace and Impressionism have a subtle texture, and so does music. Critics and practitioners have universally compared Chekhov's dramaturgy to strains of a symphony.[15] Bely (Senelick 1981: 204–5) and Fergusson (19453: 186 and 1981: 91)

---

15 The playscript as "score," "blueprint," or "scaffolding" with "signposts"—is described by many teachers, critics, practitioners and translators, as mentioned in Chapters II–III. Teacher/ practitioner Tom Markus' *How to Read a Play* (1996) also likens the work of the playwright to that of the architect and the composer, a *schematic* with the play as a *map* to performance (1). His textbook, and Hayman's—also titled *How to Read a Play*—are the only full texts I discovered that teach—with attention to space, style, character and language— how a playscript is a map to performance. Though both write about the importance of

refer to Chekhov's "curiously non-verbal dramaturgy" as "musical," as does actor/director Meyerhold. Meyerhold says Chekhov's musicality was a new element added to Russian Realism; it was a "minor embellishment in Turgenev,"[16] but was "developed by Chekhov to its furthest extent" (*Ibid.*). Meyerhold criticized the Moscow Art Theatre's (MAT) productions of *Seagull*, *Vanya* and *Cherry Orchard*. As he describes in the well-known *Meyerhold on Theatre*, the secret of Chekhov's mood lies in the *rhythm* of his language, coupled with a careful mise en scène of all theatrical elements of the play:

> Your play [*Cherry Orchard*] is like a Tchaikovsky symphony. Before all else, the direc-
> tor must get the 'sound' of it. In the third act, against a background of the stupid
> stamping of feet—this 'stamping' is what he must hear—enters Horror, completely
> unnoticed by the guests. 'The cherry orchard is sold.' They dance on. 'Sold.' Still they
> dance. And so on to the end ... A sort of irritation. Jollity with overtones of death. In
> this act there is something terrifying, something Maeterlinckian. ... (33–4)[17]

Meyerhold, who played Treplev in the MAT's original production of *Seagull* and Tusenbach in *Three Sisters*, admired Anton Chekhov, and likened him to lyric symbolist Maeterlinck. Meyerhold felt Stanislavsky's productions of Chekhov's plays ignored "how Chekhov progresses from subtle realism to mystically heightened lyricism" (33). In productions of Chekhov's last four plays, Stanislavsky added "realistic" sounds of crickets, frogs, dogs and crying children to Chekhov's plays, which both Meyerhold and Chekhov himself found annoying and superfluous.

Meyerhold wisely quotes Voltaire: "Le secret d'être ennuyeux, c'est de tout dire" (27). (The secret to being boring is to tell all.) When everything is depicted in great detail for the audience, it leaves little to the imagination. "The urge to *show* everything, come what may, the fear of mystery, of leaving anything unsaid, turns the

---

imagining the play onstage, with set, lights, actors, movement, etc., they do not cite Action as the *structure* of a play. They refer to Chekhov, Beckett and Pinter repeatedly.

16 Ivan Turgenev, (1818–1883), Russian playwright and novelist, wrote *A Month in the Country*, which is often compared to Chekhov's last four plays, in content and form, and considered a precursor to Chekhov.

17 Maurice Maeterlinck, (1862–1849) renowned Belgian symbolist poet and playwright, was especially interested in the inner technique of the actor (Stanislavsky 1948: 501). In 1904 Stanislavsky rehearsed a trilogy of Maeterlinck's one-act plays, which he felt failed, and then, in 1908, produced the successful *Blue Bird*. Stanislavsky appointed Meyerhold artistic director of a new experimental studio, as he felt the young director had "a formula for the staging of symbolist drama" (Meyerhold 20). Though it folded after two years, it was Meyerhold's springboard to a development of a "new drama" which resulted in his technique of Biomechanics and numerous stylized productions that established him as a major force in the theatre.

theatre into a mere illustration of the author's words" (30). And Chekhov's characters are *not* "illustrating" his words: they are playing Actions *underneath* the words. Chekhov is careful *not* to portray characters that respond predictably; that's what makes them so interesting, and forces the actor to contribute a creative subtext. Chekhov's pointillist style allows for a written *score* for the dialogue, but non-verbal aspects of the plays give us the characters' Actions that flow in counterpoint to what is said.

Examples of this technique are Masha's repeated insistence that she will "tear love out of [her] heart, tear it out by the roots" while she is so obviously pining for Kostya throughout *Seagull*. Her actions belie her words. The same is true of Yelena in *Vanya*, who promises to speak to Astrov about his feelings for Sonia, though Yelena is obviously drawn to him herself, and is actually intent on getting Astrov to declare his feelings for *her*, not Sonia, in the very next scene. Lopakhin promises Ranevskaya he will ask Varya to marry him in *Cherry Orchard*, and in the very next scene with Varya, he demurs and runs out of the room. The dialogue doesn't tell us what characters truly want; their *Actions* do. Contradictions between what is said at one point, and then belied in the very next instant of the play, help create the "poetry" or music of Chekhov's dramaturgy.

Gustave Flaubert (1821–80)[18] does the very same thing in his novels, especially in *Madame Bovary*. As described by my teacher (and poet) Hugh Kenner,[19] Flaubert begins every paragraph of the novel on a high note, with Emma Bovary idealistically expecting her affairs to be transcendent, and then at the end of each paragraph—literally or metaphorically—someone falls on a banana peel. The characters go from sublime hope and certainty, to complete disillusionment. This is an aspect of "Realism" on the stage too. Though Flaubert was not a physician as Chekhov was, Flaubert certainly "caricatured the requirements of Realism," writing "a satire on scientific method" (Atlas 117). In final scenes of *Bovary*, Flaubert describes in detail how Emma expects her suicide will be the "noble" way out of her amorous predicaments, but then she (humanly) suffers excruciating physical horrors after taking poison. Chekhov's characters also idealize the accomplishments and hopes of mankind, and then fall down the stairs (Trofimov) or unromantically

---

18 Flaubert is considered an originator of Realism, along with short story writer de Maupassant. Flaubert was a friend of Turgenev, and of the novelist George Sand. (See *Flaubert and Turgenev. The Complete Correspondence*, ed. and tr. Barbara Beaumont, 1985 and *Flaubert-Sand, the Correspondence*, tr. Francis Steegmuller and Barbara Bray, 1993.) Realism was a reaction to Romanticism in mid-nineteenth century France. *Madame Bovary* created a scandal when first published in 1857, as it depicted a "romantic" woman who had affairs outside her marriage, bored as she was with her rural life with a simple husband. Her woes are often comic, as her "romantic" ideals pale in the face of the "reality" of love relationships.

19 In Kenner's literature classes at UC Santa Barbara in the 1970s, which I attended.

leave their lovers in the lurch (Vershinin). The importance of objectivity—not taking the side of any one character—is paramount to both Chekhov and Flaubert, as "Realistic" writers. Senelick notes that Shakespeare too has this "negation of the writer's own ego" which comes from the writer's "authorial absence" (2005 xxxviii). This absence is obligatory for Chekhov, and helps create his inimitable style.

Chekhov on Writing: Objectivity and Nature, Grace and Rhythm

When Chekhov was twenty-three, in 1883, he wrote of his distaste for "subjectivity" in a writer, championing the objective view. He writes his older brother Alexander (also a writer): "Subjectivity is a terrible thing. It is bad in … that it reveals the author's hand and feet" (Chekhov, ed. Friedland, 1966: 69). By 1988, he insists:

> The artist should be, not the judge of his characters and their conversations, but only an unbiased witness … my business is to report the conversation exactly as I heard it, and let the jury [the readers] estimate its value. My business is merely to … illuminate the characters and speak their language … And if an artist in whom the crowd has faith decides to declare that he understands nothing of what he sees—this in itself constitutes a considerable clarity in the realm of thought, and a great step forward. (58–9)

Chekhov claims to have avoided any indication of his political or social views—a stance that flummoxed his detractors—and denied the idea that any of his characters expressed his personal outlook. "When I offer you a professor's ideas, trust me, and do not search in them for Chekhov's ideas," he wrote (17). In other words, Chekhov, like Sontag, was not fond of "interpretation," at least on the part of the artist. He also writes "I did not at all pretend to arouse attention by my stupendous views on the theatre, on literature, etc. I merely wished to make use of my information, and to present this hypnotic circle of people, which, once a man finds himself there, … makes him, in spite of himself, grumble and complain like a slave, and abuse people even at the moment when he finds himself thinking well of them" (18–19). This seems to be a basis for all of Chekhov's last four plays, which depict a certain *group* of people who respond to each other humanly and idiosyncratically, in tough circumstances. Chekhov's themes and plots involve the *ensemble* protagonist, rather than one central character, and we understand the personalities of each of these ensemble characters by virtue of their relationships to the others in the ensemble of each play.

Chekhov uses Nature to define relationships between characters as well. In 1889, when Chekhov is twenty-nine and more established as a writer, he states,

"Nature reconciles man, that is, makes him indifferent. And in this world one must be indifferent. Only those who are unconcerned are able to see things clearly, to be just, and to work" (62). This view is evidenced overtly in *Vanya* and *Cherry Orchard*, and more obliquely in *Seagull* and *Three Sisters*.[20] We may surmise that Chekhov sees Nature as a great leveler, that none of Chekhov's characters are Chekhov "himself," that he sees honor in those who admit they "don't know" and that he despises those who would presume to proselytize to the masses. In a time when Russia was undergoing political and social upheavals, this made Chekhov an iconoclast. One of his most quoted letters (1889) claims he is "not a liberal, not a conservative, not a believer in gradual progress, not a monk, not an indifferentist. I should like to be a free artist and nothing more ... My holy of holies is the human body, health, intelligence, talent, inspiration, love and the most absolute freedom ..." (63). His plays reflect this balance, humanism and clear thinking.

Chekhov himself wrote six conditions for a successful story (he was at first a short story writer) that he sent to his elder brother Alexander in 1886:

1) the absence of long passages of a politico-socio-economic nature
2) total objectivity
3) truthful descriptions of characters and settings
4) extreme brevity
5) audacity and originality, avoid clichés at all cost
6) warmth [Breyer's translation states "compassion"] (Turkov 240)

These dictums he applied as well to his plays. Their implementation in his stories and plays drew both praise and condemnation: for example, Tolstoy hailed Chekhov's stories as "an impressionistic form of writing that was completely new ... to the whole world" while Tolstoy also thought Chekhov's writing lacked a "definite point of view" and disliked his plays (Breyer 6).[21] The "brevity" and "audacity" of

---

20 Astrov in *Vanya* appears as a conservationist—he "plants forests" and points out the degeneration of his district (Act II); the plot of *Cherry Orchard* centers around the sale of this "wonderful orchard"; the first Act of *Seagull* is set by the "lovely lake"; Tusenbach, in *Three Sisters*, bids farewell to the "maples and birches ... beautiful trees!" before he goes to his death in a duel. The atmosphere of each play is subsumed in Nature, which contributes to the "mood" of every scene.

21 Tolstoy asked "Where's the drama?!" in *Vanya* and declared "Astrov and Vanya are trashy people, loafers who avoid work ... hanging around the professor's wife is wrong and immoral" (Senelick 1981: xxxvii). Tolstoy denigrated Shakespeare, and yet he said Chekhov was worse; Tolstoy also dismissed *Seagull* as "nonsense" (Magarshack 1960: 16). Senelick calls Tolstoy's objections Puritanical, a result of his refusal to "suspend disbelief" and "embarrassment at being an audience member, a refusal to admit to the playwright's

new forms, especially in Chekhov's last plays, set him apart from both the Russian intelligentsia of his time, and the flowery romanticism of the Victorian age (*Ibid.*).

Though Chekhov is considered in a line of Russian playwrights from Pushkin, Gogol, Lermontov, and is especially compared to Ostrovsky and Turgenev, his work is distinguished from his predecessors by the mix of comic and tragic elements that emerge from the true humanity he portrays onstage. In "Russian Dramatists,"[22] Meyerhold likens Pushkin to Shakespeare and the Greeks, Gogol to the seventeenth century comedy of Molière, Lermontov to the broad Spanish tragedies of Lope de Vega, Ostrovsky as creator of Theatre of Life [Realism, we may say], and Turgenev as a seed of Chekhov, who brought musicality to the Theatre of Life (Senelick 1981: 204–5). Valency writes that Chekhov's style is born of the Realism of Ostrovsky (called the father of Russian comedy) who was among the first to explore the lives of the merchant class (1966: 35–6). By modern standards, Ostrovsky is considered melodramatic (*Ibid.*). Turgenev, on the other hand, wrote characters in *A Month in the Country* with the "enigmatic quality of people ... This is the technique of Impressionism" (45) on which Chekhov draws. "Realism," for an artist like Chekhov, is not then to be taken for stark "Naturalism," or serious tragedy. Comedy may derive from the recognizable humanity—with foibles and nobility—of the characters. As Stark Young writes:

> Chekhov is like a wise, evenly balanced doctor who takes all in his stride. He can portray the human scene without bitterness, harsh theories or sentimental indulgence. For this very reason—the fact that life is so vividly apparent and expressed in him— Chekhov should never seem to be really depressing. (Chekhov 1956: xi)

While some find a serious "Realism" in Chekhov, the Impressionist quality of describing life as the artist sees it incorporates both comedy and pathos.

Chekhov shares another stylistic technique with Flaubert: both writers believe in the absolute economy of the text. Chekhov revealed his approach when he wrote "When a man spends the least possible number of movements over *some definite action*, that is grace" (emphasis added, Chekhov, ed. Bristow 1977: 367). This demonstrates Chekhov's understanding of Action as defined in this study: it

---

manipulations" (1981: xxxvii). It seems Tolstoy was not familiar with the notion Magarshack called "indirect action," which is simply the inner Actions of the characters who do not *act* the way they *speak*. This is, however, the basis of Realism. Tolstoy's dismissals of Chekhov's plays are examples of how Chekhov was often misunderstood in his lifetime.

22 Senelick explains that this article is from a letter Meyerhold wrote to English translator Calderon (Calderon's translations of *Seagull* and *Cherry Orchard* are included in the comparisons herein) who had asked Meyerhold to recommend the most interesting Russian playwrights of the time (1981: 200).

is the actor's job to express directly the Action (both physical and psychological) at any particular moment in the playscript. The actor who can play one action completely—with no extraneous movement—has strong stage presence. In Chekhov's spare writing, all allusions, repetitions and elisions are essential—they are "economic" in the sense that they contribute directly to the rhythm, meaning and themes of the plays. Chekhov is nothing if not graceful. One may edit—or "adapt"—his plays at one's peril. Every single ellipses or repetition is part of the "iron grid" of his dramaturgy. Along with telling punctuation, the plays are replete with echoes that allude to the characters and themes throughout each play, and it is *when* in the course of a play that we hear these echoes that make up the plays' "grid-iron" structures: not a line is dispensable. We may miss plot points, "mood" or character traits if a single grace note is eliminated.

Stanislavky's first stagings of Chekhov's plays were symbiotic with Chekhov's playscripts and laid a foundation for both Chekhov's and Stanislavsky's international influences on modern theatre (Markus 464). But both Meyerhold and Chekhov felt the productions were unintentional (by Stanislavsky) indictments of "Naturalism"[23] on the stage. When confronted by a MAT actor during rehearsals of *The Seagull* (1898) who insisted Stanislavky's "additives" to the play (croaking frogs, humming dragonflies, dogs barking) made them even more "realistic," Chekhov retorted that if you cut out the nose in a portrait and stick your own real nose through the canvas it may be "realistic," but the painting is ruined (Meyerhold 1969: 30). In Stanislavsky's *My Life in Art*, he quotes Chekhov's reference to Stanislavsky's *Cherry Orchard* production:

> "What fine quiet," the chief person of my play will say, he said to someone so that I could hear him. "How wonderful! We hear no birds, no dogs, no cuckoos, no owls, no clocks, no sleigh bells, no crickets." That stone was intended for my garden (420–1).[24]

Even with the "hardship" (*Ibid.*) of directing Chekhov's last play, Stanislavsky could take a joke—however incisive—sent his way. But these two strong statements by Chekhov show how strongly he believed in his art, method and the primacy of the text.

---

23 "Naturalism" is understood as pure "kitchen sink" life depicted on the stage, with every detail presented. "Realism" is a step away from this style, where the play is meant to depict a "real world" but with representational objects and sets. Realism is considered a style in itself, not just "real life" onstage.

24 Magarshack (1960: xi) notes too that Stanislavsky, playing Gayev in *Cherry Orchard,* kept catching invisible mosquitoes onstage, which prompted Chekhov to say "he (Chekhov) would write a special play in which he would make one of the characters say that there were *no mosquitoes in the locality.*"

Author and director were often at odds, and it is generally accepted that Stanislavsky brought a heavy hand to Chekhov's works, which Chekhov insisted were comedies. While Meyerhold admired Stanislavsky as an artist, he felt the director was pushed into a Naturalism born of "Meiningenism"—the Duke of Saxe-Meiningen is credited with wielding a strong directorial hand in creating "realistic" crowd scenes and "outer form" (197). Stanislavsky was impressed with Meiningen's company (The Meiningen Players) when they came to Moscow in 1890 (196–203). Meyerhold claims it was a tragedy that a man of Stanislavsky's talent and stature "was forced year after year by the pressures of a philistinism inimical to him … [to cater] to the tastes of patrons [of restaurants] and owners of banks and coffee shops" (1969: 175). Here Meyerhold refers to the pressures and patrons of the Art Theatre. He saw Stanislavsky as a brilliant actor who played Shakespeare, Molière, Pushkin and Schiller, and did not need to kowtow to the exigencies of Naturalism—which Meyerhold felt were limiting and non-theatrical—in his use of style and choice of plays.[25]

Rather than in the "naturalistic" depictions of lakes, houses, gardens or skies in the stage sets, or sounds of passing animals and insects, Meyerhold maintains that Chekhov's "mood" lies in the *rhythm* of his language, captured by the actors (32). This rhythm demonstrated to him that it is the actor who is the principal element in the theatre (*Ibid.*). How is one to create this "rhythm" when a work is not in the original language, with different words and different word sounds? This is the challenge of presenting Chekhov in translation. The key is in the underlying Actions of the characters, and in Superobjectives arrived at in the specific production. This rhythm is also created from the implementation of stage directions, attention to punctuation, syntax, pauses, word-play, allusions, quotations and song, all of which affect the actors' choice of Actions. A discussion of these elements discovered in various translations of Chekhov's last four plays will help determine how they figure in creating stage rhythm.

Structures of Action

There are other key elements of Chekhov's dramaturgy that contribute to themes, characters, and events that shape the plots. They are the use of arrivals and departures, the unseen (but present) characters and the unseen locations beyond the

---

25 Modern theorists, teachers and directors who pit Meyerhold against Stanislavsky might read the former's "The Solitude of Stanislavky" in *Meyerhold on Theatre*, pp. 175–80. Meyerhold held Stanislavsky in esteem—as Stanislavsky held Meyerhold—till the end of his life.

scenes in the play, central actions taking place offstage, the illusion of indirect action,[26] repeated echoes of words, phrases or speeches, undercutting grandiose speeches or poses, and the resultant playing of "subtext" in the circumstances of the plays, required of the actor. These eight elements are especially important in helping to define Chekhov's ubiquitous but elusive use of "mood," and they are all related to the structures of action in the plays. As Senelick paraphrases Gorky, "Chekhov managed to bring together elements that created a new kind of drama, which heightened reality to the point at which it turned into a profoundly inspired symbol" (2005: xxvii). Chekhov's dramaturgy is an inspired—or "poetic"—realism that so imitates reality, we see ourselves in its mirror.

Chekhov weaves the elements listed above into his last four masterpieces. These elements are "structures" of the Action because they propel and help define the Super-objectives of the plays. The first structure is the use of arrivals and departures of the characters. We see this in the arrival of Arkadina and Trigorin in *Seagull*, of the Professor and Yelena in *Vanya*, of the officers in *Three Sisters* and of Ranevskaya, Anya, Charlotta and Yasha in *Cherry Orchard*. In the last three plays the action is framed by the arrival and then the departure of these characters, while in *Seagull* Arkadina and Trigorin arrive at the lake house at the start of the play, and then return for a second time at the end, but amidst different circumstances. These arrivals and departures frame the plays, giving them beginnings and endings. For example, differences in the "mood" of Ranevskaya's happy return to her beloved home at the opening of *Orchard*, as compared to the tears and regret—of some characters—at the departures from the estate in Act IV, define the movement of the play. This is true for *Seagull*, *Vanya* and *Three Sisters* as well. Each character in the ensemble responds variously to these departures, which give each one an "arc" to pursue in each play. This "framing" of the movement of the plays is significant to the actor, who discovers how his or her character changes progressively with each scene or Act.

Secondly, unseen characters people all of Chekhov's plays.[27] Notably, we hear of Nina's despotic and controlling parents across the lake in *Seagull*; Sonya's mother (Vanya's sister and the Professor's first wife), eulogized throughout *Vanya*; the Colonel Prozorov, Vershinin's wife and ubiquitous Protopopov[28] (apparently

---

26 David Magarshack writes extensively on this practice in Chekhov's last four plays, which he separates from Chekhov's previous "direct action" plays (1960: 159–73).

27 Robert E. Byrd's 1995 dissertation for Educational Theatre at NYU, "The Unseen Character in the Plays of O'Neill, Williams and Albee," notes that Chekhov was one of the first playwrights to exploit the unseen character as a dramatic device (13).

28 Harvey Pitcher notes that Stanislavsky had the idea of bringing Protopopov *onstage* in the last act of *Three Sisters* (from Soviet scholar M. N. Stroeva's observation of the director's promptbook Rezhisserskie iskaniya Stanislavskogo 1973: 120). This might be another

dallying with Andrey's wife Natasha) in *Three Sisters*; and Ranevskaya's drowned son Grisha, whose ghost haunts *Cherry Orchard*, as well as the rich "Auntie" who might send money to save the estate. We see the import of these unseen characters in the behavior of the characters that *are* onstage. The absent characters influence mood and Actions, and are endemic in the plays. They are part of the characters' pasts and subtexts.

Unseen locations of the plays are also mentioned in the dialogue or referred to in the stage directions of the plays. Examples are Arkadina's acting venues and Nina's acting jobs in the provinces of Russia in *Seagull*; Vanya's map of Africa; the sisters' past life in Moscow in *Three Sisters*—not to speak of the town that goes up in flames just outside the sisters' home; Ranevskaya's digs in Paris and Trofimov's interminable university life in *Cherry Orchard*, along with the orchard itself. There are many others.

Chekhov's stage settings are confined, yet wide open—"full of lyricism and drama" (Senelick 2005: 497)—in hinting at spaces beyond the characters' views in the "real time" of the plays. The plays hold the specific locations of the characters and their pasts or future worlds beyond. We *imagine* Nina acting on rural stages and her life in a cramped apartment with her sick child, Vanya's dreams of Africa, the sisters' house and restaurants in Moscow, and the former graveyard in Act II of *Orchard*. These invisible (or partly seen) territories are part of the broad landscape of Chekhov's physical and emotional space in the plays. And, indeed, in *Orchard* we learn that soon this landscape will disappear. Chekhov's unseen landscapes invite us to conjure them in our mind's eye, and are interwoven with the dialogue in the script of the plays; they help create Chekhov's ineffable dramaturgy. Meyerhold cites Schopenhauer to explain Chekhov's art:

> "A work of art can influence only through the imagination. Therefore it must constantly stir the imagination." But it must really stir it, not leave it inactive by trying to show everything … A work of art must only give as much as is necessary to direct our imagination on the right track, letting it have the last word. (1969: 26–7)

So, the spectator is left to discover the landscapes in the plays—and what took place in them—on his or her own, without having every detail explained, or every question answered. However, the actor must develop—through his/her

---

example of Stanislavsky's misunderstanding of Chekhov's dramaturgy. Stanislavsky's staging often, apparently, missed the subtleties of the symbolism, while putting in the trivia of "realist" details. Chekhov was so upset at Nemirovich and Stanislavsky's interpretation of *Cherry Orchard* that the playwright accused these directors of not reading his plays carefully (not even once) … (Benedetti 1991).

imagination—tangible and clear-cut events that *are* explained, in detail. These hints of spaces and happenings beyond the ones "written" in the dialogue of the scripts give actors clues to the past lives of their characters, which is mandatory for acting in Chekhov: it is the actor who manifests the *behavior* based on the "unseen" in the playscript. The actor's job is to concretize the facts of the characters' past lives in playable behavior. As Stella Adler has said:

> You have to come in with a past for your character. You have to match up with what doesn't mesh … [Chekhov] … puts so much into the past of his characters that unless the actor knows how to understand that past he can't get the present or know what's going on on the stage. Each character comes in with his former life. You can't come on and expect the stage to feed you without knowing your past. (1999: 179–80)

Thus the actor has "three-fourths more to do than Chekhov put in the plays" (182). Imagining the places and lives of characters beyond the script—but based on its facts—is the actor's task; it helps him or her to create subtext. This is the art of script analysis, in which the actor needs to be expert.

Thirdly, the central actions—or events[29]—in the plays are contained in these unseen locations and the narratives surrounding them. Past or unseen events are important because they influence actors' Actions onstage and audience response. The contrapuntal arrangement of unseen characters and places defines important events in the lives of the characters, which actors explore. For example, Chekhov doesn't mention the details of Ranevskaya's life with her Paris lover—or her past husband, for that matter—but the actor must create them and know them intimately. One imagines Yelena's previous life with the Professor in *Vanya*, which affects characters we see in the present. One imagines the fanciful "Moscow" in *Sisters*—is its beauty an illusion? Is Ranevskaya's life with her lover in Paris a romantic dream? The actor must know for sure. What will Anya do when Trofimov goes back to the university? How will Varya survive work at the Ragulins? And Gaev at the bank? Chekhov leaves the answers to the "jury" of onlookers.

Other examples of events or happenings offstage are Nina's acting career and the birth of her child—not to mention her affair with Trigorin. Sale of the cherry orchard—the key and most anticipated happening in the play—happens offstage as well. These and other events necessitate that actors bring an already-lived life onto the stage: they must construct a past and appear to have responded to it. We see Chekhov's characters not always in the throes of reacting to major life

---

29   Here, the word "actions" refers to the happenings alluded to in the playscript: Yelena had a life before the start of *Vanya*, as the sisters did in *Sisters*. The major Superobjective of each play, and the individual Actions of the characters are based on these *events* (see Glossary).

events, but in the resultant state of dealing with them. [30] Of course, this is true of all Realism, but in Chekhov's plays it is especially the inner life—reactions to events the characters know about firsthand, but we, as audience, don't—that must be portrayed.

This is largely what prompts the "illusion of indirect action" (Magarshack 1960: 159–73), the fourth element mentioned as a part of Chekhov's unique dramaturgy. Chekhov observes, "It is necessary that on the stage everything should be as complex and as simple as in life. People are having dinner, and while they're having it, their future happiness may be decided or their lives may be about to be shattered" (Magarshack 1960: 118). The characters, as we do in real life, move forward, though inside they may have been broken by events; they hide or make light of their pain; they lie, vacillate, bury feelings, but go on. In their struggles to survive, Chekhov's characters have subtexts that may belie their outward utterances; this is part of the "indirection." It is a way in which Beckett's plays resemble Chekhov's: endurance is all.

Fifthly, Chekhov's characters are established by repeated behaviors: one takes snuff (Masha in *Seagull*), another complains (Telegin) or whistles (Astrov), another sings (Chebutykin), another does magic tricks (Charlotta), or plays imaginary pool (Gaev). Many have long speeches wherein they philosophize or idealize their lives—Trigorin, Astrov, Vanya, Vershinin, Gaev, Ranevskaya, Trofimov—and then, as noted earlier, they fall down the stairs, drop their money or realize that no one is listening. Characters' avowed ideas or Actions are—often comically— undercut, a sixth element. In all these cases, there is one thing taking place on the surface—often a repeated behavior—and another going on inside: this is the character's subtext. It is part of playing Actions. Thus the elements of indirect action, repeated words or behaviors, and the resultant creation of the actor's subtext, are necessarily intertwined.

Chekhov's specificity about his characters' idiosyncrasies is what makes them universal, and symbolic. Stella Adler had an exercise in her acting classes called "From the Particular to the Universal." A simple pencil, for example—an implement of *communication* throughout history—may symbolize our very culture and existence. Its import is vast, and noble. This demonstrates the importance of *endowment* (see Glossary) of props for the actor onstage. We treat a "pencil" differently if we have explored its underlying import. What *do* Olga's student papers and writing implements represent to her, not just in one conscious moment, but

---

30 As Fergusson notes, "Chekhov selects only those incidents, those moments in his characters' lives, between their rationalized efforts, when they sense their situation and destiny most directly" (1953: 175). But the incidents *offstage* spawn these events we see portrayed onstage.

subtextually? What is a *teacher*? What is the Action "to teach"? These are character questions that inform the actor working consummately on the role. They result in practical application of universal truths onstage. Though the audience may not be party to every endowment imagined by the actor, they see the *result* of this work in the character created before them onstage.

Chekhov, like all good writers, grasped how weaving seemingly small, scattered details of everyday life into a play or fiction could point up, symbolically, the underlying conceptions of life (ed. Friedland 1966: xi). As Friedland notes, "There is no doubt that his understanding of the larger relations and implications in life and art made it possible for him to see the *true significance and relativity of the particular*. It gave him orientation in the realm of observed details, and it helped to banish from his work that gritty scattering of action and characters and situation [of those writers] who refuse to see that the *particular has value and significance only in its relations*" (*Ibid.*, emphasis added). In other words, Chekhov's dramaturgy, while *seeming* to be only an impressionistic or arbitrary smattering of real-life eccentricities of his characters, is made meaningful in the poetic juxtaposition of scenes and character traits that he sets up quite *purposefully*.

We may call these repeated traits the "leitmotifs"[31] of the characters. They echo through each play and call up themes, comment on action by interrupting or confirming, ironically underlining inconsistencies of characters, or reminding us of the "truth" when a character's idealism goes too far. Repeated words, speeches or quotations are often used as leitmotifs, and the actor must recognize them and provide their subtexts whenever they occur. A poignant example of this repetition is Nina's speech from Kostya's play ("Men and beasts, lions, eagles … etc.") in Act I of *Seagull*, repeated at the end of Act IV. The words have a different meaning when Nina recites them after she has experienced her hell out in the world, and Kostya's response to them is also altered in this final scene: the characters' subtexts have changed, though the words are the same. There are character transitions as the plays progress—with new Actions—and, as Adler points out, "always in transition there is a bottom line of agony and pain" (1999: 183). Characters respond variously to this suffering. In the final scene of Act IV, Nina brings a new understanding to her role in Kostya's strange play, and to the path her life has taken since; Kostya is, perhaps, overcome with loss.

---

31   Nick Worral, in his detailed Commentary on Frayn's translation of *The Seagull* (Chekhov 2002: xii), defines this as "a term which is derived from the music dramas of Richard Wagner but which can be used to describe any (non-musical) theme associated with a particular person, situation or sentiment and which occurs in recognizable variations throughout a dramatic work." Naum Berkovsky (Senelick 2005: 483) also comments in detail on leitmotifs throughout Chekhov's canon, as a stable element of the dramaturgy.

In Chekhov's canon, characters "laugh on top of pain" (*Ibid.*). Chekhov even directs characters in his scripts to say words with "laughter through tears." He states this doesn't mean they are crybabies; he meant his last plays (except for *Sisters*, which he labeled a "Drama in Four Acts") to be comedies. He explained:

> … It is Alexeyev [Stanislavsky] who has made such cry-babies of my characters. I wanted something else. I wanted to tell people honestly: "Look at yourselves. See how badly you live and how dreary you are!" The main thing is that people should understand this. When they do, they will surely create a new and better life for themselves. I will not live to see it, but I know it will be entirely different, not like what we have now. And so long as it does not exist, I will continue to tell people: "See how badly you live, how dreary you are!" What is there in this to cry about? (Magarshack 1960: 14)

Here we see one of the few explanations Chekhov gives of his own underlying moral stance in his plays. Though the message is a serious one, it is Chekhov's use of irony and his clear depiction of characters saying one thing and doing another that brings the comedy to his canon. His characters who philosophize in long speeches (Vershinin and Trofimov, as mentioned) are likely to eat their words (or fall down the stairs!) in the next moment or next scene. These moments are often "non-verbal" comic comments on the Action, replete with subtext. As translator/critic Stark Young observes, "In Chekhov, the thought is not so often in one speech only; it is in the combination of speeches" and "there is a deceptive economy in every speech or emotional reference or transition" (Chekhov 1956: 11). The actor and the director must choreograph the subtle movement of each aria—and whole scenes—so as to portray the irony and lack of self-awareness. We will see examples of how this may be approached in Chapters VI–IX on the plays.

Biography and Dramaturgy

While it is not necessary to know Chekhov's biography to understand or act in his plays, it is helpful to know significant events in his short life that could well have affected his work.[32] Chekhov was born in 1860, the year the serfs were emancipated in Russia. He was the grandson of a serf, and beaten frequently as a child, by his father. He helped support himself, from the age of sixteen, when he was left alone in Taganrog while his parents and brothers and sister moved to Moscow.

---

32 Translator Frayn insists that it is Chekhov's "absence" and "detachment" from his characters that helps us understand his plays (Chekhov 1988: xiv). Chekhov does not take the side of any single character.

Anton eventually moved to Moscow too, and earned a medical degree, while he wrote funny short stories. He honed his writing skills by quickly producing parodies and vaudevilles, while the money he earned supported him and his family. Chekhov eventually earned the Pushkin Award for writing, and then gave it up when his friend Gorky's own award was reneged. As a doctor, Chekhov traveled to the far-off Sakhalin penal colony and remained there for six months to report on the horrible conditions. He returned to Moscow, and later lived in Yalta, writing plays for Stanislavsky, Nemirovich-Danchenko and the Moscow Art Theatre. He finally married actress Olga Knipper, had friendships with playwright Maxim Gorky, Leo Tolstoy, Impressionist painter Isaak Levitan, Vsevolod Meyerhold and the other MAT actors, as well as a wealth of artists, writers and critics of his time. He contracted tuberculosis and died at the young age of forty-four (1904). Chekhov was, by all accounts, modest to a fault, funny, reserved and extremely gracious, a lover of nature and women. He had strong social views, but did not proselytize. He almost single-handedly changed the thrust of modern theatre.

It is acknowledged that Chekhov was not a religious man in the traditional sense—it may have been beaten out of him by his father, who coerced all four brothers' incessant practice for the church choir—yet he retained a fondness for "the force of the Gospel spirit" and the liturgy (P. Callow 243). Chekhov believed that it was his study and experience as a doctor that engendered his feeling for objectivity and powers of observation (ed. Friedland 1966: 36). Always self-effacing, Chekhov revealing wrote:

> Write a story on how a young man, the son of a serf, a former shopkeeper, a chorister, a high school and university student, who was raised to respect rank, kiss the priest's hand, worship the thoughts of others, give thanks for every piece of bread, who was thrashed many times, went to school without galoshes, gave and received beatings, tortured animals, loved to eat at the home of rich relations, dissembled before God and man without the least need, solely from a sense of his own insignificance—write how that young man squeezes the slave from himself drop by drop, and how he, awakening one fine morning, senses that what flows through his veins is not a slave's blood, but that of a real human being. (Turkov 1995: 278)

Chekhov pulled himself up by his bootstraps to become what he valued: a totally free artist. Though accused of passivity and a lack of political and social commitment, he was actually free from the prejudices and formulations of many critics and writers of his time. As noted by his biographers, he was "clear, balanced and directed" and as modern as the new century (ed. Friedland 1966: xi and P. Callow 1998: 404).

With his unique use of these elements in his dramaturgy—the frame of arrivals and departures, unseen characters and locations, actions offstage, indirect action and repeated echoes in his language creating leitmotifs and subtext for his characters—Chekhov has created plays that are at once comic, poignant and "resembling sorrow only as the mist resembles the rain." Chekhov's style is practically inimitable. It is not my purpose to definitively prescribe in which "ism" Chekhov's plays may be pigeon-holed—his plays are at once Symbolist, Realist and even Naturalist or Absurd. My purpose is to apply the practical approach of the actor to the performance texts in English translations, put forward in the next four chapters. It is usually helpful to the actor to know if a scene, or the entire play, should be played with a "light" or a "dark" emphasis or style. But in Chekhov's works, it is possible that a multiplicity of modes may be applied in the same play, paying particular attention to the comic or "light" approach, as this was Chekhov's direction. This is not an obstacle for the actor, but actually a freeing process of the rehearsal period.

As an actor, it is important not to take what each character "says" as the last word on their Actions. What if Nina is tempted to return to Constantine in the final scene of *Seagull*? What if Yelena is jealous of Sonya in *Vanya*? What if Natasha is truly in love with Andrey in *Sisters*? What "if" Varya is relieved *not* to be married? And what "if" Lopakhin truly wants her very much in *Cherry Orchard*? What "if" what finally happens in the plays is *not* inevitable? Playing the scenes these ways— against the "result," as practitioners say—creates suspense and the idea that feelings of loss may *not* be akin to pain, but are more complicated than that. As is often said in the theatre, "If you're playing a miser, find his generous moment." If you're playing Arkadina, who's "cheap," or Ranevskaya, who can't hold on to a nickel, find those moments when they *are* (or approach being) generous or reasonable, and you have a real-to-life character. This is the paradox of true human behavior, and a key to acting in plays with a tragicomic "nastroenie." This is the irony of life. This is Chekhov.

References

Adler, Stella. *The Art of Acting*. Ed. Howard Kissel. New York: Applause Books, 2000.
———. *On Ibsen, Strindberg and Chekhov*. Ed. Barry Paris. New York: Alfred A. Knopf, 1999.
———. Acting Class, with Ron Burrus, Pan-Andreas Theatre, Santa Monica, CA, 1981–84.
Albee, Edward. Interview with the author. Lincoln Center, New York City, December 7, 2005.
Atlas, James. "The Prose of Samuel Beckett, Notes from the Terminal Ward," *Poetry Nation*, No. 2, 1974, 106–117. www.poetrymagazine.org.uk
Benedetti, Jean, Ed. *The Moscow Art Theatre Letters*. New York: Routledge, 1991.
Bentley, Eric. *The Life of the Drama*. New York: Atheneum, 1967.
———. *The Playwright as Thinker*. New York: Harcourt, Brace and World, 1967.
———. *The Theatre of Commitment*. New York: Atheneum, 1967.
———. *The Theory of the Modern Stage*. New York: Penguin Books, 1968.
———. *Thinking About the Playwright*. Evanston, IL: Northwestern University Press, 1987.
———. *What is Theatre?* New York: Hill and Wang, 2000.

Breyer, Christopher. "The Chekhovian Six, Principles of Writing from an Artist Outside His Time," *Performances Magazine*, Center Theatre Group, 39th Season, February 2–March 19, 2006. www.taperahmanson.com/download/CherryOrchardProgram.pdf.

Byrd, Jr., Robert E. "The Unseen Character in Selected Plays of Eugene O'Neill, Tennessee Williams and Edward Albee." Dissertation, New York University, 1995.

Callow, Philip. *Chekhov: The Hidden Ground.* Chicago: Ivan R. Dee, 1998.

Chekhov, Anton. *Anton Chekhov's Plays.* Trans. and ed. Eugene Bristow. New York: W. W. Norton & Co., 1977.

———. *Best Plays by Chekhov.* Trans. Stark Young. New York: The Modern Library, 1956.

———. *Chekhov Plays.* Trans. Michael Frayn. London: Methuen, 1988.

———. *Letters on the Short Story, The Drama and Other Literary Topics.* Ed. Louis S. Friedland. New York: Dover Publications, 1966.

———. *The Seagull.* Trans. Michael Frayn. Intro. Nick Worral. London: Methuen Drama, 2002.

———. *Three Sisters.* Acting Version. Clifford Odets. Unpublished manuscript from Phoebe Brand Carnovsky, The Group Theatre, New York City, c. 1939.

———. *Two Plays by Tchekhov.* Trans. George Calderon. New York: Mitchell Kennerley, 1912.

Cocteau, Jean. Preface, *Les Mariés de la Tour Eiffel.* Paris: Editions Flammarion, 1995. See also https://www.poetryfoundation.org/poets/jean-cocteau.

Fergusson, Francis. *The Human Image in Dramatic Literature.* Glouscester, MA: Peter Smith, 1969.

———. *The Idea of a Theatre.* Garden City, NY: Doubleday Anchor Books, 1953.

Flaubert, Gustave and Georges Sand. *Flaubert-Sand, the Correspondence.* Trans. and Eds. Francis Steegmuller and Barbara Bray. New York: Alfred A. Knopf, 1993.

Gottlieb, Vera & Paul Allain, eds. *The Cambridge Companion to Chekhov.* Cambridge University Press, 2000.

Hayman, Ronald. *How to Read a Play.* New York: Grove Press, 1977.

Hodgson, John and Ernest Richards. *Improvisation,* Methuen, London, 1966.

Kenner, Hugh. "The Flaubertian Tradition," Class at UC Santa Barbara, English Department, 1973.

Koteliansky, S. S., Trans. and ed. *Anton Tchekhov.* New York: Haskell House Publishers, 1974.

Lanskoy, Yevgeny. Interviews with author, 1999. Classes, "Structures of Action," at the Adler Conservatory, 1986–89.

Longfellow, Henry Wadsworth, *The Complete Works of Henry Wadsworth Longfellow,* "The Day is Done," Massachusetts: Ticknor & Fields, 1866.

Magarshack, David. *Chekhov the Dramatist.* New York: Hill and Wang, 1960.

Markus, Tom. *How to Read a Play.* Dubuque, IA: Kendall/Hunt Publishing Company, 1996.

Merkel, Matt S. "Reinventing Chekhov: The Journey from Realism to Impressionism in Selected Plays of Anton Chekhov." Master's Thesis, Regent University, 1998.

Meyerhold, Vsevolod. "The 225th Studio," *Tulane Drama Review,* 9:22–23, Fall, 1964.

———. *Meyerhold on Theatre.* Trans./Ed. Edward Braun. London: Menthuen & Company Ltd., 1969.

Pitcher, Harvey. *The Chekhov Play.* Berkeley: University of California Press, 1985.

Senelick, Laurence, ed. and trans. *Russian Dramatic Theory from Pushkin to the Symbolists*. Austin: University of Texan Press, 1981.

————. *The Chekhov Theatre*. Cambridge: Cambridge University Press, 1997, 2005.

Shaw, George Bernard. *Bernard Shaw: Selected Plays*. New York: Dodd, Mead & Company, 1970.

Sontag, Susan. *Against Interpretation and Other Essays*. New York: Picador USA, 2001.

Stanislavsky, Konstantin. *My Life in Art*. Trans. J. J. Robbins/Elizabeth Reynolds Hapgood. New York: Theatre Arts Books, 1948.

Taganrog Local Government, Ulitsa Petrovskaya 73, 347900, Tagnrog, Rostov Oblast taganrogcity.com

Turgenev, Ivan. *A Month in the Country*. Trans. Richard Nelson. Williamstown Theatre Festival, Massachusetts, August, 2012: "Radical Plans by Director/Translator Richard Nelson," by Charles Giuliano, July 18, 2012. https://www.berkshirefinearts.com/07-18-2012 a-day-in-the-country.htm.

————. *A Month in the Country*. Trans. John Christopher Jones. Classic Stage Company. Director, Erica Schmidt, February 2015.

Turkov, Andrei, Compiler. *Anton Chekhov and His Times*. Trans. Cynthia Carlile and Sharon McKee. Fayetteville: University of Arkansas Press, 1995.

Valency, Maurice. *The Breaking String*. New York: Schoken Books, 1983.

CHAPTER SIX

The Seagull

The Seagull is a play of infinite tenderness and compassionate understanding. That is why it is humorous as well as touching. Contrary to the common cliché, it is also full of action: no moment passes which is not dense with the subtlest interplay of human conflict …

We do not live in czarist Russia; still Chekhov is of our time. Our younger generation is not a hopeful one. For all their aches, Chekhov's people remember, yearn for, desire and dream a good life. The key to their natures is the cry, "I want to live." This informs their sorrow with a pulsing substance of experience and meaning which enriches it beyond the muscular straining and jumpiness of our young people, unconscious of any pleasure in present difficulty because they have no vision or belief in a future to which they can look forward.

—HAROLD CLURMAN, *LIES LIKE TRUTH* (131–2)

Clurman's statement was written in 1958, but is no less true today. He describes the underlying Superobjective of all Chekhov's characters: they want not only to live, but to live well, to accomplish their dreams. Chekhov's *Seagull* is his youngest play, shot through with the inflexible certainty of the young that the older generation doesn't understand them (and vice-versa), and the overwhelming "tons of love" Chekhov himself noted (Ed. Friedland 1966: 145). The play is alluring for high school or college students as well as adults, and is a captivating entrée not only into Chekhov's world, but to reading and performing dramatic literature. Chekhov's plays teach us that Action is *not* what we say, but what is beneath our

Figure 6.1: *The Seagull.* Dianne Wiest as Arkadina and Alan Cumming as Trigorin, at the Classic Stage Company, NYC, 2008. Arkadina and Trigorin are in love. Director: Viacheslav "Slava" Dolgatchev. Translator: Paul Schmidt. Photo Credit: Joan Marcus.

words and physical actions. *Seagull* is considered the first of Chekhov's master-works that typify this realist approach.

Clurman is insightful about the "action" replete in Chekhov's play. From the first moments of this "comedy," we see struggles between characters: Medvedenko pesters Masha about the necessity of money; she claims happiness "has nothing to do with money." Konstantin (Kostya) Treplev struggles to put on his new play; his mother calls it "not new forms, just old-fashioned nastiness" (Tr. Schmidt, Chekhov 1997c 120). Squabbles, fights, and tensions erupt from the first to last moments of the play, the results of conflicts over new forms of art versus old, the importance or insignificance of money and one's work, and the passions of unrequited love. The unrequited love stories involve Kostya, the young writer, in love with Nina, the young actress, who falls for the older Trigorin, a famous writer who is the paramour of Kostya's mother, famous actress Arkadina. Other entanglements concern Polina, in love with Dr. Dorn, whose passion has cooled; Dorn was once, it is hinted, Arkadina's lover. Polina is wife to cantankerous estate manager, Shamrayev. Masha is their daughter, but there is an unspoken question as to whether Shamrayev (or Dorn) is her true father. Masha's in love with Kostya, and schoolteacher Medvedenko with Masha, which brings us to Act I.

These love triangles persist through the play, but it is the passion for art—Kostya's and Trigorin's for writing and Nina's and Arkadina's for acting—that is most at issue, and defines the Superobjective, or overall Action of the play. The resulting jealousies—Kostya toward Trigorin, Arkadina towards Nina, and Polina toward any woman who comes in contact with Dorn—help create the tragicomedy throughout the piece. The claim that "nothing happens in Chekhov's plays"[1] is fundamentally inaccurate when applied to *Seagull*. Nina has her affair with Trigorin, Kostya becomes a professional writer, Masha marries Medvedenko and Trigorin returns to Arkadina: these events all happen offstage. It is the way these happenings are presented—with the elements cited in Chapter V (Structures of Action)—that gives Chekhov's dramaturgy its unique style.

One important idea to keep in mind when exploring Chekhov's canon is that his "plays of indirect action," as Magarshack calls the four masterpieces (1960: 187), are a reaction to the Romanticism, melodrama and presentational acting of the 19th century that preceded the establishment of the Moscow Art Theatre. Russia was late in developing its own style of drama, and took much from the French, as did Europe in general.[2] The tenets of the "well-made play" influenced

---

1   David Magarshack recounts how none other than Tolstoy, with other Russian critics and producers, bemoaned what they saw as a lack of action and substance in Chekhov's last plays, along with English critics, led by Desmond MacCarthy in the early 20th century (1960: 16–19). Magarshack's entire work, *Chekhov the Dramatist*, is devoted to explaining the difference between Chekhov's early plays of "direct action," where the "main dramatic action takes place onstage in full view of the audience" and Chekhov's last four plays of "indirect-action" where "the main dramatic action takes place off stage and in which the action that does take place on the stage is mainly 'inner action'" (53). The plays have been misunderstood, apparently even by director Stanislavsky (see Chapter V), from their inception.

2   Historian Prince D. S. Mirsky writes "Russian drama is entirely an importation from the West" (1926: 36). While he credits virtuoso comic actor Mikhail Schepkin (1787–1863) with bringing realism to the Russian stage (see also Senelick's *Serf Actor*, 1984), he writes: "The comic repertory … was almost entirely dominated by the vaudeville … [T]he genre was eminently unoriginal and French. It was full of a gay and lighthearted *Scribisme* … full of action and ample opportunity [for] the actors to individualize their parts"

Ibsen and many playwrights of the period (and still run rampant in film, TV and theatre today), though he and Chekhov used them to different ends. French playwright Eugène Scribe (1791–1861) developed this "pièce bien faite" based on the idea that "theatre should be a place of entertainment and not a college classroom" (Stanton vii). The well-made play depends on a plot dominated by action. It involved such features as a secret from the past hidden from characters but revealed to the audience—the *late point of attack*—in Act I; continued suspense created by exposition and ups and downs of the "hero"; a peripetia or "reversal of fortune" ("scène à faire" or obligatory scene) where the secrets are disclosed to the opposing side; and a logical and credible *dénouement* (xiv–xv).[3] Ibsen took much from Scribe in constructing his "problem plays," while Chekhov took more from the looser structures of Gogol and the everyday life of peasants, merchants and professionals propounded by Ostrovsky (Chekhov, 1977b: vii–viii). However, we see how Chekhov pokes fun at the well-made play in his use of "soliloquies, emotional duets [and] ironic curtain lines" (*Ibid.*) throughout his canon.

In each of the last four plays, I approach an explication of the playscript—a *script analysis*—based on comparisons of Chekhov's stage directions, word choices, meaning, sound and rhythm, syntax, punctuation, ellipses and pauses, and allusions/quotations/songs, and their import on Actions, in various translations. This close textual analysis is similar to a line-by-line explication of a poem, suggested by Corrigan[4] and John Crowe Ransome's and T. S. Eliot's idea of *New Criticism*, which propounds the view that one may understand a work by exploring the text alone, rather than including an historical or biographical background of the author or other interpretive aspects of criticism (Fergusson 1953: 21).[5] In this study, selected scenes will demonstrate the density of Chekhov's theatre poetry, and show how differences in translations mold the actor's approach.

Critic J. L. Styan notes that the usual methods of dramatic criticism—plot, character, theme—are inadequate to realize the texture of Chekhov's plays (1971:

(146–7). Mirsky also notes the popularity of Shakespeare in the mid-19th century, especially *Hamlet*. Chekhov was first a vaudeville writer himself, and a fan of Shakespeare. He quotes *Hamlet* repeatedly in *Seagull*. Kostya and Arkadina's relationship is frequently compared to that of Hamlet and Queen Gertrude.

3   Popular films, television series' and sit-coms use the well-made play format, which is derived from Molière and the *commedia dell'arte*, and, earlier, the Roman comedies of Plautus and Terence.

4   "To analyze these plays properly one would have to begin with the opening speech, and, making cross-relationships, work through the entire play … [as in] a critical reading of a poem" (Chekhov 1962: xxiii).

5   See also the discussion of Sontag's "Against Interpretation" in Chapter I, Definitions.

1). In the dialogue of a playscript, we must pay particular attention to the "histri-onic basis of language itself," as the language used is based on underlying Actions of the characters, and the overall Superobjective of the play as an entirety (Fergus-son 1953: 21–2). J. L. Styan emphasizes how "tracing Chekhov through his details and seeing how all the elements of his craft work together is an attempt to plumb the depth of his subtext" (1971: 1). Indeed, Martin Esslin has also expounded on Chekhov's use of subtext in his dialogue as "the greatest and most discernible impact" on modern theatre, attributing the use of "pauses, silences, and subterra-nean currents of meaning" to the work of Pinter, Mamet and English playwright Edward Bond (*Saved*), all stemming from Chekhov (Clyman 144–5).[6] This idea of subtext—Action underneath the words—put forward in previous chapters, will be explored in detail in these four chapters on the plays. The key to script analysis is to view the playscript as the practitioner (actor, director and designer) does, with an eye to the actual performance of the play.

Title and Character Names

In approaching a script, it is always best to start at the very beginning. Even the English title of the play itself—*The Seagull*—is at issue for some translators who know Russian. In notes to his translation, Senelick explains that the Russian word "Chaika" (the Russian title) means, simply, "gull" (*Anton Chekhov's Selected Plays* 2005: 135). It is incongruous that a "*sea* gull" would fly over an inland lake, like that in Chekhov's play. In French, the title of the play, *La Mouette*, is simply "the gull." However, Senelick, as in all other translations except Williams' *The Notebook of Trigorin* (an admitted "adaptation"), keeps the well-known title, while referring to just "gull" in the text of his translation. Russian has no definite articles, so the use of these in English translations are problematic, and they do affect Nina's final speech, where she calls herself "gull" or "the seagull" or "a seagull."

Moreover, Chekhov has subtitled his play "A Comedy in Four Acts." Many of the 38 translations I discovered (there are many others) *do* state "A Comedy" in the subtitle, but others print only *The Seagull*. Alex Szogyi, who claims to be the

---

6   See Peter G. Christensen's essay "Edward Bond as a Chekovian Playwright" in *Chekhov Then and Now*, ed. J. Douglas Clayton, New York: Peter Lang, 1997. Esslin too writes "The discovery that stage dialogue is a strategem to cover nakedness … is not Pinter's but was first made by Chekhov … [who knew] it is the pause which shows to the audience that the real preoccupation of the characters, the unspoken subtext, is going on beneath the surface, but … is unable to come into the open" (*Pinter* 46–7).

first American to translate Chekhov's last four plays (1968: v),[7] is the only one to label his translation of *The Seagull* a "Drama in Four Acts,"[8] while acknowledging that Chekhov himself called the play a comedy (57–63). He maintains the tone of the play is "ambiguous" yet insists the scenes in Act I, including eruptions over Konstantine's play, and in Act III, where first Arkadina pleads with Kostya not to kill himself, and then with Trigorin not to leave her, "are certainly serious scenes" (62). This is debatable. Mike Nichols' 2001 Public Theatre production in Central Park certainly underscored the comedy in these scenes: the audience howled at Nina's (Natalie Portman) studied recitation of Kostya's play—replete with strange pauses at all the repetitions—and Meryl Streep, who, as Arkadina, physically slams Kevin Kline (Trigorin) to the floor and jumps on top of him (Central Park, Summer, 2001). Though both comedy and pathos emerged throughout this production of the play, there was no loss of the "balance" Szogyi fears (*Ibid.*). He states, "Unwieldy, of many moods and many three-dimensional characters, *The Sea Gull* is a difficult, emotion-charged, exuberant, brilliantly felt work of art" (63). So, the need to challenge Chekhov's own designation of his play is unnecessary. For the actor, it is in the playing that one discovers the form and tone of particular scenes. It is helpful to note, in first reading the play, that Chekhov titled *The Seagull* a comedy.

Senelick helpfully describes associations of Chekhov's character names in footnotes to his translations, as does Bristow.[9] Bristow shows how Chekhov selected names in terms of characters' "bent or disposition." This has been a theatrical tradition since Greek and Roman drama (2). For example, Nina *Zarechnaya* means "across or beyond the river," referring to Nina's home across the lake, and her image as a water sprite, while Treplyov (a family name) incorporates the words *trepat*, meaning "to be disorganized or feverish," *trepach*, "a chatterbox" and *trepetat*, "to palpitate" (Senelick 2005: 135). Treplyov's first name, Konstantin (affectionately "Kostya"), contrarily, comes from a Latin name meaning "unwavering or firm" (3). So, Nina (variant of the Hebrew "Hannah," or "full of grace") is a graceful young water sprite and Kostya is a strong but nervous flutterer. These are actually helpful

---

7   Yet, Corrigan (famed critic and head of Yale Drama) published translations of the plays in 1962.

8   Stanislavsky thought *Seagull* a drama, and admittedly did not understand Chekhov's designation (1924: 352). Meyerhold pointed out that Stanislavsky misunderstood the tone of the plays (1969: 29–33).

9   Notes are helpful to the non-Russian practitioner: actors are researchers by nature, wholly curious about details in the originals, as Ian McKellen (Gottlieb and Allain 2000: 121–33) and Meryl Streep (The David Letterman Show, CBS, 2006) insist. Streep explained that, as an actor, she is also a scholar. Adler claimed the same (see my Introduction).

Figure 6.2: *The Seagull.* John Christopher Jones as Sorin, at the Classic Stage Company, NYC, 2008. Sorin is Arkadina's brother, and owner of their estate by the lake. Actor Chris Jones is also the translator of this rendition of the play. Director: Viacheslav "Slava" Dolgatchev. Translator: John Christopher Jones. Photo Credit: Joan Marcus.

images to keep in mind at the characters' first entrances in the play. Name meanings have an impact on physicality.[10]

"Arkadina" is a stage name from the region "Arcadia" in ancient Greece, known for its innocent pastoral people (ironically, Arkadina hates the country), and *medved* is a bear, for Medvedenko: he certainly is persistent and concerned with the fundamentals of survival. "Sorin" could come from *sorit*, to "mess up"—Arkadina's brother is always rumpled and in need of a haircut, apparently (Senelick 2005: 135). And, of

10   This includes vocal qualities; the voice is *physical*. Also, Michael Chekhov's Psychological Gesture has physical implications.

course, the audience seems pounded by the symbolism of *The Seagull*, as in Ibsen's *Wild Duck*. However, Chekhov was not a fan of Ibsen's plays, and if *Chaika* is a nod to Ibsen's duck, it is most likely an ironical one.[11] Though, on the surface, it seems Nina especially fits the "seagull" nomenclature, it is Kostya who is destroyed (like the bird he kills and throws at Nina's feet) and Trigorin who ends up with a stuffed bird he can't recall having ordered. It is comic. But then, we hear Kostya's gunshot. The names and symbols seem at once funny and sad, and often sardonic, like the play as a whole.

Hingley, in *The Oxford Chekhov*, 1964, inconsistently changes some Russian names to their English equivalent (Yelena, for example, becomes "Helen" while Masha remains Masha). The dropping of patronymics is, today, more than faintly patronizing towards the actors and audiences, as well as confusing. Many contemporary translations—excepting adaptations like Kilroy's that supplant Chekhov to Ireland—retain the common patronymics that Chekhov has written. As translator/professor Carol Rocamora (Tisch School of the Arts, NYU) explains, "Chekhov's language is beautiful and rich in rhythm, rhyme, alliteration, and onomatopoeia, and the preservation of these qualities has been a priority" in her poetic translations (Chekhov 1996: ix).[12] She also believes that actors may master the use of patronymics, which "greatly enhances the color, musicality and 'Russianness' of the language in translation" (*Ibid.*). This approach does not patronize the actor, who is capable of learning affectionate or formal uses of patronymics—the first given and second family names of characters—so they roll off the tongue as easily as other forms of speech. In an interview with Rocamora, she told me that, in rehearsing productions of Chekhov's plays, the actors particularly appreciated hearing the *sounds* of the Russian text, which Rocamora read to them (Spring, 2005). Though the Russian may not match American words or syntax, the phrasing, lilt and tone of the Russian language could be enacted by the actor. Hearing a Russian lilt in particular scenes could indeed inform the actor's Actions.

This chapter addresses the first scene of *Seagull*, then the final scene, considered one of the most challenging in the modern theatre. Selected translations are compared

---

11   P. Henry, in his Introduction to *Chaika* (1965) states "Chekhov must have compared the modest beginnings of his own reputation as a dramatist with the tremendous prestige Ibsen was enjoying all over Europe" but "symbolism" of a dead gull was "quite alien to his nature" (29). He notes friend A. F. Koni (1896) wrote "How good it is, how true that it is not she, the Seagull, who commits suicide—as doubtless any mediocre playwright would have made her do—but the young man who lives in an abstract future and cannot understand the cause and purpose of what goes on around him" (30). The "symbolism" of the seagull embraces all characters, not only Nina.

12   Her translations are, perhaps, more literary renditions, and it is fascinating for the actor to compare her work to "adaptations" of Chekhov for sound, syntax and meaning.

with regard to Stage Directions, Actions, Word Choice, Punctuation, Pauses, Rhythm and Syntax, and how character Actions may be affected by differences in the texts. The following are examples of dissimilar translations from various time periods.

The Translations, Act I, Scene 1[13]

GEORGE CALDERON, 1912

In the park of Sorin's *estate. A broad avenue runs away from the spectators into the depths of the park towards a lake; the avenue is blocked by a rough stage knocked together for amateur theatricals, concealing the lake. Bushes to right and left. A table and chairs.*

The sun has just set. On the stage, behind the curtain, which is down, are Yakov *and other workmen; coughing and hammering.*

Enter Masha *and* Medvedenko, *returning from a walk.*

MEDVEDENKO.—Why do you always wear black?

MASHA.—   I'm in mourning for my life. I am unhappy.

MEDVEDENKO.—Why? *(Reflectively)* I don't understand … You're healthy, and though your father is not rich he is quite well off. My life is far heavier to bear than yours. I'm paid only forty-eight shillings a month, minus a deduction for the pension fund; but for all that I don't wear mourning. *(They sit.)*

MASHA.—   It isn't a question of money. Even a pauper may be happy.

MEDVEDENKO.—In theory, yes; but in point of practice, there's me and my mother, two sisters and my brother, and my salary's only forty-eight shillings a month. One must eat and drink, eh? One must have tea and sugar; one must have tobacco. There's no getting round that.

MASHA *(looking round at the stage).*— The play begins very soon.

MEDVEDENKO.—Yes. Nina Zaretchnaya is to act, and the play is by Constantine Treplef. They are in love with each other and today their spirits will unite in the effort to produce a common artistic image. But my spirit and yours have no common points of contact. I love you; I cannot sit at home for longing for you; every day I come four miles

---

13 The Reader may refer to these following translations throughout the rest of this chapter.

on foot and four miles back again and meet only with a *non possumus*[14] on your part. Naturally. I have no means; we're a big family.

Why should anyone want to marry a man who cannot even feed himself?

MASHA.— Fiddlesticks. (*Taking snuff.*) I am touched by your affection, but I cannot return it; that's all.

(*Offering him the snuff box.*) Help yourself.

MEDVEDENKO.— Not for me. (*A pause.*)

MASHA.— It's very close; we shall probably have a storm tonight. You are always either philosophizing or talking about money. You think there is no greater misfortune than poverty; but I think it is a thousand times easier to wear rags and beg for bread than ... However, you wouldn't understand.

TENNESSEE WILLIAMS, 1964—*The Notebook of Trigorin*

The play opens by the lake in a section of the park on Sorin's estate. In the foreground a makeshift stage, hurriedly put together, blocks the view. There are bushes left and right of the stage. There are a few chairs and a small table. The sun has just set.

Yakov and other workmen are on the stage behind the curtain; sounds of coughing and hammering are heard. Masha and Medvedenko enter, returning from a walk.

MEDVEDENKO: Masha, tell me, why do you always wear black? [*She is obviously inattentive to him.*] You've got no reason to be depressed. You're in good health. Your father's well-off. [*He takes her hand.*]

MASHA: Don't, please don't. I'm touched by your feeling for me, I just can't return it, that's all.

MEDVEDENKO: If I were not so wretchedly poor, twenty-three rubles a month!

MASHA: It isn't a question of money. I could love a beggar if ...

MEDVEDENKO: The beggar was Constantine. Isn't that so?

MASHA: His mother treats him as one—loves him?—Oh, yes, but love can be as cruel as hate. She will despise his play this evening and make no secret of it and she'll be

---

14 "The village pedant emerges. In Russian, Medvekenko says 'indifferentism' instead of 'ravnoduszie,' indifference. Calderon writes, 'The words are so alike in English that a literal rendering would spoil the point'" (1912: 26).

coldly polite, polite as ice to Nina, you'll see. It will be clear that she's what she believes she is, the star that's the greatest in Russia. She probably thinks she's the greatest star of the world.

MEDVEDENKO: Twenty-three rubles a month is what I get.

MASHA: I think you said that.

MEDVEDENKO: Out of that twenty-three rubles, something deducted for the pension fund.

MASHA: How you do go on about money, money, and so loudly.

MEDVEDENKO: Support a witch of a mother.

MASHA: Send her away on a broomstick.

MEDVEDENKO: Two sisters, on my hands for good since they're homely as heifers.

MASHA: Then put them in a pasture.

MEDVEDENKO: My little brother—impossible to control.

MAHSA: Semyon, I think that boy would spit in the eye of the infant Jesus.

MEDVEDENKO: That he would. [*He sighs deeply.*] Still, people have to eat and drink.

MASHA: Eat, no, drink, yes. Look, you poor stupid man, you've got this appalling family on your hands, and you want me with them too? This very curious proposal of yours would not be wise to accept, sorry, but—no, Semyon.

MEDVEDENKO: Four miles here, four miles back!—And nothing but rejection from you ever. Oh, I—
[*Constantine steps out before the curtain: Masha involuntarily rises from the bench.*]

THOMAS KILROY, 1981

A lawn before the Desmond house in the West of Ireland. There is a view of a lake in the distance, between the trees. A simple wooden platform has been erected, complete with a front curtain, now closed. A sound of men working may be heard from behind the curtain.

JAMES and MARY stroll on from beneath the trees on a bright, dry summer's evening.

JAMES: And why is it you're always wearing black?

MARY: It's because I'm so sad. Black is for sadness. (*She sighs heavily.*)

JAMES: But why so? I can't make head nor tail of it. You have the full of your health. You may not be rich, I know, but at least your father is agent on the estate. Ye can't be that badly off. What more do you want? Look at me! I have to live on two pounds a week and I'm not complaining ... And that's before deductions!

MARY: Money isn't everything. Even the tinkers out on the road can be happy.

JAMES: That may all be very well if you read about it in a book. The real thing is different, I'm telling you now. I can't abide the way the well-off like to pretend they know what it is to be poor. They don't. They can't. And that's an end to it. I have to keep the mother, the sisters, the brothers and myself. There's sixpence a pound, now, duty on the tea. I'm telling you, ya don't know the half of it ...

MARY (*towards the platform*): We'll soon have the play starting.

JAMES: Ay. Lily is going to be up there speaking the poetry that Constantine has written for her. It must be marvelous for both of them. To be in love, to share their love like that. Not like the two of us. Every day of the week I walk four miles over here and four miles home again. And for what, I ask you? Nothing but cold stares. I know I'm only a schoolmaster. Who'd want to marry me anyway?

MARY: For the lord's sake, don't be an ass! (*Taking snuff.*) Of course I find your feelings for me very ah—moving. It's only that I can't feel the same way for you. That's all. (*Offering the box.*) Here! Want some snuff?

JAMES: No thanks. I feel awful this minute, so I do.

MARY: Isn't it very close all of a sudden! As if twas' going to ... It'll probably spill out of the heavens by the night. (*Pause.*) Anyway, all you ever do is lecture at me and talk about money. It's awful boring. You think there's nothing as bad as being poor. That's only because of your background. If you only knew! It's ten times easier to stand and beg on a Fair Day than to ... But, sure, what's the point in talking to you about it? You haven't a notion of what I'm ...

MICHAEL BARAKIVA, 2004

A playground outdoors in Sorin's estate. A makeshift stage has been erected, equipped with a little curtain. The sun has just set. Yakov, a servant, is hammering the last few nails into the stage. Luka, the Cook, is putting the last few stitches into the curtain. Masha and Medvedenko enter.

MEDVEDENKO:

Why do you always wear black?

MASHA:

I'm in mourning for my life. I'm unhappy.

MEDVEDENKO:

How come? (*Not understanding.*) I don't understand. You're healthy, your father's not rich but he does well for himself. My life is much worse than yours. I take home twenty-three rubles a month, and that's before deductions and taxes, but you don't see me moping and wearing black.

MASHA:

It has nothing to do with money. You can be poor and be happy.

MEDVEDENKO:

Theoretically that's possible, but I think you'd find it difficult in actuality. Look at me, for example: I have to support my mother, my two sisters, and my little brother. All we have to live on is my twenty-three rubles a month, and that's before deductions and taxes. Do you know how little that leaves for the basic necessities, not to mention sugar, tea and tobacco? It's impossible!

MASHA (*Looking at the stage*):

The play's going to start any minute now.

MEDVEDENKO:

Tonight, we will see Nina Zarechnaya in a play written for her by Konstantin Gavrilovich. They're in love. Tonight, we will witness their souls merge on the stage to create one glorious piece of art. But there's no place for my soul and your soul to meet. I love you! I love you so much I can't stay away from you. I walk five miles here and five miles back every day just to be around you, and all I get is apathy. I guess it makes sense. I'm not independently wealthy and I have the rest of my family to support. Who'd want to marry a man who couldn't take care of you?

MASHA:

It has nothing to do with that. (*Takes a pinch of snuff.*) I know how much you love me. It's touching. I just don't love you back. At all. In the least. That's all.
(*Offers him some snuff.*)
Want some?

MEDVEDENKO:

No, thank you.
(*Pause.*)

MASHA:

It's so humid. You can tell it's going to rain. All you ever do is philosophize and talk about money. To you, there's nothing worse than being poor, but I think it would be a thousand times better to be a homeless person begging on the streets than to have to … Oh, you wouldn't understand.

EUGENE K. BRISTOW, 1977a (Stage Directions Only)

The action takes place on SORIN'S *country estate.*
Between the third and fourth acts there is an interval of two years.
Act One
Part of the park on SORIN'S *estate. A broad avenue leads from the view of the audience into the depths of the park toward a lake. A platform stage—pieced together and hastily built for a home performance—has been placed across the avenue in such a way that the lake cannot be seen. To the left and right of the platform stage is shrubbery. There are a few chairs and a small table. The sun has just set. Yakov and other workmen are on the platform stage behind the lowered stage curtain. The sounds of coughing and hammering can be heard.* MASHA *and* MEDVEDENKO, *returning from a stroll, enter from the left.* …

LAURENCE SENELICK, 2005 (First Lines Only)

… MEDVEDENKO:	How come you always wear black?
MASHA:	I'm in mourning for my life. I'm unhappy.
MEDVEDENKO:	But how come? (*Thinking about it.*) I don't get it …
	You're healthy, … [etc.]

ŠTÉPAN S. ŠIMEK, 2017 (One Speech Only)

MEDVEDENKO:

That's in theory, but in real life it looks like this: there's my mother, there are my two sisters and my little brother, but my salary's still only thirteen hundred. And what about food and drink? What about tea and sugar? And tabacco, huh? You do the math!

Stage Directions

For the actor, we learn that, often, *where* you are helps define *who* you are.[15] A character's relationship with his or her environment is key to playing any scene. And the objects on the stage set—tables and chairs, a samovar, dishes, etc.—are part of this environment. Arnold Aronson notes that, like Maeterlinck, Chekhov observed that the concrete external world depicted onstage can be a manifestation of emotional states of being: "The settings are virtual roadmaps to the psyche, and so complete is the identification of the character with the décor, that if the setting were taken away the character would cease to exist" (Gottlieb and Allain 2000: 134).[16] This is why the translation of stage directions on the page of the playscript is so important to the actor, designer and director: from these simple designations of props and set pieces come the exterior *circumstances* of the play (see Appendix A). [17] As Symbolist playwright Pierre Quillard stated "Speech creates scenery like everything else" (136). The language of the translator too—like scenery on the stage—is imperative in feeding the imagination of the practitioners who will realize the play.

Chekhov's plays always include a relationship with the natural world, which changes both physically (with the seasons) and figuratively in the course of each play. Practitioners and critics often comment on Chekhov's use of progressive (or degenerative) locales in his four plays (Senelick 2005: 133 and Rocamora, Class: 2000). This is true in *Seagull*, which begins outside on Sorin's estate in summer, and ends inside during a winter storm in the "parlor/reception room" or "drawing room" Kostya has converted into his study. *The Seagull* opens on a "park," a "lawn," a "playground" or a "farm" (tr. Schmidt, Chekhov 1997b: 1), with a lake in the background, but hidden by a "rough," or "wooden," "makeshift" stage or platform "hastily pieced together for a home performance" with (not mentioned in Calderon or Williams) a curtain blocking the view of the pervasive lake.

---

15   This is true both physically and psychologically in the "real" world as well. In Communication Studies, "Proxemics" is considered the science of space and its influence on social relationships (Trenholm 106).

16   Former Chair of Columbia University Theatre Division and writer on history and theory of set design. His article, "The Scenography of Chekhov" (Gottlieb and Allain 2000), describes a short history and application of Chekhov's stage directions, with regard to the environment and style of the last four plays.

17   Senelick observes "Chekhov ... endows [real things] with significance beyond their material status" (2005: xxxviii) and quotes Leonid Andreev: "On the stage Chekhov must be performed not only by human beings, but by drinking glasses and chairs and crickets and military overcoats and engagement rings ... [which] come across as the protagonists' thoughts and sensations disseminated throughout space" (xxxix): this is another definition of the actor's "endowment" of props defined in Appendix A.

We hear construction going on. It is sunset, and, apparently, summer. Most translations tell us it is on Sorin's estate, but we soon discover it is not his stage, it is Kostya's. Calderon notes it's the scene of an "amateur" production. The weather and scene appear idyllic. In the "well-made play" it might be a love scene or an "exposition" scene. Chekhov has something else in mind: two of the characters enter, it would seem, arguing. Contrasts between the pastoral setting, the quarrelling young couple, the sounds of construction and movement around an "amateur" structure may immediately capture our interest. Masha in black is conspicuous against the rural summer scene, a visual detail that accentuates the contrasts. Why are these two at odds in such a beautiful place? Any stage direction that does not fully describe the scene—or fills it with superfluous props or sound cues not put forth by the playwright, as Stanislavsky notably did in the Moscow Art Theatre's (MAT) first production—will inhibit the circumstances of this crucial opening moment.

For the actor reading the play, or the audience witnessing the performance, are there differences between a "makeshift stage" and one "hastily slapped together" (tr. Ehre in Chekhov 1992: 19) or "knocked together" (Calderon above) for either "family" (Ehre) or "amateur theatrical" (Calderon) or "home" (Bristow above) performances? Does it matter in some translations that there is no mention for whom the structure has been built at all? Barakiva's adaptation (his appellation) includes "Luka," not mentioned in the original cast list, sewing up the hem of the curtain. When one sees a "cook" sewing the "last few stitches" of a curtain, is it necessary to write that this is for a "family" or "amateur" performance? We *see* it happening. Is including the name of a character (Luka) not designated by the playwright acceptable? If a stage is "slapped" or "knocked" together, what does this say about the ensuing production?

Since Kostya's talent for writing is at the core of the play, the style of the stage itself, the way it's installed at this location and who is actually working on it at the top of the play is, perhaps, predictive of the success of Kostya's endeavor. Kostya's reaction to the set-up is paramount. Directors have great influence on how stage directions are interpreted. Critics have discussed how this "play within a play" and its fallout affect Kostya's ultimate shooting of himself in Act IV. May we take a slipshod assemblage of the stage as a hint as to how Kostya's play may be received? It is significant, then, to the set design and to the entire production whether terms such as "haste" and "amateur" appear in the Stage Directions, along with "new" characters.

Actions, Stage Directions and Word Choice

Before characters Enter, they have a purpose. Actors learn to "cover entrances." A covered entrance is when an actor comes into a scene with a physical or inner *action* that makes sure the entrance is "justified." For instance, Masha and Medvedenko enter in mid-conversation. She may enter first, escaping him, as he is the "follower" or chaser—perhaps she is taking a snort of snuff.[18] Perhaps he trips (he is more the intellectual schoolteacher than the coordinated strongman). Some physical action that defines their relationship would be an appropriate "cover." The job for the actor is to discover what it is they've been doing immediately *before* this first entrance, as that circumstance continues as they appear onstage. What, exactly, have they been doing? How long have they known each other? Have they taken this "stroll" before? The actor answers all questions about the characters' relationship, and brings them to the present scene. The characters have lives *before* we see them enter "stage left"; as Adler stated, they bring their pasts on with them.

Most of the translations written by writers who know Russian keep the "stage left" direction written by Chekhov (see Bristow above, Senelick, Carson, Saunders/Dwyer, Rocamora and more); others just write "enter." Why does it matter from which side of the stage (Stage Left and Right refer to the *actor's* left and right) a character enters? It is a tradition in the theatre that particular stage areas (Center, Down Center, Down Right, Down Left, Up Right, etc.) are reserved for particular "types" of scenes. If Masha and Medvekenko enter from Up Left, they are likely to "cross" Down Right.[19] This area DR ("down right") may have been reserved for "love scenes" (and Chekhov may have known this), and thus the irony of the argument between the two characters would be emphasized. Also, it is traditionally considered in directing a play that certain movements onstage (blocking) are "stronger" than others. It is hypothesized that a cross from Stage Right to Left is in keeping with how Western audiences read (Left to Right for the audience), and so generally more comfortable. A long cross from Stage Left to Right by the actors is thus even stronger, as it goes against the usual expectations of the audience. An entrance, then, from Up Left would grab the audience's attention from the set and the workers putting last minute touches on Kostya's stage. The director's choice, then, to follow the Stage Directions or not (he or she is responsible for blocking), is significant—the overall staging helps define the meaning of the play. A strong entrance (where the "focus" is) from Up Left to Down Right will help the actors answer the question: What does each character want from the other at

---

18   Mike Nichol's production in Central Park, 2001, began this way.

19   *Downstage* is considered towards the audience, *Upstage* away, as stage floors used to be "raked" (tilted up in back and down towards the audience) to allow audiences to see the characters and set more clearly.

this moment? Movement—plus desire—helps define a character's purpose (see *Action*, Appendix A).

In one lively production of *Seagull* I saw, directed by Earl Gister (former head of the Yale Drama School), Masha and Medvedenko are not "arguing" at the start of the play, but are in the midst of running or playing tag. They are both happy, and obviously used to teasing and provoking each other—good friends—and even kiss as they cavort rambunctiously throughout this opening scene. Masha does not appear "unhappy" (her line may be a joke) and we only learn later (through her behavior, rather than her words) that she is in love with Kostya. Indeed, she seems to fall in love with him before our eyes, rather than to have done so before the play begins. This interpretation of the first scene made for a refreshing start to a play that has been produced so often that many theatergoers can repeat the opening lines. Gister used the American Corrigan translation, rather than the Victorian/British Garnett version, both of which are in the public domain (no royalties).[20] Gister's inventive approach underscores how a play is about the underlying Actions of the actors, rather than surface meanings of the words. This "light" touch to the first scene, Gister feels, gives room for the production to progress from excitement and happy anticipation to the pathos of the play's ending.

Senelick's opening to the play, with Medvedenko asking *"How come ...?"* instead of *"Why ...?"* contributes to the lightness and informality of the relationship between two "would-be" lovers. Senelick explains (2005: xiii) there are three separate words for *why* in Russian, and he is careful to translate them as "how come," "what for" or "why." This is an example of how the minutiae of translation affects the actors. Another is Šimek's "You do the math!" It's playful, but certainly a very contemporary turn of phrase.

In Gister's production, Masha's Action was to tease or incite Medvedenko, while Medvedenko's could have been to get the better of her by teasing back—or he could attempt to "bring her down to reality" (and "pin her down" as a marriage partner) in repeating the facts of his own poverty, and his love for her. These are character choices that depend on the tone the director and actors mean to set. In Nichols' production (Central Park, 2001), Marcia Gay Harden, as Masha, was grouchy and annoyed from the outset—she wanted to *escape* Medvedenko—which set a comic tone that followed her throughout the play.

---

20   Interview with Director Gister at The Actor's Center, New York City, Spring, 2004.

Stage Directions

CALDERON:

MASHA (*looking round at the stage*). The play begins very soon.

WILLIAMS:

MEDVEDENKO: Masha, tell me, why do you always wear black? [*She is obviously inattentive to him.*]

KILROY:

MARY (*towards the platform*): We'll soon have the play starting.

BARAKIVA:

MASHA: (*Looking at the stage*) The play's going to start any minute now.

In any case, Masha and Medvedenko have had this type of conversation before and Masha does not pay much attention to his plaints about his family: she "looks at the stage" and (in Williams above) is "obviously inattentive" from the start of the scene. At the moment where Masha changes the subject (in all but Williams' version), ignoring Medvedenko's self-flagellation about money, and points out that "the play's going to start," she begins a new *beat* (see Appendix A) in the Action. Masha diverts Medvekenko and reveals her own desire to get on to a subject she cares about: Kostya.

In William's adaptation, he alters the construct of the scene: he writes from the *top* of the scene that Masha is already "*obviously* inattentive" to the schoolteacher, and takes out Chekhov's more subtle direction to Masha to look towards the stage later on. We know from Williams' Stage Direction that we are no longer in the world of Anton Chekhov. It is too heavy a touch in Chekhov's plays to write that the characters "obviously" do anything, especially in the two-person duets like this one that opens the play. Williams employs stichomythia—the quick back-and-forth dialogue—to engage Masha in a face-to-face confrontation with Medvedenko instead of Chekhov's more elliptical encounter that leaves us wondering what is going on in her mind, and gives the actor more creative leeway. In other words, like many translators who want to "smooth out" or "clarify"[21] Chekhov's

---

21 Senelick scolds: "Reviewers … are fond of praising a translator for making the dialogue sound 'smooth.' Imagine a French translator of Mamet … or O'Neill … noted for erratic dialogue, praised for their smoothness!" Senelick claims his own translations do not "second-guess" Chekhov's choices (2005: xiv).

dramaturgy, Williams has chosen to portray the subtext of the scene explicitly. This happens with other playwright/translators who have their own inimitable styles: Williams above, Brian Friel (*Vanya*), David Mamet (*Vanya* and *Cherry Orchard*), and Tom Stoppard (*Seagull*) all change Chekhov's dialogue, punctuation and stage directions with the result of making subtext more explicit. This removes choices for actor and director, and results in dialogue that explains or instructs the viewer unnecessarily. Chekhov's own work was more oblique.

In Williams' adaptation, we learn in an instant that Medvedenko knows *for a fact* that Masha is in love with Constantine, that Masha refuses to marry Medvedenko because his family is impossible (whereas in other translations Masha claims this is *not* the reason she can't return his love), and that, by her own admission, Masha is partial to drink. This is not what Chekhov wrote. In other translations we see Masha taking snuff and drinking on the sly, but no word of the latter is mentioned explicitly in the dialogue. Williams has these two characters wrapped up before the play has hardly begun, giving the actors less room to develop their sorrows and eccentricities. It's all quite pat. In his adaptation, characters' Actions are more melodramatic: they hit us in the face. The element of surprise is lessened. Williams' focus is not on the *ensemble protagonist* who unfolds slowly to the audience throughout the play; his focus is on the "main" characters, the artists, and especially the writers, Trigorin and Kostya (*Chekhov, the Major Plays*. Trans. Ann Dunnigan 1964: xvii). Of course this is augured by his newly chosen title itself: *The Notebook of Trigorin*. Thus there is a great difference in tone and meaning in Williams' opening Stage Directions and character Actions in comparison to other translations. These variances affect the actor directly.

Punctuation, Stage Directions and Word Choice

Chekhov's use of ellipses is at issue in any translation of his last four plays. They are often combined with Stage Directions to the actor, in parentheses. In Chekhov's Russian original (ed. P. Henry, 1965) there is a stage direction, then an ellipses after Medvedenko's second line, appearing thusly (in Calderon):

Why? (*Reflectively*) I don't understand ... You're healthy, [etc.]

In different translations, other italicized Stage Directions at this point are:

– *Reflects/ Musingly/ Musing* and *Thinking about it*[22]/ *Mulling it over/ Meditatively/ He meditates*

---

22 Both from Senelick in 1977 and then 2005. This translator has obviously thought seriously about what the character is doing at this moment, and then, over 27 years' time, changed his mind! Time and fashion, with individual intuition, change translations.

- *He thinks/ Thinking hard/ Deep in thought/ In a thoughtful mood/ Thoughtfully*
- *He ponders this/ Pondering/ Wondering/ Wonderingly/ Perplexed*
- *Not understanding/ Hesitantly*

Taken together, they almost read like a poem, progressing from *reflection* to *hesitancy*. Other translators (notably Stark Young, Pam Gems and Tom Stoppard) leave out both Stage Directions and ellipses entirely. How may these differences in designation affect the actor? Greatly. The differences in word meaning are significant.

While "reflects" and "reflectively" may produce the same Action, one who "meditates" on something or is "mulling it over" and one who's "perplexed" or "hesitant" could be in different states of mind. Is "wondering" the same as "hesitant"? For example, if I "ponder," am I necessarily "perplexed"? "Musing" is not the same as being "perplexed," in any case. One may enjoy "musing," while "perplexing" problems are no fun. And just because I "ponder," it doesn't mean I don't "understand." It may seem these differences are picayune, but this is the work of the actor—and the translator. If I am "perplexed" I may get frustrated and take out my anger on Masha. If I'm "hesitant," I may hold my feelings inside and move away. There are countless physical and psychological ramifications of the actor's choice. Stage directions affect actors' Actions.

Medvedenko's Action here is also affected by ellipses after "I don't understand …". If the sentence ends in a full stop instead, that could change the Action. The ellipses show that there is definitely something unsaid going on underneath the words at this point. A period, on the other hand, indicates a completed thought. Of course, the actor may take pauses or "hesitations" regardless of the punctuation, but Chekhov's original play—with ellipses—points to the subtext here. Is Medvedenko expecting an explanation from Masha? Is he "musing" on his own, not paying attention to her? What he wants to do here, the ellipses imply, is beyond the words spoken.

Of interest is the fact that many translations skip the ellipses in Medvedenko's speech completely. Even some Russian-speaking translators do not include them, or insert them elsewhere (Calderon, Young, Magarshack, Hingley, Cook, Szogyi, Schmidt). However, some Russian speakers inconsistently *do* put an ellipses after this line of Medvedenko's—"I haven't any money, we are a large family"—yet leave *out* the ellipses in Medvedenko's second speech after "I don't understand it" and cut the clear stage direction at the end of this speech, *They sit.* (Fen)! Szogyi, a Russian speaker too, is particularly "ellipses-happy," hotly peppering his playscript both where Chekhov does and does not use ellipses (1968: 3–4).

Non-Russian-speaking "translators" also add or subtract ellipses of their own, seemingly willy-nilly: Gems, Gill, Stoppard and Barakiva do so. Van Itallie adds his own punctuation—notably a proliferation of dashes (—!), as does Stoppard, who asserts in his Introduction that his having omitted nearly all of Chekhov's Stage Directions is "the least important fact" of his English translation (Chekhov 1997d:

viii). Ironically, while claiming to write for the *actor*, Stoppard's own punctuation curbs, pushes and/or directs the actor feverishly through Stoppard's "version" (his appellation), perhaps, even more "over-instructively" than he claims Chekhov's Stage Directions do (*Ibid.*). Proving this point, Stoppard's script, remarkably, contains something present in no other translation, adaptation or version of Chekhov's plays discovered for this study: he "brackets" words throughout the playscript that, he notes in Act I, "are unspoken."[23] If this is not meant to be "overly instructive" to the theatre practitioner, what is? One imagines the bracketed words are to be "thought" rather than uttered. In any case, Stoppard's and Mamet's efforts with punctuation and syntax are marked attempts to manipulate actors' subtext.[24] Some actors may find this helpful, or just amusing. Chekhov's original Stage Directions are gentle by comparison.

To sum up, punctuation and explicit Stage Directions *do* influence the practitioner's approach to the play, and perhaps it is punctuation—unnoticed and not compared to other versions—that is even more subversively an influence.[25] If one puts three dots after a phrase on the page—or a dash, brackets, a colon, or an exclamation point—an actor will try to *justify* it. That's their job.

Word Choice and Pauses

Of note, Stoppard rationally answers the question "What is translation for?" with "the translation is for the event" (Chekhov 1997d: viii). Of course, in the theatre, this is true. Stoppard wrote his published translation for the Peter Hall Company

---

23   For instance, in Act I:
    "Sorin: ... [it] used to put all the women off [me]."
                and
    "Konstantin: ... If we can't make it new [it's] better to have none. I love my mother, I love her very much, but what a futile life [she leads] ... (1997: 4–5)"
    It's as if the translator can't trust the actor to provide the subtext—which is the actor's job.
24   Beckett is well known for having actually sued translators who change or edit his playscripts.
25   Not only actors are interested in punctuation: its import is demonstrated dramatically in the fascinating best-selling book, *Eats, Shoots and Leaves* by Lynne Truss. If any reader doubts the strength and efficacy of punctuation—critical for the playscript—note the following familiar example from Truss' page 9:
    A woman, without her man, is nothing.
    A woman: without her, man is nothing.
    Can punctuation, then, with Stage Directions, actually ever be the "*least* important fact" of a translation?
    Ironically, in Stoppard's own play, *Invention of Love*, his character A. E. Housman quips "There is truth and falsehood in a comma" (1997). The import of punctuation in English is vast, and critical in stage translations.

at the Old Vic, and when it was performed in Central Park (2001) it was heartily changed by the performers, or director Nichols (*Ibid.*). Perhaps the "*most* important fact"—or most noticeable pitfall—of Stoppard's translation for Americans is its inescapable Britishisms: a poor person is a "pauper," Masha "goes about" in mourning and declares "it's all rot"; things are "first rate," people are "out of sorts" or "cross" or "decent fellows," and some are "keen on" something they like, or have a "pretty talent." Garnett, in 1929, is old-fashioned: Medvedenko is "wretched" and "hasn't a penny to bless himself with" and "can quite understand" Masha's indifference (3–4). Other translations, even contemporary ones, can be just as stiff. The time period in which a translation is written does not always presage this stuffiness; for Americans, it is often the *Anglicism* that does.

Ostensibly, the translator's or adaptor's choice of words—along with syntax—create the most noticeable differences in various translations. In the variant translations above, for Americans, Kilroy's Irish "version" (his appellation) may be the most outspoken. In an Introduction to Kilroy's *Seagull*, the literary manager of the Royal Court Theatre, London, where the play was first performed, explains how the literary and political achievements of both Russia and Ireland echo each other at the end of the 19th century (3–6). Beyond the synergies of Russian and Irish history, it is the lilting, poetical language of the working class and peasantry that give this version its flavor. Like other translations that attempt to wind a poetic *language* into Chekhov's play, rather than depending more on Chekhov's "poetry *of* the theatre" to create the mood, Kilroy's characters tend to speak their subtext outright.[26] James and Mary wear their hearts on their tongues.

One hears the lilt in the first words spoken, as if in mid-conversation: "And why is it you're always wearing black?" James asks. Mary answers, "It's because I'm so sad. Black is for sadness. (*She sighs heavily.*)"[27] The Stage Direction here is Kilroy's, not Chekhov's. Here's a young girl who needs to express in metaphor how she feels on the inside. When James feels, he has to comment on it too: Mary pointedly offers him some snuff—"Here! Want some snuff?"—and he replies "No thanks. *I feel awful this minute, so I do*" (emphasis added). He states his precise sentiment, as if the actor's physicality or vocal tone is not enough. The result is that the character speaks his subtext. This does not create the light touch of other translations. Perhaps James is playing for sympathy, which causes Mary

---

26   Irishman Brian Friel does the same with his *Uncle Vanya*, as discussed in Chapter VII.

27   It is fascinating, for the actor and poet, to note that in these two sentences James' question is in iambic pentameter—And why'/ is it'/you're al'/ways wear'/ing black'?—and Mary's reply is anapestic, then ends with a dactyl and a final trochee: It's be-cause'/I'm so sad'/ Black' is for/sad-' ness./ The point is that Mevedenko and Masha have markedly different rhythms, which makes sense for their characters. Helpful dicussions of scansion for actors is in *The Actor at Work* by Robert Benedetti, 1970, pp. 110–22.

to change the subject, but Kilroy does not include the "pause" after James' "No thanks" as Chekhov does; it's a different kind of moment in the Kilroy version.

This extra comment on "feeling awful" is not in the Russian script; there is simply a "Pause" written, taking up a full line of the page, and centered between empty lines both above and below the "Pause." Why is this significant? Because the reader and the actor respond to how the dialogue appears on the printed page. Some translations include Chekhov's famous pauses within the paragraph next to the *dialogue*, which makes less of them than those that take up an entire three lines. Calderon, in the first group of translations above, moves a few spaces, on the same line, and writes: (*A pause.*) Bristow does the same, in brackets, but closer to Medvedenko's line [*Pause.*] Williams has no pauses at all; Frayn (a Russian speaker) does exactly as Chekhov does, giving a full three lines to the single word "Pause." Stoppard eliminates this "Pause" altogether, and throughout; he inserts his own Stage Directions and ellipses (and he calls Chekhov "overly instructive" ... !). Barakiva follows Chekhov, as does Senelick, except the latter, like Calderon, doesn't give the "Pause" the full three-line space. Certainly, a large

Pause.

on the page gets more of the reader's attention than does the one within the paragraph (a pause). See the difference? As an actor, which "pause" would *you* take to heart? This affects Actions, movement, sound, rhythm, the stage picture (just because Chekhov writes "pause" in the dialogue, it doesn't necessarily mean no one can *move*), and actors' endowments of props used in the scene. What's on the page is critical. Actors and readers respond to spacing and "readability" of the text, as well as "playability."[28]

In this opening scene, the establishment of character traits is imperative. Medvedenko is a school teacher, and plainly pedantic. He muses on how Nina and Constantine come together in

"a common artistic image" (Calderon)
"a joint artistic creation" (Senelick)
"a unique artistic endeavor" (Schmidt)
"a single sublime artistic expression"—note the alliterative "s's" (Rocamora)
"a unified work of art," (Hingley) or
"longing to create some image both can share and true to both" (Young) with
"merging souls" (Barakiva).

---

28 When this researcher pointed out to translator/playwright Jean-Claude Van Itallie that his two translations of Seagull (1977 and 1995) appeared differently on the page, and that this might affect the actor's response, he seemed amazed, and vowed for his next edition he would point this out to his editor.

Rocamora's version rolls effectively off the tongue, as the language of an academic. Calderon and Senelick, in footnotes, note Medvedenko's awkward Russian "indifferentizm" rather than simply "indifference" when speaking of Masha's apathy:

COOK: Each day I walk four miles here and four miles back and all I get from you is **indifferentism**.

CALDERON: ... meet **only with a** *non possumus*[29] on your part.

KRAMER: ... but I am met by **nothing but pococurantism** on your part ...

WILLIAMS: And nothing but **rejection** from you ever.

KILROY: ... Nothing but **cold stares**.

BARAKIVA: ... and all I get is **apathy**.

SENELICK: ... all I ever get from you is **apatheticism**.

ROCAMORA: ... just to watch you **sit around 'in mourning'**.

HINGLEY: ... it just **doesn't mean a thing to you**.

STOPPARD: ... and you **don't care**.

Calderon, to emphasize Medvendenko's knowledge of Latin, chooses "non possumus" ("we cannot," in Webster's 979) instead of "indifference," which is the word most translators choose. Only Cook and Schmidt choose the appropriately clumsy-sounding "indifferentism," which, one may argue, is as silly in English as it is in Russian. But if Medvedenko is to appear as a learned, nerdy guy—not just someone who stupidly picks the wrong form of a familiar word—"non possumus" or "pococurantism" (Kramer/Booker) stick out. Still, few in the audience will have a clue as to their meanings. Barakiva, Saunders/Dwyer and Senelick's 1977 translation go for "apathy," then Senelick changes his 2005 translation to "apatheticism," to let us know Medvedenko is trying too hard. Stoppard goes for the direct and simple "you don't care" and Rocamora, also avoiding the word completely, writes "just to watch you sit around in mourning. Who can blame you?" Is Medvedenko trying to impress Masha with his vocabulary, or just trying to get her attention? His Action will be affected by the choice of this word—it describes how he feels Masha is treating him.

Masha's reply runs from the corny "Fiddlesticks." (Calderon) or the punctuated "Fiddlesticks!" (Young), or "Oh, fiddle." (Frayn) to the honest and simple "That's not the reason." (Schmidt), "That has nothing to do with it." (Szogyi) and finally "Ridiculous." (Heim), "Don't be silly." (Senelick), "That's not important." (Magarshack) and "Oh, nonsense!" (Garnett) which, interestingly, is how most of the translations render Masha's rebuttal. Today, "Nonsense" sounds a bit dated,

---

29 "The village pedant emerges. In Russian, Medvekenko says 'indifferentism' instead of 'ravnoduszie,' indifference. The words are so alike in English that a literal rendering would spoil the point" (Calderon 1912: 26).

affected and British. Kilroy's, again, diminishes the possibility of alternate sub-texts with "For the Lord's sake, don't be an ass!" but a look at his translation is informative for any actor who may be unclear as to what is going on between the characters. Kilroy makes clear choices, and the Irish characters *tell* us how they feel.

In the other translations, Masha's words help the actor reveal or *conceal* her state of mind. "That's not the reason" is, perhaps more honest and shows some engagement, while "Ridiculous" is a true put-down. "That's all rot" from Stoppard is impossible for Americans, as it takes us out of the play when we notice it's "Brit-ish." One translation that is appealing—because it is funny but also definitive for both Masha and Medvedenko, and gives a clear rhythm—is Barakiva's:

Masha:	"It has nothing to do with that. (*Takes a pinch of snuff.*) I know how much you love me. It's touching. I just don't love you back. At all. In the least. That's all. (*Offers him some snuff.*) Want some?
Medvedenko:	No, thank you. (*Pause.*)

And the first beat is over, with the *Pause* as the final thump—or "button"—on that beat. We notice how Punctuation—with pause and stage business—gives comic meaning to this beat.

This is what actors—and directors—look for in a *beat*. There is a clear end-ing, and, though Masha goes on with this beat (humorously, as she has just stated summarily that she does *not* love him) to complain about Medvedenko's poverty consciousness, we get exactly where they're coming from up to this point. Chek-hov's dramaturgy is clear; the characters are sharply drawn, through the words, but also through their *rhythms* (short, terse sentences), attitudes, tone, movement and interaction with the surrounding environment. Much of this may be revealed if the punctuation is observed, and the pauses and ellipses are used as opportunities for playing inner Action in Circumstances. This is especially true in Nina's final speech of the play, which will now be examined.

The Translations, Act IV, Final Scene

MAGARSHACK, 1969

NINA: Why did you say that you kissed the ground on which I'd walked? I ought to be killed. [*Leans over the table.*] Oh, I'm so tired. I want to rest, rest. [*Raises her head.*] I'm a seagull. No, that's not it. I'm an actress. Yes!

[*Hearing* ARCADINA *and* TRIGORIN *laughing, she listens for a minute, then runs to the door on left and looks through keyhole.*]

He is here too. [*Returning to Konstantin.*] Oh, well, it doesn't matter. No, he didn't believe in the theatre. He was always laughing at my dreams, and little by little I stopped believing in them myself and lost heart. Besides, I had the worries of love to cope with; jealousy, constant anxiety for my little one. I grew trivial, cheap. I acted badly. Didn't know what to do with my hands, how to stand on the stage, how to control my voice. You've no idea what it feels like to know you're acting badly. I'm a seagull. No, that's not it. Remember you shot a seagull? A man came along, saw it, and just for fun destroyed it. An idea for a short story. No, I don't mean that. [*Rubs her forehead.*] What was I saying? I was talking about the stage. I'm different now. I'm a real actress. I enjoy my acting. I revel in it. The stage intoxicates me. I feel I am peerless. But now, while I've been here, I've been walking about a lot and thinking, thinking and feeling that the powers of my mind and soul are growing stronger everyday. Now I know, now I understand, that it is our calling, whether we act on stage or write, what matters is not fame, nor glory, nor the things I use to dream of. No. What matters is knowing how to endure, knowing how to bear your cross and have faith. I have faith, and it doesn't hurt so much now. And when I think of my calling, I'm no longer afraid of life.

CARNICKE, 1996

NINA

Why do you say you kiss the ground I walk on? You should have killed me. (Leans on table.) I'm so tired! I'd like to rest … to rest! (Raises her head.) I am the seagull … Not so. I am an actress. Yes! (Having heard the laughter of Arkadina and Trigorin, she listens, then runs to the left door and looks through the keyhole.) He's here too … (Returning to Treplev.) Yes … It's nothing … Yes … He didn't believe in the theatre, he always laughed at my dreams, and little by little I also stopped believing and lost heart … And then love's anxieties, jealousy, constant fear for the little one … I became petty, insignificant, I played senselessly … I didn't know what to do with my hands, didn't know how to stand on stage, couldn't control my voice. You don't understand how it feels when you're playing badly. I am the seagull. No, not so … You remember, you shot a seagull? By chance a man comes along, sees it, and because he has nothing better to do, kills it … A subject for a short story … That's not so … (Rubs her forehead.) What was I talking about? … I was talking about the stage. Now, it's not like that … I'm a real actress, I act with pleasure, with ecstasy, I'm drunk on stage, and I feel beautiful. And now, since I've been staying here, I've been walking and walking, and thinking. I think that with every day, I'm getting my inner strength back … I know now, I understand, Kostya, that in our business—whether we act or write—the important thing is not fame, not the glitter, not what I dreamed of, but the ability to endure. To know how to bear our cross and have faith. When I have faith, it's not so painful. And when I think of my vocation, then I'm not afraid of life.

PAUL SCHMIDT, 1997b

NINA: Why do you say you kissed the ground I walked on? You should have killed me instead. *(Leans on the table)* I'm so tired! I want to rest, I just want to rest! *(Raises her head)* I'm the seagull ... No, that's not it. I'm an actress. That's it.

(From the other room we hear Arkadina and Trigorin laughing.
Nina listens for a minute, goes to the left door, and looks through the keyhole.)

He's here too. *(Crosses to Konstantin)* He is, isn't he? Well, never mind. He never believed in the theatre, he laughed at all my dreams, and little by little I stopped believing in it too. And then all the emotional stress, the jealousy; I was always afraid for the baby ... I started getting petty, depressed, my acting was emptier and emptier ... I didn't know what to do with my hands, I didn't know how to hold myself onstage, I couldn't control my voice. You don't know what that's like, to realize you're a terrible actor. I'm the seagull ... No, that's not it ... Remember that seagull you shot? A man comes along, sees her, and destroys her life because he has nothing better to do ... subject for a short story. No, that's not it ... *(Rubs her forehead)* What was I saying? Oh, yes, the theatre ... I'm not like that anymore. I'm a real actress now, I enjoy acting, I'm proud of it, the stage intoxicates me. When I'm up there I feel beautiful. And these days, being back here, walking for hours on end, thinking and thinking, I could feel my soul growing stronger day after day. And now I know, Kostya, I understand, finally, that in our business—acting, writing, it makes no difference—the main thing isn't being famous, it's not the sound of applause, it's not what I dreamed it was. All it is is the strength to keep going, no matter what happens. You have to keep on believing. I believe, and it helps. And now when I think about my vocation, I'm not afraid of life.

STOPPARD, 1997d

Nina What do you mean you kissed the ground I walked on? I don't deserve to live. I'm so tired. If only I could rest—I need rest! I'm the seagull—but I'm not really. I'm an actress. Yes. (*She hears Arkadina and Trigorin laughing.*) So he's here too ... well, it doesn't matter. He never believed in the theatre—[he] always laughed at me for my dreams of being famous ... and bit by bit I stopped believing, too, and lost heart ... there were all the other things to worry about—love, jealousy ... and always the worry about the baby. I became trivial and commonplace. My work lost all meaning. On stage I didn't know what to do with my hands or how to stand, I couldn't control my voice ... You can't know what it's like when you're up there feeling you're acting so badly. The seagull. No, that's *not* me ... You remember how you once shot that seagull? A man happened to come along and see her, and having nothing much to do, destroyed her. Idea for a short story ... Wrong story, though. What was I talking about? Yes, about acting. I'm not like that anymore. I've become a real actress.

I love acting, when I'm on stage I feel drunk on the sheer joy of it, and I feel beautiful. While I've been back here I've spent a lot of time walking and thinking—and every day I've felt my spirit getting stronger. What I've realized, Kostya, is that, with us, whether we're writers or actors, what really counts is not dreaming about fame and glory … but stamina: knowing how to keep going despite everything, and having faith in yourself—I've got faith in myself now and that's helped the pain, and when I think to myself, 'You're on the stage!', then I'm not afraid of anything life can do to me.

BARAKIVA, 2004

NINA

Why did you say you worshipped the ground I walk on? You should want to kill me! *(Leans on table.)* I'm so exhausted! I wish I could rest, just rest! *(Raises her head.)* I'm the seagull. No. I'm an actress. That's what I mean. *(Sees Trigorin's cane.)* So he's here as well. *(Goes to Konstantin.)*

Well, it doesn't matter. He didn't believe in the theatre. He laughed at my dreams, and gradually, I stopped believing in them as well. I lost heart. And then there was the constant emotional strain, the insecurities, the jealousy, always being afraid for the baby. As I became pettier and pettier, my acting got worse and worse. I didn't know how to hold my hands, I didn't know how to stand on stage, I had no control over my voice. You have no idea how torturous it is to be on stage and know you're acting terribly. I'm the seagull … No, that's not it.

Do you remember, one time you shot a seagull? "One day, by chance, a man comes along, sees her, and having nothing better to do, destroys her." Subject for a short story. No, that's not it. *(Rubs her forehead.)* What was I saying?

Oh yes, the theatre. Well, I'm not like that now. I'm a real actress. I enjoy it, I'm proud of my work. I'm intoxicated when I'm on the stage. It's when I feel most myself. Ever since I've been back here, all I've done is walk and walk and think and think. I feel my soul growing stronger day after day. And now I know, Kostya. I finally get it. What matters is our work. For an artist, it's not the fame, not the glory, not any of the other things I use to dream about, that's important. The only thing that matters is knowing how to endure, how to have the strength to keep going, regardless of what happens. I believe in what I'm doing now and that belief makes everything bearable. When I think about my work, I'm not afraid of my life.

KILROY, 1981 (A Fragment)

LILY: … I'm a seagull. That's silly. It doesn't matter. Nothing matters. *(Sound of* ISOBEL *and* ASTON *off, laughing.)* I see. I see. He's here, isn't he? Aston. He has nothing but contempt for the stage. Did you know that? The horrible thing is he made me lose faith in myself. He made me feel ridiculous. So, I was quite dreadful on stage. I didn't know what to do. My voice wobbled. My hands stuck out in all directions. I was so dreadfully worried about my baby before it — A seagull. How absurd! [...] Everything's so perfectly clear. You see, dear Constantine, being a great actress or a great writer—it doesn't really matter. What matters is being able to go on with some small dignity within oneself. That's all, really I feel that, now. I'm not afraid of being alive, any more.

GEMS, 1994 (A Fragment)

You don't know what it's like, knowing you're acting appallingly. Me—the seagull. No that's not right ... remember, you shot a seagull? A man comes by and destroys it...for idleness ... idea for a short story ...

CORRIGAN, 1962 (A Fragment)

NINA ... I dried up, my acting was very bad ... I didn't know what to do with my hands or how to stand or how to use my voice ... You can't imagine what it feels like when you know you're doing a bad job.

ROCAMORA, 1996 (A Fragment)

NINA: ... And then there were the pressures of love, the jealousy, the constant worry over my little one ... I became—I don't know—mediocre, pitiful, my acting made no sense any more ...

FRAYN, 1988 and 2002 (A Fragment)

NINA [...] He didn't believe in the theatre—he did nothing but laugh at my ambitions—and gradually I stopped believing too—I began to lose heart ... Then there were the burdens of love—the jealousy, the perpetual anxiety for my little boy ... I became a paltry thing, a nonentity—my acting lost all meaning ...

WILLIAMS, 1964—*The Notebook of Trigorin* (A Fragment)

CONSTANTINE:	Trigorin has behaved like a pig, worse, pigs are killed—he kills ... [*Trigorin's laugher is heard.*] That's him, laughing out there. Mother must be performing a tragic death scene for him. [...]
NINA:	My years of attachment to him involved a child. [*Pause.*]
CONSTANTINE:	Your child and his, where is it?
NINA:	The child of a seagull is a seagull too.
CONSTANTINE:	I don't understand, where is it?

NINA: The couple to whom I—gave it when Trigorin left me—were foreigners, Kostya. By now they've returned to the other side of the world… […] And so my child will grow up in a new world. It has a lovely name—America… […] Yes, there was pettiness, triviality, anxiety, envy, discoveries that shocked me. My performances were insipid, didn't know what to do with my—empty—hands, not how to stand on the stage, sometimes a cue would have to be repeated twice before I—responded—You can imagine what it's like to feel that you're acting abominably.

As mentioned, the final scene of *Seagull* is considered a difficult one in dramatic literature. This means that it is difficult *for the actor*, especially, as well as for the translator and the director. Why should this be so? The core of the scene is Nina's return to Sorin's estate and encounter with Kostya after dramatic events have occurred in all the characters' lives, and all offstage, between Acts III and IV.[30] Nina and Kostya have both changed. He has published his writing, and is starting to become well known, but is dissatisfied with his work. Nina, while beginning her acting career, has had a child with Trigorin, but he left her and the baby died. Trigorin has returned to Arkadina, and is playing lotto in the next room as Kostya discovers Nina outside the drawing room. In a "well-made play" Nina would return to Kostya, and finally find the love that eluded them over the past two years. Chekhov sees their relationship differently, and produces an unlikely "peripetia" or "reversal of fortune": the guy, surprisingly, does *not* get the girl. Nina will likely leave for the provinces, be pestered with attentions of the bourgeois locals, and Kostya, in the final moments of the play, takes his own life. It's challenging to justify onstage why Nina returns—and departs again—and why Kostya shoots himself. If Nina and Kostya appear crazy—she repeats she's a "seagull" and Kostya rips up his papers—then the play becomes an enigma, and unrealized. The actor's job is to find the *logic* of the characters' Actions.

Word Choice

It is helpful to note Chekhov's skillful composition in beginning Act IV with the same characters who began Act I: Masha and Medvedenko. Only now, the querulous

---

30 Most "realist" plays had *three* Acts. Chekhov's *four* Acts give a more elegiac rhythm to the plays (Harrop 2000: 208). A climax in Act III allows Act IV to portray the *outcome* of significant events.

(and comic) couple is married, with a child. (Both Masha's and Nina's off-stage babies are "unseen characters" who provoke *onstage* character Actions). Masha still chases Kostya, while Medvedenko is urging her to come home to her baby. Few characters in the play have what they want, with the possible exceptions of Trigorin and Arkadina, who seem oblivious to the others' sorrows. Nina appears to have been, literally, blown into Kostya's drawing room-cum-study (books are piled on window sills), and he is elated to see her. From the first scene of Act IV with Medvedenko and Masha, "someone" (Nina) has been heard crying on the old outdoor stage set up for Kostya's play in Act I. She has been drawn back to the lake to recall her youth, among other reasons we discover later. Kostya begs her to stay, as he hasn't the power to stop loving her, but she tells him how she has managed to endure the:

> "**whirlpool**" (Garnett, Fen, Young, Bristow, Corrigan, Dunnigan, Szogyi, Heim, Ehre, Schmidt, French, Carnicke, Carson)
> "**maelstrom**" (Saunders/Dwyer, Van Itallie, Hulick, Barakiva, Senelick 2005)
> "**whirlwind**" (Senelick 1977b)
> "**merry-go-round**" (Stoppard)
> "**vortex**" (Calderon, Rocamora)
> or being "**right in it**" (Magarshack)
> in "**the thick of it**" (Gems)
> "**caught up in it**" (Cook, Gill)
> "**launched upon the world**" (Frayn)
> in "**this hectic whirl**" (Hingley)
> or having "**fallen into the same sphere**" (Kramer)

and has decided to *go on* working as an actress out in the sticks. The most common English translation of the word above—"whirlpool"—is not necessarily the most effective. The variety of terms for what Nina and Kostya have undergone is testimony to how each translator interprets the events that have ravaged these two ingénues, and of course how Nina sees the events and artistic enterprises she and Kostya are attempting. Whether lost in a "merry-go-round" (more hopeful?) or a "vortex," their pasts (and futures) are stormy.

Action, Punctuation and Rhythm

The part of Nina's speech chosen herein for comparisons is where Nina is actually shown "caught up" in the maelstrom or merry-go-round, and attempts to convince Kostya she has—or will—come out of it tolerably well. She is plagued by the vision or image of a "seagull" that both Trigorin and Kostya have placed before her earlier in the play. Most hurtfully, Trigorin has implied she may be nothing more to him than a symbol of a shot seagull (or "gull" in Senelick), a "subject for a short story." Actually, Nina explains, in part, why she has returned to the lake: she is happy to have seen that their stage—a symbol of her childhood innocence and desire to act—was still standing, and was worried that Kostya would hate her, presumably because she ran off with Trigorin. She may, on the surface, want to make amends. She can't believe Kostya would still want her: Why would he "kiss" or "worship" the ground she walks on? Her betrayal of him, she says, should have made him want to kill her. Nina may have several Actions that operate respectively throughout the scene (an actor, it is taught, can only play one Action at a time[31]), but at the end of the speech above, she directs her comments to Kostya, and wants to convince him—or calm, assure, encourage, comfort, or enlighten him—that she, and he, as artists, may ultimately find their way.

First, the largest discrepancies between translations appear between the Williams' "free adaptation" (his terms) and all the others. Williams has changed the off-stage plot: instead of Nina's baby dying, he has her give it to an American couple (how this happens is unclear). He also takes Nina's monologues and a more knowing and outwardly jealous Kostya to construct a dialogue between them in this final scene: Kostya openly calls Trigorin a "pig" and Nina states "The child of a seagull is a seagull too." Again, the result is often melodramatic. However, as in the Irish version by Kilroy, it may be helpful for the actor to explore Williams' alternately direct and then self-consciously "poetic" version for clues to possible character Actions.

Secondly, fundamental variations in punctuation between Carnicke's translation—which follows Chekhov's punctuation exactly (*Russian Text of Chaika*)—and others, with none of Chekhov's punctuation (Magarshack, Hingley, and Barakiva) or with markedly different punctuation (Stoppard, Gems) all affect possible subtexts for the actor. For example, the rhythms—or lack thereof—in Magarshack's short, prim sentences versus the thoughtful continuances and undercurrents of hills and valleys of ellipses, commas and exclamation points in Carnicke's rendition are physically arresting when we speak them, alternately, out loud. Simply, if one reads the Magarshack version with attention to periods ending each sentence (almost the only punctuation in his text) and then reads the Carnicke version, taking a short breath (for instance) at every ellipses, one sees the difference in lilt, in the build of the monologue and in the apparent emotional content of the language. And this is only by working with the breath![32] An actor, of course, would bring

---

31 Adler and Lanskoy both asked students, with regard to Action, "What are you doing *most?*" at any one time in the play: An action is not just what you do, but what you do— psychologically, to another—*most*.

32 As a Voice and Speech teacher, I work continually with the breath, on which our utterances flow, and which fills and has vital impact on whatever we say. The breath itself is a conduit of Action.

movement, eye contact, changes in volume and purpose throughout the speech. This is not to say that one could not do so with the Magarshack; it's only that the visual inflections written into the page through ellipses and commas (by Chekhov too) makes the emotional content more evident, even at a first reading. The same is true of Barakiva's short sentences and little punctuation, though his colloquial language gives the possibility for freer or varying subtexts.

Word Choice and Syntax

One of the most pronounced (pun intended) oddities written by several translators is the grammatically correct but resultantly prissy "Why do you say that you kissed the ground *on which I walked?*" (Magarshack[33]). The first reaction of the reader or actor might be to ask "Is Nina so composed at this point as to remember her schoolgirl grammar!?" This is an example of a "literary" translation, wherein the translator may not dispense with proper English on any account, and has forgotten to write for the actor and the circumstances of the play. Nina can barely keep her train of thought coherent ("I'm the gull"), let alone the command of not-ending-sentences-with-prepositions. This syntax brings attention not to Nina or Kostya, but to the translator, the worst possible snafu. This word usage peremptorily defeats the point of the scene: Nina cannot focus on what she is pursuing— her talk ("We'll sit and talk and talk" she assures him) with Kostya—because the idea of the "gull" interrupts her. Is she thinking of grammar at this instant?

Another variant regarding word choice and syntax occurs in the moments in Nina's speech when she describes how her acting was less than brilliant. It is clear that Chekhov's own descriptions may be idiomatic, since so many different accounts of Nina's bad acting run through the translations. Nina's use of her hands, stance onstage and voice are mentioned in most translations; actors would empathize with these observations. Indeed, the irony of an actress with a pivotal role onstage speaking about how lousy her performance was could not have been lost on Chekhov. Williams' mention of missed cues is familiar and suggests Nina doesn't hear or is not paying attention to what is said to her—we note that Kostya may be thinking the same thing.

Dried up, trivial, cheap, petty, insignificant, senseless, mediocre, pitiful, depressed, empty, trivial, commonplace, pettier and pettier, emptier and emptier, and worse and worse: these are the ways Nina describes her acting tribulations

---

33 Calderon's ("ground where I had walked") Garnett's ("earth on which I walked") and Cook's ("kiss the ground I trod") are equally awkward to the contemporary ear. Cook, too, has next-to-no punctuation.

across the translations. Nina cites herself doing a bad job, being a paltry thing, as a nonentity (from Frayn, markedly echoing what Arkadina calls Kostya in the fight scene with her after his unsuccessful suicide attempt), and claims she is acting abominably, badly, doing a bad job, and reveals a Britishness (or affectation) with "appallingly," "dreadfully" and "losing all meaning." "How tortuous," too, it is to "know you're acting terribly"—the alliteration is always emphatic. For the actor, the repetitions are easier to fill: Schmidt's "emptier and emptier" makes one feel empty just saying it, and Barakiva's unique "pettier and pettier … worse and worse … tortuous and terrible" all fuel the mouth (increase articulation) and the purpose of the actor. Specific observations such as "My voice *wobbled*" and "my hands *stuck out in all directions*" are also descriptive and thus effective. It will be evident to Americans that terms like "idleness," "trivial and commonplace," "paltry" and "appallingly" are particularly British, or, at least, more stiff.

The controversy (based on translations) as to whether Nina is "a" seagull or "the" seagull is easier to navigate if one considers that Nina remembers the particular story that Trigorin was to write about her. When she says in Senelick (1977 and 2005) "I'm *a* gull," and also "*a* seagull" in Calderon, Garnett, Fen, Young, Hingley, Corrigan, Dunnigan, Szogyi, Van Itallie (in 1974 and 1995) Magarshack, Bristow, Kilroy, Ehre, Saunders/Dwyer, Kramer/Booker, Carson, Rocamora, Gill and Heim (only in 2003—he used "the" in 1992), it implies she is *crazy*. She's a *seagull!* A bird! And not a woman. If, in English, she says "I'm *the* seagull" (as she does in the remaining translations, including Carnicke, Schmidt, Stoppard and Barakiva above) she could be referring specifically to the gull in Trigorin's story—not to her metamorphosis into a bird—and her Action will be different. Is she bitter about what Trigorin has reduced her to? Is she sad he sees her only that way? Importantly for the actor, what does Nina want to *do* at this moment in the play? Does she want to *punish* Trigorin? To *damn* him? To *give in* to his designation of her as this gull in his story? Even, possibly, does she want to *make fun of him*? To sardonically *control* or *resist* him? Further, what if her speech at this point is directed to or includes Kostya? Does Nina find it (hysterically) funny that she is *the* gull that Trigorin wrote about? Does she want to *engage Kostya* in *damning* or *making fun of* Trigorin? Many choices could be explored in rehearsal, based on actors' and directors' view of Nina's Superobjective in the play. Ellipses surrounding her reference to the gull allow for inner and physical Actions that depict Nina's struggle. What's clear from texts that do include Chekhov's punctuation is that there are, possibly, several beats within this speech.

Different beats—and thus different Actions—in this speech may be inferred from the fact that there are so many more ellipses (in Chekhov's original and some of the translations) for the first two-thirds of the speech in comparison to the last third. After Nina asks "What was I saying (or talking about)?" she becomes more focused and reveals her purpose to endure, go on with some small dignity, have the strength to go on no matter what happens, to have faith and/or belief. The underlying disconnection implied by the ellipses is dissolved, and Nina is able to speak directly to Kostya without interference, one can surmise, from the seagull image. In fact, Barakiva divides Nina's speech—on the page—into three, and even four separate sections—this shows her (perhaps) chastening or accusing Kostya, attacking (or pitying?) Trigorin and then herself, next reminiscing ("Do you remember, one time you shot a seagull?") and finally returning to convince Kostya of the necessity of endurance. The way the actor divides the beats of the scene defines and releases its movement, rhythm and meaning.

Action, Stage Directions and Circles of Attention

Based on punctuation, varied word choices and erratic rhythms of this speech, Nina progresses from distraction to certainty in the space of a few minutes. Chekhov's Stage Directions give us keys to her purposes. While some translations reduce Chekhov's stage directions to *"Hears Arkadina and Trigorin laughing"* (Stoppard) or *"Sees Trigorin's cane,"* (Barakiva), Chekhov describes how Nina actually goes to the door and looks through the keyhole to see Trigorin. I would stress that the core of this scene is that Nina suspects from the beginning that Trigorin is in the house, and finally gives in to her desire to make sure he's there. Throughout this scene, Nina could be in the Third Circle of Attention (see Appendix A), with her focus on Trigorin. This construct, created by Stanislavsky, is helpful in understanding Nina's Actions and agitation.

Nina has, arguably, returned to Sorin's house on the lake to see her past lover Trigorin, with whom she was enthralled from before their first meeting, and with whom she had a child. She knows he is in the next room—or may be so—from the moment she steps onto the estate, or into the study. All her movements and inner Actions could be governed by this one physical fact: right in the next room is her lover with his old paramour, Arkadina, and Nina may not—with any propriety—confront him. Indeed, her purpose in returning to the lake may hinge on this past with Trigorin, and not as much with Kostya. This is what creates the conflict between Nina and Kostya in this scene. Her struggle is not, necessarily, with a crazy vision of herself as a "seagull," but with the notion that the man she loved—and still loves, to distraction—has considered her only as a "subject for a short story" and decidedly jilted her for the older and more famous actress, Kostya's mother Arkadina. Nina's erratic behavior in this scene is explained—and acted more *specifically*, which is what the actor aims for—if Nina's Actions are directed towards the Third Circle, where this man who dumped her is casually playing cards. While

THE SEAGULL | 173

Kostya, who loves her, is indeed right there, Nina's attention is elsewhere. In this scene Chekhov clearly illustrates his statement that "People are having dinner [or playing lotto], and while they are having it, their future happiness may be decided … or shattered" (Magarshack 1960: 118). Trigorin never knows Nina has shown up, and Arkadina doesn't find out (yet) that her son has killed himself. Chekhov leaves significant events offstage; the audience imagines the fallout.

Word Choice, Syntax and Rhythm

Finally, Nina's last words in this speech are familiar. Most translations include some rendition of "what matters is not fame, nor glory, nor the things I use to dream of … What matters is knowing how to endure, knowing how to bear your cross and have faith. I have faith, and it doesn't hurt so much now. And when I think of my calling, I'm no longer afraid of life" as Magarshack writes. But, instead of just "endurance," Schmidt, Stoppard and Barakiva choose: 1) "not *applause* … [but] the *strength* to keep going"; 2) "*stamina*" and "when I think to myself, 'You're on the stage!', then I'm not afraid of anything life can do to me"; and, 3) "knowing how to *endure*, how to have the *strength* to keep going, regardless of what happens. I believe in what I'm doing now and that *belief makes everything bearable*," respectively. The difference is not only in a new "smoothness" of the word choices for modern audiences, but the resulting change in the rhythm of the speech. "*Applause*" instead of "*glory*" or "*fame*" is clear for modern audiences, as is a "*belief*" that "*makes everything bearable*," (some alliteration is preserved) but the rhythm and alliteration of "*how* to endure … *how* to bear … and *have* faith …" is lost.[34] The final, convincing claim of Nina's that, when she thinks of acting, she's not afraid of life, is dramatically "acted out" by Nina in Stoppard's version ('You're on the stage!'), but the simplicity and grammatical balance of "when I think of my work, I'm not afraid of *life*" is gone. It may be Nina's Action in this moment to comfort or enlighten *Kostya*, whom Nina has previously ignored in favor of Trigorin. At this moment she returns to the Second Circle, and sees the man who truly loves her. She may be less inclined to call out to herself 'You're on the

---

34 Magarshack warns "Garnett misses the meaning of the seagull theme (as, indeed, do most directors and actors of the play) by the mistranslation of a single word in Nina's speech in the last act, making Nina say, 'What matters is not fame … but knowing how to be **patient**', instead of 'knowing how to **endure**'. The mistranslation of a single word may … be enough to ruin a Chekhov play by reducing one of its chief characters to a state of utter idiocy …" (*The Real Chekhov* 1972: 15) Translating "*the*" as "*a*" gull may do the same to Nina.

stage!' than to connect intimately with Kostya. In any case, Stoppard's version may require a different Action.

Actions promote physical movement: a Nina who "sees Trigorin's cane" (Barakiva), and thus *surmises* his presence, may react differently from a Nina who runs across the stage, kneels on the floor and looks through a keyhole, where she can truly see him. The boisterous lotto game in the next room is ironic in comparison to the alternately charged and poignant scene between Kostya and Nina. Chekhov arranges for Kostya and Nina to hear the others; the final scene is driven by Nina's (and Kostya's) reactions to what takes place outside their space; whether remembering the past or hearing laughter in the next room, they (or she alone) may be in the "Third Circle." Translations that alter "proxemics" may miss or deflate the "pulsing substance of experience and meaning" that "informs the sorrow" of Chekhov's characters that Clurman observes. Translations that change—or delete—elements in the text, may change the rhythm of the scenes, and even the meanings inherent in Chekhov's "iron grid" of a dramaturgy.

It is the translations of Chekhov's Stage Directions, Word Choice, Punctuation, Syntax, Pauses and Rhythms in *Seagull*, and resultant Actions chosen by the actor that skew Chekhov's play from "page to stage." Clurman believes "Chekhov triumphs because the gentleness and goodness of his soul, the wit of his understanding, the acuteness of his observation are so balanced, so loving, so unemphatically honest, probing, discreet, economical and impeccably true in taste and tone that every moment of his plays is transformed into the most penetrating poetry" (1958: 134). Translators are challenged to retain Chekhov's balance and stage poetry in English to achieve the playwright's ends. Chekhov noted that he began *Seagull* "forté" and ended it "pianissimo" (*Letters* ... Ed. Friedland 1966: 146). An effective translation must hold to this musical and poetic structure. Next, the elements above and others will be explored in Chekhov's *Uncle Vanya*.

References

Adler, Stella. *The Art of Acting*. Ed. Howard Kissel. New York: Applause Books, 2000.

———. *On Ibsen, Strindberg and Chekhov*. Ed. Barry Paris. New York: Alfred A. Knopf, 1999.

———. Scene Study/Technique/Rehearsal Classes, with Ron Burrus, Pan-Andreas Theatre, Santa Monica, CA, 1981–84 and Stella Adler Conservatory, NYC, 1986–89.

Benedetti, Robert. *The Actor at Work*. Englewood Cliffs, NJ: Prentice-Hall, 1970.

Chekhov, Anton. *Anton Chekhov, Four Plays*. Trans. David Magarshack. New York: Hill and Wang, 1969.

———. *Anton Chekhov Plays*. Trans. Peter Carson. London: Penguin Books, 2002a.

————. *Anton Chekhov Selected Works*, Trans. Kathleen Cook. Moscow: Progress Publishers, 1973.

————. *Anton Chekhov's Plays*, Trans. and ed. Eugene Bristow. New York: W. W. Norton & Co., 1977a.

————. *Anton Chekhov's Selected Plays*. Trans. and ed. Laurence Senelick. New York: W. W. Norton & Co., 2005.

————. *Best Plays by Chekhov*. Trans. Stark Young. New York: The Modern Library, 1956.

————. *Chekhov: The Essential Plays*. Trans. Michael Henry Heim. New York: Modern Library, 2003.

————. *Chekhov for the Stage*. Trans. Milton Ehre. Evanston, IL: Northwestern University Press, 1992.

————. *Chekhov, Four Plays*. Trans. Carol Rocamora. Lyme, NH: Smith and Kraus, 1996.

————. *Chekhov, The Major Plays*. Trans. Ann Dunnigan. New York: Signet Classic, Penguin Books, 1964.

————. *Chekhov, The Major Plays*. Trans. Jean-Claude Van Itallie. New York: Applause Books, 1995.

————. *Chekhov Plays*. Trans. Michael Frayn. London: Methuen, 1988.

————. *Chekhov's Major Plays*. Trans. Karl Kramer and Margaret Booker. New York: University Press of America, 1997a.

————. *Chekhov, The Russian Text of Three Plays: Uncle Vanya, The Three Sisters, The Cherry Orchard*. Cambridge: University Press, 1946.

————. *The Cherry Orchard*. Adapt. David Mamet from a literal trans. Peter Nelles. New York: Grove Press, 1985.

————. *The Cherry Orchard and the Seagull*. Trans. Laurence Senelick. Arlington Heights, IL: AHM Publishing Corporation, 1977b.

————. *Four Plays by Chekhov*. Trans. Alex Szogyi. New York: Washington Square Press, 1968.

————. *The Letters of Anton Pavlovitch Tchekhov*. Trans. Constance Garnett. New York: Benjamin Blom, 1966.

————. *Letters on the Short Story, The Drama and Other Literary Topics*, Ed. Louis S. Friedland. New York: Dover Publications, 1966.

————. *Memories of Chekhov: Accounts of the Writer from his Family Friends & Contemporaries*. Ed. and Trans. Peter Sekirin. Jefferson, NC: McFarland, 2006.

————. *Notebook of Anton Chekhov*. Trans. S. S. Kotelíansky. New York: B. W. Huebsch, 1922.

————. *The Notebook of Trigorin: A Free Adaptation of Anton Chekhov's Seagull*. Adapt. Tennessee Williams. Trans. Ann Dunnigan, Ed. Allean Hale. New York: New Directions Publishing, 1997b.

————. *The Oxford Chekhov*. Trans. Ronald Hingley. London: Oxford University Press, Vol. II, 1967, Vol. III, 1964, and Vol. IX, 1975.

————. *The Personal Papers of Anton Chekhov*. Trans. S. S. Kotelíansky. New York: Lear Publishers, 1948.

————. *Plays, Anton Chekhov*. Trans. Elisaveta, Fen. Middlesex, England: Penguin Books, Ltd., 1951, 1954.

————. *The Plays of Anton Chekhov*. Trans. Constance Garnett. New York: The Modern Library, 1929.

————. *The Plays of Anton Chekhov*. Trans. Paul Schmidt. New York: Harper Collins Publishers, 1997c.

————. *Russian text of Chaika* (Seagull) http.//public-library.ru/Chekhov.Anton/chaika.htm.

————. *The Russian Text of Three Plays: Uncle Vanya, Three Sisters, The Cherry Orchard*. Ed. P. Henry. Letchworth, Hertfordshire, England: Bradda Books Ltd, 1965.

————. *The Seagull*. Adapt. Michael Barakiva. Unpublished manuscript, 2004.

————. *The Seagull*. Trans. Sharon Marie Carnicke, University of Southern California. Unpublished manuscript, 1996.

————. *The Seagull*. Dir. Mike Nichols. New York: Central Park, 2001.

————. *The Seagull*. Trans. Michael Frayn. London: Methuen Publishing Ltd., 1986.

————. *The Seagull*. Trans. Michael Frayn. Intro. Nick Worral. London: Methuen Drama, 2002.

————. *The Seagull*. Trans. David French. Don Mills, Ontario, Canada: General Publishing Co. Limited, 1977c.

————. *The Seagull*. Version. Pam Gems. London: Nick Hern Books, 1994.

————. *The Seagull*. Version. Peter Gill. Literal Trans. Helen Molchanoff. London: Oberon Books, 2000.

————. *The Seagull*. Adapt./Version. Christopher Hampton. New York: Faber & Faber, 2007.

————. *The Seagull*. Trans. Michael Henry Heim. Woodstock, IL: The Dramatic Publishing Company, 1992.

————. *The Seagull*. Version. Thomas Kilroy. London: Menthuen London Ltd., 1981.

————. *The Seagull*. Trans. Nicholas Saunders and Frank Dwyer. Newbury, VT: Smith and Kraus, 1994.

————. *The Seagull*. Trans. and Adapt. Štépan S. Šimek. Unpublished Manuscript. 2017.

————. *The Seagull*. Version. Tom Stoppard. London: Faber and Faber Limited, 1997d.

————. *The Seagull*. Version. Jean-Claude Van Itallie. New York: Applause Books, 1974.

————. *Six Plays of Chekhov*. Version. Robert W. Corrigan. San Francisco: Rinehart Press, 1962.

————. *Two Plays by Tchekhov*. Trans. George Calderon. New York: Mitchell Kennerley, 1912.

————. *Uncle Vanya*. Version. Brian Friel. New York: Dramatists Play Service, 1998.

————. *Uncle Vanya*. Adapt. David Mamet. Literal Trans. Vlada Chernomirdik. New York: Grove Press, 1988.

Chekhov, Michael. "Chekhov on Acting: A Collection of Unpublished Materials (1919–1942)." *Tulane Drama Review*. 27:63 No. 3 (T99), Fall, 1983.

————. *Lessons for the Professional Actor*. Arr. by Deirdre Hurst du Prey. New York: Performing Arts Journal Publications, 1985.

————. *On The Technique of Acting*. Ed. Mel Gordon. New York: Harper Collins Publishers, 1991.

————. *To The Actor*. New York: Harper & Row, 1953.

Clayton, J. Douglas, Ed. *Chekhov Then and Now*. New York: Peter Lang, 1997.

Clayton, J. Douglas and Yana Merzon. *Adapting Chekhov: the Text and Its Mutations*. New York: Routledge, 2013.

Clurman, Harold. *Lies Like Truth*. New York: The Macmillan Company, 1958.

Clyman, Toby W., Ed. *A Chekhov Companion*. Westport, CT: Greenwood Press, 1985.

Cocteau, Jean. Preface, *Les Mariés de la Tour Eiffel*. Paris: Editions Flammarion, 1995. See also https://www.poetryfoundation.org/poets/jean-cocteau.

Esslin, Martin. *Pinter*. New York: W. W. Norton and Company, 1976.

Fergusson, Francis. *The Idea of a Theatre*. Garden City, NY: Doubleday Anchor Books, 1953.

Gister, Earle. Interview with the author. The Actor's Center, New York City, June 8, 2005.

Gottlieb, Vera and Paul Allain, eds. *The Cambridge Companion to Chekhov*. Cambridge University Press, 2000.

Hackett, Jean, Ed. *The Actor's Chekhov: Interviews with Nikos Psachoropolous and the Company of the Willimastown Theatre Festival on the Plays of Anton Chekhov*. Newbury, VT: Smith and Kraus, 1993.

Harrop, John. *Acting*. London: Routledge, 1992.

Harrop, John and Sabin R. Epstein. *Acting With Style*. Boston: Allyn and Bacon, 2000.

Lanskoy, Yevgeny. Interviews with author 1999, "Structures of Action," Stella Adler Conservatory, 1986–89.

Magarshack, David. *Chekhov the Dramatist*. New York: Hill and Wang, 1960.

Meyerhold, Vsevolod. *Meyerhold on Theatre*. Trans./Ed. Edward Braun. London: Menthuen & Company Ltd., 1969.

Mirsky, D. S. *A History of Russian Literature*. Ed. Francis J. Whitfield. Evanston, IL: Northwestern University Press, 1999.

Rocamora, Carol. Interview with the author. New York City, January 18, 2005.

Senelick, Laurence. *Anton Chekhov*. New York: Grove Press, 1985.

———. *The Chekhov Theatre*. Cambridge: Cambridge University Press, 1997, 2005.

———. "Chekhov's Plays in English," *The North American Chekhov Society Bulletin*, Vol. IX, Spring, 2000.

———. Correspondence with author, laurence.senelick@tufts.edu, to robin.levenson@nyu.edu, Boston/ New York, March 7 and 11, 2002.

———. *Serf Actor: the life and art of Mikhail Schepkin*. Westport, CT: Greenwood, 1984.

Sontag, Susan. *Against Interpretation and Other Essays*. New York: Picador USA, 2001.

Stanislavsky, Konstantin. *My Life in Art*. Trans. J. J. Robbins/Elizabeth Reynolds Hapgood. New York: Theatre Arts Books, 1948.

Stanton, Stephen S., ed. *Camille and Other Plays*. New York: Hill and Wang, 1957.

Styan, J. L. *Chekhov in Performance*. Cambridge: Cambridge University Press, 1971.

Trenholm, Sarah. *Thinking Through Communication*, 4th ed. Boston: Pearson Education, 1995.

Truss, Lynne. *Eats, Shoots & Leaves, The Zero tolerance Approach to Punctuation*. NY: Gotham Books, 2004.

Van Itallie, Jean-Claude. Interveiw with the author. New York City, November 19, 2003.

Williams, Tennessee. *The Notebook of Trigorin: A Free Adaptation of Anton Chekhov's Seagull*. Trans. Ann Dunnigan. Ed. Allean Hale. New York: New Directions Publishing, 1997.

CHAPTER SEVEN

Uncle Vanya

Imagine this: 575 acres, 432 of them wooded, two ponds, a scraggly stream, a new house, an orchard, a piano, three horses, cows, a springless carriage, a drohzky, carts, a sleigh, horbeds, two dogs, birdhouses for starlings, and other items ... and it's farewell to Moscow! Come see us, Sasha, you can stay in the chicken coop ... There are fish in the ponds, mushrooms in the woods, the air is fresh and pure ... I shall try to pay off the mortgage in four years.

—CHEKHOV TO HIS BROTHER ALEKSANDR, JUNE, 1892

As a cholera doctor, I see the sick, and sometimes I am overcome by it all, but really and truly, they are three times easier to bear with than discussions of literature with visitors from Moscow.

—CHEKHOV TO SHCHEGLOV, (PLAYWRIGHT AND FRIEND), OCTOBER, 1892

Translator/professor Carol Rocamora writes that Chekhov's purchase of his estate in Melikhovo in 1892 served as a rich resource for his last four plays (1996: 13). More than *Seagull*, the final three plays, *Uncle Vanya*, *Three Sisters* and *Cherry Orchard*, are concerned with owning real estate in the country. Indeed, Chekhov subtitled *Uncle Vanya* "Scenes from Country Life in Four Acts."[1] This subtitle is ironic, as the "country

---

1   Magarshack states that this subtitle is an echo from Ostrovsky's plays, which dealt with the "realism" of peasant and middle class life in Russia (1972: 79). Senelick notes the subtitle is also that of Turgenev's *A Month in the* Country (1985). Both playwrights, mentioned in Chapter V, are known as precursors of Chekhov.

life" we see in *Vanya*, with family conflicts and tacit seductions, lacks the pastoral "purity" that Chekhov describes above—but it certainly has a lot to do with "paying off the mortgage," (Vanya and Sonya might be disinherited by the Professor), and, for Astrov, the overwhelming tasks of the country doctor. The bothersome "discussions of literature with visitors from Moscow" Chekhov alludes to resemble the arrival and subsequent annoyances visited on the estate by old literary Professor Serebryakov. He's a retired scholar and Sonya's father, who returns to the country with his young, beautiful wife Yelena, and disrupts the schedules and balance of the simple working lives of everyone in the house. Vanya and niece Sonya have been working hard for years to support the Professor's life in town, but now the income from the estate will no longer support a rich city life, and the Professor and Yelena have returned, it seems, to stay.

Word Choices

Vanya is the brother of the Professor's first wife, Sonya's mother, now deceased, who was an angel by all accounts. Vanya gave up property rights to provide his sister's dowry, and abandoned his own career to help Sonya on the estate. These past events begin the play (Senelick 2005: 195), as they put the characters in their present predicament: the estate may be sold out from under them by the professor to provide for his retirement. Vanya now believes the Professor's work is superfluous because the ailing academic:

chews over other people's ideas about realism, naturalism and the rest of that rubbish … pouring one empty bottle into another (Senelick 2005)

regurgitates someone else's theories on realism, naturalism, and all other kinds of ridiculous nonsense … pouring one empty vessel into another (Rocamora 1996)

[has] been regurgitating other people's ideas about realism, naturalism and all that bullshit (Schmidt 1997c)[2]

rehashed other people's ideas (Van Itallie 1995)

[has been] spewing out other people's thoughts about realism, naturalism … spilling his seed on the hard, dry ground (Columbus 2001)

---

2   An uncommon expletive, along with Lopakhin's "Shit!" in Donaghy's 2005 *Cherry Orchard*, and the "I hate that shit" in Lee's 2001 *Aunt Vanya*. Aunt Vanya (a woman in love with Yelena) explodes with "Missed him AGAIN??? FUCK! FUCK! FUCK!!" at the end of Act III, where Vanya tries to shoot the Professor. Lee's is the only translation to change the sex of one of Chekhov's characters. Like Donaghy's, Lee's adaptation strangely mixes modern quips with 19th century colloquialisms.

and for twenty-five years has been

milling the wind (Dunnigan 1964)

tilting at windmills (Hulick 1994—*Don Quixote* was known in Russia at the time)

pouring water into a sieve (Mulrine 1999a)

pouring air from one glass to another (Kramer and Booker 1997a)

pouring from empty to empty (Young 1956)

shoveling ... nothing from here to nowhere (Frayn 1988)

going to a dry well with a broken bucket (Mamet 1988)

taking nothing and making nothing out of it (Szogyi 1968)

wasting his time (Magarshack 1969)

reading and writing about stuff that any intelligent person already knows and a stupid one doesn't care about. For twenty-five years nothing but blah blah blah ... (Šimek 2017)

sprinkling academic dust on the shelves of oblivion (Poulton 1999b) (my favorite)

and finally

—let's be exact about this Mikhail—my brother-in-law is an oaf. A retired oaf. A fossilized oaf. An oaf with gout, rheumatism, migraine and a liver swollen with jealousy and frustration. An oaf ... who ... somehow tricked thousands of students into scribbling down the rubbish he lectured about art. On art! He knows as much about art as I know about surgery! For twenty-five years! (Friel 1998)

This last comment by Vanya makes Vanya's support of the professor equally absurd. These diverse examples of metaphors—with their amusing and onomatopoeic repetitions—come from Vanya's signature speech in Act I, and contain the bitterness, jealousy and moxie of the man who finally charges at the Professor with a firearm, misses, and then goes back to work for the same "oaf" of twenty-five years. The "vomiting" metaphor (chewing or regurgitating) is present in many of the translations, while some (Friel, Mamet and Gems) leave it out entirely. The speech, in its entirety, is a signal to the actor of Vanya's worldview and past and present humiliations. It follows the brief entrance and exit of the Professor— we see him and then hear Vanya's view of him—and sets up the conflict surrounding the Professor's proposed sale of the estate in Act III, which prods Vanya to attempt murder.

Still, Vanya's mother, Mariya, supports the Professor's work unconditionally, persistently perusing his prolific pamphlets. Marina, the old nanny of the family, is also supportive: she tends to chickens and the kitchen, constantly knitting and providing food for the family—she is the only character to express empathy towards the crotchety Professor (Act II). Love interests supply more conflict: both Vanya and Doctor Astrov—who cares for the local peasantry and supports reforesting the district—fall for Yelena, in spite of her indolence and marriage to the Professor. Sonya, hard worker for the estate, is secretly in love with Astrov, a diligent doctor. The indigent landowner Telegin—Waffles—had a wife who left him the day after they married, but he repeats often how he supports her still, as a matter of "pride." These circumstances define the themes and Superobjective of the play, which concern the import of family loyalty and support, of money, of beauty, of nature, of love, and having constructive work in one's life. Characters' embodiments of these themes define their Actions in the play. Actor and director choices will indicate what they feel are the most significant theme(s) in constructing a cogent Superobjective, and Vanya is entwined with all of them.

Waffles' comic bad luck in love and money is contrasted to the Professor's luck with beautiful women, and compared to Vanya's ludicrous support (like Waffles' to his absent wife) of a Professor whose authentic work in the world is nil. Sonya's hard work, plain looks and daydreams of Astrov are in contrast to Yelena's idleness, beauty and unhappy marriage to an old grouch. Vanya's disillusionment may be contrasted with Astrov's passion for preserving nature, though they both had worked hard (before Yelena and the Professor show up), and are educated. Yelena (unwittingly?) seduces them both, but admits she has more in common with the frustrated Vanya, and doesn't understand Astrov's passion for ecology. They are all a bunch of "*chudaki*" (Senelick 2005: 192)—or, in English:

kranks	(Upton 2012)
creeps	(Baker 2013)
crackpots	(Senelick 2005, 2006; Heim 2003)
"eccentrics"	(Columbus 2002b and Carson 2002a; Kramer/Booker 1997a)
idiots, eccentrics, faintly lunatic one comes to see as *normal*	(Poulton 1999b)
stupid, squalid freaks, Dr. Asinine	(as Astrov calls himself in Friel 1998)
freaks	(Schmidt 1997c)
freaks and lunatics	(Šimek 2017)
strange	(Rocamora 1996)
oddest sort of people, really odd, oddball	(Hulick 1994)
odd, ridiculous, and *freak*	(Gems 1992)
odd and *freak*	(Lee 2001)
"characters" and *some jolly "type"*	(Mamet 1988)
cranks, crackbrains and *odd oneself*	(Frayn 1987, 1988)
eccentric, foolish and *strange*	(Bristow 1977)
commonplace and queer	(Corrigan 1962)
misfits	(Szogyi 1968)
cranks	(Van Itallie 1995; Ehre 1992; Magarshack 1969)
crackpots and *odd*	(Dunnigan 1964)
odd	(Young 1939) and finally
a queer lot	(Fen 1964; Garnett 1929).

"*Chudaki*," the Russian word, is used repeatedly in *Vanya*, especially by Astrov (*Ibid.*).

This list illustrates, from Astrov's first monologue, how the translator's choice of words skews Astrov's view (and thus the audience's) of everyone on the stage. Corrigan's contradictory "commonplace and queer" is the most paradoxical—yet Chekhov's characters are exactly this: commonplace in their human foibles, and "queer" (a loaded word for contemporary audiences), for their particular obsessions and character quirks. "Queer" is also more than faintly British to the American ear, as are "odd" and "jolly type." "Eccentrics" and "strange" are euphemistic, "crackpots" is kind in an old-fashioned way, while "stupid" and "squalid freaks" are cruel. "Kranks" (misspelled and perhaps taken from Frayn's well-regarded earlier English translation?) and "cranks" implies they are grouchy as well as weird. Annie Baker's "creeps" is funny and inventive, but implies there is something icky and mean about them. Friel's "Dr. Asinine" is funny too, but this comment from Astrov is not in Chekhov's play. It does, however, establish Astrov's familiarity with nurse Marina in Act I, and his habit of self-deprecation.

Vanya is Chekhov's "chamber play" (Rocamora, Class 2000), "so compact and dramatically expressive" (Magarshack 1960: 225), the "most concise of Chekhov's plays" (Szogyi 123), Chekhov's one effort at a "well-made play" (Valency 191) and the play "mentioned least in Chekhov's correspondence" (Rocamora 1996: 17). Perhaps this is because *Vanya* is derived from Chekhov's earlier play, *The Wood Demon* (or *Wood Goblin*, from Senelick). Chekhov turned his back on *Demon* after its failure in 1889, and remolded it completely as *Uncle Vanya* sometime after *Seagull* in 1895. The differences between the two works are in changes made to Acts I and IV, and a conflation of several characters. Though Acts II and III remain mostly intact from *Demon*, the tone of the play, though still comic, has become more "contemplative," Rocamora claims (1996: 18). Contributing to this are long, often ironic speeches (like Vanya's above) wherein characters hold forth on views of themselves and the world, while their circumstances and actions reveal quite different realities. Corrigan cites T. S. Eliot's observation that "speechmaking can serve useful dramatic ends" because it gives "us a clue to the character, for we discover the angle from which he views himself" (Chekhov 1962: xxxii). Corrigan makes the point that "by contrasting the way the characters see themselves with what they do and with the way the other characters view them ... Chekhov, ... by indirection, is able to reveal the way life really is" (*Ibid.*). This makes word choice, punctuation and rhythm vital (as in Nina's monologue in Act IV of *Seagull*); these elements help the actor reveal what lies beneath language, and what characters feel about others within a scene.

Translator Curt Columbus finds *Vanya* decidedly "American" in its sensibilities: a Russian director said "Family members come for a visit, they fight, they scream, someone fires a gun, and then everyone makes up and says 'See you next

Christmas' "; it reminds Columbus of Woody Allen (Chekhov 2002b: 4). He admits this is overly simplistic, but uses it to justify "straight-forward and angular prose" in his translation (5). *Vanya*'s economy of language is particularly accessible to Americans, if the spirit of Chekhov's idiom is preserved (*Ibid.*).

Chekhov uses the same switches on the "well-made play" featured in *Seagull*: deflated curtain lines (in Act II Sonya begs Yelena to play the piano, Serebryakov says "no"); a climax/peripetia in the third act has its fallout in the fourth (Vanya's misses when he tries to shoot Serebryakov); early plot points happen offstage (Vanya gives up his rights to the estate); and unseen characters (Sonya's beloved mother) are as important to the underlying Action as those we see onstage. Another "switch" on the structure of the well-made play is the irony of characters that say one thing and do another. This is particularly remarkable in *Vanya*. An obvious example is Yelena remonstrating to Sonya in **Act II**:

> We can't get on with our lives if we don't trust people, you know.   (Friel 1998)

> You mustn't look at people like that. It's not really like you. If you can't trust people, what's the point of living?
> (*Pause.*)   (Schmidt 1997c)

> It's bad to look at someone that way. **It makes you ugly.** We have to trust or it becomes impossible to live. (*pause.*)   (Columbus 2002b)

> No more black looks. You mustn't do it – it's not like you. Be yourself again … or you'll make life impossible. (*pause.*)   (Poulton 1999b)

> … you mustn't look like that on people. It doesn't suit you. And we must *trust.* How can we live if we do not?   (Mamet 1988)

In the dialogue above, Yelena's comments are (perhaps unintentionally) specious: she soon betrays Sonya's "trust" by seducing Astrov—whom Sonya loves—in the next Act. Regarding word choice, Columbus' phrase "It makes you ugly" would surely affect Sonya deeply, as she is particularly sensitive about her looks. This phrase is not in Chekhov—no other translation includes it—but it is certainly an example of how Columbus sees Chekhov's dialogue as "straightforward" and "angular." In Columbus' "new translation" (his words)[3] Yelena takes pointed advantage of Sonya's most vulnerable trait: Sonya fears she's plain. Also, "trust" is important to the plot of the play: Sonya "trusts" Yelena to delicately sound out

---

3 Columbus' "translation" has, arguably, as many emendations as some "adaptations." This illustrates how labels of "translation," "adaptation" or "version" are problematic for English renderings of foreign scripts.

Figure 7.1: *Uncle Vanya.* Ksenia Rappoport as Elena and Elena Kalinina as Sonia from The Maly Drama Theatre, St. Petersburg, Russia. The company is on tour at the Brooklyn Academy of Music, NYC, 2010. Here in Act II, Yelena is bawling while Sonia is blissful, over their love for Astrov. Director: Lev Dodin. English Subtitles/Translation: As is commonly the case, the translator is left out of the Program and the Reviews entirely. Photo Credit: Richard Termine.

Astrov on his feelings for her (Sonya), and Yelena, soon after, betrays this trust, yielding to Astrov's romantic advances. Yet Poulton (from the Roundabout's production in 1999) leaves the word "trust" out completely. Friel cuts the speech to its essence, which he feels is "getting on with it," an Anglicism for Americans. Both Mamet and Friel leave out Chekhov's noted *pause*, changing the rhythm of the scene, and taking away the actors' opportunity to add another note. The "Pause" in the original affects both character and the audience response to Yelena's comment or rhetorical question (she asks *no* question in Chekhov's original). In any case, tragicomedy in *Vanya* is created through the juxtaposition of "duet" scenes where characters make fervent declarations, and dismiss them utterly in the next instant. Herein lies Chekhov's genius: his characters are fallible, and utterly human.

Title and Character Names

The various ways the characters address each other establishes their relationships as much as their behavior towards each other does. *Uncle Vanya*, as written in Russian, is pronounced "Dyadya Vanya," which may be translated as a childish "Unka Johnny" or "Jack" in English. "Ivan" is the character's formal name, "Vanya" the affectionate nickname. Calling the play *Uncle Ivan* would produce a different effect and connotation than Chekhov's playful (and teasing) title. The title also includes Vanya's niece Sonya, as he is *her* uncle. Astrov and Yelena address him as "Ivan Petrovich," (the first name with patronymic—one's father's name—is the common appellation in Russia), Mariya (Vanya's mother) as "Jean" (Senelick notes educated persons often referred to each other by French forms of their names [Chekhov 2005: 202–4]), and Telegin as, simply, "Vanya." Vanya calls Serebryakov "Herr Professor," revealing his attitude towards the Professor as a "mechanical" (203) stubborn German, while Telegin calls the Professor "your honor" (Chekhov 2002b: 16) or "your Excellency" (2005: 199). The Professor affectionately calls Yelena "Lenochka," but he calls his former mother-in-law Mariya "the old she-idiot Mariya Vasilyevna," (2005: 207) or the more descriptive and expository "that old fool, his [Vanya's] mother, the 'Princess of the Pamphlets,' my mother-in-law" (Chekhov, tr. Friel, 1998: 20).[4] It is typical of Friel's Irish *Vanya* to "explain" Chekhov's characters this way, just as compatriot Kilroy had characters comment on their feelings in *Seagull*: the Irish make sure their audiences "get it" when one character refers to another.

Character names in *Vanya* are suggestive, but not as symbolic as those in *Seagull* (2005: 196): Serebryakov implies "silvery" (he is old), Voinitsky (Vanya's last name) is a "warrior" (he is argumentative), Telegin is "cart"—but his nickname is usually translated as "Waffles" because of his pockmarked face (which Frayn strenuously abhors, and cuts out [Chekhov 1988: 366–7])[5]—Sofiya (Sonya's proper first name) is Greek for "wisdom" (she's wise in all but love) and Yelena, for the Greek Helen of Troy, is also sought after and extolled for her beauty. Thus Chekhov's character names may slant perspectives on these *chudaki*.[6]

Stage Directions, Act I

*The garden. Part of the veranda of the house is visible. Beneath an old poplar tree, a table set for tea. A bench, chairs. On the bench, **a guitar**. Beyond the table, **a garden swing**. It's past two in the afternoon on a **muggy, overcast day**. Marina, a slow-moving old woman, sits by the tea table, knitting a stocking. Astrov walks back and forth.*

(Paul Schmidt 1997c)

---

4 Yet Mariya worships the Professor!—Irony and juxtaposition aid comedy and character depiction.
5 Frayn states "I can think of no English nickname that suggests pockmarks." He admits the Russian *Vaflya* means "waffle," but fears listeners will think Telegin "waffles" about things, which he does not. Frayn's objection to Chekhov's nickname is confounding.
6 Senelick notes Vanya "matters most" when he *is* "Uncle Vanya"—uncle to Sonya and caretaker of the family. "When he stops trying to be Ivan Petrovich and fulfills himself as Uncle Vanya, a new life might commence (2005: 196)."

Figure 7.2: *Uncle Vanya*. Sergey Kuryshev as Vanya and Ksenia Rappoport as Elena, from The Maly Drama Theatre, St. Petersburg, Russia, on tour at the Brooklyn Academy of Music, NYC, in 2010. In Act III, Vanya attempts to charm Elena: "I'll bring you a bunch of roses … !" he promises her. Director: Lev Dodin. English Subtitles/Translation: Again, the translator is unknown. The subtitles were clear in the production, acted completely in Russian, to great comic effect. Photo Credit: Richard Termine.

As in *Seagull*, there is a progression in the physical circumstances of the play in *Vanya*. The location spirals from outside the house in Act I above, to a cramped inside (Vanya's bedroom in Act IV) during the course of the play. In Act I above, all the translations note the weather is "gray," "cloudy" or "overcast." Schmidt's translation alone adds "muggy," to anticipate the approaching storm which creates an undertow to the tetchy tempers (especially Vanya's) brewing at the start of the play; all the translations are similar to the one above. A table is set in the garden, and there is a swing and a guitar on a bench. The musical instrument and the garden swing signify a sense of fun and abandon, which is in contrast to the complaints or dour moods of those who enter this space. As Styan notes, "the swing … is waiting for someone to grace it, and it hangs there like an unfulfilled promise" (1971: 99)—this is the core of character Actions in the play. All the translations (even Mamet's) mention these props; they are useful to the actor. Telegin's guitar-playing accents scenes throughout the play. The use of music is a traditional ploy of melodrama, which Chekhov adds ironically: in counter-point to the plot, strains of music propel and underscore action and relationships.

Chekhov's settings as "roadmaps to the psyche," persist in *Vanya*. More telling Stage Directions are in **Act IV**, where Chekhov describes Vanya's cluttered room:

SCHMIDT (1997c)

Vanya's room, which also serves as the estate office. A bed in one corner. By the window, a large table with ledgers and various business papers spread out, a scale, shelves, pigeonholes, etc. A smaller table for Astrov, with drawing tools, a paint box and a file. A birdcage with a starling. A large map of Africa hangs on the wall, clearly of no use to anybody. An enormous sofa, covered in oilcloth. Left, a door leading to the rest of the house; right, a door leading to the outside entry-way. Beside the right door there's a mat, so people don't track mud into the room. Autumn weather. Quiet. Telegin and Marina sit facing each other, winding knitting wool.

COLUMBUS (2002b)

Uncle Vanya's room. On one side of the room, a bed has been set up, while the other side is laid out as a study. A large table sits near the window with account books and all kinds of papers, a writing table, old bookcase, some scales. There is a smaller table for Astrov, which is covered with drawings and paints and has a portfolio of papers leaning nearby. A small cage with two starlings. On the wall is a map of Africa, which, obviously, is of no use to anyone. A huge sofa, badly upholstered. To the left, a door leading to another chamber; to the right, a door leading to the outside, covered by an awning. Near this door is a large floor mat, so that the workmen will not track mud into the room. Autumn evening. Silence. Telegin and Marina sit opposite each other, winding a ball of yarn.

POULTON (1999b)

The estate office. It is also Vanya's room. Under the window is a big table covered in ledgers, documents and papers. There is a desk, cupboards, an abacus and some scales. Astrov's table or drawing board is covered in paints. A portfolio stands by Astrov's table. On the wall is a huge map of Africa which seems to serve no useful purpose. There is a cage with a wild bird in it. (a starling is specified but the essential thing is that it is wild and caged.) A huge sofa covered in oilcloth. There are two doors. One opens into the house. The other leads outside. By this outer door there is a mat for the peasants to stand on. It is a beautiful, still, autumn evening. Marina and Teelgin sit facing each other, winding wool.

MAMET (1988)

Same evening. Ivan Petrovich's room. Stillness. Telegin and Marina sit facing each other, winding wool.

The most interesting anomaly in a comparison of these Stage Directions is Mamet's complete deletion of Chekhov's description of the space. In plays as economic as Chekhov's, where not a word, prop or Stage Direction is wasted, this risks removing vital visual and practical aspects of Chekhov's "theatre poetry." This is a room where Vanya works and sleeps; Astrov too has his table and portfolio here. The starling in a cage (two birds, inexplicably, in Columbus' translation—is it because they must fight?) is not just a whimsical or arbitrary choice. Starlings are feisty birds that demand attention, and do not do well in enclosed spaces: they will flail against the bars till death to escape a small cage, if they have no room to fly (starlingcentral.net). They talk endlessly, and are intelligent birds. They represent Vanya himself. They are not superfluous.

More surprising is the map of Africa, to which Chekhov attached special importance (Pitcher 111). There is only one reference to it, made by Astrov in the last moments of **Act IV**. He observes:

ASTROV … There must be a heatwave over in Africa right now—something awful!
VOINITSKY I suppose so.
(Senelick 2005)

or

ASTROV … It must be hot in Africa right now. Really hot.
VANYA Probably …
(Schmidt 1997c)

or

ASTROV … It must be boiling in Africa now. I hate to think about it.
VOYNITSKY I guess so …
(Hulick 1994)

or

ASTROV … I would think down in *Africa* the heat must be *intense*.[7]
IVAN PETROVICH I think so.
(Mamet 1988)

or

ASTROV … Ah, good old Africa; I bet it is awfully hot there right now – awfully hot!
VOINITSKI … Yes, very hot.
(Šimek 2017)

---

7   Note how Mamet italicizes words, as if they should be stressed when spoken. It is perplexing (and distracting) that he uses these "word stress signals" throughout his adaptation, to prompt actors' inflections—which also suggest character Actions—and yet he ignores Chekhov's own stage directions completely, which have been written into the play purposefully to designate core themes and Actions of the play. Further, the word choice "intense" adds a modern colloquial turn unknown in Chekhov's time.

Pitcher assumes Chekhov put this map in the play to prompt this remark, to show how Astrov is, according to Chekhov's letter to his wife Olga, "reflective and even absent-minded" at this point, rather than filled with "bravura," as Stanislavsky played him (*Ibid.*). But the map is onstage for the entire Act, and is a visual aspect of the "poetry" of the entire production. It is Vanya's map, after all, and not Astrov's. Pitcher muses how Astrov must feel that there are mysterious continents that are warm (unlike Russia) where a different life can exist (*Ibid.*). But it is Vanya who put up the map in his own room, and for this reason we, as the audience, might see that though he is the "ridiculous, fumbling, grumbling, ineffectual, self-pitying Vanya," he too yearns for another world, and that, for all his weakness, never loses his sense of dignity (Corrigan 1962: xvi).

By the end of the play, the audience is aware that most characters have done just the opposite of what they said they will do in their dialogue, so the map of Africa—and its revelations—tend to "throw the whole thing into scale" (Valency 189). That is, the map screams "Look at all of you in cold, pitiless Russia! There are other places, on another side of the earth, where things are done differently, where life may be transformed. Get out! Or, at the very least, *dream.*" The map portrays a possible Superobjective of the play: to escape dreary lives and petty troubles and dream of or pursue an extraordinary future. Translations—or adaptations (like Mamet's)—that ignore this vital prop, or other descriptions of settings that poetically and psychologically charge Chekhov's dramaturgy, do so at the peril of the production. In other words, a play—and thus a translation—is not dialogue alone. Chekhov's Circumstances, enacted by the actor, create his poetry. When Circumstances are removed from a playscript, the poetry is whittled as well.

Chekhov has an earlier "map scene" in his play: Astrov describes the disappearance of the forests of the district to Yelena in Act III, with the help of his charts. They are Astrov's "personal prop," he carries them around, and they help define who he is. They are also included in the Stage Directions. Ironically, Sonya is the one who is truly fascinated with Astrov's work. Astrov knows from the start that Yelena will pay little attention to his forests, but he is hopelessly captivated by her beauty. This scene, wherein Yelena and Astrov seduce each other, is one of the strongest examples of how words on the surface do *not* reflect underlying Actions of the characters. This makes the pauses, ellipses and italicized words (throughout Mamet's adaptation) significant, as their "paralanguage"[8] informs what is beneath the speech.

---

8   "Paralanguage," in the field of Communication, is all the sounds, breaths, stresses on particular words, inflections, elongation of words, volume, rate of speech and all physical attributes of the voice and body that accompany speech. They are indicators—or revealers and sometimes concealers—of Action.

At the start of the scene, Astrov explains deforestation to Yelena in great detail. Hilariously, in Britain's Donmare Warehouse production of *Vanya*,[9] while Astrov's long speech is going on, Yelena moves behind him, next to him, touches him, breathes on him, does everything possible to engage him, but, when he responds, she coyly stops and looks at the map as if shyly paying attention to it. While Astrov's words are about the flora and fauna of the forest, he can't help responding to Yelena's proximity. On the surface, Yelena is listening to Astrov's lecture on the destruction of nature, but her (unwitting?) *Action* can be to seduce him—to pounce on him—at all costs. Like Nina in the "third circle," taken with Trigorin in the next room in Act IV of *Seagull*, Astrov and Yelena do not always admit their true purposes. Finally, however, Astrov states outright that he sees Yelena is not listening, and she explains her thoughts are elsewhere. The audience is anticipating that Yelena, as she promised Sonya, will ask Astrov how he feels about Sonya. She does, bluntly, and, seeing he does not love Sonya, tells Astrov he should leave. Astrov responds differently than expected:

The Translations, Act III, Scene 3

SCHMIDT (1997c)

ASTROV: […] *(Beat)* There's just one thing I'd like to know: why did *you* want to have this little talk? *(Looks at her, points his finger)* **You're really clever, aren't you?**
YELENA: What do you mean?
ASTROV: *(Laughs)* Really clever. All right, so Sonya's suffering; it's possible, let's assume she is, but why were you so eager to find out how I felt about her? *(Stops her from interrupting and continues with intensity)* No, please, don't look surprised. You know exactly why I come over here everyday. And you know exactly who I come to see, too. Oh, no, **sweetheart**, don't give me one of those looks. **I'm not some dumb kid—**
YELENA: *(Bewildered)* I don't know what you mean.

COLUMBUS (2002b)

ASTROV: […] … There's just one thing I don't understand: why did it have to be you who asked all those questions? *Looking into her eyes, wagging his finger)* **You're very sneaky!**
YELENA: What does that mean?
ASTROV: *(laughing)* Yes, sneaky! Let's suppose Sonya is suffering, I'll give you that as a possibility, but why are you so interested? *(interrupts her, quickly)* Please, don't give me that surprised look, you know very well why I've been here ever single day. Why I'm here and who I come for, you know very well! My **sweet little fox,** you don't need to look at me like that, **I'm an old hand at this.**

---

9 Brooklyn Academy of Music, New York, Spring, 2003.

ASTROV: **You're a real little weasel, aren't you?** You've got sharp claws under your soft fur. And you need some fresh meat. I've been coming over here for the last month—I dropped everything to come **sniffing around after you**—and you love it, don't you? You really love it. All right, here I am! I'm yours—you knew that without any little talks. *(Holds out arms)* I give in. Come on, take me! **Sink your claws into me!**

YELENA: Have you lost your mind?

FRIEL (1998)

ASTROV: Come on, Elena.

ELENA: How should I know why—

ASTROV: Stop fluttering those innocent eyes at me. Neither one of us is a novice at this game. I come here every day to see you, my **beautiful young falcon**—

ELENA: Mikhail, I—

ASTROV: You don't like "falcon"? You're right. Too free. Too ethereal. Because you're solidly of the earth, aren't you? Grounded and guarded. **What about a weasel**, smooth and silky and hungry for victims? Yes, I throw everything up and **come panting over here** just to gaze at you. You know I do. And you love it! God, how you love to have me here on my knees! So forget your devious questions and your **bogus** concern for Sonya. I confess! Take me! **Devour me!**

ELENA: You are out of your mind, Mikhail.

YELENA: Fox? I don't understand you at all.

ASTROV: **You beautiful, fluffy little minx.**

You need some prey, a victim! I haven't done a thing for a whole month, tossed it aside, **hungrily searching for you**, and you loved every second of it. So what are you waiting for? You should have known that without those ridiculous questions. *(tilts his head back, exposing his neck)* I submit. Go on, **devour me!**

YELENA: You've lost your mind!

MAMET (1988)

ASTROV: [...]Yet you call me here for an "interrogation" ...

YELENA: I don't understand.

ASTROV: *Oh* yes ... *Oh* yes ... and I walk into - your trap. *Didn't* I, now ...? All *worry* over the poor girl's feelings. "What do you feel, as a Man, Dear Doctor?" "Why have you been *coming* here the whole month, every day? Could we know your true feelings?" Alright! Alright! ... I'll *tell* you, and *without* the charade. I confess it. I'm yours. I *surrender*, I'm *yours*, **take me away.**

YELENA: Are you out of your mind?

POULTON (1999b)

ASTROV: [...] But what's your interest in this? Why the inquisition? What do you really want out of me?

YELENA: I don't know what you mean.

ASTROV: *(wags his finger at her)* Oh yes you do! It's a pity Sonya finds my presence painful. I'm sorry for that. But it isn't Sonya who needs the answers, is it? *(stops her answering)* Come on! Oh that expression! If you could see yourself! You know very well why I'm here – why I'm here every day – who the attraction is – you **beautiful bird of prey**!

YELENA: Bird of –

ASTROV: **Weasel then – teeth or talons – what's the difference?** When are you going to pounce? Come on! For a whole month I've been helpless – letting everything go to pot to run after you – And you love it! You need no inquisition to be sure of me. I give in! Here I am. On a plate. **Eat me!**

YELENA: You're mad!

Word Choice and Sound

One of the most notable differences in translations in this section of the play is the reference to Yelena as a bird of prey, and/or a "weasel." In most of the 34 translations, I've discovered, Astrov refers to Yelena as a "fluffy weasel." Claws and teeth play a part in most translations. But Yelena is also seen as a:

wild little minx	(Baker 2013)
pretty minx with soft pretty fur	(Van Itallie 1995)
beautiful, fluffy polecat	(Carson 2002a; Ehre 1992)
fluffy lynx	(Hulick 1994)
silky-smooth ferret	(Frayn 1987)
fluffy little ferret	(Kramer/Booker 1997a)
beautiful, sleek ferret	(Upton 2012)
beautiful, furry little beast of prey	(Magarshack 1969)
an irresistible and entrancing predator	(Gems 1992)
my dear vulture and *fluffy little ferret*	(Šimek 2017)

The words chosen are also notable for their sounds, as well as their images of sleek cats, feral ferrets or wily weasels: the alliterative "s's" in "*silky-smooth ferret*" and fricatives[10] in "*fluffy ferret*," as well as popping plosives in "*beautiful beast of prey*"

---

10 Fricatives are vocal sounds that result from pushing air through the teeth and forward or shaped lips, such as *f, v, s, sh,* and *ch*. Plosives are letters *p, b, d, t, k,* and *g* that "explode" on the lips or in the throat.

and lolling "l's" in "real *little* wease*l*," and even "r's" in "dea*r* vultu*r*e" help Astrov to bare his teeth or growl and seduce Yelena with the resonance, quality and tone of his voice alone. Some translations also combine the bird imagery ("sweet sparrow-hawk" in Frayn) of Yelena with that of Astrov as "no gosling" (Dunnigan) or "fledg-ling" (Kramer/Booker) or a "wise owl" (Heim) an "old chicken" (Senelick) and "old sparrow" (Hulick). These sounds and images are helpful to the actor: they help define Actions *physically*, with voice and body, as well as imaginatively, with animal personification. It is only in comparison with other translations that Mamet's and others' sparse, and perhaps less rich, renditions may be recognized as less vivid.

Word Meaning

There are differences in qualities between birds and "fluffy" rodents; some trans-lations use both, others just one animal, and, with Mamet, none of the above. A "beautiful young falcon" may be less huggable than a furry mammal. The verbs are also connotative: see the difference between the common (among the translations) "Devour me!" and the simple (and suggestive) "Eat me!" Mamet's more generic "take me away" is less evocative. Being "clever" (most common among translations) and being "sneaky" are also divergent: "clever" sounds British and more affected to the American ear, whereas "sneaky" is more colloquial and practically onomatopoeic. On the other hand, referring to oneself as "not some dumb kid" is more down to earth than "I'm an old hand at this;" the latter is more polite. One is tempted to combine lines from Schmidt and Columbus, to make the Astrov who calls Yelena "sneaky" be the same one who tells her he is not a "dumb kid." That translation would dispense with worn out phrases like "aren't you clever" and "I'm an old hand" and go right for the gullet. Mamet dispenses with all the animals and pleasantries, but images are lost.

Punctuation

Once again, Mamet's italicized words suggest Action to the actor. His "*Oh*, yes ... *Oh*, yes ..." and "*Didn't* I, now ..." could suggest tall waves of pitch variances, up and down the scale, which could result in sarcasm and an appearance of mimicry on Astrov's part (to tease? to demean? to humiliate? to crush?). Mamet does have Astrov "mimic" Yelena when he repeats her words in quotes: "What do you feel, as a Man, Dear Doctor?", etc. If Mamet believes, like Stoppard, that all Stage Directions should be omitted "on the ground that instructions to actors ... and to designer ... nowadays seem over-instructive" (Chekhov 1997d: viii), why so "over-instruct" the actor's inflections with unexplained capitalizations (Man and Dear Doctor) and *italicizations* on every other *word*? The rampant ellipses, too, in

Mamet's version, are not Chekhov's, and encourage the actor to find a physical/vocal "end" to the phrases where they appear. This is not *necessarily* unhelpful ... but it ... *you* know ... can *influence* the actor whose *job* it is to find his/her *own* way ... to *perform* dialogue based on his or her chosen Action ... (!). Words are meant to evoke Action, but belabored punctuation says more about the writer than the character or the performer. With a graceful and precise writer like Chekhov, enhancing (and inventing) punctuation and deleting stage directions and descriptive images may reveal mistrust on the part of the translator or adaptor, and even a misunderstanding or dismissal of the Russian's clear dramaturgy. Or, it may be simply a desire to do things differently than those who have come before. Still, it is hard to improve on Chekhov. Drastic emendations, one might conclude, are a habit of an apprehensive writer, who may not trust that the creativity and contribution of actors or directors will do justice to his or her rendition of Chekhov's play, without the "help" of inflated textual signals.

Since the late 19th century, with the rise of the "auteur" director, directors and actors interpret and evoke the text based on their own time and sensibilities. "When a script is written, it has already been directed *once*." Producer/writer/director Joseph Mankiewicz (1909–1993) recognized this, according to fellow film director Walter Hill.[11] It means that the original playwright (or screenwriter) has a vision that is written peremptorily into the text: the language, to a greater or lesser extent, suggests to the actor (and director) "how" to behave or to navigate the play. This is no less true (and perhaps goes double) for the translated playscript. While a playscript for the stage does not always have the narrative—and sometimes florid—descriptions of locale present in a screenplay,[12] the dialogue, with specific punctuation, word choice and stage directions, forms the design for the stage, as a screenplay describes the look of a film. The five translations above vary greatly: an Astrov, for example, who goes "sniffing around," comes "panting over" to see Yelena or just summarily "surrenders" himself without these descriptions, could each be played variously. Mamet's directness and lack of animal metaphors alone puts forth a different man—with, possibly, different Actions—than one who describes Yelena as a fox, weasel, minx, falcon or bird of prey.

Final Word Choice and Sound

Chekhov's life on Melikhovo may have influenced his "Scenes of Country Life." The finale of the play could reveal another part of Chekhov's life, regarding his religious

---

11   Hill was interviewed on the Leonard Lopate Show, WNYC, June 20, 2006.

12   Unless it is written by George Bernard Shaw, well-known for exhaustive notes included in his playscripts.

training. Sonya's plaints and comforts expressed to her Uncle Vanya in her final speech are, on the surface, in the realm of the spirit rather than the body. Her last words are:

The Translations, Act IV, Final Scene

SCHMIDT (1997c)

(Telegin plays softly)
We'll rest! We'll hear the angels singing, we'll see the diamonds of heaven, and all our earthly woes will vanish in a flood of compassion that overwhelms the world! And then everything will be calm, quiet, gentle as a loving hand. *(Wipes away his tears with her handkerchief)* Poor Uncle Vanya, you're crying ... *(Almost in tears herself)* I know how unhappy your life has been, but wait a while, just a little while, Uncle Vanya, and you and I will rest. *(Embraces him)* We will, I know we will.
We hear the night watchman outside the house, tapping his stick as he makes his rounds. Telegin continues to play quietly; Mrs. Voinitsky makes a note in the margin; Marina knits her stocking.) We'll rest. I know we will.
THE CURTAIN FALLS SLOWLY.

ROCAMORA (1996)

[...] I have faith, I have faith ... [...] *(Through tears.)* You have known no joy in your life, but wait, Uncle Vanya, wait ... We shall rest ... *(Embraces him.)* We shall rest! [...] We shall rest!

FRIEL (1998)

(... Yefim, off, sings a haunting folksong)
And I believe, too, that the angels will sing for us and the sky will be festooned with stars as bright as diamonds and all the misery of this life, all the terrible things we've had to endure, they will be swept away in a great wave of mercy and understanding. And for the first time ever we will know what it is to be peaceful and at rest. *(She wipes away his tears. She is on the verge of tears herself.)* Poor Uncle Vanya; God help you; you're crying. You've had a very unhappy life—I do know that. But be patient. Endure.
And peace will come to us. Listen to me, Uncle Vanya. Believe me. Peace will come to us. *(She kisses the top of his head. Then they pick up their pens and begin writing. Silence—except for the scraping pens, the crickets, Yefim off.)*

SENELICK (2005)

[...] I believe, believe ... [...] *(Through tears.)* You've known no joy in your life, but wait, Uncle Vanya, wait ... We shall be at rest ... *(Embraces him.)* We shall be at rest! [...] We shall be at rest!

SENELICK (2006)

[...] We'll be at peace! [...] We'll be at peace!

The first two translations above are variant, while the last three are similar, except in 2006 Senelick decided to change his "We shall be at rest!" (common to many translations) to "We'll be at peace!" Why? Senelick is a Russian speaker and Chekhov scholar who has written extensively on Chekhov's life and dramaturgy, as well as the nature of translating Chekhov's plays. He explains that Chekhov's last words for Sonya in Russian are *my otdokhnyom*, and it contains "soft, aspirated sounds" that "We shall rest" or (worse, he writes) "We will rest," with the final plosive "t," cannot match (2005: xiv). In other words, the hard "t" in "res<u>t</u>" will never have the same effect as Chekhov's soft "mmm"—recalling "Mama" or a comforting "hum" or "mmm" in the mouth—at the end of the play. His second-best choice is the extended "sss" sound of "peace." Friel may have had the same idea. Schmidt, on the other hand, goes for the soft "wuh" sound of a repeated "w" (and rounded lips, as in a kiss) in "I know we will." Both Schmidt and Friel delete "faith" or "belief," leaving out religious connotations of the words completely: "I know we will" is Sonya's conviction, but not necessarily faith in God.

Most translations state something like "We shall hear the angels, we shall see heaven all diamonds ..." (Senelick 2005, 2006), but it is striking to view the following variants of this famous short phrase all together:

> ... We shall hear the angels sing. We shall see heaven shining in all its radiant glory. (Corrigan 1962)
> ... We shall hear choruses of angels and see the heavens ablaze in diamonds ... (Ehre 1992)
>> ... all the heavens covered with stars like diamonds ... (Fen 1954)
>> ... all Heaven lit with radiance ... (Garnett 1929)
>> ... all heaven bright with many stars, shining like diamonds ... (Magarshack 1969)
>> ... the heavens sparkling with diamonds ... (Rocamora 1996; Heim 2003)
>> ... the heavens sparkling like diamonds ... (Mulrine 1999a)
>> ... the heavens like bright diamonds ... (Szogyi 1968)
>> ... the heavens streaming with diamonds ... (Hulick 1994)
>> ... the heavens spread out before us like a field of diamonds ... (Columbus 2002b)
>> ... the heavens all sparkling like jewels ... (Dunnigan 1964)
>>> ... the diamonds of heaven ... (Schmidt 1997c)
>>> ... the sky filled with diamonds ... (Van Itallie 1995)
>>> ... the sky sparkling with diamonds ... (Lee 2001)
>>> ... the sky shimmering with diamonds ... (Poulton 1999b)
>>> ... the sky all dressed in diamonds ... (Frayn 1988a)
>>> ... the sky will be festooned with stars as bright as diamonds ... (Friel 1998)
>>>> ... the whole sky shining like diamonds ... (Bristow 1977)
>>>> ... the whole sky studded with diamonds ... (Kramer/Booker 1997a/ Šimek 2017)
>>>> ... the whole sky paved with diamonds ... (Carson 2002a)
>>>> ... the whole sky starry with glory! ... (Gems 1992) and, finally,
> ... We shall rest to the songs of the angels. In a firmament arrayed in jewels. .... (Mamet 1988b)

When "heaven" is replaced with "sky" or "firmament," and "diamonds" with "radiance," "jewels" or "glory," the meanings and sounds—not to mention the variant syntaxes—possibly change the purpose and tone of the actor's utterance. Why "firmament" instead of "sky" or "heaven"? Certainly "heaven" has religious connotations. Some translators, regardless of their time period, seem to want to avoid this; others insist on a mention of "heaven." Interestingly, this seems to have little to do with whether or not the translator—or adaptor—has a knowledge of Russian. It seems an individual choice, and varies across the translations. "Heavens" is, today, an anachronism; it affects the actor.

Sonya's "faith" or "belief," it seems, eluded Chekhov himself, as he stated he was not a believer. This came, no doubt, from his "religious" father's beatings and repeated early morning practicing of church hymns forced on Anton and his brothers. Are we to believe that Sonya's promises of "peace" or "rest" are imminent? Or, like much of the dialogue in the play, are they only her fervent prayers for a reality that does not come to pass? The key to this speech, unfortunately, may be in the ferocity and hyperbole of Sonya's description of heaven, which is so exaggerated as to appear as a desperate—however well-meaning—attempt to rouse Vanya from his final despair. Sonya, like all the characters, may be grasping for the impossible—uttering much more than she actually believes—like the "Africa" of Vanya's hopeful but incongruous map.

Stella Adler called *Vanya* "the most fantastically beautiful play" (1999: 246). If *Seagull* is Chekhov's poem to youth, ultimately, with Vanya in the title role, *Uncle Vanya* is a requiem to middle age. Though its sympathies lie with all the characters, it is the young Sonya, not unlike Nina in *Seagull*, who attempts to comfort her defeated uncle. Adler believes that both Kostya and Vanya are "idealists, country adolescents supplanted by decayed, glamorous men from the city … [Vanya] is coming to the end of his life and has never lived." In Chekhov's next play, youth and middle age are both presented, as the effects of time are lived before our eyes. Language, rhythm, scene directions and punctuation, as well as allusion and song, are no less important in *The Three Sisters*.

References

Adler, Stella. *On Ibsen, Strindberg and Chekhov*. Ed. Barry Paris. New York: Alfred A. Knopf, 1999.

Chekhov, Anton. *Anton Chekhov, Four Plays*. Trans. David Magarshack. New York: Hill and Wang, 1969.

———. *Anton Chekhov Plays*. Trans. Peter Carson. London: Penguin Books, 2002a.

———. *Anton Chekhov Selected Works*. Trans. Kathleen Cook. Moscow: Progress Publishers, 1973.

————. *Anton Chekhov's Plays*, Trans. and Ed. Eugene Bristow. New York: W. W. Norton & Co., 1977.

————. *Anton Chekhov's Selected Plays*. Trans. and Ed. Laurence Senelick. New York: W. W. Norton & Co., 2005.

————. *Aunt Vanya*. Adapt. David Karl Lee. Unpublished manuscript, Ant Farm Productions for the New York Chekhov Festival, New York City, 2001.

————. *Best Plays by Chekhov*. Trans. Stark Young. New York: The Modern Library, 1956.

————. *Chekhov: The Essential Plays*. Trans. Michael Henry Heim. New York: Modern Library, 2003.

————. *Chekhov for the Stage*. Trans. Milton Ehre. Evanston, IL: Northwestern University Press, 1992.

————. *Chekhov, Four Plays*. Trans. Carol Rocamora. Lyme, NH: Smith and Kraus, 1996.

————. *Chekhov, The Major Plays*. Trans. Ann Dunnigan. New York: Signet Classic, Penguin Books, 1964.

————. *Chekhov, The Major Plays*. Trans. Jean-Claude Van Itallie. New York: Applause Books, 1995.

————. *Chekhov Plays*. Trans. Michael Frayn. London: Methuen, 1988a.

————. *Chekhov's Major Plays*. Trans. Karl Kramer and Margaret Booker. New York: University Press of America, 1997a.

————. *Chekhov, The Russian Text of Three Plays: Uncle Vanya, The Three Sisters, The Cherry Orchard*. Cambridge: University Press, 1946.

————. *The Complete Plays, Anton Chekhov*. Trans. Laurence Senelick. New York: Norton, 2006.

————. *Four Plays by Chekhov*. Trans. Alex Szogyi. New York: Washington Square Press, 1968.

————. *The Letters of Anton Pavlovitch Tchekhov*. Trans. Constance Garnett. New York: Benjamin Blom, 1966.

————. *Letters on the Short Story, The Drama and Other Literary Topics*, Ed. Louis S. Friedland. New York: Dover Publications, 1966.

————. *Memories of Chekhov: Accounts of the Writer from his Family Friends & Contemporaries*. Ed. and Trans. Peter Sekirin. Jefferson, NC: McFarland, 2006.

————. *Notebook of Anton Chekhov*. Trans. S. S. Koteliansky. New York: B. W. Huebsch, 1922.

————. *The Notebook of Trigorin: A Free Adaptation of Anton Chekhov's Seagull*. Adapt. Tennessee Williams. Trans. Ann Dunnigan. Ed. Allean Hale. New York: New Directions Publishing, 1997b.

————. *The Oxford Chekhov*. Trans. Ronald Hingley. London: Oxford University Press, Vol. II, 1967, Vol. III, 1964, and Vol. IX, 1975.

————. *The Personal Papers of Anton Chekhov*. Trans. S. S. Koteliansky. New York: Lear Publishers, 1948.

————. *Plays, Anton Chekhov*. Trans. Elisaveta, Fen. Middlesex, England: Penguin Books, Ltd., 1951, 1954, 1964.

————. *The Plays of Anton Chekhov*. Trans. Constance Garnett. New York: The Modern Library, 1929.

————. *The Plays of Anton Chekhov*. Trans. Paul Schmidt. New York: Harper Collins Publishers, 1997c.

————. *The Russian Text of Three Plays: Uncle Vanya, Three Sisters, The Cherry Orchard*. Ed. P. Henry. Letchworth, Hertfordshire, England: Bradda Books Ltd., 1965.

————. *The Seagull*. Version. Tom Stoppard. London: Faber and Faber Ltd., 1997d.

————. *Six Plays of Chekhov*. Version. Robert W. Corrigan. San Francisco: Rinehart Press, 1962.

————. *Uncle Vanya*. Adapt. Annie Baker. Literal Trans. Margarita Shalina. New York: Samuel French, 2013.

————. *Uncle Vanya*. Trans. Curt Columbus. Chicago: Ivan R. Dee, 2002b.

————. *Uncle Vanya*. Trans. Michael Frayn. London: Methuen London Ltd., 1987.

————. *Uncle Vanya*. Version. Brian Friel. New York: Dramatists Play Service, 1998.

————. *Uncle Vanya*. Version. Pam Gems. London: Nick Hern Books, 1992.

————. *Uncle Vanya*. Adapt. David Mamet. Literal Trans. Vlada Chernomirdik. New York: Grove Press, 1988, also by Samuel French, 1988b.

————. *Uncle Vanya*. Trans. Stephen Mulrine. London: Nick Hern Books, 1999.

————. *Uncle Vanya*. Version. Mike Poulton. Unpublished manuscript from Roundabout Theatre production, New York City, Brooks Atkinson Theatre, August 31, 1999.

————. *Uncle Vanya*. Štěpan S. Šimek. Unpublished Manuscript. 2017.

————. *Uncle Vanya*. Adapt. Andrew Upton. Unpublished manuscript sent to this author, 2012.

————. *Uncle Vanya and Other Plays*. Trans. Betsy Hulick. New York: Bantam Books, 1994.

————. *Wild Honey*. Version of the untitled play. Trans. Michael Frayn. London: Methuen London Ltd., 1984.

Lopate, Leonard. "The Leonard Lopate Show," WNYC Radio, Interview Walter Hill, June 20, 2006.

Magarshack, David. *Chekhov the Dramatist*. New York: Hill and Wang, 1960.

————. *The Real Chekhov*. London: George Allen & Unwin, Ltd., 1972.

Rocamora, Carol. Interview with the author. New York City, January 18, 2005.

————. "The Living Chekhov," and Classical Drama courses at NYU, 1998–2000, New York University.

Senelick, Laurence. *Anton Chekhov*. New York: Grove Press, 1985.

Styan, J. L. *Chekhov in Performance*. Cambridge: Cambridge University Press, 1971.

Valency, Maurice. *The Breaking String*. New York: Schoken Books, 1983.

CHAPTER EIGHT

The Three Sisters

It is very Chekhovian when you are reaching out to somebody but they can't understand you and you don't understand them.

—(ADLER 1999: 240)

... there is a collision between what the actor is truly doing onstage and what the text is saying.

—ELIZABETH LeCOMPTE[1] (ALLEN 2000: 154)

Chekhov's *Three Sisters* is considered his most difficult play.[2] Chekhov thought so too: he spent the longest amount of time on it of any of his plays (Trans. Senelick

1   Elizabeth LeCompte, Artistic Director of New York City's "The Wooster Group," "deconstructed" Paul Schmidt's translation of *Sisters* and called the play *Brace Up!* (Trans. Schmidt 1992).

2   From Szogyi (Chekhov 1968: 204). Brustein notes it is the "gloomiest" or "darkest" of Chekhov's plays (157, 167), as does Gilman (142); Kataev relates that it "dumbfounded and depressed" Chekhov's contemporaries (256); Magarshack writes of the complexity of the new "chorus element" of the play (1960: 233); Pitcher describes it as a "complex emotional symphony" (1985); Valency pronounces the "theme of *The Three Sisters* [to be] so elusive as to be almost indefinable" (241). It is the one full-length play of Chekhov's canon that he called a "drama."

2005: 241),[3] and described difficulties to sister Masha and writer Gorky (Magarshack 1960: 226). To Olga Knipper[4] he wrote, "It is not a play, but a sort of tangle. There are a great many characters—perhaps I shall get in a muddle and give it up" (Styan 148). Luckily for the theatre, Chekhov did not give it up, intent on writing what many consider his most eloquent masterpiece.[5] *Sisters* was the first play Chekhov wrote specifically for actors of the Moscow Art Theatre, and one that most typifies his realist/symbolist/impressionist style.

Part of the "muddle" on the page is what Magarshack calls the "chorus element" and the "indirect action" of the dialogue (1960: 226, 233). Characters speak of trivial concerns, they don't respond to each other, they sing, whistle, and quote poetry and prose (in Russian, Latin and French), all of which seem to have little to do with the plot of the play. As Adler notes above, characters "reach out" to each other without connecting, and, as LeCompte describes, the actors' Actions "collide" with words in the text. But in performance—where one hears intonation and sees characters' behavior—the actors' utterances reveal "subtext" (see Appendix A) to the audience that contributes to the meaning and themes of the productions. Chekhov's "collisions" are calculated.

As noted in Chapter V, "all allusions, repetitions and elisions are essential," as they provide echoes or "leitmotifs" for the characters throughout the play. *Sisters* is Chekhov's most fearless example of these character behaviors or instances of "indirect action" (Magarshack 1960), also remarked upon as:

"concentration and ordering of detail in all departments of theatre"   (Styan 3)
"intonation and rhythmic variation" and "interpolation of dialogue" (Nilsson 178)[6]
"the arrangement of interlaced stories" and "artful inconsequentiality of dialogue"
(Valency 211, 238)

and

---

3   Chekhov unprecedently directed the MAT's staging of the fire scene in Act III himself (1901) and made numerous emendations to his script for the new 1902 published edition (Magarshack 1960: 231).

4   Chekhov's wife-to-be and prominent actress in the MAT. He wrote the *Sisters*' "Masha" for her to play.

5   Valency praises *Sisters* as "the flower of impressionism in the drama" (219); Jarrell extols it as "[Chekhov's] crowning work ... the culmination of his whole writing life. *Uncle Vanya* is the nearest thing, but nothing ... is as good as *Three Sisters*." (1969, 113). Pitcher sees it as "the fullest statement of Chekhov's own 'philosophy of life'" (1985, 213). Ehre writes "it may be Chekhov's supreme achievement" (13). Gilman claims, "While *Sisters* may not be the greatest drama ever written, it would be hard to establish that it isn't" (145).

6   In *Anton Cechov, Some Essays*, ed. Eekman 1960.

"symbols and leitmotifs ... expressed in terms of ... Vuillard 'spots'[7] ... found in bizarre, grotesque, homey touches in a speech, a mannerism, a trait, an incident" giving "the randomness and personalness of real life."   (Tr. Jarrell 105–6)

These symbols and leitmotifs are both visual and aural. In performance, Chekhov's "mechanism," as Szogyi describes it (Chekhov 1968: 204), also results in "oeillades [eyeballing] and tentative gestures that pass between characters" both "beneath and between the lines" (Senelick 1997: 3). His "drama of collocation" (58) is "music, not acting" (62), as described here in Chapter V. The key to playing such a mosaic-like script is in playing Actions: cryptic dialogue, sounds and song are clarified when enacted with underlying purpose. Gesture and sound together come from humans playing Actions: the result is appropriate vocal inflection and expressive movement.

In a seminal and often-referenced essay on Chekhov, Nils Ake Nilsson[8] quotes Stanislavsky's partner at the MAT, Nemirovich-Danchenko:

When someone speaks to me I hardly understand the words he pronounces at all. To be quite honest the words don't exist for me. I disown them completely. They never show me what the human soul in reality wants. But the sounds—they affect me. Do you follow me? The sounds of the voice. By them I am always able to discern whether a man is happy at heart or not.

(Eekman 170)

Nilsson holds that it is the intonation of the human voice that most connotes meaning (*Ibid.*). And what gives our voices intonation? It is the purpose behind the words. We stress important words, take breaths, use volume, inflection, rate of speech, pitch—all the elements that form "intonation"—because we want to *do* something to someone at the moment of utterance. That is Action. And it is what creates Chekhov's music. This will be apparent in scenes in various translations that follow.

---

7   Adaptor Jarrell links French painter Vuillard's work—an "uncanny visual counterpart"—to Chekhov's method: "In certain of [Vuillard's] indoor and outdoor scenes of French domestic life, the foundation areas on the canvas are made less emphatic by the swarms of particles that mottle the walls with rose-printed paper, the rugs with swirls, the lawns with pools of sun and shade. From such variation and variegation comes his cohesion. Vuillard commingles plaids and dappled things as non sequitur as the jottings in Chebutykin's notebook [officer who loved the three sisters' mother, and may have fathered Irina]."

8   Emeritus Professor of Slavic Languages and Literatures at the University of Stockholm, Sweden, and writer on Russian literature (Jackson 1993: 257). Laurence Senelick also cites him as his teacher (1997: 5).

It is helpful to define the characters' relationships in *Sisters* in order to understand their Actions, and the plot of the play. The ensemble of characters—more numerous than in Seagull or Vanya—may be grouped together in "trios," like the "three sisters" themselves (Adler 1999: 271). For example, Irina, the youngest and most hopeful sister, is in a love triangle with Tusenbach, the romantic German Baron, and Solyony, the "neurotic and satanic" officer (*Ibid.*). Both are desperately in love with her. Irina disdains Solyony, and admires but does not love Tusenbach, whom she finally agrees to marry late in the play. This propels Solyony to challenge Tusenbach to a duel that the "Byronesque" officer may not refuse, and Solyony kills him. Irina's Action to grab "true love," Tusenbach's to attain a "pure" love with Irina, and Solyony's to possess a sensual love with her, all feed into the possible Superobjective of the play: "to reach the 'symbolic' Moscow," or quixotic goal, each character yearns for. None is successful.

Another prominent trio in the play includes the artistic Masha (a lapsed concert pianist), her rather dull, pedant, Latin-teacher husband Kulygin (one person, besides Natasha, who does *not* want to go to Moscow), and the "lieutenant colonel battery commander" Vershinin, a "philosopher"-type, who becomes Masha's lover, and then leaves her at the end of the play, when the regiment pulls out of the small town. Masha has grown cynical, having already wrecked her life by marrying a man who, though a teacher (like the Professor in *Vanya*), is a philistine. She yearns for love with someone whom she thinks has vision. Vershinin, who knew the three sisters' father in Moscow, describes a world of the future, melting Masha's brusque demeanor every time he opens his mouth. Kulygin cannot compete, but remains surprisingly loyal to Masha, despite her indiscretion with the colonel. When Vershinin leaves, Kulygin is right there—sporting a funny mustache—to cheer Masha up. He is an example of how persistence and plodding may win out: Masha goes home with Kulygin at the end of the play.

A third trio is formed when lower-class usurper Natasha marries the three sisters' brother Andrey, a violinist ("he plays like an angel") and prospective professor who never makes it back to the university. Andrey "relaxed and got fat" (282) once his father, the general, died: Andrey is an "Oblomov"[9] character. His rival, a

---

9   "Oblomov" is a familiar Russian type of the late 19th century who, though full of potential, is ineffectual and lazy, throwing away his gifts on easy wealth. He is a character created by Russian novelist Goncharov (1812–91), and has become a symbol of the old Russian aristocracy. Prince Mirsky (historian) describes him as "the embodiment of the whole side of a Russian soul ... or the soul of the Russian gentry—its sloth and ineffectiveness. He has a high sense of values. He is open to generous aspirations but incapable of effort or discipline" (191). This is Andrey, much like Vanya, Dr. Dorn in *Seagull* and Gaev in *Orchard*.

district official, the never-seen Protopopov, is a social "climber" like Natasha, who manages to father at least her second child, and move into the Prozorov home in the course of the play. In fact, like the Professor in *Vanya*, Natasha and Protopopov eventually disinherit Andrey and his sisters by the last Act, and the family is literally put out of the house. The theme of "disinheritance" that is seen at a distance in *Seagull* (Nina's rich father left her nothing) and almost accomplished in *Vanya* (the Professor wants to sell the estate) is practically settled by the end of *Sisters*. The aristocracy is losing to the new middle class.

Not all the events mentioned above (family life in Moscow, death of the general, Masha's marriage to Kulygin, Natasha's marriage to Andrey and affair with Protopopov, Solyony's altercation with Tusenbach) are shown explicitly in the text of the play, though they are mentioned, and the upshots of them are inferred. They—and other events, particular to each character—are the keys to playing the Actions of the play. Actors must decide how important events—beginning with *past* occurrences, antecedent to the play itself—drive their Actions, and so create the world of the play. Happenings endemic to the play have shaped every character before he or she appears on the stage.

Valency writes, "themes in *Sisters* are all but indefinable" (241), but this assertion is untrue for the actor. If it were true, Chekhov's plays would be unactable! And they would certainly not be as affecting as they have been for over one hundred years. What seems mysterious on the page is illuminated in the playing. The goals of the character become the actor's Actions, which are absolutely clear and "definable." Actions evoke the themes in the text; playable Actions come from a comprehensive analysis of that text. As in the previous plays, Stage Directions set up the Circumstances for the characters. The Circumstances feed the actor: again, we know how to behave when we know exactly where we are—in terms of season, surroundings, rooms, objects and our current purpose in a space. As before, a brief look at the various translations of Stage Directions in *Sisters* will help shed light on the Circumstances of the characters:[10]

---

10   Title and character names are common in *Three Sisters*, so a section need not be devoted to them. However, Senelick notes the family name *Prozorov* suggests "insight," *Vershinin* suggests "summit," *Solyony* means "salty," and *Protopopov* means "descended from archpriests" (2005: 248). Bristow (in Chekhov 1977) notes that *Olga* comes from a word meaning "holy," *Masha* is a variant of *Mary* from the Hebrew for "bitter," *Irina* is from the Greek word for "peace," *Andrey* is from *Andrew* which means "manly" and that Protopopov was a contemporary critic that Chekhov despised (2005: 101).

Figure 8.1: *The Three Sisters Come and Go*. Jackie Lowe, Claire Lebowitz and Liza Cassidy are "following the lives of three archetypal women of Chekhov's plays … through the lens of Beckett's comic take on the existential dilemma … Each of the sisters is obsessed with being the most unhappy." From the inventive Theaterlab, NYC, in 2010, this fanciful and engaging production included pieces of all Chekhov's last four plays, from the women's points of view. It was conceived and directed by Orietta Crispino. Dramaturgy and Photo Credit are from Marco Casazza.

The Translations, Act I, Scene 1

MICHAEL HENRY HEIM (2003)

The PROZOROV *house. A drawing room with columns. A ballroom[11] is visible in the background. Noon. It is table is* **sunny and cheerful** *outside. A table in the ballroom is* **being set for lunch.**

DAVID MAMET (1990a)

The Prozoroff's house—a parlor. Mid-day. The table is **being set for breakfast.** OLGA, MASHA, *and* IRINA.

---

11   A ballroom—some translations name it a "reception room"—was a standard in upper-class homes in 19th century Russia (Chekhov 1977: 103).

OLGA, *in the dark-blue uniform of a girls' second-ary-school teacher, is correcting exercise books, first standing still, then pacing back and forth.* MASHA, *in a black dress, is sitting with a hat in her lap, reading a book.*
IRINA, *in a white dress, is standing lost in thought.*

Stage Directions

Three Sisters has been described as a play about the passing of time (Chekhov, tr. Carson 2002: xxix; Gilman 150–5). Changes of the seasons and times of day reveal significant progressions in the play. Most of the 37 translations I discovered, except Mamet's, reflect Chekhov's concerns with these given circumstances in Act I. Most, except Mamet's, begin similarly to Heim's translation above. Inexplicably, Mamet retains the same Stage Directions as other translators for Acts II and III, and is especially detailed in ACT IV below. Here Friel has taken a few liberties:

The Translations, Act IV, Scene 1

DAVID MAMET (1990a)

The old garden of the Prozoroff house. A long avenue of firs, at the end of which a river is visible. On the other side of the river, a forest. On the right, the terrace of the house; here, bottles and glasses on the table—it is evident that champagne has just been drunk. It is twelve o'clock noon. From the street, PASS-ERS-BY walk through the garden to the river occasionally; five or so SOLDIERS walk through rapidly.
CHEBUTYKIN, *in a benign mood which does not leave him throughout the entire act, is sitting in an armchair in the garden waiting to be called; HE is in a [military] cap and has a stick.* IRINA, KULYGIN *with a decoration around his neck and no mustache, and* TUZENBACH, *standing on the terrace, are seeing off* FEDOTIK *and* RODE, *who are walking down [the steps];* BOTH OFFI-CERS *are in field dress.*

BRIAN FRIEL (1981)

*Almost two years have passed. Autumn. Noon. Diluted sunshine—the first snow of winter is imminent. The old garden of the Prozorov house. Stage left a **garden swing**. Stage right the verandah of the house. On the verandah a table with glasses and empty champagne bottles. In the distance a long avenue of fir trees beyond which one can see the river. Beyond the river is a wood.*
*Chebutykin sits at the table, **drinks champagne**, and reads his paper. He is in a benevolent mood which lasts throughout the entire Act. He is waiting to be summoned for the duel. His army cap and stick are on the table beside him. Irina, Kulygin (Wearing a decoration round his neck and with his mustache shaved off) and Tusenbach emerge from the house. Fedotik and Roddey are with them. They all stand on the steps of the verandah to say goodbye. Fedotik and Roddey are in field uniform.*

Act I began on a "sunny and cheerful" day ("bright" or "happy" in some translations) in the spring, at "Midday," and, as Olga's opening lines tell us, it is May. Act II is in the same house, but at eight o'clock in the evening, one year later. We know this because Natasha has had a baby, "Bobik;" she and Andrey have gotten married after Act I. Act III takes place "after two in the morning" in the much smaller space that is now a shared bedroom for Irina and Olga, during the upset of a fire in the town. It must be another year later, as Natasha has had a second child, Sofia. Natasha goes off for a "ride" with the elusive Protopopov, and the intimation is that she has continued an affair with him, and her second child "Sofotchka" (affectionate for "Sofia") is actually theirs. In Act IV above we are told only that, again, it is twelve o'clock noon and the army is dressed up and moving out. There has been a party or toasts, we see, from the champagne. We, as audience, soon learn it is autumn, when Masha mentions "it'll snow any moment" and "the migrant birds are starting to fly … ". Friel, above, notes the season and time frame—"almost two years have passed"—explicitly in the Stage Directions, but, in the other translations I have unearthed, Chekhov lets dialogue and actions of the characters alone suggest the passage of time. Costumes define the season too.

Indeed, it is largely Natasha's breeding—the only woman who has born children during the play—that keeps the audience abreast of how long the soldiers and the Prozorovs have been together and longed for the unattainable. Also, it is Natasha who defines a major plot line, since one could describe *Three Sisters* as a play about a family (Olga, Masha, Irina and Andrey) that is disinherited by a lower class girl (Natasha) who marries their brother and takes over their home. Or, as Gilman remarks: like Beckett's *Godot* is about someone who *doesn't* come, *Sisters* is about how a family does *not* get to Moscow (161). While plot and themes are not "indefinable" as Valency suggests, they are malleable, depending on each character's point of view—for the whipped Andrey, social climber Natasha, positivist Kulygin, rejected Solyony, overworked Olga and yearning Irina or bored then lovelorn Masha—the events have special significance. *Sisters* could also be seen as a play where the military comes to town—then the military leaves town. In any case, the family is "invaded" and seems not to be the better for it.[12]

---

12 Thus we see a relationship between Chekhov and the plays of Harold Pinter, whose plays have invaders as well.

   Notably, a Lithuanian production in 2017 sets the play in a situation parallel to Chekhov's Imperial Russia at the start of the 20th century where "the intrusion of the military force into civilian routine … was anticipating WW I … We look at the Central Europe's political and ideological landscape and the shift to intellectual apathy, so similar to Chekhov's mood at the time of the play. … Our Sisters are stuck in the 2017 town of Vilnius and dreaming of Moscow or Bruxelles … [with] the army marching away towards Poland at the end of the play." Chekhov seems infinitely malleable indeed. (yanaross.com)

Stage Directions set the mood, alert the set designer and describe character behavior. Mamet's short description in Act I does not tell us that there are "columns" or a ballroom behind the three sisters, who are noticeably clad in stark colors—blue, black and white—which could have symbolic meaning. His short statement gives us no feeling of the expanse of the house: this is crucial to the plot, as, by the end of the play, the sisters and Andrey are put patently outside of the house. It is helpful to know at the start what kind of real estate is relinquished to Natasha and the impalpable Protopopov. The colors have import too: Masha (like Masha in *Seagull*) is clad in black throughout (also in mourning for her life?); Olga might stay in blue, as she continues to be a schoolmistress; and Irina's white dress may be her "leitmotif" for a purity that is lost in the course of the play. Also, Mamet's first Act takes place at "breakfast," while other translations mention "lunch." Why? This change is never explained.[13]

Though a small addition, Friel's note in Act IV that Chebutykin actually *drinks* champagne as he reads his paper could imply he does this a lot, and even that he drunk the other glasses of drink on the table as well. It is not the first time in the play he is alleged to be alcoholic. Again, Chekhov's original is more discreet than Friel's overt description. Also, Friel adds a "garden swing"—as appears in *Vanya*—to this set, though it is not present in any other translation. Friel provides set answers to questions that the actors in the play might provide with their own contributions, while, on the other hand, Mamet hides or changes information (in Act I) that Chekhov, it seems, gives the actor from the start. It seems, as Carnicke notes in Chapter III, Mamet and Friel are attempting to put directorial choices into the text. The point is, they are different from Chekhov's choices. Mamet's is an "adaptation," Friel's, a "version."

The import of word choice, syntax, punctuation, song or allusions and the attendant repetitions, echoes and character traits they propound in the script are evident in almost every "beat" of *Three Sisters*. Perhaps because of this, the play, in general, has particularly varied and diverse renditions, among all the translations in this study. The final moments of Act III demonstrate this plainly:

The Translations, Act III, Final Scene

ROCAMORA (1996)

IRINA: *(From behind the screen.)* Olya![14] Who is knocking on the floor?
OLGA: It's the doctor, Ivan Romanich. He's drunk.
IRINA: **What a bewildering night!**

---

13   Perhaps Mamet recalls how households in *Vanya* and *Cherry Orchard* have been turned upside down, and mealtimes attenuated to suit new arrivals. But Mamet makes no mention of this at the start of *Sisters*.

14   "Olya" is the affectionate nickname for "Olga."

Pause.

Olya! *(Peers out from behind the screen.)* Did you hear? They're taking the brigade from us, they're moving it somewhere far far away.

OLGA: It's only **a rumor.**

IRINA: And then we shall be left alone ... Olya!

OLGA: What?

IRINA: Dearest, darling, I respect the baron, I admire him, I do, he's a fine person, I'll marry him, I'll agree to it, only then let's go to Moscow! I beg of you, let us go! There is no place on earth for us but Moscow! Let's go, Olya! Let's go!   [END]

ODETS (1939)

Irina

(Behind the screen)

Olga, who is that knocking on the floor?

Olga

It's the doctor. He is drunk.

Irina

What a terrible[15] **night!**

PAUSE.

Olga! *(Looking out from behind the screen)* Have you heard? They are taking the brigade away from us, transferring them far away.

Olga

That's only **a rumor.**

Irina

Then we shall be alone ... Olga!

Olga

Yes?

Irina

Darling, I respect and esteem the Baron, he is a fine man. I consent to marry him, only let us go to Moscow.

I beg you, let us go! Nothing in the world is better than Moscow. Let us go, Olga! Let us go!   [END]

McGUINNESS (1990b)

(the stage is empty)

IRINA: Olia, who is knocking on the floor?

OLGA: The doctor, Ivan Romanych, drunk.

IRINA: **This dark night.**

(Silence.)

Olia?

(Looks from behind the screens.) Have you heard?

The brigade's being moved from here. They're being posted somewhere far away.

OLGA: **Hearsay, only hearsay.**

IRINA: We'll be on our own then. Olga?

OLGA: What?

IRINA: My dear, I respect the Baron, I do, I value him. A good man. I will marry him, I will accept, but we must go. Moscow, there's nowhere better on this earth. We must go, Olia. We must go.

[END]

---

15 Phoebe Brand's script (she played Irina) has the word "restless" crossed out and "terrible" written in. Her son, Stephen Carnovsky, kindly gave a copy of Clifford Odets' little known translation to me for these comparisons.

MAMET (1990a)

IRINA: *(Behind the screen.)* Olga ... What is that?

OLGA: *(Behind the screen.)* It's Dr. Ivan Romanych.

IRINA: What?

OLGA: It's Doctor Ivan Romanych. Knocking on the floor.

IRINA: Why is he doing that?

OLGA: He's drunk.

IRINA: **... what a night.** *(Pause.)*

OLGA: *What?*

IRINA: *(Looks out from behind the screen.)* Olga ...

OLGA: What?

IRINA: Did you hear?

OLGA: ... Did I ...?

IRINA: ... that the Brigade is being transferred.

OLGA: I heard it. Yes. It's **only gossip.**

IRINA: ... because we'd all be alone. *(Pause.)* Olga.

OLGA: Yes.

IRINA: Olga ... *(Pause.)* The *Baron* ...

OLGA: Yes. The Baron?

IRINA: He is a good man?

OLGA: Yes.

IRINA: He's a good man. *(Pause.)* I can marry him.

OLGA: Yes?

IRINA: I'll marry him.

OLGA: You will.

IRINA: I'll agree to marry him. Only. Can we go to
  Moscow? Can we leave here? Olga? Please. *(Pause.)*
  Olga ...
   CURTAIN. END OF ACT III

Word Choice, Sound, Syntax and Punctuation

Once again, Mamet's word choice, syntax and punctuation vary strikingly from
the other translations/adaptations/versions.[16] He has interpolated Irina's short

---

16 Rocamora calls her rendition a "translation," Odets' is referred to (by Senelick 1997: 183)
as a text Odets "prepared" with an "idiomatic ... American" flavor, McGuinness calls
his a "version," and Mamet labels his an "adaptation." Mamet cites Chernomirdik and
McGuinness cites Cullen as "literal" translators.

speech at the end of the act with responses from Olga, which, perhaps, make Irina's dependence on Olga's reactions even more studied. For the actor, this whispered, broken and "secret" sister-conversation might be especially fun to play. Mamet adds ellipses throughout the short scene as well as at the very end ("Olga …") that Chekhov never put in. The fact that Mamet left the scene "unfinished" with these ellipses is perhaps more portentous than the others, and makes the oncoming Act IV even more of a jolt into the mid-day sunlight.

The word "rumor," appearing in most of the 37 translations, has been changed by Mamet to the even more colloquial (and condemning) "gossip"—which also contains the sharp "plosives" of "g" and "p" sounds. McGuinness' "hearsay" is jarring as courtroom jargon. "Bewildering night" (this more literary word choice is typical of Rocamora) is an anomaly, while the "terrible" or "restless" night of Odets (changed by the actor), with "dark night" and "what a night" are all used variously in other translations across the 37 mentioned herein. Stark Young (1956) chooses "What a torn-up night!" Each word reflects a different feeling in the character regarding the conflagration (both fire and character conflicts) that has just taken place. McGuinness' lack of exclamation points and ellipses, with shorter sentences, changes meaning and tone—the more evocative punctuations ("!" and "…") are preponderant in Irina's last speech in Chekhov's Russian original (Chekhov 1946: 85). Indeed, McGuinness' version is the most short and clipped of any translation, while Mamet's is one of the most extended. This does influence the character's Actions in the scene: in Mamet, Irina's decision to marry the Baron seems more thoughtful, and is decided before our eyes, with coaxing from the crafty Olga. In McGuinness, Irina makes a snap decision, seemingly at the instant she discovers that they—Olga and all three sisters—will be "on their own" when the Baron and his regiment leave town. The simple "stichomythia" (short, back-and-forth dialogue) of Mamet's more protracted exchange, versus longer speeches in McGuinness, skew the scenes differently. This is discovered in the playing of the scenes. So, this short "beat" is a clearly identifiable example of how various renditions of *Three Sisters* carry different tones and Actions for the actor, based on word choice, syntax, punctuation, sound and scene structure.

Translations of the "good-bye" scenes between the two sets of star-crossed lovers in Act IV are also diverse, and portray especially telling nuggets of Actions that demonstrate the themes and purpose of the play: Irina, Tusenbach, Masha and Vershinin all ache for love that escapes them through lack of feeling for the available partner, or the circumstance of departure. Chekhov seems particularly interested in how characters arrive and depart throughout his last four plays, and these two farewell scenes between Irina and Tusenbach and then Vershinin and Masha are templates of his tragicomic genre.

First, Irina and Tusenbach are only ill-matched because Irina is not in love with the Baron; their educations, temperaments and world views are compatible. (One recalls similarities between Astrov and Sonya in *Vanya*.) But Irina agrees to marry him at the end of Act III. In Act IV, it is over a year later and she hasn't married him, but is about to. She says, after this decision, she felt great relief and

> **her soul lightened** (Mamet1990a)
> **her soul had wings** (Jarrell 1969)
> **she'd become happier** (Szogyi 1968)
> **cheerful** (Wilson 1984)
> **joyous and free** (Rocamora 1996)
> **light-hearted** (Magarshack 1969)
> **brightened up and breathed easy** (Heim 2003)
> **was less depressed** (Schmidt 1997b)
> **her spirits soared** (Cook 1973), and, in most translations, she
> **felt light enough to fly into the blue** (Markus 1996) or
> **as if my heart had grown wings, and I cheered up, and felt light as a feather** (Šimek 2014)
> **sprouted wings** (Senelick 2005) of some sort, and also **felt a weight lifted.**

Certainly having a "*lightened* soul" is different from being "less depressed"—the first is a spiritual event, and the second is amusing in its negative slant—it is less than superlative. (Question: Do you love me? Answer: Well, you make me less depressed …!) She has, in any case, accepted her fate and is looking towards the future. While she tells him, finally, she can never love him, he too accepts his fate, knowing that he may be killed in the duel with Solyony, a fact he does not disclose to Irina. Tusenbach's good-bye to her is one of the most tender in modern dramatic literature. His plea she "say something" to him of her love—she cannot—and his observation of the beautiful birch trees before he leaves for the duel are both touching and ironic, because of what follows: Natasha's subsequent vow to cut down these same trees adds a sinister irony to Tusenbach's death.

Next, Masha and Vershinin, also temperamentally well-matched, are both married to others, and Vershinin must leave with the regiment. Their "farewells" are in contrast to Irina's and Tusenbach's: Irina and Tusenbach are allowed a private conversation, while in the Masha/Vershinin "farewell," Olga speaks to Vershinin before Masha shows up. During this exchange, Vershinin looks at his watch no less than four times, and mentions how late he is another four times (in Senelick, Carson, Schmidt, Rocamora and most of the early translations). How much does his leaving Masha affect him, if he can't stop looking at his watch? Some translations lessen the number of times he looks at his watch (Friel and

Wilson), or replace Chekhov's many "pauses" between Olga and Vershinin with "Silences" (McGuinness). But Vershinin's glances to his watch betray his inner conflict: will he make it back to his post on time? Will he see Masha? It is comic that he is "in the third circle of attention" (see Appendix A) during what should be a poignant farewell to her; this may twist our idea of the "romantic" colonel. He may be more concerned with his job (his wife? how his affair looks to others?) than with Masha. The comparison of four translations begins with Vershinin's final words to her:

The Translations, Act IV

SCHMIDT (1997b)

VERSHININ: I came to say goodbye …
MASHA: *(Looking him in the face)* Goodbye … *(A prolonged kiss.)*
OLGA: Now, now, that's enough … *(Masha sobs violently.)*
VERSHININ: Write me … don't forget. Let me go—I've got to go … Olga Sergeyevna, take her—I've got to go … I'm late. *(Shaken, kisses Olga's hand, embraces Masha once again, and goes away quickly)*
OLGA: Now, now, Masha! Stop, dear … *(Enter Kulygin.)*
KULYGIN: *(Embarassed)* It's all right, let her cry, it's all right … Masha dearest, my sweet Masha … You're my wife, and I'm happy, no matter what happened … I'm not complaining; I haven't a single reproach to make to you—Olga is my witness … Let's start over again just the way it was before. I'll never say a single word about this, never …
MASHA: *(Holding back her sobs)* "Beside the sea there stands a tree, and on that tree a golden chain … a golden chain …" I'm going crazy …
"Beside the sea … a golden chain."
OLGA: Calm down, Masha, calm down. Give her a drink of water.
MASHA: I won't cry anymore.

McGUINNESS (1990b)

VERSHININ: I've come to say goodbye to you.
MASHA: Goodbye to you. *(There is a long kiss exchanged between them.)*
OLGA: Now, now, enough, enough. *(MASHA weeps with violence.)*
VERSHININ: Write to me … Do not forget. Let me go … Time … Olga Sergeevna, here, her … Must go … Late, late, I'm … *(Deeply distressed, he kisses OLGA's hand, embraces MASHA once more and exits.)*
OLGA: Now, Masha, enough. Don't, loved one. *(KULYGIN enters in confusion.)*
KULYGIN: It's going to be all right. Weep, let her. My Masha, dear, good, my wife, you are mine and I am happy, come what may. I will not complain. You will not hear one word of blame from me. Olga, be my witness to that. We will live again as we did before, and not one word, not one syllable, will you hear— *(MASHA suppresses her sobs.)*
MASHA:
I saw the shore that strides the sea,
A green oak, green oak, oh green oak tree,
A chain of gold embracing thee.
I am going mad.

KULYGIN: She's not going to cry anymore ... that's good.[17] *(A muffled shot is heard in the distance.)*

MASHA: "Beside the sea there stands a tree, and on that tree a golden chain ... an educated cat ... a golden tree ..." I'm all confused. *(Takes a drink of water)* My life is a disaster ... I don't need anything anymore ... I'm all right now ... What difference does it make? What does that mean, "beside the sea ..."? Why can't I get it out of my head? I'm all confused. *(Irina comes in.)*

OLGA: Calm down, Masha. That's a good girl ... Let's go lie down.

MASHA: *(Angrily)* I won't go in there. *(Sobs, but stops immediately)* I'm not going into that house ...

IRINA: Let's just sit here for a moment; we don't have to say anything. I'm going away tomorrow, remember. *(Pause.)*

KULYGIN: Yesterday I took this away from one of the boys at school. *(Takes out a fake beard and mustache and puts it on)* It looks just like the German teacher.

OLGA: *(Laughing)* It really does. *(Masha cries.)*

IRINA: Don't, Masha!

KULYGIN: Exactly like him.

[END]

The shore that strides
A green, green oak.

OLGA: Calm, Masha, calm. Give her a drink of water.

MASHA: Not crying any more.

KULYGIN: She's stopped crying. She's very good. *(The dull sound of a gunshot heard from far away.)*

MASHA: I saw the shore—a green, green oak, a chain of gold, chained. Green cat. Green oak. All confused, everything. *(Drinks water)* This foul thing, my life ... I need nothing now, I'll be calm in a moment. It's of no matter. Why the shore? What does that mean? Why is that word stuck in my head? My brain's drowning. *(IRINA enters.)*

OLGA: Calm, Mahsa. Be a good girl. We'll go inside—*(MASHA speaks angrily.)*

MASHA: I am not going in there. *(Sobs, but stops immediately.)* I do not go into that house any more, I will not go in.

IRINA: Come on, we'll sit down for a short while, we don't need to talk. Tomorrow I'm leaving here, you know. *(Silence.)*

KULYGIN: Yesterday I took this beard and moustache away from a boy in the third year. *(Puts on moustache and beard.)* I look like the German teacher. *(Laughs)* Don't I? I do. Those boys, such comedians.

MASHA; Yes, you do look like that German of yours. *(Olga laughs.)*

OLGA: Yes. *(Masha cries)*

IRINA: Enough, now, Masha.

KULYGIN: The image of him.   [END]

---

17   Ironically, this "shot" is the one that kills Tusenbach, just after Kulygin tells Masha "that's good."

FRIEL (1981)

VERSHININ. I came to say goodbye.

MASHA. Goodbye. *(Pause as they look at each other. Then suddenly they embrace. A long kiss. Olga looks away.)*

OLGA. Please! Please! For God's sake—please! *(Masha sobs loudly.)*

VERSHININ. Write to me, my darling. And when you think about me—*(Masha flings her arms around him. Pause.)* I have got to leave now, Masha. Olga, please. I must go. I'm late already. *(Olga takes Masha, still sobbing, in her arms. Vershinin takes Olga's free hand and kisses it. Then he leaves. Masha emits a long, loud anguished howl.)*

OLGA. Shhhhh, my darling, please ... please, my darling, shh ... *(Kulygin enters. He is so embarrassed, so totally defeated, that even his clichéd and protective speech patterns fail him. He cries quietly. As he cries.)*

KULYGIN. Let her cry ... doesn't matter ... let her cry ... doesn't matter at all ... My Masha, my good kind Masha, you are my wife and I am happy no matter what ... Oh Jesus Christ ... I'm not complaining—really, I'm not—not blaming you at all—not in the slightest. Isn't that right, Olga? Have I ever complained, Olga? Ever? What we'll do is—what we'll have to do is—we'll have to go back to the way we used to be before—before—And I promise you, my darling, I promise you I'll never ever make any reference to—to—ever say a single word about—about ... *(He breaks down.)*

MASHA. "A green oak grows by a curving shore

And on that oak a gold chain hangs;

And on that oak a gold chain hangs ..."

I think I'm going mad, Olga.

MAMET (1990a)

VERSHININ. I've come to say goodbye. *(OLGA walks away a little. Pause.)*

MASHA. Farewell. *(Beat. A prolonged kiss.)* *(OLGA clears her throat. They look to her for a moment. MASHA sobs.)*

VERSHININ. Write me. Don't forget me. Don't forget me. *(HE kisses Olga's hands. Embraces Masha again.)* Don't forget me. *(Exits.)* *(Pause.)*

OLGA. Shhh. Masha. Shhh, now. Come now, Darling.

KULYGIN. *(Enters.)* It's all right. Let her cry. No. No. *(Pause.)* Masha. You're my wife. My good, kind Masha. My wife. And I reproach you with *nothing*. Do you hear me? *Nothing. (To Olga.)* As you will witness. *(To Masha.)* We'll begin again. And no one will say one word of what has occurred. Not a word, not a *reference* ...

MASHA. ... I'm going mad ...

OLGA. Calm yourself, Masha. Please. Calm yourself. Get her some water.

MASHA. I don't need it.

KULYGIN. No. She doesn't need it. She's no longer crying. No. *(Distant sound of a shot.)*

MASHA. Why should I need anything. My life is finished. Really. I'll be calm. In just a moment. You must forgive me. My head is spinning now. My *thoughts* ... *(Enter Irina.)*

OLGA. Shhh. Masha. That's a clever girl. You calm yourself now. Come up to my room.

MASHA. No I will *not*. I'm not going in there. And I'm not going in the house. No.

IRINA. All right, then. We'll sit here. We'll be silent. *(Pause)* I'm off tomorrow, you know.

"A green oak grows by a curving shore …"

OLGA. Shhhh, my love, shhhh—easy, easy—don't talk—*(To Kulygin.)*—A glass of water.

MASHA. No more crying.

KULYGIN. No more crying. All over and done with. All finished. *(Distant sound of a gunshot.)*

MASHA. "A green oak hangs by a golden shore—a hanging shore—And on that chain a green oak curves—a green chain curves—a gold oak hangs—" I've got it all mixed up. *(Drinks water.)* It's all a mess, all a confusion. Just give me a minute— I'll be all right in a minute. No more crying. What's that line again? "A green oak hangs by a golden shore"—what's that supposed to mean? If I can't get those lines out of my head, Olga, I think I'll go mad. *(Irina enters.)*

OLGA. No, you won't. You're better already. You're fine now.

MASHA. No more crying.

OLGA. Good. Now, give me your hand. We'll go inside together.

MASHA. *(With sudden anger and lucidity.)* I am not going into that house! *(Sobbing again, softly.)* I'm not going into that house ever again.

IRINA. All right. That's all right. We'll all just sit here for a while and not speak at all.

KULYGIN. I took this beard and moustache from a boy in the third form yesterday. *(He puts it on.)* Look, Masha. Look. Who's this? Who am I? OLGA. Who?

KULYGIN. Our German master! *(Laughs.)* Isn't this exactly what he's like, Masha?

MASHA. Yes.

KULYGIN. There!

KULYGIN. I can make myself into a German Master. Would you like to see it? *(Puts on a false moustache and beard. Postures.)* I took them yesterday off a boy in the second-form.

MASHA. You look like him.

OLGA. You look exactly like him! *(Masha weeps.)*

KULYGIN. Funny, those boys.

OLGA. Come, Masha.

KULYGIN. *(To himself.)* I look so much like him.

[END]

OLGA. Very like him.

KULYGIN. Like him? It's him! *(In heavy German accent.)*

"I look and I say to me: who is beautiful three sisters what sits in those garden—ja?"

(Irina laughs. Then Olga. Finally Masha. The laughter lives for a few seconds and then dies.

Now Masha cries again, quietly and in resignation.)   [END]

Song and Allusion

One of the most overt differences in these renditions of the final moments between Masha and Vershinin is Mamet's complete deletion of the song of the "green oak tree" that is one of Masha's leitmotifs throughout the play. Senelick (2005) and Carson (2002a) explain that the song—or poem—is from Pushkin's fable or fairy-tale entitled *Ruslan and Lyudmila* (1820) that is "known to every Russian school-child" (2002a: 354). Senelick likens it to the popular Edward Lear poem "The owl and the pussycat went to sea, in a beautiful pea-green boat …"[18] In any case, Masha hums and sings or chants this poem three times in Act I, and here at the end of the play—except in Mamet's lone adaptation, where he, inexplicably, takes out this echoing reference in Act IV after *including it*, as do all other translations, in his first Act. The lack of consistency—even more than the blatant deletion—is puzzling.

---

18   Tom Markus' funny American adaptation transplants the three sisters to "a garrison town in the American West in the twilight of the 19th century" (Markus 1996: 485). Therein, the sisters want to get to *Charleston*—the "elegant city celebrated in *Gone with the Wind*"— and Masha's poem is changed to Tennyson's haunting "The Lady of Shalott." Renamed "Marcie" (also a nickname of Mary), she recites

On either side the river lie

Long fields of barley and of rye,

That clothe the wold and meet the sky …

'I am half-sick of shadows' said the Lady of Shalott.

The charm and calming "th" sounds of the poem, along with Lady *Sh*alott, seem fitting for the character. The creation of the play in American idiom and history is singular, a refreshing anomaly among the 37 renditions.

It is significant that Masha recalls (in all but Mamet's rendition) the song she remembers from years ago—before her affair with Vershinin. The poem is about a girl kidnapped by a wizard on her wedding night, and then found by her husband after years of adventures (Senelick 2005: 253). Perhaps Masha relates it to her "abduction" by Kulygin. The song returns to her when she sees there is no way to keep Vershinin in her life. What upsets her, one intuits, is that her life is now, "just the way it was before" Vershinin. The force of Chekhov's comment on reminiscence and irony in life and love may be lost when this poem is cut from Masha and Vershinin's final scene.

Sound and Rhythm

What also seems to be ignored by many translators is the *sound* of the poem in English. Schmidt's iambic quarter meter—

"Beside' the sea' there stands' a tree,'
and on' that tree'a gol'den chain' ..."—

is easy to chant in English, like a child's nursery rhyme. Others, such as "I saw the shore that strides the sea, a green oak, green oak, oh, green oak tree ..." from McGuinness, or "A green oak grows by a curving shore ..." from Friel, have more complicated cadences, so it seems they would be difficult for Masha to utter in her present state of disarray. It's also more humorous if Masha can repeat the first two lines of the poem—which we recognize from Act I—and then botch up those simple lines with "an educated cat." The *sounds* and "speakability" for the actor must be considered, rather than the literal *meaning* of the Russian text. To leave out Masha's attempts to sing or chant the poem altogether, as Mamet does here in Act IV—inconsistent with his inclusion of the poem in Act I—loses the allusion to childhood, to Masha's relationship with Vershinin, and her attitude towards Kulygin. Chekhov's repetitions are always purposeful.

Stage Directions

Other anomalies are Friel's additions of his own descriptive Stage Directions, for example, at Vershinin's departure:

Olga takes Masha, still sobbing, in her arms. Vershinin takes Olga's free hand and kisses it. Then he leaves. Masha emits a long loud anguished howl.

In Friel's "version," it seems Masha does not get her final hug from Vershinin, present in all the other renditions: Friel cuts out the final embrace between Masha and Vershinin, and lets the last touch be between *Olga* and Vershinin, rather than the two lovers. This could be effective (what does it say about the Olga/Vershinin relationship?), but it is not in the original. Friel also gives coaching to Kulygin, wholly missing from other translations, and, apparently, from Chekhov's Russian play:

(Kulygin enters. He is so embarrassed, so totally defeated, that even his clichéd and protective speech patterns fail him. He cries quietly. As he cries. […])

This is a complete concoction on the part of the "version" writer. In Friel's version, we read that Kulygin has witnessed the heated goodbye of Masha and Vershinin, and that he is crushed by it. Chekhov did not include this observation, so hugely sentimental. These are choices meant for the actors and director. Again, it seems an attempt to direct the play from the desk of the "version"-writer.

Next, Friel deletes both a "pause" in this scene, and Irina's line that she is "going away" (Schmidt), "leaving" (McGuinness) or "off tomorrow" (Mamet):

FRIEL:
IRINA. All right. That's all right. We'll all just sit here for a while and not speak at all.

SCHMIDT:
IRINA. … we don't have to say anything.
I'm going away tomorrow, remember. *(Pause.)*

McGUINNESS:
IRINA. Tomorrow I'm leaving here, you know.

(Silence.)

MAMET:
IRINA. *(Pause)* I'm off tomorrow,
you know.

Cutting out "Pauses," as Friel does, or changing their syntax, as Mamet does, changes rhythm and "beats" of the scenes. The new "beat" here, beginning after the lines above, could be Kulygin's attempt to try to get Masha to laugh about his German beard and mustache, in order, of course, to win her back. The "Pause" or "Silence" before this beat allows the actors to respond to Irina going away. Dropping the line completely, as Friel does, removes a vital plot point: Irina too is departing. The others don't have time to muse over the fact of her departure, and what it will do to them. And Mamet's *Pause*—placed *before* Irina's line about leaving—begins the "beat" on a different thought, which may change the Action for Irina: maybe she's just "off work" the next day. Actually, she's leaving the district.

Yet another addition by Friel is a speech at the end of the scene, where he has Kulygin speak in a "heavy German accent" and directs Irina, Olga and Masha how to "laugh." For some theatre practitioners, this is helpful; it could be fun for the actors. For others, it is anathema, like stage managers' notes added in a version of a previously produced play: they should be summarily cut out. Such liberties with the script may help "clarify" what the translator believes were Chekhov's intentions, but it is vital to note that they are not in Chekhov's original. Manipulating characters, leaving out repeated phrases or songs, changing interstices of Chekhov's "grid" of a dramaturgy and adding or replacing dialogue is more risky in Chekhov than in works of other playwrights. In *Three Sisters* especially, it drives home McKellen's observation: "we don't do Chekhov; we do *translations* of Chekhov."

There are more anomalies in the renditions above that skew relationships between characters. Mamet's last words from Vershinin—"Don't forget me. Don't forget me. Don't forget me."—are not in other translations, and they abandon Chekhov's choice for more clumsy (and ironic) last words from this "romantic" hero: "I'm late." In explicating Chekhov's plays, it is useful to know his views on the themes he tackles. Two notes from Chekhov reveal what the playwright thinks about this subject of love:

> Love. Either it is a remnant of something degenerating, something which once has been immense, or it is a particle of what will in the future develop into something immense; but in the present it is unsatisfying, it gives much less than one expects.
> *Notebook of Anton Chekhov*, 1896 (tr. Kotelian: Woolf 1921: 65–6)

> The one incontestable truth about love is that it is a mystery and all that is written about it is not a solution but a series of questions that remain unanswered.
> From Chekhov's short story "About Love," 1898 (Jarrell 1969: 105)

It is significant that there are no happy marriages in Chekhov's plays. The relationships of all the couples in *Three Sisters* reflect these two assertions above. While both couples, Irina/Tuzenbach and Masha/Vershinin, are suited to each other as far as their backgrounds (educated upper class) and temperaments are concerned, Irina's lack of attraction to Tuzenbach and the fact that Masha and Vershinin are both married to others makes their loves almost impossible in the present. Andrey ends up miserable, pushing the baby carriage of a child that may not be his own. Only Natasha—seen as one of Chekhov's most vicious and unyielding characters— seems content, but, notably, not with her husband. So, what may seem like minor or negligible differences among various translations of Chekhov's plays may wholly tinge the strong themes he puts forward: "Don't forget me" may suggest a "romantic" belief in "the power of love" while "I'm late" suggests a more practical and possibly selfish concern. Which is the Vershinin Chekhov wants to leave his audience with? The actor may provide inflection and underlying purpose, but is still at the mercy of the translator (McKellen in Gottlieb and Allain 2000: 122).

Impossible love may be a symptom of a deeper theme: the search for transcendence in a vulgar world. These citations describe a larger Superobjective for the play:

> That's how the three sisters feel: trapped. They were born in Moscow, but their father took them to live in a provincial town three hundred miles away. […] Here the symbol is Moscow. It is not a city. It is an idea to which you can attach hope.
>
> (Adler 1999: 262)

> "To Moscow!" says Irina …
> "So why don't they just go," says the perplexed spectator. […]
> "But my dear," a friend explained to me, "this is not the Moscow train station, or Moscow, some commodity. This is symbolic Moscow … They don't yet sell tickets to this station."
>
> (*Novosti dnia*, Feb. 2, Mar. 3, 1901; op. cit., Chudakov 1983: 162)

Indeed, where the three sisters and their brother want to go, there is, as yet, no train stop.

If *Seagull* is filled with "tons of love," as Chekhov stated, *Sisters* is heaving with the desire to escape. Just like *Vanya*'s map of Africa suggests an unknown world of which the play's characters may only dream, Moscow reminds the three sisters of a happier time, and is, as Adler suggests above, their symbol for the hope of a fulfilled life. As Clurman noted, their cry, as with characters in the previous plays, is always "I want to live!" whether it is for true love, art, or meaningful work. Olga is exhausted by her teaching job, yet she accepts a promotion at the school. Irina lets go of her dream of true love in Moscow to marry Tusenbach, only to lose him too, and so also takes on what may be a dreary teaching position. Masha is dashed by the loss of Vershinin, but seems strangely hopeful as she laughs at Kuligin's mustache and agrees to go home with him in the last moments of the play. None of them does "escape." But, as the *Novosti dnia* article above observes, there is no more a "ticket to this station" of hope than there is a trip to Africa for Vanya, Astrov or Sonya. It is in accepting their present lives that the three sisters will endure.

References

Adler, Stella. *On Ibsen, Strindberg and Chekhov*. Ed. Barry Paris. New York: Alfred A. Knopf, 1999.

Allen, David. *Performing Chekhov*. London: Routledge, 2000.

Brustein, Robert. *The Theatre of Revolt*. Boston: Little, Brown and Company, 1964.

Chekhov, Anton. *Anton Chekhov, Four Plays*. Trans. David Magarshack. New York: Hill and Wang, 1969.

————. *Anton Chekhov Plays*. Trans. Peter Carson. London: Penguin Books, 2002.

————. *Anton Chekhov Selected Works*, Trans. Kathleen Cook. Moscow: Progress Publishers, 1973.

————. *Anton Chekhov's Plays*, Trans. and ed. Eugene Bristow. New York: W. W. Norton & Co., 1977.

————. *Anton Chekhov's Selected Plays*. Trans. and ed., Laurence Senelick. New York: W. W. Norton & Co., 2005.

————. *Anton Chekhov's Three Sisters*. Trans. Štěpan S. Šimek. Unpublished manuscript: 2014.

————. *Best Plays by Chekhov*. Trans. Stark Young. New York: The Modern Library, 1956.

————. *Chekhov: The Essential Plays*. Trans. Michael Henry Heim. New York: Modern Library, 2003.

————. *Chekhov for the Stage*. Trans. Milton Ehre. Evanston, IL: Northwestern University Press, 1992.

————. *Chekhov, Four Plays*. Trans. Carol Rocamora. Lyme, NH: Smith and Kraus, 1996.

————. *Chekhov, The Major Plays*. Trans. Ann Dunnigan. New York: Signet Classic, Penguin Books, 1964.

————. *Chekhov, The Major Plays*. Trans. Jean-Claude Van Itallie. New York: Applause Books, 1995.

————. *Chekhov Plays*. Trans. Michael Frayn. London: Methuen, 1988.

————. *Chekhov's Major Plays*. Trans. Karl Kramer and Margaret Booker. New York: University Press of America, 1997a.

————. *Chekhov, The Russian Text of Three Plays: Uncle Vanya, The Three Sisters, The Cherry Orchard* Cambridge: University Press, 1946.

————. *Four Plays by Chekhov*. Trans. Alex Szogyi. New York: Washington Square Press, 1968.

————. *Notebook of Anton Chekhov*. Trans. S. S. Koteliansky and Leonard Woolf. New York: B. W. Huebsch, 1922.

————. *The Oxford Chekhov*. Trans. Ronald Hingley. London: Oxford University Press, Vol. II, 1967, Vol. III, 1964, and Vol. IX, 1975.

————. *The Personal Papers of Anton Chekhov*. Trans. S. S. Koteliansky. New York: Lear Publishers, 1948.

————. *Plays, Anton Chekhov*. Trans. Elisaveta, Fen. Middlesex, England: Penguin Books, Ltd., 1951, 1954.

————. *The Plays of Anton Chekhov*. Trans. Constance Garnett. New York: The Modern Library, 1929.

————. *The Plays of Anton Chekhov*. Trans. Paul Schmidt. New York: Harper Collins Publishers, 1997b.

————. *The Russian Text of Three Plays: Uncle Vanya, Three Sisters, The Cherry Orchard*. Ed. P. Henry. Letchworth, Hertfordshire, England: Bradda Books Ltd., 1965.

————. *Six Plays of Chekhov*. Version. Robert W. Corrigan. San Francisco: Rinehart Press, 1962.

————. *Three Sisters*. Trans. Sharon Marie Carnicke, University of Southern California. Unpublished Manuscript, 1979.

———. *Three Sisters*. Version. Brian Friel. New York: Dramatists Play Service, 1981.

———. *The Three Sisters*. Adapt. Christopher Hampton. UK: Samuel French, 2004/2015.

———. *The Three Sisters*. Trans. Randall Jarrell. London: Collier-Macmillan Limited, 1969.

———. *The Three Sisters*. Adapt. David Mamet. Trans. Vlada Chernomirdik. New York: Samuel French, 1990a.

———. *Three Sisters*. Version. Frank McGuinness. Literal Trans. Rose Cullen. London: Faber and Faber Limited, 1990b.

———. *Three Sisters*. Acting Version. Clifford Odets. Unpublished manuscript from Phoebe Brand's script, given to me by Stephen Carnovsky. The Group Theatre, New York City, c. 1939.

———. *Three Sisters*. Trans. Paul Schmidt. New York: Theatre Communications Group, 1992.

———. *Three Sisters*. Trans. Lanford Wilson. Lyme, NH: Smith and Kraus, 1984.

Chudakov, A. P. *Chekhov's Poetics*. Trans. Edwina Jannie Cruise and Donald Dragt. Ann Arbor: Ardis, 1983.

Eekman, Thomas. *Anton Čechov*. Leiden, Netherlands: E. J. Brill, 1960.

Gilman, Richard. *Chekhov's Plays*. New Haven: Yale University Press, 1995.

Gottlieb, Vera and Paul Allain, eds. *The Cambridge Companion to Chekhov*. Cambridge University Press, 2000.

Jackson, Robert Louis. *Reading Chekhov's Text*. Evanston, IL: Northwestern University Press, 1993.

Kataev, Vladimir. *If Only We Could Know!* Trans./Ed. Harvey Pitcher. Chicago: Ivan R. Dee, 2002.

Magarshack, David. *Chekhov the Dramatist*. New York: Hill and Wang, 1960.

Markus, Tom. *How to Read a Play*. Dubuque, IA: Kendall/Hunt Publishing Company, 1996.

Mirsky, D. S. *A History of Russian Literature*. Ed. Francis J. Whitfield. Evanston, IL: Northwestern University Press, 1999.

Pitcher, Harvey. *The Chekhov Play*. Berkeley: University of California Press, 1985.

Ross, Yana. Lithuanian actor: CV/Performances in *Three Sisters* at yanaross.com, 2017.

Senelick, Laurence. *The Chekhov Theatre*. Cambridge: Cambridge University Press, 1997, 2005.

Styan, J. L. *Chekhov in Performance*. Cambridge: Cambridge University Press, 1971.

Valency, Maurice. *The Breaking String*. New York: Schoken Books, 1983.

CHAPTER NINE

The Cherry Orchard

McKellen: Chekhov provides much more satisfying characters to play because you
            have such details that you don't need to guess. I think his instruction to
            Stanislavsky was that you should *not* guess, because the material is all
            there[1] ...
            There are so many themes going on in Chekhov's plays, but in such a
            delicate way, always rooted and expressed in the text. [...]
Gottlieb: So complexity is the key dimension of the characters?
McKellen: Yes. I would find it very hard to write about Chekhov, but I don't find
            it very difficult to act.

               Actor Ian McKellen to Critic Vera Gottlieb (2000: 128–9)

McKellen makes two points presented in this study: the actor's work is embedded
in Chekhov's texts, and writing about Chekhov is harder than just *doing* it onstage.
Details of word choice, punctuation and other written exigencies *on the page* of
translations are of utmost importance to the actor, as they propel this *doing* known
as Action. McKellen is arguing for the detailed Script Analysis this study propounds. Like human beings in "real" life, Chekhov's characters are complex. They

---

1   When actors from the MAT would ask Chekhov about his characters he often responded
    that it was "all there" in his script. Script analysis, requisite for the actor, is a development
    of Stanislavsky technique.

do one thing and say another. They put forward strong points of view, and then they disavow these views. They begin the plays advancing one thing, and, by the final curtain, they are *doing* the exact *opposite* thing. Deep convictions are undercut. And it's very funny.

This paradox is a key to Chekhov's last play, *Cherry Orchard*. More than any of his full-length creations, this one combines comedy with tragedy so "delicately" that we laugh "through tears" and cry while we laugh. Translators Kramer and Booker claim that "This sense of emotions simultaneously comic and serious, or situations which suddenly veer from one extreme to another, reaches its apex in *The Cherry Orchard*, where virtually every moment is infused with a double feeling" (Chekhov 1997a: 13). The problem of which style Chekhov should be played in is a moot point. McKellen notes:

> I remember speaking to Russian director Efros[2] ... [who] made the point that Chekhov is not exclusively a naturalistic playwright, and that there are many many styles within his writing. *You'd be hard put to know that from reading translations!* Once you realize that you may be killing the effect of a Chekhov play by resolutely playing it in only one style, *then* you have a chance of unlocking its richness. ... Michael Frayn[3] makes Chekhov's play [*Orchard*] into an English comedy ... Looking around for the possibility of different styles of presentation can be very helpful. (first emphasis added, 124)

McKellen's observation is spot-on. In some translations, including those from British, Irish and American playwrights, Chekhov takes on the tone and feel of an English drawing room or an American domestic drama rather than the "*poetic comedy* of exquisite balance" described by J. L. Styan (1971: 244). Chekhov's *Orchard* demonstrates this balance with less pathos than his drama *Three Sisters*, and with more objectivity towards the characters. Jean-Louis Barrault (1910–1994)[4] insists Chekhov's *Orchard* leaves behind a sense of impartiality, as his characters are ambiguous, with no conventional heros (Chekhov 2005: 627). For this reason,

---

2 Anatoly Efros is an iconoclast Russian director, who set his "non-naturalistic" 1975 *Cherry Orchard* in a graveyard replete with family portraits (Gottlieb and Allain 2000: 189).

3 Russian speaker Frayn, is considered by some to be the "best" translator of Chekhov into English (See Rayfield 1994: 44–5 and Ryapolova, "English Translations: a Russian view," in *Chekhov on the British Stage*, ed. Patrick Miles, 1993: 233–5). Still, for Americans, his British-isms are impossible to overcome.

4 Renowned French director/actor of the postwar era, known for highly stylized pieces, notably Ionesco's *Rhinoceros* in 1978 (Cohen 1981: 140). He played Trofimov in *Cherry Orchard* (1954), and wrote the article "Pourquoi *La Cerisaie*?" ["Why The Cherry Orchard?"] (tr. Senelick, Chekhov 2005: 620).

many consider *Orchard*, rather than *Sisters*, to be Chekhov's masterpiece, his best-loved play, and his most universal.[5]

Styles in Chekhov's last four plays are defined so much by the imprints of the text that any departure from Chekhov's "grid" may tilt the poetic balance. As Styan puts it, "if production allows either the heroics of prophecy [Trofimov's 'future'] or the melo-drama of dispossession [Ranevskaya's loss of the orchard], then all of Chekhov's care for balance is set at naught and the fabric of his play torn apart" (245–6). Styan writes:

> Farce, which prohibits compassion for human weakness, and tragedy, which demands it, are close kin. The truth is that *The Cherry Orchard* is a play which treads the tightrope between them, and results in the ultimate form of that special dramatic balance we know as Chekhovian comedy. (245)

But it is not just the production that could distort Chekhov's style and meanings; the translated script itself may twist Chekhov's score more endemically than any actor's performance alone. This has been demonstrated in *Seagull*, *Vanya* and *Three Sisters*, and it is also true for the play that "treads the tightrope" as gracefully as *Cherry Orchard*.

Title and Character Names

Characters in *Orchard* are subject to more vaudevillian antics than those in any of the last four plays. They are almost all clowns. As with *Seagull* and *Uncle Vanya*, *Cherry Orchard*, as a comedy, has character names that resonate with ironic meanings and associations. The start of Act I could be the beginning of a play by Molière. The play begins with an inverted take on the popular well-made play and commedia dell'arte device of having servants, or lower class characters—in this case Lopakhin, Dunyasha and Yepikhodov—reveal the exposition in the first scene.[6] The mistress of the house is returning for the first time in five years, but Lopakhin has just been asleep and Dunyasha has taken on the airs of a "lady"

---

5   Carson states it is best-loved and most frequently performed (Chekhov 2002a: xxx); Tyrone Guthrie notes it exceeds critical and popular acclaim of the other plays; Pitcher sees it as much richer than its predecessors and not in any sense partisan (159, 166); Styan proclaims it the supreme achievement of the naturalistic movement (1971: 239); Kataev says it is the most celebrated play of 20th century world drama (268).

6   Senelick likens themes in *Orchard* to those in Beaumarchais' *Marriage of Figaro*, where the clever servant outwits his less capable master; the idea of the social misfit or "misanthrope" variously fits Lopakhin, Charlotta the governess, Dunyasha and the social climber servant

rather than the servant girl she is. Yepikhodov, a clerk ("bookkeeper" in Senelick; "money manager" and "accountant" in Donaghy) who also puts on airs, is known as "twenty-two misfortunes" in Calderon (1912), Young (1956), Gielgud (1963), Cook (1973) and Van Itallie (1995, 1979), or:

"two-and-twenty misfortunes" (Garnett 1929; Fen 1954; Corrigan 1962)
"Endless Misfortune" (Mamet 1985)
"twenty-two disasters" (Ehre 1992; Kramer/Booker 1997a; Heim 2003)
"Two-and-Twenty Hard Knocks" (Bristow 1977)
"Two-and-twenty Troubles" (Dunnigan 1964)
"twenty-two troubles" (Szogyi 1968; Senelick 1977; Carnicke 1980)
"Twenty-two Calamities" (Magarshack 1969)
"Twenty Times Trouble" (Hulick 1994)
"Tons of Trouble" (Senelick 2005)
"Double Trouble" (Schmidt 1997c)
"The Walking Disaster" (Mann 2000)
"The Walking Accident" (Carson 2002)
"Disasters by the Dozen" (Frayn 1988)
"Mister Disaster" (Rocamora 1996)
"Mister Misery" (Logan 1950)
'Million Miseries' (Griffiths 1978)
[misfortunes] "Never come singly" (Guthrie/Kipnis 1965)
"Simple Simon" (Hingley 1964)
"Two Left Feet" (Sherman 2006) and the inimitable current
"Yepikhodork" (Donaghy 2004)

Peter Gill's 1978 "version," has *no* nickname at all, while in Chay Yew's 2004 "adaptation," he is cut completely from the text. Gill—who considers his play a "version"—mentions only that people do call Epikhodov (variant spelling) names because he is "unlucky," and that he is a fool. Yew dispenses with comic characters in his adaptation, so Yepikhodov and his eccentricities don't fit in.

Senelick relates that the literal translation of Yepikhodov's nickname is "twenty-two misfortunes," but the chosen designation in particular translations makes a difference to audiences and actors. The nomenclatures with "two-and-twenty"—even those with "twenty-two"—are literal, and sound old-fashioned.

Yasha, Firs (out of his "serf" element) and even Varya, who longs for something beyond her housekeeping (Chekhov 2005: 317).

"Tons of Trouble" is more contemporary, but Schmidt's "Double Trouble"—a true
American metaphor—may well bring a smile. This is possibly also true of "The
Walking Disaster" and "The Walking Accident," both contemporary attempts at
new names. "Yepikhodork" also brought howls from the audience (spring 2005
at the Atlantic Theatre Company, New York City), but the word "dork" was not
known in 19th century Russia. "Mister Disaster" may be a bit cute and labored,
"Mister Misery" and "Million Miseries" are not true of Yepikhodov (he's actually
rather upbeat) though they are onomatopoeic. "Simple Simon" does not describe
Yepikhodov's problem, and "Never come singly" is grammatically awkward and
takes too much thought. Gill's solution—like Mamet's with the "golden chain"
poem in *Three Sisters*—is no solution at all. Cutting out Chekhov's chosen character nickname altogether seems unnecessarily dismissive. Cutting characters from
the script (as Yew does) changes style and themes—and thus Actions—entirely.

Here are another three translations that put Dunyasha's response to Yepikhodov in Act I in context:

FRAYN (1988)

DUNYASHA: To tell you
the truth, he's proposed to
me.

LOPAKHIN: Ah!

DUNYASHA: I don't know
what to say ... He's all right,
he doesn't give any trouble,
it's just sometimes when
he starts to talk – you can't
understand a word of it. It's
very nice, and he puts a lot
of feeling into it, only you
can't understand it. **I quite
like him** in a way, even.
He's madly in love with me.
He's the kind of person who
never has any luck. Every
day something happens.
They tease him in our part
of the house – they call him
Disasters by the Dozen ...

SHERMAN (2006)

I have to tell you a secret.
Yepikhodov's proposed
to me.

Oh dear.

I'm not sure what to do
... He's nice.
But sometimes, when
he starts talking, it's all
gibberish – I mean, it
sounds alright at first,
there are always a few
flowery phrases, but then
finally it stops making
sense.
**I don't actually dislike
him.** And he *is* madly
in love with me. But
he's so accident-prone.
Every day there's another
drama. The staff call him
Two Left Feet.

DONAGHY (2004)

Yepikhodov proposed to
me.

You're kidding.

He's nice and all, I mean
he says nice things - I
mean I think they're nice
things. I don't under-
stand half of what comes
out of his mouth. Which
I shouldn't hold against
him.
**But then he's such a loser,
too!** I mean, everyone says
so.
Behind his back. They call
him **Yepikhodork.**

Notice how Lopakhin responds variously ("Ah" is in most translations) to Dunyasha's news that Yepikhodov has asked her to marry him, and the Britishness of Frayn's *I quite like him.* Frayn too adds ellipses at the end, and dashes not present in the others (he is the one Russian speaker of the three). Donaghy's *He's such a loser* brought laughs in performance (2005), but some may argue it is not exactly Chekhov's turn of phrase. Still, in performance, contemporary audiences respond to familiar idiomatic language regardless of the period in which the play is set (Donaghy's Atlantic Theatre production was—purposefully, we must assume—costumed in Edwardian dress, though the language was pointedly contemporary).

Other names of Chekhov's characters are also resonant with aspects of their personalities. Most significantly, "Lyubov"—for Lyubov Andreevna Ranevskaya—means "love," about which she is rather indiscriminate. Her brother Gaev—for Leonid Andreevich Gaev—has the ironic "Leo the Lion" in his first name, and the Russian *gaer* or clown for his last (Chekhov, tr. Senelick, 1977: 163 and Rayfield 1994: 48, respectively). Lopakhin may be derived from the Russian *lopat* for "shovel"—he is always at work and earthy. Strangely, Griffiths' version calls Lopakhin by the first name "Alexander," an upper class name. Perhaps this comes from his patronymic "Alexeyevich," but it is a paradoxical coupling with his given name, Yermolay, which is decidedly rural (Rayfield 1994: 48). The constant borrower/neighbor's last name, Simeonov-Pishchik (a funny sound in English too) means *pishchat* or "to chirp," so that Bristow says his name might be "Squeak" while Senelick calls him "Tweet" (Chekhov 2005: 323). He is always squeaking around Lyubov for money. Bristow relates that *Yepikhodov* incorporates a Russian word meaning "run" or "speed," and this character (Double Trouble or Walking Accident) is always running into things and knocking them over (1977: 163). Firs is appropriately named after Saint Thyrsus, martyred in 251 A.D. (Chekhov 2005: 323).

In the theatre, the names suggest possibilities for physical actions for the characters: Lopakhin "waves his arms" in Chekhov's script, and this, with his name Yermolay, suggests a working class guy, while Gaev could have clownish qualities (with a lionish mane?) and the squeaky Pishchik could "fly in" and peck at Lyubov like a hummingbird. These physical actions also suggest the underlying *psychological* Actions of the characters. Thus the names aid the actor's practical research on character.

Two interesting associations make *The Cherry Orchard* the perfect name for the play. In Russian, there are, according to Senelick, two ways to pronounce the title *Vish'nevy sad*: with the accent on the first syllable—"an orchard of cherries"—or the accent on the second syllable—*Vishnev'y sad*—which means "a cherry orchard" (Chekhov 2005: 323). Chekhov chose the latter, because, as Stanislavsky explains, an "orchard of cherries" brings in profits, but a "*cherry* orchard" does nothing but "preserve within itself and its snow-white blossoms the poetry of the life of the masters of olden times" (*My Life in Art*, 417). In other words, Chekhov thought the former was commercial, and the latter only beautiful. This is true in the play, as we discover that no one sells the cherries anymore, and they have forgotten (Firs, the ex-serf tells us) the recipe for the wonderful jam that used to be made. Further, this researcher discovered that there are two kinds of cherries in Russia: the *sweet* ones, called, *chereshnya* and the *sour* variety, called *vishnevy*.[7] So, Chekhov has named his play for a "Sour Cherry Orchard"[8] that is beautiful, but brings in no money. The irony of the title predicts that of the Superobjective (to save the orchard) and echoes character conflicts in the play.

Every character in *Orchard*, as in the other plays, has leitmotifs or traits that are contradictory. Lyubov, returning to her childhood home with her young daughter Anya, says she wants to keep the cherry orchard, but she is generous to a fault— she gives away gold coins she can ill afford to hand out, and literally spills money onto the ground in Act II. She repeatedly borrows money from Lopakhin, once a peasant, and now a thriving member of the middle class. Money is an issue for the landowner Simeonov-Pishchik, who is just as insistent on borrowing money from Lyubov. Gaev is Lyubov's brother, another member of the upper class, educated, but constantly playing his imaginary billiard shots and making grand speeches that make the rest of his family wince. He repeatedly claims that they may get money to save the orchard from their rich Aunt, but does nothing to procure the amount they need to pay the mortgage. Ironically, it is all the aristocratic characters who need money, and seem powerless to do anything about it, while the characters who work—Varya, the older adopted daughter who runs the house, her keys always hooked to her waist, Charlotta, Anya's Governess and an eccentric circus per-former, and the businessman Lopakhin—are aware that they must be productive in the "real" world. Trofimov, the perpetual student, and Anya are "above love" (or so Trofimov insists) but agree that they must work for the future.

McKellen points out that themes are so rich that actors can rehearse the play alternately with "points of concentration" on various aspects of theme or character:

> You would be alert to what is said about money: knowing how much money you earned … how much you have in your pocket … *every* character has some prob-lem with money. Whether they've got it or not … the whole play seems to be about

---

7   From Russian Janna Krylov, and Administrative Asst. Genya Aotman in the Slavic Studies Dept. at New York University (July 27, 2006).

8   Rayfield notes "*vishnia* means the sour, or Morello cherry, which is … cooked before it is eaten, as opposed to the sweet cherry (*chereshnia*). Really, the play should be called *The Sour-Cherry Orchard*" (1994: 136).

money! *Or* … the past—and you then discover that they all talk about the past non-stop. [Or] … *the future*—and they all talk about the future! Or … in a run-through, your point of concentration is one particular character … the thing uppermost in your mind as an actor was *that* character. You might find yourself *ignoring* him, but you would *know* you were ignoring him—and why. Once that's been done with all of the characters … you then realize as an actor that you can go on being Lopakhin—who I was—whether you are saying your lines to Trofimov, or to Ranevskaya, or to Dunya-sha. It doesn't matter—you go on being yourself. There's no end to the ways in which you can tell the story.

(Gottlieb 2000: 129)

This is testimony to the fact that the actor's *Action*—linked to what McKellen is calling the "point of concentration"—determines the turn of any one scene, and the force of the play as well. Chekhov's plays—especially *Cherry Orchard*—are so layered that the many concerns of the characters may be highlighted separately and the play remains intact. McKellen says Chekhov appeals to him especially because the Russian's plays cannot be realized in production *unless* every part has been worked on fully (129–30). The actor depends so much on the clues embedded in the script, that the particular translation—ideally, containing all Chekhov's intimations—is pivotal to the actor's preparation. Once again, McKellen substantiates the necessity of script work for the actor.

Cherry Orchard has also been called a "simple" play by critics because its plot is simple: the estate of the orchard will be sold out from under the longtime land-owners if they can't get the money together to pay the mortgage, or find a way to make the orchard pay for itself. Lopakhin has a way to let Lyubov and Gaev keep the estate—to break it up into the popular "dachas" for tourists, but this is abhorrent to the brother and sister who grew up on the land. Because they can't do anything, they lose it all. The intrigue of the play is *how* they manage to do "nothing" about this huge event—the sale of the orchard—and how each character manages to deal with the outcome.

Senelick describes how characters' speech patterns reflect their Actions: Lyubov uses diminutives and words of affection, along with vague adjectives like "some kind of" (2005: 322); Gaev's words are thick with platitudes; Pishchik grasps for breath (he has high blood pressure) while Lopakhin molds his words to fit the character he is addressing: blunt with servants, ingratiating to the aristocrats (*Ibid.*). With Varya he is teasing and possibly embarrassed (he yells "Moo!" at her) and often facetious (*Ibid.*). Yasha, servant to Lyubov, is obsequious towards her, but opportunistic in his Actions. He is rude to the older Firs, who, for all his senility, is in charge of the servants and takes good care (unlike Yasha) of his master Gaev and mistress Lyubov. It is Yasha who repeatedly calls Firs—and Firs applies the term to himself at the end of the play—"nedo'tyopa." The term

Figure 9.1: *The Cherry Orchard*. Katherine Alt Keener as Mme. Ranevskaya (Lyubov) and Sue-Ellen Mandell as Gayev, Columbia University Theatre, NYC, 2017. In Act I, Lyubov is joyful, returning to her childhood nursery. Brother Gayev looks on happily in the background, in this gender-bending production of the University MFA Directing Program. Director: Mark Herbert Barford. Translator: Paul Schmidt. Photo Credit: Abo Huang.

means anything from a "wash-out" to a "flibbertigibbet" and is described at the end of this chapter. It is perhaps, as Senelick suggests, the term Chekhov meant to sum up inchoate qualities in all of the characters (*Ibid.*). Like the "chudaki" in *Vanya*, all the characters are multi-layered, eccentric and still changing as human beings.

I have read and/or seen 36 extant renditions of *Cherry Orchard*. First, Stage Directions that put forward *circumstances* (see Appendix A) of the characters will be compared and explored.

The Translations, Stage Directions, Act I

PAUL SCHMIDT (1997c)

A room they still call the nursery. A side door leads to Anya's room. Almost dawn; the sun is about to rise. It's May; the cherry orchard is already in bloom, but there's a chill in the air. The windows are shut. Enter Dunyasha with a lamp, and Lopakhin with a book in his hand.

TOM DONAGHY (2004)

A train whistle is heard in the near distance. Lights up.

Dawn. A room that is still called the nursery. One of the doors leads to Anya's bedroom.

It's May; the cherry trees are in bloom, but there is frost on their branches.

The train whistle blows again. Closer this time.

Dunyasha enters with a candle. Lopakhin follows, clutching a book.

TREVOR GRIFFITHS (1978)

Black.

A slow gathering of light reveals a single cherry tree in flower. The image steadies; holds. A long way away, the sound of a steel cable groaning under stress.

Closer, though still distant, a train whistles its approach.

Silence.

Fade to black.

Black.

Tape: (LOPAKHIN's *voice*): (first line of play in Russian)

Early dawn light reveals the old nursery, several doors leading from it, one to Anya's room. May. Frost. Shut windows. LOPA-KHIN, *late thirties, strong-shouldered, bearded, in suit, white shirt, light calf-skin boots, sprawls uneasily in a winged chair, an open book across his chest, sleeping fit-fully. The sound of the train's whistle wakes him.* DUNYASHA *comes in, carrying a lit candle, as* LOPAKHIN *fumbles for his watch.*

CHAY YEW (2004)

Spring.

Early morning.

Downstage in a corner is a round marble table with several black lacquer stools. On One stool is a bouquet of white ying fa (prunus yedeonsis) blossoms.

As the audience enters the theatre, they see LIAO *is asleep on a chair with his head on the table. On the table is a hard covered book. Next to him is a gramophone that is continuously playing a record that has ended. A scratch. A click. A scratch. A click.*

Sound of a train pulling into the station.

Screeching brakes.

Upstage, QING *carries a lantern and looks out expectantly into the street.*

Silence.

Suddenly, QING *coughs violently, waking* LIAO.

JOSHUA LOGAN (1950)

The children's parlor and part of the gallery surrounding the big house, on Wisteria Plantation.

It is at first glance a room that has been lived in for generations. The furniture and the decorations have been changed and added to many times. It is an elegant room but shows signs of disrepair. Elaborately carved moldings are still evident. There is a crystal chandelier. The ceilings are tall, the wallpaper is old.

There are also many reminders of the children who have lived in this room—an elaborately carved child's piano, several children's chairs, a children's table, and some old toys. On a shelf are two stuffed animals made of felt; they are pretty bedraggled now. One is a frog; he wears a frock coat and a small sword and pistol are attached to his belt. The other is a mouse who wears a white satin dress and a bridal veil.

In the upstage wall there are two very tall French windows with jalousies or two-battened blinds. Above them is a fan-shaped West Indian blind. There is also one of these windows in the right wall through which the sun is seen to rise during the first act.

There is an archway in the upper left wall which leads to the hall and the rest of the house. In the wall are two more windows opening onto the gallery.

When the blinds are open, the long gallery which surrounds the house can be seen, with part of the tall, fluted columns that surround the house and the banisters between them. Above the banisters are the wisteria vines with their thick, tortuous trunks and silver bark. Beyond the vines, which practically screen out any view of the outside, can be seen the purple flowers in spring, the heavy leaves in summer, the thinned out leaves of autumn and the bare, web-like sprigs of winter.

When the curtain goes up it is dark, before dawn, in the month of April. A faint light reveals the room and then from the hall the light of a lamp carried by someone approaching can be seen. A Negro woman can be heard singing:

Oh, dere's fo' and twenty elders on deir knee-ees,
Oh, dere's fo' and twenty-elders on deir knee-ees.
The all rise together and face the risin' sun,
Singing, "Lord, have mercy … if you plee-eese."
A train whistle is heard not too far off.

DOLLY MAY, *a young Negro girl, enters. She is carrying a lamp, which gives the room more light. Now we can see that there are rain stains on the wallpaper of the walls and of the ceiling. The wisteria vine has grown across the gallery and entered the room and broken part of the fan-shaped blind above one of the windows.*

DAVID MAMET (1985)—There are no Stage Directions for Act I at all.

Stage Directions

As with the last three plays, the settings of Chekhov's original *Cherry Orchard* are tellingly progressive in their own way. The play begins in a room that *used to be* a nursery (see Schmidt above), on an early morning in May (in most of the translations). It proceeds in Act II to a field (or meadow) that *used to be* a graveyard near sunset, where the Action of the entire act is static and contemplative. It switches dramatically in Act III to a party scene in a drawing room downstage of a ballroom in the evening, with unlikely couplings of guests swirling madly through the two rooms while, offstage, the estate is being auctioned away. Finally, the last scene of Act IV is in the same room as Act I, but stripped and packed up to be vacated. The "nursery" is no more. In this last Act, no one would even suspect that the room *used to be* a nursery. It is important that the spectator see the orchard in Acts I and IV, and many productions have gone so far as to set the entire play amidst white blossoms.[9] Stanislavsky remembers that Chekhov wanted a

---

9   For examples: Andrei Serban's 1977 *Cherry Orchard*, Vivian Beaumont Theatre, NY and Giorgio Strehler's *Il giardino dei ciliegi*, Piccolo Teatro di Milano, 1974.

cherry branch actually "pushing into the room from the orchard" and wrote to Stanislavsky "Act 1, cherry blossom seen through the windows, an utterly white orchard. And the ladies in white dresses" (Rayfield 1994: 36, 38). As in all of Chekhov's last four plays, nature's encroachment on the Action is an elemental part of his dramaturgy.

However, Chekhov did not specify anything approaching the detail described in Logan's *Wisteria Trees*, where the play is transplanted to the American South. Logan has taken on the style of plays that were modern in the 1950s, more like those of Lillian Hellman, Eugene O'Neill, Tennessee Williams[10] or Lorraine Hansberry—that is, American Realism. The detailed set description resembles too the narrative prefaces of George Bernard Shaw: sets are explained in detail, and scene directions are explicit.

In Logan's play, characters are transformed to conform to the social hierarchies and relationships of the American South at the end of the 19th century. The play resembles *Gone with the Wind* more than any play by Chekhov. For examples, "Miss Lucy" (Lyubov) is portrayed as a sweet but patronizing mistress who cannot help but coddle the servants, and Gavin (Gaev) is too "friendly" with the black tenants on his land to collect rent from them. The character Firs is now "Scott," an African-American (Negro, at the time) "house" servant on the plantation, whose final scene at the end of the play is cut out entirely: Chekhov's tone of impartiality toward his characters is lost, as the play ends with a tearful, sentimental "good-bye" to the orchard from "Lucy" (Lyubov) and brother "Gavin" (Gaev), rather than the ironic note sounded by their faithful servant left alone in the house. Today, Logan's play probably might not be done because of the "politically incorrect" diminution of the servants; characters are twisted to fit into stereotypes of a by-gone Southern "gentility." Charlotta has become "Cassie, the Negro nurse" and Dunyasha is the flighty young black servant easily wooed by "Jacques" (Yasha).[11] One thing retained in Logan, from Chekhov's letter to Stanislavsky, is the protuberance of the tree (the purple wisteria, in this version) into the house in the opening scene. Of note is what Yew's re-formation has in common with Logan's version: though separated by over fifty years and two cultures, both replace Chekhov's dramaturgy with a sentimentality and melodrama not present in the original.

Yew's "adaptation," titled *A Winter People*, changes the setting to an estate in the Republic of China in 1935, during the last days of the Nationalist

---

10   Williams is considered more of a lyric or poetic Realist, more like Chekhov, and O'Neill went through an Expressionist period, but both had detailed, Realist settings with many props.

11   This role was played by a young Ossie Davis, and "Miss Lucy" by Helen Hayes, New York City, 1950.

Government. Firs has become a female octogenarian, and a character called "Wu" merges Charlotta and Dunyasha as a third daughter of Lyubov, who is re-named "Mme. Xia." She is now a singer returning from a concert career in San Francisco (thus the gramophone), rather than Paris. The daughters are redolent of *Three Sisters*, with Wu unhappily married to "Zhou" (like Masha to Kuligin). The play is loosely based on *Cherry Orchard*, and set amidst an industrializing China where women have only just stopped binding their feet. The "Passer-by" in Act II has become a Communist Soldier, the distant sound of the "breaking string" is replaced with a "sad cry of a bird" and the many "Silences" are not in Chekhov's original. Dialogue dispenses with many of Chekhov's careful undercuttings and counterpoints, and staging is choppy, with "parts of the stage" designated for duos rather than ensemble scenes. Act II is verbally and visually split into abrupt two-person confrontations. Ming (Varya) is bitter towards her mother at the loss of the orchard, which she sees as her legacy. Irony and Comedy seem sacrificed to Melodrama. The Logan and Yew translations are examples of extreme adaptations that dispense with Chekhov's dramaturgy, and loosely borrow his plot and characters; their inclusion in this study shows the imaginative efforts of translators to, perhaps, grab on to Chekhov's cachet, if not his style. Chekhov's humanity crosses cultures.

The first scene description above from Schmidt's translation, with few discrepancies, is the one given by most of the 36 translations noted in this study. The others reproduced above are departures from Chekhov's clear description. Donaghy, Griffiths and Yew add the sound of a train, and in Griffiths and Yew the scene opens with the Lopakhin character (Liao in Yew's adaptation) asleep on the stage. What this eclipses for the audience is a moment to see the stage unpeopled—to note the "nursery" that will undergo a drastic change by Act IV. Opening the play with the empty set was an innovation for Chekhov and Stanislavsky; it was purposeful on Chekhov's part. Griffiths' directions are more like those in a screenplay, with the explicit "fade to black" and added "voice-over" of Lopakhin speaking Russian (in Griffiths' script the Russian line is written in the Russian Cyrillic letters). Once again, unlike any of the other translators, Mamet has chosen *no* stage directions, while, as in his *Three Sisters*, he includes them in subsequent Acts. Where are Mamet's characters at the start of the play? He leaves it a mystery—or up to the stage director and designer—until Act II. Once again, since "*where* we are is *who* we are," Mamet's actor is left in the lurch for Act I. Set directions in Chekhov vitally affect actors' Actions.

Before comparisons of the final scene of *Orchard*, a discussion of Act II is important. More than any other single section of Chekhov's last four plays, Act II of *Cherry Orchard* is a precursor to modern drama: it is antecedent to Beckett's

Waiting for Godot,[12] as Gilman mentions, with its "lonely road at evening" ("A country road. A tree." are the only designations for Beckett's set) and "eventful immobility" (121, 159). Rayfield notes too that Chekhov's symbolism of the "eloquent but betrayed cherry orchard" is resounded in the "gaunt, leafless tree" in *Godot*'s sparse setting, but it cannot inspire the two tramps "Didi" and "Gogo"—so much like Chekhov's "nedo'tyopa" characters—to hang themselves (1994: 129). Indeed, the "tramp" in Act II of *Orchard* also heralds these vaudeville replants. *Cherry Orchard*'s comic/tragic contradictions are facts in Ionesco, Artaud, Pirandello and works of other modern dramatists as well. While Ibsen prompted Arthur Miller's style (the "problem play"), Chekhov begot another line of playwrights from the Absurdists and the avant-garde through to Harold Pinter.

Fergusson describes Chekhov's Act II as an "agon" of the plot—a contest between conflicting characters, from Greek ritual enactments of struggle—where "we see most clearly the divisive purposes of the characters, the contrasts between their views of the Cherry Orchard itself" (1953: 180). It has been seen as scenes of "stasis," with no Action. If Chekhov's last four masterpieces are "plays of indirect action," (Magarshack 1960: 264), Act II of *Orchard* is the clearest example of this structure. As Fergusson explains, it is composed of "many moments—composed, interrelated, echoing each other—when the waiting and loafing characters in Act II get a fresh sense (one after the other, each in his own way) of their situation on the doomed estate" (186). The stage directions, with the unusual outdoor setting, are integral to the poetry of the entire Act.[13]

The Translations, Act II, Scene One

PAUL SCHMIDT (1997c)

An open space. The overgrown ruin of an abandoned chapel. There is a well beside it and some large stones that must once have

TREVOR GRIFFITHS (1978)

Black.

Charlotte's voice on tape delivers first line in Russian [...] *Lights up, revealing a stage-wide*

---

12 Beckett steals conversations from Act II of *Orchard*:
    Trofimov: What were we talking about?
    Gayev: About pride.
    Trofimov: We talked a lot yesterday, but we didn't agree on anything. [...]
    Gayev: You'll die just the same, whatever you do. (etc.) (Peace 133)
        We hear junkets similar to this one between Didi and Gogo in *Waiting for Godot*. As Esslin points out, "In a purposeless world ... dialogue, like all action, becomes a mere game to pass the time" (1968: 86).

13 Chekhov himself found this second act most difficult to write. He feared it was "boring and monotonous, like a spider web" (S. D. Balukhaty, "*The Cherry Orchard:* A Formalist Approach," in *Chekhov*, ed. Jackson, p. 145; originally *Problem dramaturgicheskogo analiza. Chekhov*, tr. James Karambelas, London: 1927, chap. VII, pp. 148–61).

been grave markers. An old bench. Beyond, the road to the Gayev estate. On one side a shadowy row of poplar trees; they mark the limits of the cherry orchard. A row of telegraph poles, and on the far distant horizon, on a clear day, you can just make out the city. It's late afternoon, almost sunset. Carlotta, Yasha, and Dunyasha are sitting on the bench; Yepikhodov stands nearby, strumming his guitar; each seems lost in his own thoughts. Carlotta wears an old military cap and is adjusting the strap on a hunting rifle.

cyc. [cyclorama], *dark blue. A guitar strums. A crow barks overhead, once, twice; is answered by another. More lights reveal* YASHA *(smoking a long thin cigar), and* DUNYASHA *(powdering her face in a mirror), seated on a crude old country bench:* EPIKHODOV *standing, leg up on a tilted gravestone, playing a love song on a guitar; and Charlotte, in hunting clothes and cap, shortening the canvas sling on her rifle. They sit or stand, absorbed, separate, facing out. Behind them, set into the remnant of a wall, a traveller's shrine with a faded blue and gold icon of the Virgin Mary. It's twenty minutes to sunset. A full moon is already faintly silvering their skin.*

CHAY YEW (2004)

Summer.
At the end of the summer afternoon.
At one corner of the stage, XIA, HAN and LIAO are in the house talking.
At another corner of the stage, WU is sitting on a bench beneath the trees in the garden. While sewing her lotus shoes, WU sings a Cole Porter song.
QING is fanning WU.

DAVID MAMET (1985)

A field. The sun will soon be down. Charlotta, Yasha *and* Dunyasha *are sitting on the bench:*
Epihodoff *is standing near and playing the guitar.*
Charlotta *has taken a rifle from off her shoulders and is adjusting the buckle on the strap.*

The scenes in this Act, set in a "field," "meadow" or "countryside" in other translations, are as evocative as the opening park-with-a-lake scene in *Seagull*. Notice how Schmidt has set the Act in, simply, an "open space" rather than a "field" or a "meadow." It is, despite this difference, Schmidt's translation that mirrors most of the other 35 renditions. Just like the stage directions from Act I, which express that the room *used to be* or is "still called" the nursery, here there are stones and the "*ruin* of an *abandoned* chapel" which describe what the landscape *used to* be. The past is clearly represented. Styan notes that Chekhov wanted a peaceful scene—one of dissolution—but not a funereal one (1971: 274). Chekhov wrote "There is no cemetery—there had once been one, but two or three gravestones leaning in disorder are all that remain" (*Ibid.*). Like the lake behind the makeshift stage in *Seagull*, the background with telegraph poles, a glimpse of a city far away on the horizon with a part of the orchard visible through or by the poplar trees is important for the tone of the Act. It is ironic to be standing on a former gravesite while one moralizes about the future (as Trofimov does in this Act), and to reminisce about the death of one's child (as Lyubov does), surrounded by old tomb-stones. The telegraph poles also signal the future, as does the city in the distance. The contrast between the petty concerns of the servants at the start of the Act, every single character's troubles, and the vastness of the outdoors with the orchard that will be transformed at the end is a theatrical poem with visual, verbal and musical dimensions.

Fergusson writes that when music is played in Chekhov, it signals the audience to raise its eyes from the characters in the foreground up to the wider setting (1953: 181). Yepikhodov is strumming his guitar in Schmidt—and with his foot evocatively on a gravestone in Griffiths—while in Yew, the sister called "Wu" is singing Cole Porter. It is the *sound* that compels us to see the entire scene as an entity, or stage picture. This is helpful at the start of the Act, because we are more likely to notice the inconsistencies in the speeches and behavior of these "nedo'tyopa" characters who follow. Music, Brecht too has demonstrated, is an element that helps the audience see stage action objectively. The wider setting of the scene includes the distant town on the horizon, the telegraph poles, the ruined chapel and the edge of the orchard itself. Chekhov wrote that there is love for humanity in the creation of the telegraph and the steam engine (Hingley 1950: 180):

> An interest in scientific development is a well-established feature of Chekhov's outlook … "He liked looking at new buildings of original construction and at large sea-going steamers," Kuprin recalls in his reminisces of Chekhov: "He took a lively interest in all the latest technical inventions, and was not bored by the company of specialists."
>
> (1950: 177)

So, the inclusion of a telegraph line in the landscape of Act II of *Cherry Orchard* is significant. It presents the future, as does the town in the distance, while the tilted gravestones look back over the past. When these settings are changed or ignored, as Griffiths does with the substitution of the blue cyc (pronounced "sike") and, in Mamet's adaptation, once again Chekhov's poetry is eroded. Griffiths also puts into his beginning stage directions some character directives that Chekhov mentions later (Yasha's cigar and Dunyasha's compact), but Griffiths adds his own direction about the characters' demeanors ("absorbed") and the Virgin Mary icon. Yew, with Cole Porter and Wu's lotus shoes, also adds his own directorial choices. These touches, along with Mamet's deletions, may rob the actors of their own choices, prescribe different Actions for the characters and obscure or omit symbols that create Chekhov's careful composition. They may push to the foreground what Chekhov only hinted at in relief.

Mamet includes the objectifying music and the magical (twilight) time of day, but refuses to paint the backdrop. Intriguingly, he explains in his "Notes on *The Cherry Orchard*" that, like an actor, he consults what the characters *do* and the *way* that they do it, in determining what the play is all about (Chekhov 1985: vii). This is the actor's research. But Mamet foists his conclusions on the entire play, stating the play is simply a "series of scenes about sexuality, and, particularly, frustrated sexuality" (x). Many of Mamet's own original plays are about sexuality, but, unlike *Seagull* or *Vanya*, *Orchard* is not much about sex, though it is about love. In fact, numerous critics have noted how there is not one sex "triangle" in the play. (Maybe Dunyasha and Yasha, but Yasha quickly loses interest …). Mamet's effort to take *Orchard*'s themes and Superobjective away from the main plot—involving the sale of the land—is reductive, and ignores character complexities.

For example, Styan notes Chekhov's craftsmanship is evidenced by the progress of the settings (which Mamet leaves out) and the meaning of the cherry orchard itself, which is more than a "place." "It represents an inextricable tangle of sentiments, which together comprise a way of life … [so] an audience finds that the orchard grows from a painted backcloth to an ambiguous, living poetic symbol of *any* human life in a state of change" (1971: 241). And Fergusson reminds us how the play—with Act II as a significant element in the composition of the work—cannot be "reduced to either one emotion or one idea: [the images and feelings in the play] indicate an action and a scene which is 'there' before the rational formulations, or the emotionally charged attitudes, of any of the characters" (1953: 184). That is, the whole play may not be reduced to the Action "to pursue sex," as Mamet suggests. It is, rather, for Fergusson and others, a "poem of the suffering of change." *Orchard* is more than a "compilation of brilliant scenes" (Mamet 1985: xiii). Characters pursue individual Actions, and may not be conscious of attractions to other characters (like Trofimov towards Anya, for example, or Lopakhin towards Lyubov), but the play may not be reduced to the search for sexual fulfillment alone. In any case, Mamet's cutting of Chekhov's evocative and substantive stage directions—and continually cutting or changing "Pauses" which redefine the beats of the play—may help substantiate Mamet's take on the overall Action,[14] but

---

14 Mamet states that the play has no "through-action" ("Superobjective"—see Appendix A) (xii). Fergusson maintains that the play's Superobjective, which "all the characters share by analogy and suffer through, while moods shift and their perceptions alter," is "to save the Cherry Orchard" (1953: 176). Like *Sisters'* objective "to get to Moscow," "saving the orchard" is unrealized. This does not mean there is no "through-line." The cherry orchard is, rather—like going to Moscow—"an idea to which you can attach hope" (Adler 1999: 262).

they rob the play of Chekhov's original structure, and thus, possibly, Chekhov's underlying meanings.

Change of Scene/A Traveler

Two more anomalies among translations may be mentioned. In the original production of *Cherry Orchard* at the MAT, Stanislavsky asked Chekhov to change the ending of Act II, and he did so. The first performance of the play ended with a scene between unlikely compatriots Firs and Charlotta. Charlotta describes how her parents were circus performers, as she does at the top of the Act in Chekhov's published play, and Firs tells a strange story of how he spent two years in jail for a murder he did not commit, a story which was cut out completely. Emily Mann, in her adaptation, has actually put back Chekhov's original scene at the end of the Act.[15] Mann states that it "redefines the play," but that may be an exaggeration. What it does do is end Act II on an even more funny and ironic note—Firs describes how something alive was twitching or "jerking" around in a bag—rather than the romantic episode with Anya and Trofimov running down to the lake (pursued by Varya). Plus, we get more information about Firs, and understand how Charlotta likes him: another relationship is revealed.

Another strange incident in this Act is the arrival of the:

"Passerby"	(Hingley 1964; Guthrie/Kipnis 1965; Szogyi 1968; Bristow 1977; Gill 1978; Frayn 1988; Rocamora 1996; Carson 2002)
"Tramp"	(Fen 1954; Corrigan 1962 Senelick 1977; Gill 1978; Ehre 1992; Kramer/Booker 1997a)
"Vagrant"	(Griffiths 1978; Van Itallie 1979, '95; Hulick 1994; Mann 2000)
"Stranger"	(Young 1956; Dunnigan 1964; Sherman 2006
"Wayfarer"	(Garnett 1929; Cook 1973)
"Homeless Man"	(Schmidt 1997c; Donaghy 2004) or
"Hiker"	(Magarshack 1969),

while in one adaptation he is cut out completely (Logan 1950). A "Wayfarer," "Stranger," "Passerby" or "Hiker" may have no ill intent; a "Tramp," "Vagrant," or "Homeless Man" are not usually welcome. The nomenclature of this outsider

---

15 English director Mike Alfreds did so also, describing the cutting of this scene a "dubious intervention" of Stanislavsky (Stuart Young in *Chekhov on the British Stage*, ed. Patrick Miles, 1993, 181).

Figure 9.2: *The Cherry Orchard.* Katherine Alt Keener as Mme. Ranevskaya and Sue-Ellen Mandell as Gayev, Columbia University Theatre, NYC, 2017. In Act II, Sister Lyubov Andreyevna and brother Gayev are wistful. Director: Mark Herbert Barford. Translator: Paul Schmidt. Photo Credit: Abo Huang.

describes how the characters may see him. Varya is afraid of him and screams; Lyubov gives him a gold coin; Lopakhin exclaims on the Vagrant's rudeness, though the stranger only sings and asks for a few kopeks. The man himself is drunk, begging for money, asking directions to the train station. Is he an augur of the future? A former prisoner out of jail? (These travelers were common in Russia at the time.) Certainly he's not just a "hiker" out for a walk. He bespeaks the poverty and social upheaval in the country, brought on by the "Emancipation" of the serfs Firs has just denigrated a moment before. Before that, the company heard the famous "breaking string," also an unsettling occurrence. This one strange character—outside the circle of the cherry orchard but as much "nedo'tyopa" as the others—presages another possibility for the future, reminds us of the past, and underscores the omens of this open landscape. The diversity in name choices for him is testimony to varying points of view of each translator, adaptor or version-writer.

The stasis and portent of Act II is in great contrast to Act III, with its wild party, culminating in Lopakhin's announcement that he bought the orchard; this is the "peripety" (from "peripeteia") or "reversal of fortune" in the traditional Greek plot scheme. Act IV of the play, like the last Acts of Chekhov's other masterpieces, is, structurally, an "epiphany" as Fergusson explains: after the "agon" of Act II, and

Figure 9.3: *The Cherry Orchard.* Daniel Stompor as Anya with Katherine Alt Keener as Mme. Ranevskaya in Act III. Columbia University Theatre, NYC, 2017. Lyubov, in Anya's arms, realizes the estate has been sold. Director: Mark Herbert Barford. Translator: Paul Schmidt. Photo Credit: Abo Huang.

the climax of Act III, the characters are seen in a "new and ironic light" in the last Act (1953: 176–7). The play ends with the most ironic plot point of all: while everyone in the family departs for a new life, the old servant Firs is left alone in the house. Before he enters for this final scene, we notice the empty stage of Act IV, in sharp contrast to the opening scene of the play. Everyone has gone; we wonder what could possibly happen next.

The Translations, Act IV, Scene One

SENELICK (2005)

First act setting. Neither curtains on the window, nor pictures on the wall, a few sticks of furniture remain, piled up in a corner as if for sale. A feeling of emptiness. Near the door to the outside and at the back of the stage are piles of suitcases, traveling bags, etc. The door at left is open, and through it we can hear the voices of VARYA and ANYA. LOPAKHIN stands, waiting. YASHA is holding a tray of glasses filled with champagne. In the hallway, YEPIKHODOV is tying up a carton. Offstage, at the back, a murmur.

It's the peasants come to say good-bye.

GRIFFITHS (1978)

Black.

Tape: (YASHA'S voice): << [in Russian] >> *Lights up, harsh and bright on the bare white nursery. Nothing of furniture or decoration remains save for a huddle of pieces in a corner marked 'sale'. Trunks, bags and bundles mound about the door and the back wall.*

LOPAKHIN stands in the middle of the room, staring at the door, which is open. YASHA stands by the window, a tray of champagne and glasses in his hands. The glasses are full and flattening.

Odd voices-VARYA'S, ANYA'S-flit through the house. […]

MAMET (1985)

A hum of voices is heard offstage.

The "feeling of emptiness" is stated explicitly in Chekhov's play, as it is common among most of the translations, which follow Senelick's description above. Translator Carson sensually renders "The sense of emptiness is palpable" (Chekhov 2002: 333). Noticeably, this statement is missing in Griffiths. More noticeably, none of the stage setting for Act IV at all—save a "hum of voices"—is rendered in Mamet. Again, in Mamet's adaptation, the actors are left to the imagination of the set designer, without help from Chekhov. Act IV is played in this altered space, no longer the "nursery" it was.

In the final scene, Firs has been inadvertently left locked in the house after the sale of the estate, when everyone else has gone. The others believe he has been taken to the hospital, but due to Yasha's negligence (Lyubov's champagne-swilling, social-climbing servant) Firs is left ill, in the old nursery, which has been practically excoriated since Act I. His situation is sad and comic at the same time. As Clurman observes, Chekhov's plays "are deeply affecting even as they provoke laughter; they make us smile even as we feel our hearts ready to break" (Corrigan 1962 x). We may also say, with Chekhov's friend Gorky, that the essence of Chekhov is "laughter through tears." Firs' fate epitomizes this essence. He is not unlike the sympathetic Charlie Chaplin or Buster Keaton.

Stage Directions

In determining the actor's Action for the last scene, we may divide it into "beats" (see Appendix A). It begins with an empty stage, after the others have left for the train station; none are scheduled to return to the estate (with the possible exception of Yepikhodov, whom Lopakhin appoints estate manager). There is, intriguingly, an opening "beat" created only by the empty nursery, sheared of its curtains, no more pictures on the walls, with the furniture (including Gayev's beloved bookcase?)[16] shoved into a corner, "as if for sale," and trunks, suitcases and bundles in a pile by the doorway. One recalls the first scene of the play also began with an empty stage.

The Translations, Act IV, Final Scene

GEORGE CALDERON (1912)

[Exeunt. The stage is empty. One hears all the doors being locked, and the carriages driving away. All is quiet. Amid the silence the thud of the axes on the trees echoes sad and lonely. The sound of footsteps. Firs *appears in the doorway,* R. *He is dressed, as always, in his long coat and white waistcoat; he wears slippers. He is ill.]*

FIRS *(going to the door L. and trying the handle).*—Locked. They've gone. *(Sitting on the sofa.)* They've forgotten me. Never Mind! I'll sit here. Leonid Andreyitch is sure to have put on his cloth coat instead of his fur. *(He sighs anxiously.)* He hadn't me to see. Young wood, green wood! *(He mumbles something incomprehensible.)* Life has gone by as if I'd never lived. *(Lying down.)* I'll lie down. There's no strength left in you; there's nothing, nothing, Ah, you … **job-lot!**

He lies motionless. A distant sound is heard, as if from the sky, the sound of a string breaking, dying away, melancholy. Silence ensues, broken only by the stroke of the axe on the trees far away in the cherry orchard.

---

16 In Act I, Gayev makes an impassioned speech to an old bookcase ("cupboard" in Senelick) in the nursery, expressing his feeling for its "ideals of virtue and justice" nurturing "decency and social consciousness." The irony of Gayev's bookcase now up for sale with the other furniture would not be lost on Chekhov.

TREVOR GRIFFITHS (1978)

They leave.

The room is empty, save for a solitary chair on the back wall. Sound of doors being locked, carriages leaving.

Silence.

An axe hits a tree, once, twice, three times.

Slow, shuffling footsteps. FIRS *enters, in jacket, white waistcoat, as ever,*

but with slippers. He's ill. He crosses to the door, tries the handle.

Firs Locked. They've gone.

There's a solitary chair left, its back broken. FIRS *painfully drags it into the middle of the room, sits on it.*

They forgot me. Never mind. I'll sit here for awhile.

He picks up the cloth that covered TROFIMOV'S *overshoes, shivering a little, places it over his head and ears. The axe starts up again, closer.*

I don't imagine for one minute he's put is fur coat on ... No, no ... he'll be wearing his thin one ... *(He blows on his hands.)* ... If I don't see to it ... mmm? These green lads ...

Mutters, unintelligibly, for a moment. The axe persists, closing in.

... It's gone ... gone ... as if I'd never lived it ... *(Looks at the floor.)* I might lie down in a minute. You've no strength left in you, have you ... you've nothing left, eh ... nothing ...

He begins to rock backwards and forwards in the chair, slowly at first, but

the arcs grow longer, the legs lifting front and back.

You silly old nothing. Silly old nothing. Silly old nothing.

The axe pounds towards the house. FIRS *rocks on, muttering.*

*Tape: (*FIRS'S *voice):* << [in Russian] >> *(Over and over.)*

Cut, abruptly.

He topples to the floor, felled. The axe stops. A distant sound is heard. It's the sound of a snapping string.

BLACK

PAUL SCHMIDT (1997c)

(The stage is empty. We hear the sound of the door being locked, then the carriage as they drive away. It grows very quiet. In the silence, we hear the occasional sound of an ax chopping down the cherry trees, a mournful, lonely sound. Then we hear steps. Enter Firs from the door, right. He wears his usual butler's livery, but with bedroom slippers. He's very ill.)

FIRS: *(Goes to the door, tries the handle)* Locked. They're gone. *(Sits on the sofa)* They forgot about me. That's all right. I'll just sit here for a bit … Leonid Andreyich probably forgot his winter coat. *(A worried sigh)* I should have looked … He's still all wet, that one … *(Mumbles something we can't make out)* Well, it's all over now, and I never even had a life to live … *(Lies back)* I'll just lie here for a bit … No strength left, nothing left, not a thing … Oh, you. **You young flibbertigibbet**. *(Lies there, no longer moving)*

(In the distance we hear a sound that seems to come from the sky, a sad sound, like a string snapping. It dies away. Everything grows quiet. We can hear the occasional sound of an ax on a tree.)

CURTAIN

TOM DONAGHY (2004)

They exit. The stage is empty. One can hear all the doors being locked, and the carriages driving away. After a moment, footsteps are heard. Firs appears from the door on the right. He is dressed, as always, in a jacket with a white waistcoat, and slippers on his feet. He is ill.

Firs walks to the door, jiggles the handle; it's locked. He looks out the window, sees carriages moving into the distance, shrugs, and sits down on the sofa. Once there, he notices Gayev's coat has been left on a chair. He shakes his head in disgust, sighs, and mutters. He then lies down, trying to get comfortable. Soon, he is still.

A distant sound is heard, as if from the sky: the doleful sound of a string breaking. Silence sets in, and then an ax is heard. It's chopping a tree far away in the orchard ...
Curtain.

Word Choice

While the translations of this final scene may differ with regard to the elements mentioned above, perhaps they are distinguished most of all by word choice in Firs' final pronouncement. Firs assesses himself as a good for nothing, a silly old nothing, an old muddler, a pathetic old fool, a silly idiot, a silly galoot, a sillybilly, an addlepate, a job-lot, a nincompoop, an absolute wash-out, a duffer, daft, half-chopped, half-baked, a bungler, a lunkhead, a booby, a numskull, some kind of clown, useless lumber and, possibly, a silly young cuckoo or a young flibbertigibbet, though these latter nomenclatures may be directed at Gayev who went out without the proper coat. Why are there so many different (self-) assignations to Firs? What do they have in common, and how are they different? We may begin with discovering the sounds of the words.

Word Sounds

One cannot but note the plosives in nearly every translation. Plosives are considered p's and b's, t's and d's and (farther back in the throat) hard g's and k's. These are the sounds made by "a complete closure of two organs of articulation [the lips], behind which air pressure builds up and is released suddenly" (Rodenburg 247). The last word out of Firs' mouth in the play—and perhaps his last word ever—is one with plosives, which may signify the expulsion of one's last breath. Putting aside meaning for a moment, we see that "flibbertigibbet" has the most syllables and plosive sounds of "b" and "t," and might be the hardest—or most surprising—to say. (Here, the "f" and "g" sounds are fricatives, where "the escaping air-stream makes considerable friction" [*Ibid.*].) "Addlepate" has three plosives, and of course the two syllables of "bungler," "booby," "cuckoo," "(nin)compoop," "galoot," "job-lot" or "some kind of clown" could also be exploded out of the mouth with considerable force.

It is significant that this last explosion of air is also the last sound out of the mouth of the oldest character, in a play where sound is considered extremely important to the poetry and mood of the whole play.[17] Perhaps the b and p sounds

---

17 Nils Ake Nilsson's "Intonation and Rhythm in Chekhov's Plays" in *Anton Cechov 1860–1960, Some Essays*, ed. T. Eekman, Leiden, Netherlands: E. J. Brill, 1960, pp. 168–80.

(try saying them over and over in your mouth) could mimic the stuttering, almost drooling, or escape-back-to-baby-blubbering of a man on his last legs. It may be helpful to consider too the difference in a man who expires (or seems to be on the verge of doing so) by repeating Griffiths' "silly old nothing" (ending in the nasal "nng") over and over, versus the quick, (bitter?) release of air on "booby," "bungler," "nincompoop" or "clown." The sound in each is different and each one has different connotations with regard to meaning. Also, the action of a man who thinks himself a "nincompoop," "sillybilly," "booby" or a "clown" may be different than the one who thinks of himself as truly "good for nothing."

Word Meaning

It is helpful to consider meaning. It may be obvious at first glance that an "addlepate," "silly galoot," or "job-lot" are disparagements from another age, and another country—though "addlepate" is chosen by an American translator, Ann Dunnigan. An addlepate is, literally (from the German "adel"), a manure-head (shithead), or, also colloquially, a confused, silly harebrained person (Webster's 17). The term "addlebrained" may be more familiar (and polite), if dated, to most Americans. A galoot is an awkward, silly person, and a job-lot is a quantity of miscellaneous or mixed up items (*Ibid.* 581, 768)—a strange adjective (to the modern ear) to attach to a person, chosen by one of Chekhov's very first English translators, George Calderon. Today, it may be said that such words would make Firs sound like an intellectual or wordsmith, which he is not. Yet "sillybilly" is a mild and affectionate remonstrance given to a child, a "young flibbertigibbet" can't sit still or stop gossiping (and is usually a woman according to Webster's 543), "half-baked" is usually applied to ideas, a "washout" implies elimination due to a tie in a competition, while Firs may indeed be a bungler, booby or—quite literally—a pathetic old fool or clown as seen by the other characters. The questions may be how much self-understanding one wants to attribute to Firs, what word he might actually use as a matter of course (he calls Yasha this same adjective in Act III) and what sound and meaning the playwright or director wants echoing in the ears of the audience as the final verbal declaration of the play.

It is important in any analysis of a scene to first understand the circumstances, which include situation (all have left the house) and setting. The furniture and props are tools for the actor; they are real objects that define the place. Stella Adler said frequently, "The props don't lie—*you* lie!" This was meant to illustrate the fact that if the actor could handle real objects as they were meant to be used, he or she would help create truth on the stage. The props are there to help the actor, as well as to inform the audience. They are important to Firs. In Griffiths' version, the translator gives Firs a cloth that is covering Trofimov's shoes to put over his head (to shield his eyes? As a shroud?) and a broken rocking chair, not in Chekhov's original script. These are set, costume and directorial choices that may have been discovered in the first production of this version, and incorporated into Griffiths' text. They may complement the director's vision of the play, but are not from Chekhov's original script.

Sound Effects

As we view the stage set, we hear the sounds: the turn of the key in the lock, and the carriages—we may assume horse carriages—driving away, the sound of wheels and gallops and neighing fading into the distance. We might also hear the sounds of excited voices, perhaps some are even calling "Good-bye!" until they too fade away. It must be noted that as the audience hears the sounds, they imagine the action, and see in their mind's eye the carriage with the characters escaping down the road. Chekhov then tells us that there is "Silence" or it "grows very quiet." We must ask, how many times are we asked to watch a silent stage, unpeopled with actors? As mentioned regarding Act I, this is an anomaly in the theatre: it must be an important moment. It is helpful to the actor to label beats or scenes, to understand their essence. This prelude to Firs' entrance might be called "The Leave-Taking." Then the Silence gives us a moment to watch the entire stage, and to perhaps notice how different it now appears, compared to the opening scene with all its energy of arrival. The parting voices were happy; this shorn nursery, if not sad, is at least wistful, emptied of the human traffic that filled it moments ago. Finally, we hear the occasional crack of an ax on a tree; some of the translations describe this sound as "lonely, sad, mournful." It is the poetry of the sights and sounds of the action that fills us—however briefly—in this moment. And then we hear something else.

As the first note of a musical movement, we first hear the sound of Firs' approaching steps. The translations mention he is in slippers, which are not part of his usual livery. We may hear the sound of the swishing slippers before we actually see the character. We had thought that all had departed, but the sound signals there is something alive still left in the house. Firs enters in the formal livery of his servant's station, but with the shoes of a man in his pajamas—the incongruity is comic, as Firs has been throughout the play. He is often the "comic relief," the butt of jokes, the hanger-on who doesn't hear well, and so his responses to the action are often wacky. He may be considered, as many of Chekhov's characters are, from the author's first published works, a "vaudeville" character. When we see Firs (as with Chaplin and Keaton), we are prepared to laugh.

Firs crosses the stage, to the opposite door. We see he is ill. The actor must make the decision of exactly *how* he is ill: is he sniffing? Coughing? Dizzy, or simply out of sorts? His walk may be comic, but his illness is real. We don't know whether to laugh at him, or cry. This is the core of Chekhov's style; his works are the precursors to all modern tragicomedy. Firs' flawed humanity is capped in this final scene. Firs tries the door, is unsuccessful, and we see he is locked in. To make it absolutely clear, he talks to himself: "Locked. They're gone." We might label this new beat "Firs Alone," "Firs is Ill" or "Firs Scolds Master," to place it in the overall action of the play. Labeling scenes helps the actor to find the appropriate action in the story—a compilation of events—of *The Cherry Orchard*. Of course the labels are up to the actor, depending on his/her determination of the overriding essence of each scene.

Action

What is Firs' Action upon entering the scene? Did he hear "The Leave-Taking"? He is partially deaf, but he knows the master and mistress are leaving. His physical action is to, possibly, follow his master, Gayev, out of the house, but, as often happens to him, he is too late. Where was he just before everyone left? In the kitchen? Taking a nap? Ironing Gayev's shirts? Where he is coming from, both geographically and psychologically, helps determine the actor's Action. Chekhov doesn't tell us explicitly; it is part of the actor's job to make this decision for every entrance and exit they make. Firs could want "to take care of the master," which is often what moves him in the play; it is one of his reasons for living. His *obstacles* to this action are his infirmities. These obstacles—whatever the actor decides they are, physically and mentally—are a great help to the actor, because they intensify the characters' Action. It is harder to pull the door handle when one is ill; it's harder to walk, it's harder to think with a stuffed head. Firs' attempt to do his job—"take care of the master"—is compounded by his infirmities, and they give the actor the opportunity for physical actions that are comic, poignant and real.

Firs sits down when he realizes he's not going to get out the door. Perhaps the obstacle he tries to overcome—his illness—gets the better of him at this moment. He would never sit in the master's or mistress' presence, but he can afford to do so now. His ruminations about Gayev's coat are still part of his action "to take care." He takes out his frustration on himself ("I should have looked," "If I don't see," "He hadn't me to see," etc.), and then on Gayev ("He's still all wet, that one," "These green lads," "Young wood, green wood!" etc.). How many ways can he "take care" of the master? He can warn him, he can scold him, he can browbeat himself. "To browbeat" is an especially good choice because it is physical as well as psychological. This language that the actor uses to describe the Action to himself is critical. The actor finds the words that move him the most; these words will evoke the actor's contribution. It is understood that Chekhov's words in the script—those chosen by the translator in the text of the play, and spoken by the actor—must be spoken as the *result* of how the actor chooses to describe his psycho-physical movement through the scene. And this is why the translation is so important: its words—along with the circumstances of the play—move the actor to find the appropriate Actions (such as "to browbeat") for his or her character. As mentioned early on, words have private connotations and meanings for everyone, and one's talent is in one's choice.

Punctuation/Rhythm

Chekhov gives Firs the chance to go to and fro with his recriminations by the addition of ellipses. These helpful and telling pieces of punctuation give the actor the meaning and rhythm of Firs' monologue. Translators who leave them out (like Hingley or Donaghy), or change their placement (like Van Itallie, among others), do so at the peril of the actor. In English or Russian, Firs must have those moments (indicated by ellipses) to scold or blame, first himself, then the master, and finally the life itself that was so illusive it could never be lived. The non-verbal struggle in these ellipses points to a thought process and subtext underneath the words. There is a build in Firs' speech, from frustration with the doorknob, to scolding himself, reproving Gayev and finally damning the life he himself didn't lead. What does he say (also in Chekhov's original) when he "mumbles," or "mutters unintelligibly"? Does he tell a joke about Gayev? Admonish himself or Gayev further? Grapple with senility or fever? In any case, there are transitions or intensifications in the ellipses, where Firs' focus switches from Gayev to himself, and then, losing strength and ending with, possibly, a final recrimination.

Word Choice and Sound

Is Firs' final breath about himself, or his master? Schmidt's use of the words "You *young* flibbertigibbet" points to Gayev, as does Guthrie's "silly *young* cuckoo." Firs is old; he would think of Gayev as young. "Job-lot!" and "silly old nothing," along with the other translations, could well be Firs' view of himself. The choice is the actor's. Certainly the choice of translation is significant for this moment of the play. In Donaghy's adaptation the beats, without words, are only suggested, and it is up to the actor to create the beats and Actions on his own, and silently.

The first three translations above are similar in word choice before the final "nedo'tyopa," (a transliteration of the Russian for Firs' final verbal pronouncement in the scene) but they are not the same. When we say, in English, "I *should* have ...!" it is particularly strong. As humans, we often see a better way after the fact: "I shoulda, woulda, coulda!" The direct recrimination of "should" is stronger than the passive "If I don't see to it" or more British "He hadn't me to see." Does Firs whine? Is he fearful? Is self-pity involved? How aware of his circumstances is he? How long might he wait for someone to return? Will they ever? It may add to the comedy and the meaning of the play if Firs is, indeed, oblivious (as he seems to be) to all consequences of the locked door. The actor has to know, though Firs may not.

Sounds of the words, paralanguage (breaths, grunts, etc., especially in Donaghy) and connotations (like "should have" vs. "he hadn't me to see") will inform how the actor will handle the text in terms of cadence and non-verbal expressions. When he finally lies down, or falls over (in Griffiths), is he dead? Many translations note he "lies motionless," or "unmoving" while Griffiths goes so far as to "fell" Firs like the cherry trees. Chekhov might have been stunned to see Griffiths' implication that Firs dies, since Chekhov writes nothing of the sort. None of the translations except Griffiths' goes as far as to imply Firs' death. The ending is ambiguous—perhaps even more so in Donaghy—and it is the actor's choice of physical action that is left to insinuate Firs' last moment. These are choices for the actor and director.

There is a change at the end of the scene. Firs finally decides to lie down or lie back, and spit out his favorite retort in the play—the Russian "nedo'tyopa." As mentioned above, this word has significance because Firs uses it earlier in the play, at least twice, as an insult to Yasha. The English word chosen in the translation is intrinsic to discovering the Action chosen by the actor. As mentioned, one may see the difference between a "job-lot," "Silly old nothing. Silly old nothing. Silly old nothing" and a "Young flibbertigibbet." Is Firs addressing himself or Gayev with this final admonition? Many English translations from various time periods choose "good for nothing." But the Russian word may not be so harsh as that. A good for nothing may be indolent and slothful, but a "flibbertigibbet" is simply flighty. The latter term, as the final word, might point up the irony of Firs' circumstances; the former could hit a much more serious note. Firs wants to reprove either his master or himself with this last word, but the tone of the scene will be different, depending, in part, on this one last instance of word choice.

Fergusson states that Chekhov chooses the scenes in characters' lives "between their rationalized efforts, when they sense their situation and destiny most directly" (1953: 175). Firs is poignantly at this point of "sensing his situation" in this final scene. Firs doesn't accomplish his Action. But like Nina in *Seagull*, Sonya and Vanya in *Uncle Vanya*, and the three sisters, he makes the (final?) effort to endure. At the very end, we hear the ax on the cherry trees, and Chekhov's "snapping" or "breaking" string. What are we to think? We may laugh at Firs, as we bemoan his outcast state. We see Fergusson's view of Chekhov's work as a "theatre-poem of the suffering of change" quite eloquently expressed, and we are left to answer the questions it poses on our own.

References

Adler, Stella. *On Ibsen, Strindberg and Chekhov.* Ed. Barry Paris. New York: Alfred A. Knopf, 1999.

Chekhov, Anton. *Anton Chekhov, Four Plays.* Trans. David Magarshack. New York: Hill and Wang, 1969.

———. *Anton Chekhov Plays.* Trans. Peter Carson. London: Penguin Books, 2002.

———. *Anton Chekhov Selected Works.* Trans. Kathleen Cook. Moscow: Progress Publishers, 1973.

———. *Anton Chekhov's Plays.* Trans. and ed. Eugene Bristow. New York: W. W. Norton & Co., 1977.

———. *Anton Chekhov's Selected Plays.* Trans. and ed. Laurence Senelick. New York: W. W. Norton & Co., 2005.

———. *Best Plays by Chekhov.* Trans. Stark Young. New York: The Modern Library, 1956.

———. *Chekhov: The Essential Plays.* Trans. Michael Henry Heim. New York: Modern Library, 2003.

———. *Chekhov for the Stage.* Trans. Milton Ehre. Evanston, IL: Northwestern University Press, 1992.

———. *Chekhov, Four Plays.* Trans. Carol Rocamora. Lyme, NH: Smith and Kraus, 1996.

———. *Chekhov, The Major Plays.* Trans. Ann Dunnigan. New York: Signet Classic, Penguin Books, 1964.

———. *Chekhov, The Major Plays.* Trans. Jean-Claude Van Itallie. New York: Applause Books, 1995.

———. *Chekhov Plays.* Trans. Michael Frayn. London: Methuen, 1988.

———. *Chekhov's Major Plays.* Trans. Karl Kramer and Margaret Booker. New York: University Press of America, 1997a.

———. *Chekhov, The Russian Text of Three Plays: Uncle Vanya, The Three Sisters, The Cherry Orchard.* Cambridge: University Press, 1946.

———. *The Cherry Orchard.* Trans. Martin Sherman. Unpublished manuscript for the Music Center production in Los Angeles, California, 2006.

———. *The Cherry Orchard.* Trans. Sharon Marie Carnicke. Copywright 1980.

———. *The Cherry Orchard.* Adapt. Tom Donaghy. Unpublished draft. December 2004.

———. *The Cherry Orchard.* Version. Pam Gems. UK: Oberon Classics, 2007.

———. *The Cherry Orchard.* Version. Sir John Gielgud. New York: Theatre Arts Books, 1963.

———. *The Cherry Orchard.* Version. Peter Gill, from a literal trans. Ted Braun. London: Oberon Books Ltd., 1978.

———. *The Cherry Orchard.* Version. Trevor Griffiths/Trans. Helen Rappaport. London: Pluto Press Ltd., 1978.

———. *The Cherry Orchard.* Trans. Tyrone Guthrie and Leonid Kipnis. Minneapolis: University of Minnesota Press/Minnesota Theatre Company, 1965.

———. *The Cherry Orchard.* Joshua Logan. *The Wisteria Trees, based on Anton Chekhov's The Cherry Orchard.* New York: Random House, 1950.

———. *The Cherry Orchard*. Adapt. David Mamet from a literal trans. Peter Nelles. New York: Grove Press, 1985.

———. *The Cherry Orchard*. Adapt. Emily Mann. New York: Dramatists Play Service, 2000.

———. *The Cherry Orchard*. Trans. Jean-Claude Van Itallie. New York: Dramatists Play Service, 1979.

———. *The Cherry Orchard*. Chay Yew. *Adaptation: A Winter People*. Unpublished Draft, September 28, 2004.

———. *The Cherry Orchard and the Seagull*. Trans. Laurence Senelick. Arlington Heights, IL: AHM Publishing Corporation, 1977.

———. *Four Plays by Chekhov*. Trans. Alex Szogyi. New York: Washington Square Press, 1968.

———. *The Oxford Chekhov*. Trans. Ronald Hingley. London: Oxford University Press, Vol. II, 1967, Vol. III, 1964, and Vol. IX, 1975.

———. *Plays, Anton Chekhov*. Trans. Elisaveta, Fen. Middlesex, England: Penguin Books, Ltd., 1951, 1954.

———. *The Plays of Anton Chekhov*. Trans. Constance Garnett. New York: The Modern Library, 1929.

———. *The Plays of Anton Chekhov*. Trans. Paul Schmidt. New York: Harper Collins Publishers, 1997c.

———. *The Russian Text of Three Plays: Uncle Vanya, Three Sisters, The Cherry Orchard*. Ed. P. Henry. Letchworth, Hertfordshire, England: Bradda Books Ltd., 1965.

———. *Six Plays of Chekhov*. Version. Robert W. Corrigan. San Francisco: Rinehart Press, 1962.

———. *Two Plays by Tchekhov*. Trans. George Calderon. New York: Mitchell Kennerley, 1912.

———. *Uncle Vanya and Other Plays*. Trans. Betsy Hulick. New York: Bantam Books, 1994.

Cohen, Robert. *Theatre*. Palo Alto, CA: Mayfield Publishing Company, 1981, 1983.

Esslin, Martin. *The Theatre of the Absurd*. Garden City, NY: Anchor Books, 1961; Penguin Books, 1968.

Fergusson, Francis. *The Idea of a Theatre*. Garden City, NY: Doubleday Anchor Books, 1953.

Gottlieb, Vera and Paul Allain, eds. *The Cambridge Companion to Chekhov*. Cambridge University Press, 2000.

Hingley, Ronald. *Chekhov, A Biographical and Critical Study*. London: Allen and Unwin, 1950; New York: Barnes and Noble, 1966.

Jackson, Robert Louis. *Chekhov*. Englewood Cliffs, NJ: Prentice-Hall, 1967.

———. *Reading Chekhov's Text*. Evanston, IL: Northwestern University Press, 1993.

Kataev, Vladimir. *If Only We Could Know!* Trans./Ed. Harvey Pitcher. Chicago: Ivan R. Dee, 2002.

Magarshack, David. *Chekhov the Dramatist*. New York: Hill and Wang, 1960.

Miles, Patrick, ed. and trans. *Chekhov on the British Stage*. Cambridge: Cambridge University Press, 1993.

Peace, Richard. *Chekhov*. New Haven: Yale University Press, 1983.

Rayfield, Donald. *The Cherry Orchard, Catastrophe and Comedy*. New York: Twayne Publishers, 1994.

Rodenburg, Patsy. *The Right to Speak*. New York: Routledge, 1992.

Stanislavsky, Konstantin. *My Life in Art*. Trans. J. J. Robbins/Elizabeth Reynolds Hapgood. New York: Theatre Arts Books, 1948.

Styan, J. L. *Chekhov in Performance*. Cambridge: Cambridge University Press, 1971.

CHAPTER TEN

A Body of Beauty

The words, the words, the words—they speak for themselves.

—SAMUEL BECKETT

The farther he goes the more good he does me. I don't want philosophies, tracks, dogmas, creeds, ways out, truths, answers, nothing from the bargain basement. He is the most courageous, most remorseless writer going, and the more he grinds my nose in the shit the more I am grateful to him.

He's not fucking me about, he's not leading me up any garden path, he's not slipping me a wink, he's not flogging me a remedy or a path or a revelation or a basinful of breadcrumbs, he's not selling me anything I don't want to buy—he doesn't give a bollock whether I buy or not—he hasn't got his hand over his heart.

Well, I'll buy his goods, hook, line and sinker, because he leaves no stone unturned and no maggot lonely. He brings forth a body of beauty ...[1]

—HAROLD PINTER, 1954, IN A LETTER TO A FRIEND ON SAMUEL BECKETT

I've discovered 145 plays in English, "translated" or "adapted" from, or fashioned into "versions of" or "based on" Chekhov's last four masterpieces (see Appendix B).

---

[1]	Richard Ouzounian, "He left 'no maggot lonely,'" *Toronto Star*, Apr. 9, 2006. Printed in *Beckett at 60.*
	Also see Charles A. Carpenter's *Modern British, Irish and American Drama: A Descriptive Chronology, 1865–1965.* http://bingweb.binghamton.edu/~ccarpen/Pinter.htm.

Many more exist. A variorum of all four of Chekhov's plays and differences in their myriad renditions would be beyond the realm of this study—or, perhaps, any one study—but the selections of examples provided herein put forward several conclusions: Translation—or adaptation or version-writing—seems to depend largely on the background and tastes of the translator, and less on the original work. Comparing translations is a helpful way to begin an interrogation of a foreign play. And perhaps the truest statement that can be made on the issue of "translation" for the stage, versus "adaptation," or "version," "based on," "inspired by" or other constructs of the original text is that of translator Neil Bartlett (Chapter III): it depends on what kind of night out in the theatre one is looking for.

Secondly, and nonetheless, an understanding of the dramaturgy of a particular work is of great value to the translator or adaptor. Indeed, play translator Johnston insists nothing less than a full dramaturgical interrogation is required of the translator. Johnston eschews even the "duality" of the theatre (as written and performed artwork), since this seemingly egalitarian view "imposes a deformation on the play by ignoring the patterns for performance which are encoded in its scripting" (57–8). It is vital that students of theatre and literature in general understand this distinction between works meant to be read, and those meant for performance, in any period of history. Plays must be read differently than other works of literature—as performance blueprints—taking into consideration too when and where they were written. This study has attempted to demonstrate, as examples, these "patterns for performance" that Chekhov has encoded, not always fully recognized by some critics or translators. A "word for word translation" of a play denies the nature of dramatic art: It is Action—the desires of the characters and overall movement and purpose of the work in its entirety—that is the basis of a theatre piece, and not words. A misunderstanding of play translation as a reconfiguration of words alters Chekhov's—and others'—delicate and nuanced playscripts. Thus, a practical knowledge of the notion of Action—whether it is called the "energy" fueling a play (Gooch/Boswell), "wearing the language of the play like clothes" (Gooch), "reflecting the subtle currents of human life" (Brook) or by other similar metaphors—is imperative for the translator.

For example, in *Seagull, Vanya, Sisters* and *Orchard*, the translators' choices of words, scene and stage directions, punctuation, ellipses and pauses, syntax, sounds, rhythms, song and allusions most definitely influence the actor's view and practice of possible Actions in the scenes of the plays. This is especially true when whole structures have been altered, as when Ronald Hingley cuts all ellipses in the last scene of Nina's speech in *Seagull*, when David Mamet switches or cuts character speeches, when he and Tom Stoppard use repeated emphases (with italics) changing syntax and punctuation, and when Tom Donaghy completely cuts all words in Firs' last scene of *Orchard*. Notably, however, there could conceivably be less or little change in the actors' Actions when all the words have been omitted in a scene (like Firs' last speech), than when entire scenes have been *restructured* with new words, syntax and punctuation, as Mamet and Brian Friel have done in Acts III and IV of *Sisters*, respectively. These examples, and others herein, support the idea that plays are based on Actions and *not* words. The notion of Action may provide a "descriptive vocabulary"—suggested by Susan Sontag—for the form of a play.

Stage Directions—altered or left out—also change the circumstances of the plays, and thus the character Actions. These changes occur most peremptorily in Mamet's *Sisters* and *Orchard*, Griffiths' *Orchard*, Yew's *Winter People* and Logan's *Wisteria Trees*. Complete character changes or transpositions—as in Yew's *People* and Lee's *Aunt Vanya*—also change the tenors of the plays. It is the rhythm that changes abruptly with new sentences, punctuation and variant word choices, and is most noticeable in Thomas Kilroy's *Seagull* and Friel's *Vanya* and *Sisters*. In Poulton's *Vanya*—"sprinkling academic dust on the shelves of oblivion"—and Friel's "fossilized oaf" speech, both spoken by Vanya about the Professor, these witty observations give Sonya's uncle a new sheen. Halley Feiffer's *Moscow Moscow* ... is constructed of almost *all* under-the-breath utterances delivered directly as the unspoken and scatological *subtext* of each of the characters, to uproarious effect. So, this is not to say the writing in such "versions" is inappropriate or unengaging, only that Chekhov did not make the same direct observations. They may well be in keeping with the "spirit" of the play. However, word choice, additions, added or subtracted punctuation and changes in other elements mentioned in the four chapters on the plays change rhythm—and thus meaning too—irreversibly. This is one element that is vital and often overlooked in the translation of plays. As David Hare notes, he spends more time "thinking about rhythm" than "meaning," and Senelick declares flatly that "harmony and rhythm" is the greatest loss in English translations of Chekhov's major plays (2005: xii). Action helps create rhythm and inflection, along with word sounds and pauses in speech. Investigation into this aspect of play translation is lacking, and warranted in future studies. Our speech rhythms come from our purposes or Actions in speaking. As a voice and speech teacher, I'm particularly sensitive to this important aspect of the play in English translation.

Thirdly, this exploration has upheld—with critics and practitioners—the primacy of the actor in the theatre. In translated texts, as other plays, it's the actor who brings the play to its targeted audience. Since the translator, as Corrigan notes, must write for the actor just as the original playwright does, it is fitting that concluding statements for this study include the import of acting and Action on the stage.

Chekhov wrote:

> If one were to deny that self-examination and intention are present in the creative process, one would be forced to conclude that the artist creates spontaneously, without thinking, in a state of temporary insanity.[2]

Laypersons may think of the actor's art in this way. After all, acting is everywhere. Often without our notice, actors portray "real people" and surround us through the media of television, film, commercials and print ads, political messages and speeches, as well as theatrical productions. We are all daily bombarded with advertising, even if we don't watch television, or see films or theatre. This tends to diminish the standing of the art of the actor in comparison to that of the playwright, director or designer. It seems that everyone can *do* acting. We all do it to some extent in our "real" lives: communication researchers note how we role-play in different semantic environments every day.[3] Thus, it is not surprising that the layperson may confuse the art of the actor with an ability to only "create spontaneously" or just "play oneself."

Nothing is farther from the truth. The idea that acting requires little work, preparation or study comes from a misunderstanding of the art of creating characters onstage. Both acting and public speaking require performance skills that are not necessarily "natural" to everyone, and that must be learned from experience or formal training; there *is* a creative process. Further, learning these skills is helpful to the layperson as well as the actor. Teacher Ron Burrus stated in class that once we know what to do skillfully onstage, we know what *not* to do in our daily lives: the theatre is about conflict, and that is the last thing we want to experience in real life. Learning about "Action"—its theory and praxis—can help us to communicate empathetically.

Some practitioners don't go in for "theories" of acting. They see what they assume are Stanislavsky's methods, for example—or how they are presented—as inhibiting.[4] However, as Bernard Beckerman states, "Unthinking practice does not avoid theory. It merely acts upon old-fashioned 'theory,' even though such 'theory' may be no more than a residue of unexamined premises and reflex habits. *Theory is inescapable because fundamental propositions always underlie accumulated artistic*

2   Anton Chekhov, Letter to A. S. Suvorin, qtd. in Natalia Pervukhina, *Anton Chekhov: The Sense and the Nonsense* (New York, 1993), p. 39.

3   See Erving Goffman's *The Presentation of Self in Everyday Life, Interaction Ritual* and *Relations in Public*.

4   Prof. Stephen Wangh of NYU's Tisch Shool of the Arts Experimental Theatre Wing expressed this concern to me, for example.

practice" (5, emphasis added). Theatre practice comes from somewhere; what we do comes from our experiences and those who helped shape them. Robert Cohen[5] believes an understanding of acting theory is helpful to the student:

> Pedagogy founded on a communicated theoretical base ... may have ... long-lasting value, both as a means of instruction and as a support for artistry and the free-flow of creative imagination. Well-defined and well-conveyed acting theory provides motivation and discipline to artistic and intellectual processes. It provides a language for artistic and intellectual collaboration. It lends structure to creativity and confidence to imagination. It leads to intellectual connections with other thinkers—in and out of the theatre—and to other modes of thought. It dignifies the process it informs and intensifies the student's search for artistic value. It is a strong basis for further growth. I should make clear, however, that I am speaking of *practical* theorizing. (2002b: 20–1)

Lending "*structure to creativity and confidence to imagination*" is key to teaching the arts. The idea that the artist "creates spontaneously, *without thinking*, in a state of temporary insanity" is not helpful to the artist or the audience. It is important to recognize that theatre artists work from a theoretical basis, whether individuals acknowledge that theory or not. Teacher/director Yevgeny Lanskoy stated, "If acting is a mystery, it's not a profession." The "practical theory" of Action, with its strong basis in Greek thought, psychology and stage practice, provides this "language for artistic and intellectual collaboration," and a basis for growth. It dignifies the process of the actor and the public speaker as well, and so that of Communication Studies, Theatre and Theatre Education as scholarly and artistic enterprises. It is a way to approach theatre and communication practice, and a way to see the world.

Fourthly, teaching acting as a *practical* psychology—with the notion of Action[6]—is valuable for students in general, and not just those pursuing skills in stagecraft. It promotes "conflict resolution" as well as taking responsibility for what one does, by defining conflict itself: the student sees that Actions may be

---

5   As a Director and university acting teacher, Cohen writes he is pressured into being a combination of "dramaturg, pedagogue, visualist, critic, composer, theorist, editor, acting coach, translator and universal scholar of worldwide cultures, politics and traditions" (2002b: 3). Such is the praxis of theatre. This is also no less true for the Communication Studies teacher.

6   Teacher Yevgeny Lanskoy translated the titles of books by Russian theorist Pyotr Yershov as *Directing as a Practical Psychology* and *Technology of the Actor*. They describe more structures of Action beyond those in this study. These are books on directing actors in the theatre, and, unfortunately, have not been translated into English. Acting teacher Tim Craig also gives excellent classes based on Structures of Action theory and practice in Los Angeles.

controlled. When we do so on the stage, in "playing," we see the import of applying the lessons of "Action" to real life. Interpersonal behavior can change when we become consciously aware of *why*, or *to what end* we do something in the world. The key word here is "consciously": communication studies scholars note actions are often a result of "mindless processing" (Trenholm 49) or automatic behavior that happens without the benefit of thought or reflection. As teacher Lanskoy also stated, when it is done effectively onstage, "Action *does you*." In real life too, we may often be unaware of our own behavior as it happens.

The good news is that techniques of acting and drama can be taught—they are not "mysteries"—and good acting classes are classes in life skills: they encourage *conscious* behavior. Learning about playing Actions inevitably leads to the discovery that conflict in life may be avoided, by choosing different "Actions" or purposes. Whether one pursues an acting career, learns to appreciate theatre from the inside, or becomes more conscious of motivations and personal power, acting and the nature of Action are helpful in learning to navigate "conflict resolution," self-awareness and, as purported in communication studies, an "other-oriented" approach to the world (Beebe 4). This is significant to the field of education, where teaching conflict resolution and communication skills has become not just a way of dealing with classroom management for the teacher, but of preparing young people for their futures in the job market. Communication skills are the number one capability employers look for in potential employees (8–9). Not surprisingly, students involved in art classes or performance groups—drama, dance, fine arts and music—score higher on SAT tests.[7] Teaching acting and theatre skills may be among the most valuable ways to address literacy (including media literacy), aggression, self-expression, self-discipline, intercultural communication, group-building and tolerance in the schools. Teaching drama—involving language skills—has the added advantage of addressing both reading and oral communication. It is as important as any subject in the curriculum.

To that point, playwright and translator Tom Stoppard[8] wrote the following in his play, *The Invention of Love* (1997), about poet A. E. Housman and translation:

> Flowers, animals and rocks being the work of nature, their sciences are exact sciences, and must answer to the authority of what can be seen and measured. Literature, however, being the work of the human mind with all its frailty and aberration, and of human fingers which make mistakes, the science of textual criticism must aim for degrees of likelihood, and the only authority it might answer to is an author who has

---

7   Stanley Kaplan Test Preparation. I wrote materials for Kaplan in the 1990s.

8   Described as "the best playwright in the English language" by veteran actor Brian Cox on "Charlie Rose," PBS Channel 13, October 27, 2006.

been dead for hundreds or thousands of years. But it is a science none the less, not a sacred mystery. Reason and common sense, a congenial intimacy with the author, a comprehensive familiarity with the language ... concentration, integrity, mother wit and repression of self-will—these are a good start for the textual critic. In other words, almost anybody can be a botanist or a zoologist. Textual criticism is the crown and summit of scholarship. (38)

Though Stoppard is writing about translating ancient poetry, his words may be applied to the work of the play translator—and the script explorations of the actor—in modern works as well. The literary and dramatic nature of drama are not impenetrable, but require an understanding of human nature, "intimacy with the author" and an aim for "degrees of likelihood" rather than definitive answers. Searching for possibilities, instead of certainties, is not a bad thing; just the *attempt* to translate culture and explore possibilities of language and theatre poetry is part of what makes "textual criticism"—or script analysis—a "crown and summit of scholarship." The exploration of the playscript by the actor to glean clues to performance is as valuable as any "scholarly" a pursuit by the critic whose eyes may never leave the page. Indeed, the study of drama "on its feet" is imperative for a comprehensive understanding of the work.

I've noted that translating is not just a redistribution of words in another language, but the much more problematic transposition of culture. The translator—especially for the stage—is engaged in a practice that may reinterpret an entire text for the sensibilities of an audience unknown to the original playwright. In today's world, and notably in the United States, effective intercultural communication has become *de rigueur* in every aspect of our lives.[9] If the translator "adapts" a play that, for example, might "smooth over" the Russian-ness of Chekhov, or changes words so that the character(s) may play different Actions, who is to say but that the new concoction is not a *mis*representation of the author's original intention? Of course, any play may be reinterpreted onstage to represent something other than what the original playwright may have "intended," even if the original is in English. But the matter has what may be called "politically incorrect" implications when it is a foreign playwright whose work is renegotiated. Respectful intercultural communication is said to follow not the well-known Golden Rule, but, rather, the *Platinum Rule*: Do unto others as *they* would have you do unto *them*. So it's important to treat others not as *you* would like to be treated, but, rather, as *they* would like to be treated (Beebe 125). This is a shift from Katherine F. Philips'

---

9   Itntercultural communication includes gender communication as well, since men and women have their own "cultures" and ways of using and perceiving language. This involves the entire population, regardless of geography or enthnicity.

1663 idea that the translator was, for example, to "write to Corneille's sense, as it is supposed Corneille would have done *if he had been an Englishman*" and from Dryden's 17th century directive to get the foreign writer to "speak in one's own tongue." Corneille was not an Englishman, and Chekhov was no American. Play translators must address the question of whether or not to "change" the nationality of the original writer to conform to sensibilities of the audience. Once again, there is no one answer to this question.[10] For the actor and other practitioners, notes from the translator on variant word meanings and cultural annotations in a text could help immensely in making choices for performance. Discerning "Action" in the playscript, however, is the key for both translators and practitioners in contributing to the choices that create the particular "night out in the theatre" they envision.

In New York City and the U.S., both professional and amateur productions of all four plays take place every season. The annual "Chekhov Now" festival in Manhattan puts on inventive renditions of the plays; the Brooklyn Academy of Music sponsors Russian (The Maly Drama Theatre) and international interpretations (Sam Mendes' "The Bridge Project"); the Wooster Group revived their deconstruction of *Three Sisters* known as *Brace-Up!*; the new *Moscow Moscow Moscow Moscow Moscow Moscow* by Halley Feiffer slashes through the subtext of Chekhov's *Three Sisters*,[11] as does Aaron Posner's *Stupid Fucking Bird* with *Seagull*, and tributes to the canon throughout the United States are produced regularly in regional theatres: *The Fourth Sister, Vanya Masha Sonia and Spike, The Three Sisters Come*

---

10   Playwright Annie Baker coyly states in her *Uncle Vanya* Preface that her play "could be called a translation or an adaptation, depending on how you define the terms ... The goal was to *create a version that would make Chekhov happy*; to create a version that sounds to our contemporary American ears the way the play sounded to Russian ears during the play's first productions in the provinces in 1898. We will never know if that goal was achieved, but it was the guiding principle behind this text" (emphasis added). How Chekhov was played in the "provinces," versus the city, and why this is of import is indeed "unknown."

What would have made Chekhov happy might be gleaned from page one of my book. He asked: "Why do you want my work to be published in America? And in a lady's—which means an atrocious—translation?" (Chekhov 1975: xv) Just saying.

Baker's choice of the word "creeps" for the *chudaki* in *Vanya* is unique among all the translations I have encountered. Also, in Soho Rep's 2012 show, Merritt Wever as "Sonya" touched the audience with such pathos in her monologues, it was startling.

11   This hysterically funny, affecting and salacious contemporary play inspired by Chekhov's *Three Sisters* was presented at famed Chekhov director Nikos Psacharopoulas' Williamstown Theatre Festival. Nikos was Artistic Director for 33 years, before his death in 1989, and was known as a Chekhov aficionado. The show does start "*forte*" as a comedy, and ends surprisingly "pianissimo." Modern and classical styles are mixed; this is not necessarily a disadvantage to the production.

& *Go, Neva, The Chekhov Dreams* (on Theatre Row in February 2018 in NYC), and other shows "based on" or "inspired" by Chekhov's life or canon are examples. Arthur Allan Seidelman's film "The Sisters" came out in 2006 with Mary Stuart Masterson, Eric McCormack, and Rip Torn. Playwright Martin Sherman also wrote a new translation of *Cherry Orchard* for Los Angeles' Ahmanson Theatre with Annette Bening as Lyubov in winter 2006. Actor Susan Sarandon told me she had received no less than three new scripts of modern adaptations of Chekhov's plays in 2012. Playwright Lee Blessing's comedy *Uncle*—inspired by *Vanya*—was staged in Iowa and Arkansas in 2015 and 2016. Currently, another new movie version of "The Seagull" with Annette Bening as Arcadina, Saoirse Ronan as Nina, Elisabeth Moss as Masha, Mare Winningham[12] as Polina and Brian Dennehy as Sorin, with Stephen Karam's film adaptation, is at the movies. Finally, at this moment (June 2018) "an Epic New Symposium Celebrates Chekhov's Resonance in the 21st Century" in Portland, Oregon, with Štěpán Šimek's new "accessible to a millennial audience" translations of the last four plays.[13] Chekhov is everywhere.

Chekhov's canon and earlier Vaudevilles are played and studied in colleges and universities to help students learn styles of farce as well as Realism. In December 2017 I saw a gender-bending production of *Cherry Orchard* at Columbia University's Graduate MFA Directing Program.[14] Chekhov is a useful learning tool even outside the theatre or drama classroom because his plays teach both the value and incomprehensibility of language. There is no better demonstration of the import of human fallibility and relationships than Chekhov's plays. Chekhov's lessons can be fun and surprising to teach. They are nuanced and exploratory rather than definitive. They provide students with options for true critical thinking. Arguably,

---

12   Mare Winingham and I—along with Val Kilmer and Kevin Spacey, with many others—had the same inspiring drama teacher, Robert Carrelli, at Chatsworth High in Los Angeles. See "Waldman, Tom, Los Angeles Times …" herein.

13   A report from writer Bennett Ferguson from Willamette Week and the symposium website from Lewis and Clark College states: "In Šimek's translation of *the Three Sisters*, for example, the character of Masha—a delightfully cynical wife who spurns her buffoonish husband for a soldier—uses the word 'shithole.'" Šimek explains, "I thought 'Masha is a character who is very direct. Masha is a character who calls a spade a spade,' … So I used a contemporary word that expresses who she is and how she speaks." Again, Chekhov sparks the use of extreme language registers in translation. www.petensemble.org/event/chekhov-in-the-21st-century-a-symposium/

14   Director Mark Bruford's *Orchard* had Varya actually in love with Petya—with whom she is always fighting—rather than Lopakhin. He convinced us that there is justification for this singular interpretation in Paul Schmidt's contemporary translation.

Chekhov and the notion of Action could benefit every Humanities teacher's curricula.

Actors, translators and educators might realize common interdisciplinary goals and join together to promote continued exploration of the nature of translation of dramatic literature and its relationship to acting praxis and theory. Plays must be seen as templates for performance. The play doesn't exist until it is acted.[15] The plays of Chekhov, like those of all great writers, deserve translations in every generation. The fact that his canon tackles underlying complexities of human communication—broaching questions about aesthetics and language—makes exploration vital, especially for the artist and the educator. Esslin writes of Theatre of the Absurd—of which Chekhov is a precursor—"Paradoxically, the theatre that attacks language, and above all language that is beautiful and poetical for its own sake, is a deeply poetical theatre, only its poetry is a poetry of situation, movement, and concrete imagery, not one of language ... *Waiting for Godot* or *The Chairs* prove this point" (1971: 9). This is true of Chekhov too. Besides Beckett and Ionesco, Chekhov's legacy is found in Williams, Odets,[16] O'Neill, Pirandello, Albee, Pinter, Wasserstein,[17] and many writers dealing with the irony of the human condition. Chekhov is truly our contemporary.

The beauty survives in Chekhov's works regardless of the translations, which he dryly disdained (p. 1 herein). Beauty is created—as Chekhov actor Annette Bening pointed out to Charlie Rose—from characters that, at least, "try" amid overwhelming obstacles.[18] This comes through even "in translation." For all their foibles, Chekhov's characters have purpose, and they push through living. They have Action. They teach that Beckett's "I can't go on. I'll go on"[19] is a way to approach life; it is humorous as well as "wistful." It admits to human suffering, yet proposes a way to surmount it. Russian film director Nikita Mikhalkov ("Unfinished

15 Playwright Gore Vidal also stated this truism on the Leonard Lopate Show, WNYC, Nov. 10, 2006.

16 Odets' *Awake and Sing*, re-produced in 2006 by Lincoln Center Theatre and the National Asian American Theatre in 2013, NYC.

17 Wasserstein called her own play, *Sisters Rosensweig*, a "rip-off" of Chekhov's *Three Sisters* (WNYC Radio, Aug. 13, 2004).

18 "Charlie Rose" PBS Channel 13, Oct. 27, 2006. She played Ranevskaya in Sherman's version of *Orchard* at The Music Center in Los Angeles, 2006. Bening noted of *Adler on Ibsen, Strindberg and Chekhov*: "Stella speaks better about Chekhov than anybody." Bening later told me that it was husband Warren Beatty who was a student of Stella's. Adler continues to have great influence on the contemporary actor.

19 From the last line of Beckett's well-known trilogy, *The Unnameable*, translated into English in 1958.

Piece for the Player Piano")[20] said "the greatness of Chekhov lies in being anti-ideological and anti-pedagogical. His characters hurry in search of answers they never find."[21] Ironically, we are inspired by these characters, and learn from the questions their circumstances pose. They exist in translation, and only the actor can create them onstage. With Chekhov, as actors and audiences, we share the most confounding experiences we can know. There is no artist more inspirational to other artists. Chekhov lives on in the words of his translators and the Actions of the actors onstage.

References

Albee, Edward. Interview with the author. Lincoln Center, New York City, December 7, 2005, NYU in 2004 and Oklahoma City University, Spring 2008.

Beckerman, Bernard. *Dynamics of Drama*. New York: Drama Book Specialists, 1979.

———. "The Play's the Thing But What's a Play?" in Hobgood, Burnet M., ed. *Master Teachers of Theatre*. Board of Trustees, Southern Illinois University, 1988, pp. 32–33.

Beebe, Steven A., J. Susan, and Diana I. Ivy. *Communication, Principles for a Lifetime*. Boston: Pearson Education, 2007.

Brook, Peter. *The Empty Space*. New York: Avon Books, 1968.

———. Interview with Genista McIntosh, Royal National Theatre/Olivier Theatre, November 5, 1993. Also at: website-archive.nt-online.org.

Burrus, Ron. Classes in Technique, Rehearsal, Scene Study, 1980–83, 1986–89, Los Angeles. Interviews, New York City and Los Angeles, 2001–present.

"Charlie Rose" TV Show. Annette Bening. PBS Channel 13, October 27, 2006.

Chekhov, Anton. *Anton Chekhov's Selected Plays*. Trans. and ed., Laurence Senelick. New York: W. W. Norton & Co., 2005.

———. *Aunt Vanya*. Adapt. David Karl Lee. Unpublished Manuscript, Ant Farm Productions for the New York Chekhov Festival, New York City, 2001.

———. *The Cherry Orchard*. Adapt. David Mamet from a literal trans. Peter Nelles. New York: Grove Press, 1985.

———. *The Cherry Orchard*. Adapt. Tom Donaghy. Unpublished draft. December 2004.

———. *The Cherry Orchard*. Chay Yew. Adaptation: *A Winter People*. Unpublished Draft. September 28, 2004.

———. *The Cherry Orchard*. Joshua Logan. *The Wisteria Trees*, based on Anton Chekhov's *The Cherry Orchard*. New York: Random House, 1950.

———. *The Cherry Orchard*. Version. Trevor Griffiths/Trans. Helen Rappaport. London: Pluto Press Ltd., 1978.

20 It is said this 1977 film is based on Chekhov's first play, *Platonov*, a romantic romp with plot elements of *Seagull* and *Vanya* evident in the characters and story.

21 McNulty, Charles. "Simple, Inspiring, Misread." *Los Angeles Times*, Feb. 12, 2006.

————. *Moscow Moscow Moscow Moscow Moscow Moscow*. Adaptor Halley Feiffer. From Chekhov's *Three Sisters*. Williamstown Theatre Festival, July 26–August 6, 2017. Director Trip Cullman.

————. *The Oxford Chekhov*. Trans. Ronald Hingley. London: Oxford University Press, Vol. II, 1967, Vol. III, 1964, and Vol. IX, 1975.

————. *The Seagull*. Version. Tom Stoppard. London: Faber and Faber Limited, 1997.

————. *Three Sisters*. Version. Brian Friel. New York: Dramatists Play Service, 1981.

————. *The Three Sisters*. Adapt. David Mamet. Trans. Vlada Chernomirdik. New York: Samuel French, 1990.

————. *Uncle Vanya*. Adapt. Annie Baker. Literal Trans. Margarita Shalina. New York: Samuel French, 2013.

————. *Uncle Vanya*. Version. Brian Friel. New York: Dramatists Play Service, 1998.

————. *Uncle Vanya*. Version. Mike Poulton. Unpublished Manuscript from Roundabout Theatre production, New York City, Brooks Atkinson Theatre, August 31, 1999.

Cohen, Robert. *More Power to You*. New York: Applause Theatre and Cinema Books, 2002a.

————. Cohen, Robert and John Harrop. *Advanced Acting*. Boston: McGraw Hill, 2002b.

Craig, Timothy. "Acting for the Eye: Making Acting Visual." Unpublished Manuscript, n.d., circa 2000.

Goffman, Erving. *Interaction Ritual: Essays in Face to Face Behavior*. New Brunswich, NJ: Transaction Publishers, 1967.

————. *The Presentation of Self in Everyday Life*. New York: Anchor Books, 1959.

————. *Relations in Public*. New York: Basic Books, 1971.

Johnston, David, ed. *Stages of Translation*. Bath, England: Absolute Classics, 1996.

Lanskoy, Yevgeny. Interviews with the author, 1999, and Classes, "The Structures of Action," at the Stella Adler Conservatory, 1986–89.

McNulty, Charles. "Simple, Inspiring, Misread." *Los Angeles Times*, February 12, 2006.

Odets, Clifford. *Awake and Sing*. National Asian American Theater, Walkerspace at Soho Rep., NYC, August 2013.

————. Lincoln Center Theatre, Vivian Beaumont Theatre, New York City, Spring 2006.

Ouzounian, Richard. "He left 'no maggot lonely,' " *Toronto Star*, April 9, 2006.

Pervukhina, Natalia. *Anton Chekhov: The Sense and the Nonsense*. New York: Legas, 1993.

Sontag, Susan. *Against Interpretation and Other Essays*. New York: Picador USA, 2001.

Stoppard, Tom. *The Invention of Love*. New York: Grove Press, 1997.

Trenholm, Sarah. *Thinking Through Communication*, 4th ed. Boston: Pearson Education, 1995.

Wangh, Stephen. *An Acrobat of The Heart*. New York: Vintage Books, 2000.

————. Interview with the author. Classroom Observation. New York University, March 2003.

Yershov, Pyotr. *Directing as a Practical Psychology* and *Technology of the Actor* as taught by Yevgeny Lanskoy, 1986–1989. Structures of Action course, Stella Adler Conservatory, New York City.

Bibliography

Aaltonen, Sirkku. *Time-Sharing Onstage: Drama Translation in Theatre and Society.* Clevedon: Multilingual Matters, 2000.

Adler, Stella. *The Art of Acting.* Ed. Howard Kissel. New York: Applause Books, 2000.

———. Interview with Russell Vanderbrouke, *Yale Theatre*, 8(2 and 3), Spring, 1977.

———. *On Ibsen, Strindberg and Chekhov.* Ed. Barry Paris. New York: Alfred A. Knopf, 1999.

———. "The Reality of Doing," *Tulane Drama Review*, IX(1): 136–155, Fall, 1964.

———. Scene Study/Technique/Rehearsal Classes, with Ron Burrus, Pan-Andreas Theatre, Santa Monica, CA, 1981–84 and Stella Adler Conservatory, NYC, 1986–89.

———. *The Technique of Acting.* New York: Bantam Books, 1988.

Albee, Edward. Interview with the author. Lincoln Center, New York City, December 7, 2005, NYU in 2004 and Oklahoma City University, Spring, 2008.

Aldridge, Joyce Spivey. "The Tradition of American Actor Training and Its Current Practice in Undergraduate Education." Dissertation, University of Colorado, 1993.

Allen, David. *Performing Chekhov.* London: Routledge, 2000.

Aristotle. *Aristotle's Poetics.* Trans. S. H. Butcher. Intro. Francis Fergusson. New York: Hill and Wang, 1961.

———. *Aristotle's Theory of Poetry and Fine Art*, Trans. S. H. Butcher, 4th ed., London: Macmillan & Co. Ltd., 1932.

Arrowsmith, William and Roger Shattuck, eds. *The Craft and Context of Translation.* Austin: The University of Texas Press, 1961.

Artaud, Antonin. *The Theatre and Its Double.* Trans. Mary Caroline Richards. New York: Grove Press, 1958.

Atlas, James. "The Prose of Samuel Beckett, Notes from the Terminal Ward," *Poetry Nation*, No. 2, 1974, 106–117. www.poetrymagazine.org.uk.

Austin, J. L. *How to Do Things With Words*. Cambridge: Harvard University Press, 1975.

Baines, Roger, Cristina Marinetti, and Manuela Perteghella. *Staging and Performing Translation: Text and Theatre Practice*. New York: Palgrave Macmillan, 2011.

Baker, George Pierce. *Dramatic Technique*. Boston: Houghton Mifflin, 1976.

Baker, Paul. *Integration of Abilities: Exercises for Creative Growth*. New Orleans: Anchorage Press, 1977.

Bakhtin, M. M. *Speech Genres and Other Late Essays*. Austin: University of Texas Press, 1986.

Ball, William. *A Sense of Direction*. New York: Drama Book Publishers, 1984.

Barricelli, Jean-Pierre. *Chekhov's Great Plays*. New York: New York University Press, 1981.

Barthes, Roland. *Image Music Text*. London: Fontana Paperbacks, 1984.

Barton, Robert. *Style for Actors*. Mountain View, CA: Mayfield Publishing Company, 1993.

Bassnett, Susan. "Translating for the Theatre: The Case Against Performability," *TTR: Traduction, Terminologie, Redaction*, 4(1), 1st Semester, 1991.

Beale, Simon Russell. Interview with the author. Brooklyn Academy of Music, March 9, 2003.

Beebe, Steven A., J. Susan, and Diana I. Ivy. *Communication, Principles for a Lifetime*. Boston: Pearson Education, 2007.

Beckerman, Bernard. *Dynamics of Drama*. New York: Drama Book Specialists, 1979.

———. "The Play's the Thing But What's a Play?" in Burnet M. Hobgood, ed. *Master Teachers of Theatre: Observations on Teaching Theatre by Nine American Masters*. Board of Trustees, Southern Illinois University, 1988.

Bellos, David. *Is That a Fish in Your Ear?* New York: Faber and Faber, 2011.

Benedetti, Jean, ed. *The Moscow Art Theatre Letters*. New York: Routledge, 1991.

———. *Stanislavski*. New York: Routledge, 1990.

———. *Stanislavski and the Actor*. New York: Routledge, 1998.

———. *Stanislavski: An Introduction*. London: Methuen, 1982.

Benedetti, Robert. *The Actor at Work*. Englewood Cliffs, NJ: Prentice-Hall, 1970.

———. *Seeming, Being and Becoming*. New York: Drama Book Specialists, 1976.

———. *The Actor in You*. Boston: Allyn and Bacon, 1999.

Bentley, Eric. "Are Stanislavsky and Brecht Commensurable?" *Tulane Drama Review*, 9: 69–76, Fall, 1964.

———. *The Brecht Memoir*. Evanston, IL: Northwestern University Press, 1985.

———. *The Life of the Drama*. New York: Atheneum, 1967.

———. *The Playwright as Thinker*. New York: Harcourt, Brace and World, 1967.

———. *The Theatre of Commitment*. New York: Atheneum, 1967.

———. *The Theory of the Modern Stage*. New York: Penguin Books, 1968.

———. *Thinking About the Playwright*. Evanston, IL: Northwestern University Press, 1987.

———. *What is Theatre?* New York: Hill and Wang, 2000.

Bersley, Tracy. Interview with the author. New York University, Spring, 2004.

Billington, James H. *The Icon and the Axe*. New York: Vintage Books, 1970.

Billington, Michael. "His Genius is to Find the Drama Between the Words," *The New York Times,* July 15, 2001.

Bitsilli, Peter. *Chekhov's Art*. Ann Arbor: Ardis Publishers, 1983.

Blessing, Lee. Interview with the author. Rutgers University, May, 2004; phone Interview, July, 2017.

———. *Uncle*, World Premiere by New Ground Theatre, Davenport, IA, 2016.

———. *Uncle*, Reading at the Arkansas New Play Festival, Theatre Squared, Fayetteville, 2015.

Bogart, Anne. *Anne Bogart: Viewpoints*. Eds. Michael Bigelow Dixon and Joel A. Smith. Lyme, NH: Smith and Kraus, 1995.

———. Letter to the author, September, 2006.

Boleslavsky, Richard. *Acting, The First Six Lessons*. New York: Theatre Arts Books, 1963.

Bond, Will. Interview with the author. Anne Bogart's SITI Company at the New York Theatre Workshop, New York City, 1998.

Bosworth, Patricia. "Despise a Guy for 50 Years? Put Him in a Play," *The New York Times*, April 19, 1998.

Brand, Phoebe. Interview with the author. Manhattan Plaza, New York, NY, May, 2005.

Brantley, Ben. "Chekhov is Recast ..." *The New York Times*, May 1, 2000.

———. "Pinter the Actor Meets Pinter the Writer," *The New York Times*, July 19, 2001.

———. "Streep Meets Chekhov ..." *The New York Times*, August 13, 2001.

Brecht, Bertolt. *Brecht on Theatre*. Trans. and ed. John Willett. New York: Hill and Wang, 1964.

———. "Notes on Stanislavsky," *Tulane Drama Review*, 9:157–166, Fall, 1964.

Brestoff, Richard. *Acting Under the Circumstances*. Lyme, NH: Smith and Kraus, 1999.

———. *The Great Acting Teachers and Their Methods*. Lyme, NH: Smith and Kraus, 1995.

Breyer, Christopher. "The Chekhovian Six, Principles of Writing from an Artist Outside His Time," *Performances Magazine*, Center Theatre Group, 39th Season, February 2–March 19, 2006. www.taperahmanson.com/download/CherryOrchardProgram.pdf.

Brietzke, Alexander Kendrick. "Nothing is But What is Not: Chekhovian Drama and the Crisis of Representation." Dissertation of Stanford University, 1992.

Brislin, Richard. *Translation: Applications and Research*. New York: Gardner Press, 1976.

Brodsky, Joseph. "Homage to Chekhov," Poem in *The New Yorker*, August 7, 1995.

Brook, Peter. *The Empty Space*. New York: Avon Books, 1968.

———. Interview with Genista McIntosh, Royal National Theatre/Olivier Theatre, November 5, 1993a. Also at: website-archive.nt-online.org.

———. *The Open Door*. New York: Random House, 1993b.

———. *The Shifting Point*. New York: Harper & Row, 1987.

Brooks, Cleanth. *The Well Wrought Urn*. New York: Harcourt, Brace, Jovanovich, 1975.

Brown, Richard P. *Actor Training 1*. New York: Drama Book Specialists, 1972.

Bruder, Melissa, et al. *A Practical Handbook for the Actor*. New York: Vintage Books, 1986.

Bruehl, Bill. *The Techniques of Inner Action*. Portsmouth, NH: Heinemann, 1996.

Bruford, W. H. *Chekhov and His Russia*. New York: Oxford University Press, 1947.

———. *Anton Chekhov*. London: Bowes and Bowes, 1957.

Brustein, Robert. *The Theatre of Revolt*. Boston: Little, Brown and Company, 1964.

———. "The Heritage of the MXAT," *The New Republic*, 217.6–7, 29–31, August 11, 1997.

———. "Idiots and Ivanov," American Repertory Theatre, www.amrep.org, February 17, 2003.

Burke, Kenneth. *A Grammar of Motives*. New York: Prentice-Hall, 1954.

———. *Philosophy of Literary Form.* New York: Vintage Books, 1957.

———. *Language as Symbolic Action.* Berkeley: University of California Press, 1966.

Burrus, Ron. Classes in Technique, Rehearsal, Scene Study, 1980–83, 1986–89, Los Angeles. Interviews, New York City and Los Angeles, 2001-present.

Byrd, Jr., Robert E. "The Unseen Character in Selected Plays of Eugene O'Neill, Tennessee Williams and Edward Albee." Dissertation, New York University, 1995.

Callow, Philip. *Chekhov: the Hidden Ground.* Chicago: Ivan R. Dee, 1998.

Callow, Simon. *Being an Actor.* New York: St. Martin's Press, 1984.

Campbell, Christopher. *Platform Papers on Translation*, Royal National Theatre, November 11, 2003.

Carey, Dean. *Masterclass.* Portsmouth, NH: Heinemann, 1995.

Carnicke, Sharon Marie. *Checking Out Chekhov.* Boston: Academic Studies Press, 2013.

———. "The Nasty Habit of Adaptations," Conference: "Chekhov the Immigrant: Translating a Cultural Icon," Colby College, October 8–9, 2004.

———. "Stanislavsky Uncensored and Unabridged," *Tulane Drama Review,* T137, 13, Spring, 1993, 22–37.

———. *Stanislavsky in Focus.* Australia: Harwood Academic Publishers, 1998.

———. *The Theatrical Instinct.* New York: Peter Lang, 1989.

Carnovsky, Morris. *The Actor's Eye.* New York: Performing Arts Journal Publications, 1984.

———. "Statement to House on UnAmerican Activities Committee," n. d., 1950s.

Carpenter, Charles A. *Modern British, Irish and American Drama: A Descriptive Chronology, 1865–1965.* http://bingweb.binghamton.edu/~ccarpen/Pinter.htm.

Chaikin, Joseph. *The Presence of the Actor.* New York: Atheneum, 1972.

"Charlie Rose" TV Show. Annette Bening. PBS Channel 13, October 27, 2006.

Chekhov, Anton. *Anton Chekhov, Four Plays.* Trans. David Magarshack. New York: Hill and Wang, 1969.

———. *Anton Chekhov Plays.* Trans. Peter Carson. London: Penguin Books, 2002a.

———. *Anton Chekhov Selected Works*, Trans. Kathleen Cook. Moscow: Progress Publishers, 1973.

———. *Anton Chekhov's Plays.* Trans. and ed. Eugene Bristow. New York: W. W. Norton & Co., 1977a.

———. *Anton Chekhov's Selected Plays.* Trans. and ed. Laurence Senelick. New York: W. W. Norton & Co., 2005.

———. *Anton Chekhov's Three Sisters.* Trans. Štěpan Šimek. Unpublished Manuscript. August 2014.

———. *Aunt Vanya.* Adapt. David Karl Lee. Unpublished manuscript, Ant Farm Productions for the New York Chekhov Festival, New York City, 2001.

———. *Best Plays by Chekhov.* Trans. Stark Young. New York: The Modern Library, 1956.

———. *Chekhov, The Early Plays.* Trans. Carol Rocamora. Lyme, NH: Smith and Kraus, 1999.

———. *Chekhov: The Essential Plays.* Trans. Michael Henry Heim. New York: Modern Library, 2003.

———. *Chekhov for the Stage.* Trans. Milton Ehre. Evanston, IL: Northwestern University Press, 1992.

———. *Chekhov, Four Plays.* Trans. Carol Rocamora. Lyme, NH: Smith and Kraus, 1996.

———. *Chekhov, The Major Plays.* Trans. Ann Dunnigan. New York: Signet Classic, Penguin Books, 1964.

———. *Chekhov, The Major Plays.* Trans. Jean-Claude Van Itallie. New York: Applause Books, 1995.

———. *Chekhov Plays.* Trans. Michael Frayn. London: Methuen, 1988a.

———. *Chekhov's Major Plays.* Trans. Karl Kramer and Margaret Booker. New York: University Press of America, 1997a.

———. *Chekhov, The Russian Text of Three Plays: Uncle Vanya, The Three Sisters, The Cherry Orchard.* Cambridge: University Press, 1946.

———. *Chekhov, The Vaudevilles.* Trans. Carol Rocamora. Lyme, NH: Smith and Kraus, 1998.

———. *The Cherry Orchard.* Trans. Martin Sherman. Unpublished manuscript for the Music Center production in Los Angeles, California, 2006.

———. *The Cherry Orchard.* Trans. Sharon Marie Carnicke. Copyright 1980.

———. *The Cherry Orchard.* Adapt. Tom Donaghy. Unpublished Draft, December, 2004.

———. *The Cherry Orchard.* Version. Pam Gems. UK: Oberon Classics, 2007.

———. *The Cherry Orchard.* Version. Sir John Gielgud. New York: Theatre Arts Books, 1963.

———. *The Cherry Orchard.* Version. Peter Gill, from a literal trans. Ted Braun. London: Oberon Books Ltd, 1978a.

———. *The Cherry Orchard.* Version. Trevor Griffiths/Trans. Helen Rappaport. London: Pluto Press Ltd., 1978b.

———. *The Cherry Orchard.* Trans. Tyrone Guthrie and Leonid Kipnis. Minneapolis: University of Minnesota Press/Minnesota Theatre Company, 1965.

———. *The Cherry Orchard.* Joshua Logan. *The Wisteria Trees, based on Anton Chekhov's The Cherry Orchard.* New York: Random House, 1950.

———. *The Cherry Orchard.* Adapt. David Mamet from a literal trans. Peter Nelles. New York: Grove Press, 1985.

———. *The Cherry Orchard.* Adapt. Emily Mann. New York: Dramatists Play Service, 2000.

———. *The Cherry Orchard.* Trans. Jean-Claude Van Itallie. New York: Dramatists Play Service, 1979.

———. *The Cherry Orchard.* Chay Yew. *Adaptation: A Winter People.* Unpublished Draft, September 28, 2004.

———. *The Cherry Orchard and the Seagull.* Trans. Laurence Senelick. Arlington Heights, IL: AHM Publishing Corporation, 1977b.

———. *The Complete Plays, Anton Chekhov.* Trans. Laurence Senelick. New York: Norton, 2006.

———. *Dear Writer ... Dear Actress ... The Love Letters of Olga Knipper and Anton Chekhov.* Sel., Trans. and Ed. Jean Benedetti. Great Britain: Methuen Drama, 1996.

———. *Four Plays by Chekhov.* Trans. Alex Szogyi. New York: Washington Square Press, 1968.

———. *The Letters of Anton Pavlovitch Tchekhov.* Trans. Constance Garnett. New York: Benjamin Blom, 1966.

———. *Letters on the Short Story, The Drama and Other Literary Topics*, Ed. Louis S. Friedland. New York: Dover Publications, 1966.

———. *Memories of Chekhov: Accounts of the Writer from his Family Friends & Contemporaries.* Ed. and Trans. Peter Sekirin. Jefferson, NC: McFarland, 2006.

———. *Moscow Moscow Moscow Moscow Moscow Moscow*, Adapt. Halley Feiffer. *Three Sisters*, Williamstown Theatre Festival, July 26–August 6, 2017. Director Trip Cullman.

———. *Notebook of Anton Chekhov*. Trans. S. S. Koteliansky and Leonard Woolf. New York: B. W. Huebsch, 1922.

———. *The Notebook of Trigorin: A Free Adaptation of Anton Chekhov's Seagull*. Adapt. Tennessee Williams. Trans. Ann Dunnigan. Ed. Allean Hale. New York: New Directions Publishing, 1997b.

———. *The Oxford Chekhov*. Trans. Ronald Hingley. London: Oxford University Press, Vol. II, 1967, Vol. III, 1964, and Vol. IX, 1975.

———. *The Personal Papers of Anton Chekhov*. Trans. S. S. Koteliansky. New York: Lear Publishers, 1948.

———. *Plays, Anton Chekhov*. Trans. Elisaveta Fen. Middlesex, England: Penguin Books, 1951, 1954, 1964.

———. *The Plays of Anton Chekhov*. Trans. Constance Garnett. New York: The Modern Library, 1929.

———. *The Plays of Anton Chekhov*. Trans. Paul Schmidt. New York: Harper Collins Publishers, 1997c.

———. *Russian text of Chaika* (Seagull). http://public-library.ru/Chekhov.Anton/chaika.htm.

———. *The Russian Text of Three Plays: Uncle Vanya, Three Sisters, The Cherry Orchard*. Ed. P. Henry. Letchworth, Hertfordshire, England: Bradda Books Ltd, 1965.

———. *The Seagull*. Adapt. Michael Barakiva. Unpublished manuscript, 2004.

———. *The Seagull*. Trans. Sharon Marie Carnicke, University of Southern California. Unpublished manuscript, 1996.

———. *The Seagull*. Dir. Mike Nichols. New York: Central Park, 2001.

———. *The Seagull*. Trans. Michael Frayn. London: Methuen Publishing Ltd, 1986.

———. *The Seagull*. Trans. Michael Frayn. Intro. Nick Worral. London: Methuen Drama, 2002.

———. *The Seagull*. Trans. David French. Don Mills, Ontario, Canada: General Publishing Co. Ltd., 1977c.

———. *The Seagull*. Version. Pam Gems. London: Nick Hern Books, 1994.

———. *The Seagull*. Version. Peter Gill. Literal Trans. Helen Molchanoff. London: Oberon Books, 2000.

———. *The Seagull*. Adapt./Version. Christopher Hampton. New York: Faber & Faber, 2007.

———. *The Seagull*. Trans. Michael Henry Heim. Woodstock, IL: The Dramatic Publishing Company, 1992.

———. *The Seagull*. Version. Thomas Kilroy. London: Methuen London Ltd., 1981.

———. *The Seagull*. Trans. Nicholas Saunders and Frank Dwyer. Newbury, VT: Smith and Kraus, 1994.

———. *The Seagull*. Trans. and Adapt. Štěpán S. Šimek. Unpublished Manuscript. 2017.

———. *The Seagull*. Version. Tom Stoppard. London: Faber and Faber Ltd., 1997d.

———. *The Seagull*. Version. Jean-Claude Van Itallie. New York: Applause Books, 1974.

———. *Six Plays of Chekhov*. Version. Robert W. Corrigan. San Francisco: Rinehart Press, 1962.

———. *Three Sisters*. Trans. Sharon Marie Carnicke, University of Southern California. Unpublished Manuscript. 1979.

————. *Three Sisters*. Version. Brian Friel. New York: Dramatists Play Service, 1981.

————. *The Three Sisters*. Adapt. Christopher Hampton. UK: Samuel French, 2004/2015.

————. *The Three Sisters*. Trans. Randall Jarrell. London: Collier-Macmillan Ltd., 1969.

————. *The Three Sisters*. Adapt. David Mamet. Trans. Vlada Chernomirdik. New York: Samuel French, 1990a.

————. *Three Sisters*. Version. Frank McGuinness. Literal Trans. Rose Cullen. London: Faber and Faber Ltd., 1990b.

————. *Three Sisters*. Acting Version. Clifford Odets. Unpublished manuscript from Phoebe Brand Carnovsky, The Group Theatre, New York City, c. 1939.

————. *Three Sisters*. Trans. Paul Schmidt. New York: Theatre Communications Group, 1992.

————. *Three Sisters*. Trans. Lanford Wilson. Lyme, NH: Smith and Kraus, 1984.

————. *Two Plays by Tchekhov*. Trans. George Calderon. New York: Mitchell Kennerley, 1912.

————. *Uncle Vanya*. Adapt. Annie Baker. Literal Trans. Margarita Shalina. New York: Samuel French, 2013.

————. *Uncle Vanya*. Trans. Curt Columbus. Chicago: Ivan R. Dee, 2002b.

————. *Uncle Vanya*. Trans. Michael Frayn. London: Methuen London Ltd., 1987.

————. *Uncle Vanya*. Version. Brian Friel. New York: Dramatists Play Service, 1998.

————. *Uncle Vanya*. Version. Pam Gems. London: Nick Hern Books, 1992.

————. *Uncle Vanya*. Adapt. David Mamet. Literal Trans. Vlada Chernomirdik. New York: Grove Press, 1988, also by Samuel French, 1988b.

————. *Uncle Vanya*. Trans. Stephen Mulrine. London: Nick Hern Books, 1999a.

————. *Uncle Vanya*. Version. Mike Poulton. Unpublished manuscript from Roundabout Theatre production, New York City, Brooks Atkinson Theatre, August 31, 1999b.

————. *Uncle Vanya*. Trans. Štěpan S. Šimek. Unpublished Manuscript. 2017.

————. *Uncle Vanya*. Adapt. Andrew Upton. Unpublished manuscript sent to this author, 2012.

————. *Uncle Vanya and Other Plays*. Trans. Betsy Hulick. New York: Bantam Books, 1994.

————. *Wild Honey*. Version of the untitled play. Trans. Michael Frayn. London: Methuen London Ltd., 1984.

Chekhov, Michael. "Chekhov on Acting: A Collection of Unpublished Materials (1919–1942)." *Tulane Drama Review*, 27:63 No. 3 (T99), Fall, 1983.

————. *Lessons for the Professional Actor*. Arr. by Deirdre Hurst du Prey. New York: Performing Arts Journal Publications, 1985.

————. *On The Technique of Acting*. Ed. Mel Gordon. New York: Harper Collins Publishers, 1991.

————. *To The Actor*. New York: Harper & Row, 1953.

Chilewska, Anna. "The Assessment of Translations: Examples from Chekhov, Zoshchenko and Sienkiewicz." M. F. A. Thesis. University of Alberta, Canada, 2000.

Chinoy, Helen Krich, ed. "Reunion: A Self-Portrait of The Group Theatre," *Educational Theatre Journal*, 28:4, December, 1976.

Chudakov, A. P. *Chekhov's Poetics*. Trans. Edwina Jannie Cruise and Donald Dragt. Ann Arbor: Ardis, 1983.

Chukovsky, Kornei. *Chekhov the Man*. Trans. Pauline Rose. London: Hatchinson & Company Publishers, n.d., circa 1940s.

Clark, Virginia P., et al., eds. *Language*. New York: St. Martin's Press, 1985.

Clayton, J. Douglas, ed. *Chekhov Then and Now*. New York: Peter Lang, 1997.

Clayton, J. Douglas and Yana Merzon. *Adapting Chekhov: The Text and Its Mutations*. New York: Routledge, 2013.

Clifford, John. "Translating Moments, Not Words," www.teatrodomundo.com, February 9, 2005.

Clurman, Harold. *Lies Like Truth*. New York: The Macmillan Company, 1958.

———. *The Naked Image*. New York: The Macmillan Company, 1967.

———. *The Fervent Years*. New York: Harcourt, Brace, Jovanovich, 1975.

———. *The Collected Works of Harold Clurman*. Eds. Marjorie Loggia and Glenn Young. New York: Applause Books, 1994.

Clyman, Toby W., ed. *A Chekhov Companion*. Westport, CT: Greenwood Press, 1985.

Cocteau, Jean. Preface, *Les Mariés de la Tour Eiffel*. Paris: Editions Flammarion, 1995. See also https://www.poetryfoundation.org/poets/jean-cocteau.

Coger, Leslie. "Stanislavsky Changes His Mind," *Tulane Drama Review* 9:63–68, Fall, 1984.

Cohen, Robert. *More Power to You*. New York: Applause Theatre and Cinema Books, 2002a.

———. *Theatre*. Palo Alto, CA: Mayfield Publishing Company, 1981, 1983.

Cohen, Robert and John Harrop. *Advanced Acting*. Boston: McGraw Hill, 2002b.

———. *Creative Play Direction*. Englewood Cliffs, NJ: Prentice-Hall, 1974.

Cole, David. *Acting as Reading*. Ann Arbor: The University of Michigan Press, 1992.

Cole, Toby, compiler. *Acting, A Handbook of the Stanislavski Method*. New York: Crown Trade Paperbacks, 1983.

Cole, Toby and Helen Krich Chinoy, eds. *Playwrights on Playwriting*. New York: Hill and Wang, 1968.

———. *Actors on Acting*. New York: Three Rivers Press, 1970.

———. *Directors on Directing*. Indianapolis: Bobbs-Merrill Educational Publishing, 1976.

Coquelin, Constant. *Art and the Actor*. Trans. Abby Langdon Alger. New York: Dramatic Museum of Columbia University, 1915.

———. *The Art of Acting*. New York: Dramatic Museum of Columbia University, 1926.

———. *The Art of the Actor*. Trans. Elsie Fogerty. London: George Allen & Inwin, 1932.

Corrigan, Robert W., ed. *New American Plays*. New York: Hill and Wang, 1965.

———. "Some Aspects of Chekhov's Dramaturgy," *Educational Theatre Journal,* 7:108–114, May, 1955.

———. *The Theatre in Search of a Fix*. New York: Delacorte Press, 1973.

———. *Theatre in the Twentieth Century*. New York: Grove Press, 1963.

———. "Translating for Actors." *The Craft and Context of Translation*. Eds. William Arrowsmith and Roger Shattuck. Austin: The University of Texas Press, 1961 pp. 95–106.

———. *The World of the Theatre*. Glenview, IL: Scott, Foresman and Company, 1979.

Craig, Timothy. "Acting for the Eye: Making Acting Visual." Unpublished Manuscript, n.d., circa 2000.

Croft, Giles. *Platform Papers*. London: Royal National Theatre, 1989 and 1991.

Dace, Wallace. *Elements of Dramatic Structure*. Manhattan, KS: AG Press Paperback, 1972.

Danchik, Roger L. "The Distinction Between the Written and Performed Dramatic Text from Suzanne Langer's Perspective," Dissertation, NYU, 1991.

Denby, David. "Classville, Robert Altman's 'Gosford Park,'" *The New Yorker,* January 4, 2002.

Diderot, Denis and William Archer. *The Paradox of Acting and Mask or Faces?* New York: Hill and Wang, 1963.

Dobbin, James G. "A Director's Analysis of *Uncle Vanya*." M. F. A. Thesis. University of Calgary, Canada, 1993.

Dolgatchev, Slava. "Workshop in Acting." NYU, Department of Music and Performing Arts, 2004.

Drake, Sylvie. "Stella Adler: Last of Theatre Dynasty," *The Los Angeles Times,* December 22, 1992.

Driver, John and Jeffrey Haddow. *Chekhov in Yalta.* New York: Helen Merrill, 1982.

Dukore, Bernard R. *Dramatic Theory and Criticism.* New York: Holt Rinehart and Winston, 1974.

Edel, Leon. *Literary Biography.* Bloomington: Indiana University Press, 1973.

Edwards, Christine. *The Stanislavsky Heritage.* New York: New York University Press, 1965.

Eekman, Thomas. *Anton Cechov.* Leiden, Netherlands: E. J. Brill, 1960.

Eisen, Donald G. "The Art of Anton Chekhov: Principles of Technique in His Drama and Fiction."

Dissertation, University of Pittsburgh, 1982.

Emeljanow, Victor, ed. *Chekhov, The Critical Heritage.* London: Routledge & Kegan Paul, 1981.

Epstein, Sabin R. and John D. Harrop. *Basic Acting.* Boston: Allyn and Bacon, 1996.

Esslin, Martin. *An Anatomy of Drama.* New York: Hill and Wang, 1976a.

———. *The Field of Drama.* London and New York: Methuen, 1987.

———. *Pinter.* New York: W. W. Norton and Company, 1976b.

———. *Reflections.* Garden City, NY: Anchor Books, 1971.

———. *The Theatre of the Absurd.* Garden City, NY: Anchor Books, 1961; Penguin Books, 1968.

Evreinov, Nicolas. *The Theatre in Life.* Trans. Alexander I. Nazaroff. New York: Benjamin Blom, 1970.

Fan, Jiayang. "Buried Words: Han Kang and the Complexity of Translation." *The New Yorker,* January 15, 2018.

Feingold, Michael. "Gull Talk," *The Village Voice,* August 21, 2001.

Ferguson, Bennett Campbell. *Willamette Week, Portland News.* "An Epic New Symposium Celebrates Chekhov's Resonance in the 21st Century." June 27, 2018. http://www.wweek.com/arts/2018/06/27/an-epic-new-symposium-celebrateschekhovs-resonance-in-the-21st-century

Fergusson, Francis. *The Human Image in Dramatic Literature.* Gloucester, MA: Peter Smith, 1969.

———. *The Idea of a Theatre.* Garden City, NY: Doubleday Anchor Books, 1953.

———. "The Notion of Action," *Tulane Drama Review,* 9:85–87, Fall, 1964.

Filho, Souza. *Language and Action.* Amsterdam: John Benjamins Publishing Company, 1984.

Flaubert, Gustave and Georges Sand. *Flaubert-Sand, the Correspondence.* Trans. and eds. Francis Steegmuller and Barbara Bray. New York: Alfred A. Knopf, 1993.

Fletcher, Beryl S., et al. *A Student's Guide to the Plays of Samuel Beckett.* London: Faber & Faber, 1978.

Flood, Alison. "Tolstoy thought Chekhov 'worse than Shakespeare.'" *The Guardian*, UK, July 11, 2011.

Fornes, Maria Irene, et al. *Orchards*. New York: Broadway Play Publishing, 1987.

Forsythe, James. *Tyrone Guthrie*. London: Hamish Hamilton, 1976.

Friedberg, Maurice. *Literary Translation in Russia*. University Park, PA: The Pennsylvania State University Press, 1997.

Friel, Brian. *Translations*. London: Faber and Faber Limited, 1981.

Gagen, Jean. " 'Most resembling unlikeness, and most unlike resemblance': Beth Henley's *Crimes of the Heart* and Chekhov's *Three Sisters*," *Studies in American Drama*. 4:119–128, 1989.

Gauss, Rebecca. "Studios of the Moscow Art Theatre." Dissertation, University of Colorado, 1997.

Gilles, Daniel. *Chekhov, Observer Without Illusion*. New York: Funk & Wagnalls, 1967.

Gilman, Richard. *Chekhov's Plays: An Opening into Eternity*. New Haven: Yale University Press, 1995.

Giona, Dana. "A Translator's Tale" (with Richard Wilbur), *American Theatre Magazine*, New York: TCG, April 2009.

Gister, Earle. Interview with the author. The Actor's Center, New York City, June 8, 2005.

Glenn, Stanley. *A Director Prepares*. Encino, California: Dickenson Publishing Company, 1973.

———. *The Complete Actor*. Boston: Allyn and Bacon, 1977.

Goffman, Erving. *Interaction Ritual: Essays in Face to Face Behavior*. New Brunswick, NJ: Transaction Publishers, 1967.

———. *The Presentation of Self in Everyday Life*. New York: Anchor Books, 1959.

———. *Relations in Public*. New York: Basic Books, 1971.

Gold, Sylviane. "Stella the Great ..." *The Wall Street Journal*, December 15, 1983.

Gorchakov, Nikolai M. *Stanislavsky Directs*. Trans. Goldina, Miriam. New York: Funk and Wagnalls, 1954.

Gordon, Marc. "Stanislavsky in America: Russian Émigré Teachers of Acting." Dissertation, Cambridge: Tufts University, 2002.

Gordon, Mel. "Nine Misconceptions About Stanislavsky and His System," *Soviet and European Performance*, 9 (2 and 3), Fall, 1989.

———. *The Stanislavksy Technique: Russia*. New York: Applause Theatre Book Publishers, 1987.

Gottlieb, Vera. *Chekhov and the Vaudeville*. Cambridge: Cambridge University Press, 1982.

———. and Paul Allain, eds. *The Cambridge Companion to Chekhov*. Cambridge University Press, 2000.

Granville-Barker. *On Dramatic Method*. New York: Hill and Wang, 1967.

Gross, Alex. "And What About the ATA?" [American Translation Association] language.home.sprynet.com/trandex/theata.htm, January 28, 2005a.

———. "Some Major Dates and Events in the History of Translation," www.accurapic.com, January 28, 2005b.

———. "Translation: The Human Utility," language.home.sprynet.com January 28, 2005c.

———. "Translation Theory: Some Images and Analogies for the Process of Translation." language.home.sprynet.com/trandex/images.htm, April 26, 2005d.

————. "Hermes—God of Translators and Interpreters," language.home.sprynet.com, April 26, 2005d.

Grossman, Edith. *Why Translation Matters.* New Haven and London: Yale University Press, 2010.

Grotowski, Jerzy. *Towards a Poor Theatre.* New York: Simon and Schuster, 1968.

Gunn, Drewey Wayne. "More Than Just a Little Chekovian," *Modern Drama,* 33:313–321, No. 3, September, 1990.

Guthrie, Tyrone. *A Life in the Theatre.* New York: McGraw-Hill Book Company, 1959.

Hackett, Jean, ed. *The Actor's Chekhov: Interviews with Nikos Psachoropolous and the Company of the Williamstown Theatre Festival on the Plays of Anton Chekhov.* Newbury, VT: Smith and Kraus, 1993.

Hagen, Uta. *A Challenge for the Actor.* New York: Charles Scribner's Sons, 1991.

————. *Respect for Acting.* New York: Macmillan Publishing Company, 1973.

————. Posters on the doors of the Lucille Lortel Theatre, January 15, 2004. Quotes and stories of Uta Hagen.

Hanne, Michael. *The Power of the Story.* Providence, Rhode Island: Berghahn Books, 1994.

Hall, Edward T. *The Silent Language.* New York: Anchor Books Doubleday, 1959.

Hamon-Sirejols, Christine. *Anton Pavlovitch Tchekhov, La Cerisaie.* Paris: Presses Universitaire de France, 1993.

Hampton, Wilborn. "Frielizing Chekhov to Widen His Appeal," *The New York Times,* February 16, 2003.

Hare, David. *The Guardian.* "David Hare on Young Chekhov: 'thrilling sunbursts of anger and romanticism'" October 5, 2015. [the guardian.com]

Harrop, John. *Acting.* London: Routledge, 1992.

Harrop, John and Sabin R. Epstein. *Acting With Style.* Boston: Allyn and Bacon, 2000.

Hayakawa, S. I. *Language in Thought and Action.* New York: Harcourt Brace Jovanovich, 1939.

Hayman, Ronald. *How to Read a Play.* New York: Grove Press, 1977.

Heilman, Pamela Sue. "The American Career of Maria Ouspenskaya (1887–1949): Actress and Teacher." Dissertation, Louisiana State University, 1999.

Hensher, Philip. "Incomparable Naturalism," *The Atlantic Monthly,* January, 2002.

Hingley, Ronald. *Chekhov, A Biographical and Critical Study.* London: Allen and Unwin, 1950; New York: Barnes and Noble, 1966.

————. *A New Life of Anton Chekhov.* New York: Alfred A. Knopf, 1976.

Hirsch, Foster. *A Method to Their Madness.* New York: W. W. Norton and Company, 1984.

Hoberman, Barry. "Translating the Bible," *The Atlantic Monthly,* February, 1985.

Hobgood, Burnet M., ed. *Master Teachers of Theatre.* Board of Trustees, Southern Illinois University, 1988.

Hodge, Alison, ed. *Twentieth Century Actor Training.* London: Routledge, 2000.

Hodgson, John and Ernest Richards. *Improvisation,* Methuen, London, 1966.

Hoffman, Theodore. "Stanislavsky Triumphant," *Tulane Drama Review* 9:9–17, Fall, 1964.

Hohman, Valleri. "Translating Chekhov for the American Stage," University of Illinois, Urbana Champaign, 2010. www.academia.edu/16792347/Translating_Chekhov_for_the_American_Stage.

Holden, Stephen. "Grand But Idle in Old Russia," *The New York Times,* February 22, 2002.

Hornby, Richard. *The End of Acting.* New York: Applause Theatre Books, 1992.

Houghton, Norris. *Moscow Rehearsals.* London: George Allen & Unwin, Ltd., 1938.

Hull, Lorrie. *Strasberg's Method.* Woodbridge, CT: Ox Bow Publishing, 1986.

Izzo, David Garrett. *Aldous Huxley and W. H. Auden On Language.* West Cornwall, CT: Locust Hill Press, 1998.

Jackson, Robert Louis. *Chekhov.* Englewood Cliffs, NJ: Prentice-Hall, 1967.

———. *Reading Chekhov's Text.* Evanston, IL: Northwestern University Press, 1993.

Janecek, Gerald, ed. *Andrey Bely.* Lexington, KY: The University Press of Kentucky, 1978.

Johnston, David, ed. *Stages of Translation.* Bath, England: Absolute Classics, 1996.

Jones, David Richard. *Great Directors at Work.* Berkeley: University of California Press, 1986.

Jones, Ellis. *Acting.* London: Hodder Headline PLC, 1998.

Jones, Robert Edmond. *The Dramatic Imagination.* New York: Theatre Arts Books, 1994.

Kaplan, David. *Five Approaches to Acting.* New York: West Broadway Press, 2001.

Karam, Stephen. "Stephen Karam on Giving the Last Word in the *Cherry Orchard*" Theater-mania, www.theatermania.com/broadway/news/stephen-karam-on-chekhov.

Kataev, Vladimir. *If Only We Could Know!* Trans./Ed. Harvey Pitcher. Chicago: Ivan R. Dee, 2002.

Katzer, Julius, ed. *A. P. Chekhov.* Moscow: Foreign Languages Publishing House, n.d.

Kazan, Elia. "Outline from Elementary Course in Acting, 1935," *Tulane Drama Review,* T104, 28:34–37, Winter, 1984.

Kenner, Hugh. "The Flaubertian Tradition," Class at UC Santa Barbara, English Department, 1973.

Kerr, Walter. *Thirty Plays Hath November.* New York: Simon and Schuster, 1968.

Kerwin, William, ed. *Brian Friel, A Casebook.* New York: Garland Publishing, 1997.

Kirby, Michael. "Nonsemiotic Performance," *Modern Drama,* March 1982, pp. 105–111.

Kirk, Irina. *Anton Chekhov.* Boston: Twayne Publishers, 1981.

Kirsch, Adam. "Chekhov in American," *The Atlantic,* July, 1997.

Konijn, Elly A. *Acting Emotions.* Amsterdam: Amsterdam University Press, 2000.

Koteliansky, S. S., Trans. and ed. *Anton Tchekhov.* New York: Haskell House Publishers, 1974.

Krasner, David, ed. *Method Acting Reconsidered.* New York: St. Martin's Press, 2000.

Kvale, Steiner. *Interviews.* Thousand Oaks, CA: Sage Publications, 1996.

Lahr, John. "The Great Guskin," *The New Yorker,* March 20, 1995.

———. "Life After Death," *The New Yorker,* November 6, 1995.

———. "Sea of Love," *The New Yorker,* August 20 and 27, 2001.

Langer, Susanne K. *Feeling and Form.* New York: Charles Scribner's Sons, 1953.

Lanskoy, Yevgeny. Interviews with the author, 1999, and Classes, "The Structures of Action," at the Stella Adler Conservatory, 1986–89.

Law, Alma and Mel Gordon. *Meyerhold, Eisenstein and Biomechanics.* Jefferson, NC: McFarland & Company, 1996.

Lawson, Mark. "The World's Second Best Dramatist," *The Guardian (UK),* September 21, 2001.

Lee, Josephine. "Disciplining Theatre and Drama in the English Department," *Text and Performance Quarterly,* 19(2), April, 1999.

Lazar, Paul. Interview with the author. Brooklyn, NY, April 16, 2003.

Leiter, Samuel L. *From Stanislavsky to Barrault*. New York: Greenwood Press, 1991.

Lessing, Gotthold Ephraim. *Emilia Galotti*. Adapter/Director Michael Thalheimer. Brooklyn Academy of Music, NYC, October 2005.

Levenson, Robin Beth. "Mamet on Acting," Letter to Editor, *American Theatre Magazine*, September, 1996.

———. "Afraid to Lie," Unpublished paper, Dr. Richard Schechner's Directing Course, New York University, Tisch School of the Arts, Spring, 1999.

———. "American Royalty," Unpublished paper, Lowell Swortzell's Methods and Materials Course, New York University School of Education, Spring, 2000.

Levin, Irina and Igor. *The Stanislavsky Secret*. Colorado Springs: Meriwether Publishing, 2002.

———. *Working on the Play and the Role*. Chicago: Ivan R. Dee, 1992.

Lewis, Robert. *Method or Madness?* New York: Samuel French, 1958.

———. "Emotional Memory," *Tulane Drama Review*, T16:54–61, Summer, 1962.

———. "Would You Please Talk to Those People?" *Tulane Drama Review* 9:104–113, Fall, 1964.

———. *Advice to The Players*. New York: Harper & Row, Publishers, 1980.

———. *Slings and Arrows*. New York: Stein and Day, 1984.

Linklater, Kristin. *Freeing the Natural Voice*. UK/USA: Drama Publishers, 1976.

———. Workshop with MFA students, Columbia University at American Communication Association Conference, NYC, 1998.

Logan, Brian. "Whose Play is it Anyway?" *Guardian*, March 12, 2003.

Logan, Joshua. *The Wisteria Trees, based on Anton Chekhov's The Cherry Orchard*. New York: Random House, 1950.

Lopate, Leonard. "The Leonard Lopate Show," WNYC Radio, Interview Walter Hill, June 20, 2006.

Longfellow, Henry Wadsworth, *The Complete Works of Henry Wadsworth Longfellow*, "The Day is Done," Massachusetts: Ticknor & Fields, 1866.

Mabley, Edward. *Dramatic Construction*. Philadelphia: Chilton Book Company, 1972.

Maegd-Soep, Carolina De. *Chekhov and Women*. Columbus, OH: Slavica Publishers, 1987.

Magarshack, David. *Chekhov*. New York: Grove Press, 1952.

———. *Chekhov the Dramatist*. New York: Hill and Wang, 1960.

———. *The Real Chekhov*. London: George Allen & Unwin, Ltd., 1972.

———. *Stanislavsky*. Westport, CT: Greenwood Press, 1975.

Malague, Rosemary. "Getting at 'the Truth:' A Feminist Consideration of American Actor Training." Dissertation, City University of New York, 2001.

Malcolm, Janet. *Reading Chekhov*. New York: Random House, 2001.

———. "Three Journeys," *The New Yorker*, October 29, 2001.

Mamet, David. *Writing in Restaurants*. New York: Penguin Books, 1986.

———. *Some Freaks*. New York: Penguin Books, 1989.

———. *True and False*. New York: Vintage Books, 1999.

———. Interview, David Mamet, "The Leonard Lopate Show," WNYC Radio, February 12, 2007.

Markus, Tom. *How to Read a Play*. Dubuque, IA: Kendall/Hunt Publishing Company, 1996.

Marowitz, Charles. *The Act of Being*. New York: Taplinger Publishing Company, 1978.

———. *The Other Way*. New York: Applause Books, 1999.

———. *Prospero's Staff*. Bloomington: Indiana University Press, 1986.

Marsh, Cynthia. "Three Sisters as a Case Study for Making Foreign Theater or Making Theater Foreign." *Chekhov for the 21ˢᵗ Century* by Carol Apollonio and Angela Brintlinger. Bloomington, IN: Slavica Publishers, 2012.

McCaslin, Nellie. Interview with the author. New York City, June 2, 2003.

McGaw, Charles. *Acting is Believing*. New York: Holt, Rinehart and Winston, 1975.

McKellen, Ian. "The Test of Time," *The Observer Magazine*, April 13, 1975.

McMillan, Eric. "The Greatest Literature of All Time." *Translations*. January 28, 2005. www.editoreric.com/greatlit/info/translations.html.

McNulty, Charles. "Simple, Inspiring, Misread." *Los Angeles Times*, February 12, 2006.

McTeague, James H. *Before Stanislavsky*. New Jersey: The Scarecrow Press, 1993.

Meisner, Sanford. *On Acting*. New York: Vintage Books, 1987.

Meister, Charles W. *Chekhov Bibliography*. Jefferson, NC: McFarland & Co., 1985.

Mekler, Eva. *The New Generation of Acting Teachers*. New York: Penguin Books, 1988.

———. *Masters of the Stage*. New York: Grove Weidenfeld, 1989.

Mekler, Nancy. Interview with the author. Brooklyn Marriott Hotel, November, 2004.

Mendes, Sam. Interview with the author. Brooklyn Academy of Music, March, 2003.

Merkel, Matt S. "Reinventing Chekhov: The Journey from Realism to Impressionism in Selected Plays of Anton Chekhov." Master's Thesis. Regent University, 1998.

Merlin, Bella. *Beyond Stanislavsky*. New York: Routledge, 2001.

———. *Konstantin Stanislavsky*. New York: Routledge, 2003.

Meyerhold, Vsevolod. "The 225th Studio," *Tulane Drama Review*, 9:22–23, Fall, 1964.

———. *Meyerhold on Theatre*. Trans./Ed. Edward Braun. London: Methuen & Company Ltd., 1969.

Midgette, Anne. "Finding the Musical Romance in a Chekhov Play," *The New York Times*, December 14, 2002.

Miles, Patrick., ed. and trans. *Chekhov on the British Stage*. Cambridge: Cambridge University Press, 1993.

Miller, Arthur. Interview, Leonard Lopate Show, 2000.

Mirsky, D. S. *A History of Russian Literature*. Ed. Francis J. Whitfield. Evanston, IL: Northwestern University Press, 1999.

Mitchell, John D. (with Trans. Alan UpChurch) *Staging Chekhov: Cherry Orchard*. New York: Institute for Advanced Studies in the Theatre Arts, 1991.

Miller, Arthur. Interview. "The Leonard Lopate Show," WNYC Radio, 2000.

Mitter, Shomit. *Systems of Rehearsal*. London: Routledge, 1992.

Monos, Jim. "The Use of Stanislavsky Techniques in Professional Actor Training in New York City." Dissertation, City University of New York, 1981.

———. *Professional Actor Training in New York City*. Shelter Island, NY: Broadway Press, 1989.

Moody, A. David. *Thomas Stearns Eliot, Poet*. Cambridge: Cambridge University Press, 1994.

Moore, Irene. Interview with the author. New York City, February 28, 2002.

Moore, Sonia. *The Stanislavski System.* New York: The Viking Press, 1974.

———. *Stanislavski Revealed.* New York: Applause Theatre Books, 1991.

Morgan, Joyce Vining. *Stanislavski's Encounter with Shakespeare.* Ann Arbor: University of Michigan Press, 1984.

Morrison, Hugh. *Acting Skills.* London: A & C Black (Publishers) Limited, 1992.

Mueller-Vollmer, Kurt and Michael Irmscher. *Translating Literatures, Translating Cultures.* Berlin: Erich Schmidt, 1998.

Murdock, Michael Julian. "The Humor of Anton Chekhov." Dissertation, University of Wisconsin, 1971.

Nabokov, Vladimir. *Lectures on Russian Literature.* New York: Harcourt Brace Jovanovich, Publishers, 1981.

Nemirovsky, Irene. *A Life of Chekhov.* London: The Grey Walls Press Ltd., 1950.

Nikolarea, Ekaterina. "Performability vs. Readability." *Translation Journal,* 6(4): 1–21, October, 2002. www.accurapid.com/journal/22theater.htm.

Noice, Tong and Helga Tong. *The Nature of Expertise in Professional Acting.* Mahwah, NJ: Lawrence Erlbaum Associates, Publishers, 1997.

Odets, Clifford. *Awake and Sing!* National Asian American Theater, Walkerspace at Soho Rep., New York City, August 2013.

———. Lincoln Center Theatre, Vivian Beaumont Theatre, New York City, Spring 2006.

Olson, Elder, ed. *Aristotle's "Poetics" and English Literature.* Chicago: University of Chicago Press, 1965.

"One Snappy, One Not So," (no author listed) *The New York Times,* February 16, 2003.

Ong, Walter J. *Orality and Literacy.* London: Routledge, 1997.

Ormsby, Eric. "Still a Great Translation," *New York Sun,* November 3, 2004.

Ouzounian, Richard. "He left 'no maggot lonely,'" *Toronto Star,* April 9, 2006.

Pang, Cecilia Jessica. "The Angst of American Acting: An Assessment of Acting Texts." Dissertation. Berkeley: University of California, 1991.

Peace, Richard. *Chekhov.* New Haven: Yale University Press, 1983.

Pennington, Michael. *Are You There, Crocodile?* London: Oberon Books Ltd., 2003.

Pervukhina, Natalia. *Anton Chekhov: The Sense and the Nonsense.* New York: Legas, 1993.

Peter, John. *Vladimir's Carrot.* Chicago: University of Chicago Press, 1987.

Pitcher, Harvey. *The Chekhov Play.* Berkeley: University of California Press, 1985.

———. *Chekhov's Leading Lady.* New York: Franklin Watts, 1980.

Poggi, Jack. "The Stanislavsky System in Russia," *Tulane Drama Review.* 28:124–133, T104, Winter, 1984.

Pohorlak, Frank. "Proponents for a Literal Translation of the New Testament," www.concordant.org.

Postlewait, Thomas. *Interpreting the Theatrical Past.* Iowa City: University of Iowa Press, 1989.

Postman, Neil. *Crazy Talk, Stupid Talk.* New York: Delacorte Press, 1976.

Priestly, J. B. *Anton Chekhov.* London: International Textbook Company Ltd., 1970.

Pritchett, V. S. *Chekhov, A Spirit Set Free.* New York: Random House, 1988.

Rabassa, Gregory. Interview on "The Leonard Lopate Show," WNYC AM radio, July 11, 2005.

Rayfield, Donald. *The Cherry Orchard, Catastrophe and Comedy.* New York: Twayne Publishers, 1994.

———. *Anton Chekhov.* London: Harper Collins Publishers, 1997.

———. *Understanding Chekhov.* Madison: University of Wisconsin Press, 1999.

Rayner, Alice. *To Act, To Do, To Perform.* Ann Arbor: The University of Michigan Press, 1994.

Redgrave, Michael. *The Actor's Ways and Means.* New York: Theatre Arts Books, 1966.

Remnick, David. "The Translation Wars," *The New Yorker,* November 7, 2005, pp. 98–109.

Renner, Pamela. "Lessing is More," Village Voice, October 4, 2005.

Rexroth, Kenneth. "The Poet as Translator." *The Craft and Context of Translation.* Eds. William Arrowsmith and Roger Shattuck. Austin: The University of Texas Press, 1961, pp. 22–37.

Rich, Elisabeth T. "Chekhov and the Moscow Stage Today …" *Michigan Quarterly Review* 39:4, Fall, 2000.

Richards, Thomas. *At Work With Grotowski on Physical Actions.* London: Routledge, 1995.

Roach, Joseph R. *The Player's Passion.* Ann Arbor: The University of Michigan Press, 1993.

Roberts, J. W. *Richard Boleslasky.* Ann Arbor: UMI Research Press, 1981.

Rocamora, Carol. Interview with the author. New York City, January 18, 2005.

———. "The Living Chekhov," and Classical Drama courses at NYU, 1998–2000, New York University.

Rockwood, Jerome. *The Craftsmen of Dionysus.* Glenview, Illinois: Scott Foresman and Company, 1966.

Rodenburg, Patsy. *The Right to Speak.* New York: Routledge, 1992.

Roose-Evans, James. *Experimental Theatre.* New York: Avon Books, 1970.

Rose, Marilyn Gaddis, ed. *Translation in the Humanities.* Binghamton: State University of New York, n.d.

———. *Translation Spectrum.* Albany: State University of New York Press, 1981.

Rosenblatt, Louise M. *The Reader, The Text, The Poem.* Carbondale: Southern Illinois University Press, 1978.

Rosenfield, Paul. "Stella Adler's Teaching Actors How to Imagine," *The Los Angeles Times,* August 15, 1982.

Ross, Yana. Lithuanian actor: CV/Performances in *Three Sisters* at yanaross.com, 2017.

Rossi, Alfred. *Astonish Us in the Morning.* London: Hutchinson and Company, 1977.

Rostovskaya, Alla Grigorievna. "Teaching Chekhov's Plays: A Cross-Cultural Approach. A Reference Guide to Curriculum and Methodology for the Teaching of a Special Author in Translation on the Undergraduate Level." Dissertation, Stony Brook: State University of New York, 1991.

Rotté, Joanna. "Stella Adler: Teacher Emeritus," *Journal of American Drama and Theatre,* City University of New York, 11:3, Fall, 1999.

———. *Acting With Adler.* New York: Limelight Editions, 2000.

Russell, Douglas A. *Period Style for the Theatre.* Boston: Allyn and Bacon, 1987.

Russel-Parks, Shelley McKnight. "A Phenomenological Analysis of the Actor's Perceptions During the Creative Act," Dissertation, Florida State University, 1989.

Sacharow, Lawrence. "Enemies: A Russian Love Story," *American Theatre,* January, 2004.

———. "For Russians, A Process of Constant Rediscovery," *The New York Times,* December 2, 2001.

————. Interview with the author. Fordham University, New York, NY, May 12, 2003.

————. "Students Get Taste of Acting's Raw Power," *The New York Times*, August 20, 2000.

————. "Uncertainty is the Most Lethal Weapon," *The New York Times*, December 3, 2001.

Saint-Denis, Michel. "Stanislavsky and Shakespeare," *Tulane Drama Review* 9:77–84, Fall, 1964.

————. *Training for the Theatre: premises and promises*. London: Heinemann, 1982.

Sanders, Edward. *Chekhov*. Santa Rosa, CA: Black Sparrow Press, 1995.

Sapir, Edwards. *Selected Writings …*. Ed. P. B. Mandelbaum. Berkeley: University of California Press, 1949.

Sarraute, Nathalie. *L'Usage de la Parole*. Paris: Editions Gallimard, 1980.

Scammell, Michael. "The Servile Path–Translating Vladimir Nabokov," *Harper's Magazine*, www.findarticles.com.

Schechner, Richard. "Already Reworking the Classics of Modern Realism," *The New York Times*, Feb. 13, 2000.

————. *Performance Theory*. New York: Routledge, 1988.

Schechner, Richard and Lisa Wolford, eds. *The Grotowski Sourcebook*. New York: Routledge, 1997.

Schlusberg, Julian S. *Lessons for the Stage*. Hamden, Connecticut: Archon Books, 1994.

Schmitt, Natalie Crohn. *Actors and Onlookers*. Evanston, IL: Northwestern University Press, 1990.

Scolnicov, Hannah and Peter Holland. *The Play Out of Context*. Cambridge: Cambridge University Press, 1989.

Segal, Robert. "Writer Hampton Transforms 'The Seagull' On Stage," All Things Considered, NPR News, October 3, 2008.

Senelick, Laurence, ed. and trans. *Russian Dramatic Theory from Pushkin to the Symbolists*. Austin: University of Texas Press, 1981.

————. *Anton Chekhov*. New York: Grove Press, 1985.

————. *The Chekhov Theatre*. Cambridge: Cambridge University Press, 1997, 2005.

————. "Chekhov's Plays in English," *The North American Chekhov Society Bulletin*, Vol. IX, Spring, 2000.

————. Correspondence with the author, laurence.senelick@tufts.edu, to robin.levenson@nyu.edu, Boston and New York, March 7 and 11, 2002.

————. *Serf Actor: the life and art of Mikhail Schepkin*. Westport, CT: Greenwood, 1984.

————. Ed. *Wandering Stars, Russian Émigré Theatre, 1905–1940*. Iowa City: University of Iowa Press, 1992.

Shapiro, G. "Memories of Joseph Chaikin and Hume Cronyn," *The New York Sun*, September 18, 2003, p. 16.

Shaw, George Bernard. *Bernard Shaw: Selected Plays*. New York: Dodd, Mead & Company, 1970.

Sherbinin, Julie W. de. and Ralph Lindheim, eds., *The Bulletin of the North American Chekhov Society*, NACS, Ed., 1992–2000, 2013–17. This publication contains many articles regarding the nature of translations of Chekhov's plays and prose. Online at Chekhbul.com/issues.

Shewey, Don. "Chekhov's Stories Through Eyes of Seven Playwrights," *The New York Times*, August 25, 1985.

Simmons, Ernest J. *Chekhov: A Biography*. Chicago: The University of Chicago Press, 1962.

Simon, John. "Women of No Importance," *New York Magazine*, February 24, 1997.

Smeliansky, Anatoly. *The Russian Theatre After Stalin*. Trans. Patrick Miles. Cambridge University Press, 1999.

———. "The Russian Connection," American Repertory Theatre, www.amrep.org, February, 17, 2003.

Smith, Wendy. *Real Life Drama: The Group Theatre and America, 1931–1940*. New York: Alfred A. Knopf, 1990.

Sontag, Susan. *Where the Stress Falls*. New York: Farrar, Straus and Giroux, 2001.

———. *Against Interpretation and Other Essays*. New York: Picador USA, 2001.

Spolin, Viola. *Improvisation for the Theater*. Evanston, IL, 1963.

Spoto, Daniel. *The Kindness of Strangers, The Life of Tennessee Williams*. New York: Da Capo Press, 1997.

Stanislavsky, Konstantin. *An Actor's Work. A Student's Diary*. Trans. and ed. Jean Benedetti. New York: Routledge, 2008.

———. *An Actor Prepares*. Trans. Elizabeth Reynolds Hapgood. New York: Theatre Arts Books, 1948a.

———. *My Life in Art*. Trans. J. J. Robbins/Elizabeth Reynolds Hapgood. New York: Theatre Arts Books, 1948b.

———. *Building a Character*. Trans. Elizabeth Reynolds Hapgood. New York: Theatre Arts Books, 1949.

———. *The Seagull Produced by Stanislavsky*. Trans. David Magarshack. London: Dennis Dobson Ltd., 1952.

———. "Director's Diary," *Tulane Drama Review*, 9:38–41, Fall, 1964.

———. *Stanislavsky's Legacy*. Ed. and trans. Elizabeth Reynolds Hapgood. New York: Theatre Arts Books, 1968.

———. *Creating a Role*. Trans. Elizabeth Reynolds Hapgood. New York: Theatre Arts Books, 1961.

———. *Konstantin Stanislavsky, Selected Works*. Compiled, Korneva Oksana. Moscow: Raduga Publishers, 1984.

Stanton, Stephen S., ed. *Camille and Other Plays*. New York: Hill and Wang, 1957.

States, Bert O. "The World on Stage," *Great Reckonings in Little Rooms*. Berkeley, 1985, pp. 19–47.

Steiner, George. *After Babel*. New York: Oxford University Press, 1998a.

———. *Language and Silence*. New Haven: Yale University Press, 1998b.

———. *Real Presences*. Chicago: The University of Chicago Press, 1989.

Stoppard, Tom. *The Invention of Love*. New York: Grove Press, 1997.

Strasberg, John. *Accidently On Purpose*. New York: Applause Books, 1996.

———. Interview with the author. New York City, April 1, 2003.

Strasberg, Lee. *A Dream of Passion*. New York: Plume/Penguin Books, 1987.

———. *Strasberg at The Actor's Studio*. Ed. Robert H. Hethmon. New York: The Viking Press, 1968.

———. "Working With Live Material," *Tulane Drama Review*, 9:117–135, Fall, 1964.

Styan, J. L. *The Elements of Drama.* Cambridge: Cambridge University Press, 1969.

———. *Chekhov in Performance.* Cambridge: Cambridge University Press, 1971.

———. *Drama, Stage and Audience.* Cambridge: Cambridge University Press, 1975.

Sullivan, John T. "Stanislavsky and Freud," *Tulane Drama Review.* 9:90–111, Fall, 1964.

Taganrog Local Government, Ulitsa Petrovskaya 73, 347900, Tagnrog, Rostov Oblast taganrogcity.com/chekhov's legacy.

Tairov, Alexander. *Notes of a Director.* Trans. William Kuhlke. Coral Gables, FL: University of Miami Press, 1969.

Taylor, Philip. *Researching Drama and Arts Education.* London: The Falmer Press, 1996.

Thomson, David. "The Idea Is to Intimidate With Words. And Silence." *The New York Times,* July 15, 2001.

Toporkov, Vasily Osipovich. *Stanislavsky in Rehearsal.* Trans. Christine Edwards. New York: Theatre Arts Books, 1979.

Trenholm, Sarah. *Thinking Through Communication,* 4th ed. Boston: Pearson Education, 1995.

Truss, Lynne. *Eats, Shoots & Leaves, The Zero tolerance Approach to Punctuation.* New York: Gotham Books, 2004.

Tulloch, John. *Chekhov: A Structuralist Study.* New York: Barnes and Noble Books, 1980.

Turgenev, Ivan. *A Month in the Country.* Trans. John Christopher Jones. Classic Stage Company, New York City. Director, Erica Schmidt, February 2015.

. ———. Trans. Richard Nelson. Williamstown Theatre Festival, Williamstown, Massachusetts, August, 2012: "Radical Plans by Director/Translator Richard Nelson," by Charles Giuliano, July 18, 2012. https://www.berkshirefinearts.com/07-18-2012 a-day-in-the-country.htm.

Turkov, Andrei, compiler. *Anton Chekhov and His Times.* Trans. Cynthia Carlile and Sharon McKee. Fayetteville: University of Arkansas Press, 1995.

Upton, Carole-Anne, ed. *Moving Target: theatre translation and cultural relocation.* Manchester: St. Jerome Publishing, 2000.

Valency, Maurice. *The Breaking String.* New York: Schoken Books, 1983.

Vakhtangov, Yevgeny. *The Vakhtangov Sourcebook.* Ed. and Trans. Andrei Malaev-Babel. London and New York: Routledge, 2011.

Van Itallie, Jean-Claude. Interview with the author. New York City, November 19, 2003.

Veltman, Chloe. "The Roots of Translation," American Repertory Theatre. www.amrep.org, website, Feb. 9, 2003.

Waldman, Tom. "Chatsworth Teacher Gives Students Push to Stardom," Los Angeles Times. Nov. 26, 1987.

Wangh, Stephen. *An Acrobat of the Heart.* New York: Vintage Books, 2000.

———. Interview with the author. Classroom Observation. New York University, March, 2003.

Wellek, Rene and D. Nona. *Chekhov: New Perspectives.* Englewood Cliffs, NJ: Prentice-Hall, 1984.

Williams, Tennessee. *Memoirs.* New York: Bantam Books, 1975.

———. *Stopped Rocking and Other Screenplays.* New York: A New Directions Book, 1984.

———. *The Notebook of Trigorin: A Free Adaptation of Anton Chekhov's Seagull.* Trans. Ann Dunnigan. Ed. Allean Hale. New York: New Directions Publishing, 1997.

Webster's Encyclopedic Unabridged Dictionary of English. New York: Portland House, 1989.

Worral, Nick. *Modernism to Realism on the Soviet Stage.* Cambridge University Press, 1989.

Yeremin, Yuri. "A Muscovite on the Banks of the Charles," American Repertory Theatre, www. amrep.org, October 25, 1999.

Yershov, Pyotr. *Directing as a Practical Psychology* and *Technology of the Actor* as taught by Yevgeny Lanskoy, 1986–1989, Structures of Action course, Stella Adler Conservatory, New York City.

Yew, Chay. *A Winter People.* New Adaptation of Anton Chekhov's *The Cherry Orchard*, Unpublished Draft, September 28, 2004.

Young, Stark. *The Theatre.* New York: Hill and Wang, 1966.

Yusim, Marat. *Passing the Torch—Basic Training: Stanislavsky's School of Acting and Directing.* New York: Marat Yusim, 2006.

Zarrilli, Philip B. *Acting (Re)Considered.* London: Routledge, 1995.

Zatlin, Phyllis. *Theatrical Translation and Film Adaptation, a Practitioner's View.* UK, USA, Canada: Multilingual Matters Ltd., 2005.

Zubarev, Vera. *A Systems Approach to Literature, Mythopoetics of Chekhov's Last Four Plays.* Westport, CT: Greenwood Press, 1997.

Zuber, Ortrun, ed. *The Languages of Theatre.* Oxford: Pergamon Press, 1980.

Glossary

The following terms are arranged in a logical, rather than alphabetical, order. The terms are interdependent, and are all related to "structures of Action" in a play. They are practical definitions for the actor's analysis of the playscript.

For the purposes of this exploration, **Action** is defined as "movement plus desire" or "movement with purpose" for the actor playing a character onstage.[1] The nature of Action is necessarily psycho-physical; that is, it is a "movement" of the psyche and the body that is *internal* as well as *external*.[2] It is what the character wants to accomplish, whether consciously or unconsciously. An action must be "doable" or "playable." It is often defined with an active verb, such as *I want to convince, to comfort, to help, to escape, to attack, to reveal, to teach.* It must also carry within it an "end" (Rotté 2000: 82–3, 110–27): "*I want to escape* this prison in order *to save* my child's life." The grammatical object of the sentence must be included in the Action so the actor may "experience the doing" and justify the Action (*Ibid.*). Action may also be expressed as or related to concepts of intention, purpose,

---

1   Defined by Yevgeny Lanskoy, teacher at the Stella Adler Conservatory in his classes "Structures of Action," 1987–1990.

2   *Ibid.*; see also Carnicke, *Stanislavsky in Focus*, Ch. 7, "Action and the Human Body in Role," 147–66; Stanislavsky, *An Actor Prepares*, Ch. 3, "Action," 31–50; and Irina and Igor Levin, *Working on the Play and the Role*, p. 179.

objective/superobjective, spine, through-line, motivation, justification, task, goal, aim, will, wish, want, need, desire, influence, inner technique, subtext, appetency, meaningful doing and histrionic sensibility.[3]

It is important to understand that **Action** in the playscript is a result of **Conflict**. Director/teacher Marat Yusim explains:

> On the bottom of human needs … and any human activities [or] human actions, there is always a certain open or hidden conflict between a man and his surroundings … Conflict first of all is shock, a collision, a disruption of the status quo, a breaking of the rules. It's a clash of opposing ideas, characters and circumstances, a clash of opposing feelings, actions, aspirations and passions, a clash of opposing forces that spring from the contradictions of real life. The essence of a dramatic conflict could be expressed by the struggle between man and his fate, between man and the world, between love and hate, between new and old, between the beautiful and the ugly, between the transcendent and the mundane, the progressive and the conservative, between the good and the evil, and so on. We can see the completion and evaluation of this struggle in the events of the play. (351–2)

Thus the conflict(s) in Chekhov's plays must be determined in order to discover the Actions of the characters. The **Superobjective** of the play is the overall Action of the piece as a whole, based on the main conflict of the play (see Chapter IV).

Activity is not to be confused with **Action.** An activity is the physical movement or "business" (a conventional behavior, such as smoking, often using a hand prop) that accompanies an **Action** onstage. For example, dancing itself is an activity; a character may be dancing and also have a separate **Action.** In Ibsen's *A Doll's House* Nora "dances to save her life": while rehearsing her tarantella for her husband Torvald, she attempts to distract his attention from the letter in the mailbox, which she believes stamps (pun intended) her and Torvald's doom. Her larger action (or objective) is to save her husband's life: she is fulfilling it at this moment by distracting Torvald; she does this through the activity of dancing. Now, the *manner in which* she dances comes from her purpose, her action. If she were dancing to amuse herself, the tenor and movement of the dance would be markedly different. Thus, it is understood that **Actions** and **Activities** are evoked by the **Given Circumstances** of the play. These are the contextual "givens" of any play onstage. They are the setting and situation of the play as set by the playwright. More specifically, given circumstances may include the playwright's stage directions, "place, time, relationships, illnesses and physical restrictions, past, present, future, fears, challenges, dreams, and the psychological characteristics

---

3   "Histrionic sensibility" is coined by Francis Fergusson, *The Idea of a Theatre*, pp. 250–5.

involved."[4] The place or "where"[5] includes props, set and scenery in the space, and any meanings with which the character(s) may endow them, in accordance with the action of the play.[6]

Endowment refers to the physical properties (props) or psychological meanings that the actor gives to the given circumstances onstage in order to help **Justify** the chosen actions for the play. Actor/teacher Uta Hagen states: "Almost nothing in our characters' life *is* what it *is*—but we must make it so! We *endow* the given circumstances, our own character, our relationship to others in the play, the place, each object we deal with, including the clothes we wear. All must be endowed with the physical, psychological or emotional properties which we want in order to *send us richly into action from moment to moment*" (emphasis added, Hagen 1973: 116–17). For example, an actor may endow a plastic flower with the texture and scent of a real flower, and may treat it with the delicacy it evokes for her as a missive from her beloved in the play. **Endowment** thus induces behavior. Stella Adler uses the term "personalization" for the same concept. The flower is placed tenderly in a vase, or it is ripped to shreds, depending on the actor's personalization of the object. Adler advises "Personalize the props you use by endowing them with *some quality that comes from you*" (emphasis added, Adler 1988: 60). By using one's imagination to endow objects and characters onstage, the actor is engaged in **Justification**. This is the "reason" an actor has for doing an Action. It gives the actor the "end" or "objective" of an Action and forces the actor to think creatively about the play. Stella Adler writes "The justification is not in the lines; it is in you. What you choose as your justification should agitate you. As a result of the agitation you will experience the action ..." (48). Justifying an Action is "imaginative rather than logical" as it "arises from the actor's insight into the nature of the circumstances" (Rotté 2000: 103) as put down by the playwright. Thus justification allows the actor to explore the themes of the playwright and leads to the **Actor's Contribution**.

Actor's Contribution. As a creative artist, the actor makes choices of Action that contribute to the rhythm and the meaning of the play as a whole. Adler maintains that the actor's "talent" is in his or her choice. It is not only the job of the director to define the themes in a particular production; the actor is crucial to and collaborative in creating the specifics of performance that define theatricality. "The actor experiences him or herself as a person creating situations, not someone

---

4   Doug Moston, "Standards and Practices" in *Method Acting Reconsidered*, ed. David Krasner.

5   Coined by Viola Spolin in *Improvisation for the Theatre*.

6   Michel Saint-Denis points out that "it is not important to find out what a character *thinks*, but what a character thinks in a *situation* related to the play" (*Training for the Theatre*, 191).

reciting lines" (105). Adler often stated "anyone can speak English out loud."[7] Speaking words is not the actor's job; "the real actor will ask: 'What can I give the play? What can I contribute? What truth can I find and reveal?'" (188). This was also Stanislavsky's ethic. A good example of the actor's contribution is Bernard Beckerman's remembrance of Judith Anderson in the role of Lady Macbeth, in the scene after her visit to Duncan's death chamber. Beckerman describes how Anderson, after summoning all her strength to place the bloody daggers next to the murdered boys, "retched violently, projecting in that abdominal contraction her utter revulsion at the murder" (Beckerman 1979: 158). This is an example of the *actor's* contribution, as distinguished from the playwright's, since the act of retching is not indicated in the text. It shows the audience in the most histrionic way exactly how Lady Macbeth feels about what she and Macbeth have just done. The idea and the execution of it (the *activity* of retching, and its accompanying *Action*) were contributed creatively by the actor. Defining and describing possibilities for the actor's contribution—especially as regards the playscript—is central to this study.

Text is the words written in the **Playscript**. The difference between the two is that while the text is simply the words on the page, the term "playscript" implies the entire poetry of the drama which is beyond the page: words, gesture, given circumstances (see above), lights, costume and sound. A playscript may also be described as the performance text. The text is a *map* of the action of the play; the playscript includes the entire *territory*. A director's promptbook—the director's script with notes on blocking (movement), character and every aspect of the production—would ideally contain elements and explication of the playscript as well as the text. Stanislavsky kept detailed promptbooks of his productions of Chekhov's plays, wherein he wrote copious directions to the actors, set designers, sound technicians, etc., and, indeed, described almost every movement and gesture of the characters (1952).

Subtext refers to the Inner Monologue and Mental Images of the actor *underneath* the dialogue of the text (Benedetti 1998: 153). Subtext is the deeper, "real" meaning of the words. When it is understood that the dialogue of a play is the *last* thing the author has set down—though it is the first thing the actor and readers see—and that it is the result of constructing a story, characters and overall play structure, we may understand that dialogue is just the tip of the iceberg in creating a character (Brestoff 1999: 4). The actor must do the subtextual work of recreating the Actions the playwright has structured into the fabric of the play. Subtext—this underlying dialogue or monologue in the mind—is created by the actor (see Actor's Contribution) to give Action to his or her words. It may be noted

7   Stella Adler, *Acting Technique* class, 1981.

that the actor's subtext is a further "translation" of the text from "page to stage" and moves the actor (providing Action) on the stage. We see how the ideas of Subtext, Action and Given Circumstances (which create subtext and propel action) are inextricably intertwined.

Event(s) are the large happenstances that affect all the characters in the play. They propel the action. They create the circumstances. Some precipitating event (sometimes called the "inciting" event) precedes the opening of the play, while one or more take place in the course of the drama. We may see how "events" are precipitated by, contain or result in "conflict." We may judge whether an occurrence in the playscript is truly an event by gauging whether it indeed affects every character, or has the potential of doing so. For instance, Hamlet's sighting of the Ghost of his father could be considered an event. Though this happening may not initially affect every character, the proceedings that follow as a result of Hamlet's sighting do affect every personage. Yevgeny Lanskoy maintained that we may only experience two or three true "events" in our lives, regardless of what happens to us: an event is an occurrence that, once it happens, changes us forever. A car accident, a divorce, or a death may seem like affecting events, but if they don't change us in a fundamental way, they are not to be considered as events in the theatrical sense. "Change" for the character is a change in Action, based on event.

Beats are the units of Action in a scene or act of a play—"a short segment of a script which has a complete purpose" (Hull 325). Beats are a tool for the actor in script analysis. Beats add up to the overall superobjective of the character (the large Action that is the character's purpose in the whole play), and are the increments of Action that make up the spine of the play, the through-line of action. Beats may be long or short; they change when the intention of a character changes, or possibly when the tact by which the character approaches his task changes. Beats are not defined by the text alone, but by the changes in Action in the playscript. They may change, for example, when a character exits or enters the scene.

Tempo-Rhythm is a term coined by Stanislavsky to describe the actor's overall pace (the tempo) and the varying rhythms (inner beat) within that pace. Stanislavsky writes in *Building a Character* that tempo-rhythm can be marked by body movement, and also by words, syllables and sounds. Even thoughts and imagination are described as "subject to movement and consequently there must be tempo and rhythm in them." (192). Tempo-Rhythm is particularly significant to this study because the rhythm and sound of words from various translations may influence Action. Diction (both the choice of words and the sounds they produce in the mouth), and syntax all create meaning for the actor, and are affected by his or her choice of Actions. Elements of sound, syntax, word choice and rhythm are examined in the chapters on the plays as discrete areas of comparison between translations.

Scansion is the method of "scanning" a text, including noting the rhythm, sounds, syntax, intonation and inflection of the words. It is also described as "the name for analyzing rhythm syllable-by-syllable" (Benedetti 1970: 111). It is normally used for poetry, as a metrical analysis of the verse (*Webster's* 1274). I maintain that Chekhov's text is a form of poetry: the poetry of the theatre.[8] His text, even in translation, has rhythm, sometimes known as *cadence*.

Cadence is established by the alternation of stressed and unstressed syllables, which create a "beat" underlying a prose speech. (Cadence is not to be confused with the "beats" which are units of Action in the playscript. Action may indeed influence cadence, however.) Variations in cadence are based on differences in language and syntax, (Benedetti 1970: 116) which are noted and compared in this study. The detailed work of textual analysis an actor might do for each play may be described as "scansion" for the playscript to determine how the actor might approach the text in performance. Iambic pentameter in Shakespeare's plays, for example, creates a certain cadence in his lines. But prose can do this too.

Finally, Stanislavsky came up with the four "**Circles of Attention**" to help the actor focus on *where*, psychologically, he or she is at any one moment. These "Circles" may be considered a "structure" of Action, as they are an idea that helps the actor define his or her purpose in the play. The First Circle is where one is involved only with oneself, and the small space around one's body. Talking to oneself, regarding one's hands or face in a mirror, etc. would be in the First Circle. The Second Circle, where most scenes in Realism are played, is when the actor is engaged with a partner or partners or objects on the stage, or with the audience; the focus is on what is happening in the space one is actually in, physically, at the moment. For example, in the last scene of *Seagull,* when Nina addresses Kostya specifically, they are both in this Second Circle. When actors are in the Third Circle, they are focused on something *outside the space* they are actually in. If I am speaking to you but constantly consulting my watch (as Vershinin does in the final scene of *Three Sisters*), I can be physically *with* you, but my mind is in the Third Circle, where I have a future appointment. In "real life" we are often in this Third Circle, just walking through the streets of New York City, for example.[9] Lanskoy described the Fourth Circle as "with God," (Class 1988) or far out on "another planet," or, possibly, psychologically disturbed. In practice, the Fourth Circle may be close to the *First*. When we are alone, we may "phase out" from the outside world.

---

8   Robert Benedetti insists that "most of the *principles* of poetry analysis are also applicable to prose" in his text *The Actor at Work,* p. 111.

9   This is called "mindless processing" in the field of Communication—see Trenholm, p. 49.

References

Adler, Stella. *The Art of Acting*. Ed. Howard Kissel. New York: Applause Books, 2000.

———. Interview with Russell Vanderbrouke, *Yale Theatre* 8, nos. 2 & 3, Spring 1977.

———. *On Ibsen, Strindberg and Chekhov*. Ed. Barry Paris. New York: Alfred A. Knopf, 1999.

———. "The Reality of Doing," *Tulane Drama Review*, Vol. IX, No. 1, Fall 1964, 136–155.

———. *The Technique of Acting*. New York: Bantam Books, 1988.

———. Scene Study/Technique/Rehearsal Classes, with Ron Burrus, Pan-Andreas Theatre, Santa Monica, CA, 1981–84 and Stella Adler Conservatory, NYC, 1986–89.

Aristotle. *Aristotle's Poetics*. Trans. S. H. Butcher. Intro. Francis Fergusson. New York: Hill and Wang, 1961.

———. Aristotle's Theory of Poetry and Fine Art, Trans. S. H. Butcher, 4th ed., London: Macmillan & Co. Ltd., 1932.

Ball, William. *A Sense of Direction*. New York: Drama Book Publishers, 1984.

Beckerman, Bernard. *Dynamics of Drama*. New York: Drama Book Specialists, 1979.

———. "The Play's the Thing But What's a Play?" in Hobgood, Burnet M., ed. *Master Teachers of Theatre: Observations on Teaching Theatre by Nine American Masters*. Board of Trustees, Southern Illinois University, 1988.

Benedetti, Jean. Ed. *The Moscow Art Theatre Letters*. New York: Routledge, 1991.

———. *Stanislavski*. New York: Routledge, 1990.

———. *Stanislavski: An Introduction*. London: Menthuen, 1982.

———. *Stanislavski and the Actor*. New York: Routledge, 1998.

Benedetti, Robert. *The Actor at Work*. Englewood Cliffs, NJ: Prentice-Hall, 1970.

———. *The Actor in You*. Boston: Allyn and Bacon, 1999.

———. *Seeming, Being and Becoming*. New York: Drama Book Specialists, 1976.

Boleslavsky, Richard. *Acting, The First Six Lessons*. New York: Theatre Arts Books, 1963.

Brestoff, Richard. *Acting Under the Circumstances*. Lyme, NH: Smith and Kraus, 1999.

———. *The Great Acting Teachers and Their Methods*. Lyme, NH: Smith and Kraus, 1995.

Carnicke, Sharon Marie. "Stanislavsky Uncensored and Unabridged," *Tulane Drama Review*, T137 Spring, 1993.

———. *Stanislavsky in Focus*. Australia: Harwood Academic Publishers, 1998.

Coger, Leslie. "Stanislavsky Changes His Mind," *Tulane Drama Review* 9:63–68, Fall 1984.

Fergusson, Francis. *The Idea of a Theatre*. Garden City, NY: Doubleday Anchor Books, 1953.

———. "The Notion of Action," *Tulane Drama Review*, 9:85–87, Fall 1964.

Gordon, Mel. "Nine Misconceptions About Stanislavsky and His System," *Soviet and European Performance*, Vol. 9, Nos. 2 and 3, Fall 1989.

———. *The Stanislavksy Technique: Russia*. New York: Applause Theatre Book Publishers, 1987.

Hagen, Uta. *A Challenge for the Actor*. New York: Charles Scribner's Sons, 1991.

———. *Respect for Acting*. New York: Macmillan Publishing Company, 1973.

———. Posters on the doors of the Lucille Lortel Theatre, Jan. 15, 2004. Quotes and stories from students, colleagues and well-wishers.

Hull, Lorrie. *Strasberg's Method*. Woodbridge, CT: Ox Bow Publishing, 1986.

Krasner, David, ed. *Method Acting Reonsidered.* New York: St. Martin's Press, 2000.

Lanskoy, Yevgeny. Interviews with the author, 1999, and Classes, "The Structures of Action," at the Stella Adler Conservatory, 1986–89.

Levenson, Robin Beth. "Afraid to Lie," Unpublished paper, Dr. Richard Schechner's Directing Course, New York University, Tisch School of the Arts, Spring, 1999.

Merlin, Bella. *Beyond Stanislavsky.* New York: Routledge, 2001.

———. *Konstantin Stanislavsky.* New York: Routledge, 2003.

Moore, Sonia. *The Stanislavski System.* New York: The Viking Press, 1974.

———. *Stanislavski Revealed.* New York: Applause Theatre Books, 1991.

Rotté, Joanna. *Acting With Adler.* New York: Limelight Editions, 2000.

Saint-Denis, Michel. "Stanislavsky and Shakespeare," *Tulane Drama Review* 9:77–84, Fall 1964.

———. *Training for the Theatre: premises and promises.* London: Heinemann, 1982.

Spolin, Viola. *Improvisation for the Theater.* Evanston, IL, 1963.

Stanislavsky, Constantin. *An Actor Prepares.* Trans. Elizabeth Reynolds Hapgood. New York: Theatre Arts Books, 1948.

———. *An Actor's Work. A Student's Diary.* Trans. and ed. by Jean Benedetti. New York: Routledge, 2008.

———. *Building a Character.* Trans. Elizabeth Reynolds Hapgood. New York: Theatre Arts Books, 1949.

———. *Creating a Role.* Trans. Elizabeth Reynolds Hapgood. New York: Theatre Arts Books, 1961.

———. *Konstantin Stanislavsky, Selected Works.* Compiled by Korneva Oksana. Moscow: Raduga Publishers, 1984.

———. *The Seagull Produced by Stanislavsky.* Trans. David Magarshack. London: Dennis Dobson Ltd., 1952.

———. *Stanislavsky's Legacy.* Ed. and Trans. Elizabeth Reynolds Hapgood. New York: Theatre Arts Books, 1968.

Toporkov, Vasily Osipovich. *Stanislavsky in Rehearsal.* Trans. Christine Edwards. New York: Theatre Arts Books, 1979.

Yusim, Marat. *Passing the Torch—Basic Training: Stanislavsky's School of Acting and Directing.* New York: Marat Yusim, 2006.

The Cited Plays and Their Translators, 145 Renditions

a = adaptation   v = version   b = based on (all others are considered "translations")

THE SEAGULL – 38 renditions

George Calderon, 1912
Constance Garnett, 1929
Stark Young, 1939 (1956)
Elisaveta Fen, 1954
Robert W. Corrigan, 1962 (v)
Ann Dunnigan, 1964
Tennessee Williams, 1964 (b)*
Ronald Hingley, 1967
Alex Szogyi, 1968
David Magarshack, 1969
Kathleen Cook, 1973
Jean-Claude Van Itallie, 1974 (v)
Eugene K. Bristow, 1977
David French, 1977
Laurence Senelick, 1977
Thomas Kilroy, 1981 (v)
Michael Frayn, 1988
Milton Ehre, 1992
Michael Henry Heim, 1992

Pam Gems, 1994 (v)
Betsy Hulick, 1994
Nicholas Saunders/Frank Dwyer, 1994
Jean-Claude Van Itallie, 1995 (v)
Sharon Carnicke, 1996
Carol Rocamora, 1996
Karl Kramer, 1997
Paul Schmidt, 1997
Tom Stoppard, 1997 (v) **(tr. Joanna Wright)
Peter Gill, 1999 (v) (tr. Helen Molchanoff)
Peter Carson, 2002
Michael Frayn, 2002
Michael Henry Heim, 2003
Michael Barakiva, 2004 (a)
Laurence Senelick, 2005
Christopher Hampton, (v.) 2008
David Hare, 2015
Aaron Posner, 2016 (a) *Stupid Fucking Bird*
Štěpán S. Šimek, 2017

The Notebook of Trigorin, based on the translation of Ann Dunnigan.

**Stoppard mentions Joanna Wright as "literal" translator, but only in his Introduction.

UNCLE VANYA – 34 renditions

Constance Garnett, 1929
Stark Young, 1939
Elisaveta Fen, 1954
Robert W. Corrigan, 1962 (v)
Ann Dunnigan, 1964
Ronald Hingley, 1964
Alex Szogyi, 1968
David Magarshack, 1969
Christopher Hampton, 1971 (tr. Nina Froud)
Kathleen Cook, 1973
Eugene K. Bristow, 1977
Laurence Senelick, 1977
Michael Frayn, 1988
David Mamet, 1988 (a) (tr. Vlada Chernomirdik)
Milton Ehre, 1992
Pam Gems, 1992 (v)
Betsy Hulick, 1994

Jean-Claude Van Itallie, 1995 (v)
Carol Rocamora, 1996
Karl Kramer, 1997
Paul Schmidt, 1997
Brian Friel, 1998 (v)
Stephen Mulrine, 1999
Mike Poulton, 1999 (v)
Karl L. Lee (*Aunt Vanya*), 2001 (a)
Peter Carson, 2002
Curt Columbus, 2002
Michael Henry Heim, 2003
Laurence Senelick, 2005
Craig Lucas, 2007
Annie Baker, 2012 (v) (tr. Margarita Shalina)
Andrew Upton, 2012 (a)
Štépan S. Šimek, 2017 (tr.) & (a)
Richard Nelson, 2018 (trs. Pevear/Volokhonsky)

THREE SISTERS – 37 renditions

Constance Garnett, 1929
Stark Young, 1939 (& 1956)
Clifford Odets, 1939 (acting version)
Elisaveta Fen, 1954
Robert W. Corrigan, 1962 (v)
Ann Dunnigan, 1964
Ronald Hingley, 1964
Alex Szogyi, 1968
Randall Jarrell, 1969 (tr. Paul Schmidt)
Tom Markus, 1996 (a)
David Magarshack, 1969
Katherine Cook, 1973
Eugene K. Bristow, 1977
Laurence Senelick, 1977
Sharon Carnicke, 1979
Brian Friel, 1981 (v)
Lanford Wilson, 1984
Michael Frayn, 1988
David Mamet, 1990 (a) (tr. Vlada Chernomirdik)

Frank McGuinness, 1990 (v) (tr. Rose Cullen)
Milton Ehre, 1992
Paul Schmidt, 1992
Betsy Hulick, 1994
Jean-Claude Van Itallie, 1995 (v)
Richard Schechner, 1995 (a) (tr. Michele Minnick)
Carol Rocamora, 1996
Karl Kramer, 1997
Paul Schmidt, 1997)
Peter Carson, 2002
Michael Henry Heim, 2003
Christopher Hampton, 2005
Laurence Senelick, 2005
Craig Lucas, 2005
Sarah Ruhl, 2009
Marina Brodskaya, 2010
Štépan S. Šimek, 2014
Halley Feiffer, 2017(a) *Moscow, Moscow, Moscow, Moscow, Moscow, Moscow*

THE CHERRY ORCHARD – 36 renditions

George Calderon, 1912

Constance Garnett, 1929

Stark Young, 1939

Joshua Logan (*Wisteria Trees*), 1950 (b)

Elisaveta Fen, 1954

Robert W. Corrigan, 1962

Sir John Gielgud, 1963 (v)

Ann Dunnigan, 1964

Tyrone Guthrie/Leonid Kipnis, 1965

Ronald Hingley, 1967

Alex Szogyi, 1968

David Magarshack, 1969

Kathleen Cook, 1973

Eugene K. Bristow, 1977

Laurence Senelick, 1977

Trevor Griffiths, 1978 (v) (tr. Helen Rappaport)

Laurence Senelick , 2005

Peter Gill, 1978 (v) (tr. Ted Braun)

Sharon Carnicke, 1980

Mamet, 1985 (a) (tr. Peter Nelles)

Michael Frayn, 1988

Milton Ehre, 1992

Betsy Hulick, 1994

Jean-Claude Van Itallie, 1995 (v)

Carol Rocamora, 1996

Karl Kramer/Margaret Booker, 1997

Paul Schmidt, 1997

Emily Mann, 2000 (a)

Peter Carson, 2002

Michael Henry Heim, 2003

Tom Murphy, 2004

Tom Donaghy, 2004 (a) (tr. Ronald Meyer)

Chay Yew, 2004 (a) *Winter People*

Martin Sherman, 2006 (v) (tr. Svetlana Darsalia)

Pam Gems, 2007 (tr. Tania Alexander)

Stephen Karam, 2016

Index

Y

Z